Grasping Gallipoli

Terrain, Maps and Failure
at the Dardanelles, 1915

GRASPING GALLIPOLI

TERRAIN, MAPS AND FAILURE AT THE DARDANELLES, 1915

by

Peter Chasseaud and Peter Doyle

Front jacket picture: The British fleet bombarding the
Dardanelles defences (Peter Chasseaud)

Fist published in 2005

This edition published in 2015
by Spellmount, an imprint of The History Press
The Mill, Brimscombe Port
Stroud, Gloucestershire, GL5 2QG
www.thehistorypress.co.uk

British Library Cataloguing in Publication Data.
A catalogue record for this book is available from the British Library.

ISBN 978 0 7509 6226 1

Typesetting and origination by The History Press
Printed in Great Britain

Contents

List of Maps

Glossary

Admiralty	Government Department dealing with Naval administration, also containing Naval Staff
ANZAC	Australian and New Zealand Army Corps
AWS	Admiralty War Staff, London
Battery	Set of guns or howitzers under a single command and control
BEF	British Expeditionary Force (France and Belgium)
CID	Committee for Imperial Defence (London)
CIGS	Chief of the Imperial General Staff (London)
C in C	Commander in Chief
DAQMG	Deputy Assistant Quarter-Master General (a Staff Officer)
Dardanelles Commission	Enquiry set up by Asquith in 1915 to investigate the Gallipoli fiasco
DMO	Director of Military Operations (and Intelligence)
First Lord of the Admiralty	Political head of the Navy, a Cabinet Minister
First Sea Lord	Professional head of the Navy, the senior Naval officer
FO	Foreign Office, London
GHQ, Egypt	Maxwell's Headquarters
GHQ, MEF	General Headquarters, Mediterranean Expeditionary Force
GOC	General Officer Commanding
GSGS	Geographical Section of the General Staff (MO4), War Office, London
HUMINT	Human Intelligence
IMINT	Imagery Intelligence (Aerial Photography in 1914–18)

MEF	Mediterranean Expeditionary Force (Hamilton's Force)
MG	Machine Gun
MI	Military Intelligence (War Office; in 1914–15 MO)
MO	Directorate of Military Operations and Intelligence at War Office (split at end of 1915)
NID	Naval Intelligence Division, Admiralty, London
OS	Ordnance Survey, Southampton
Photogrammetry	Science of accurate plotting of points and lines (mapping) from aerial photos
Porte	*La Sublime Porte*: the Ottoman Court at Constantinople; the Turkish Government
psc	Passed Staff College; a professionally trained staff officer who had passed through the Staff College at Camberley
RNAS	Royal Naval Air Service
RND	Royal Naval Division
RNVR	Royal Naval Volunteer Reserve
SIGINT	Signals Intelligence
TOPINT	Topographical Intelligence
War Council	Cabinet Committee, including Chiefs of Staff, dealing with strategic direction of war
War Office/WO	Government Department in London dealing with Army administration, also containing General Staff

Foreword

Home to Ardagh, Constantinople, 19 November 1876, speaking of the Crimean War [TNA(PRO) WO 33/29, Reports & Memoranda – Constantinople & Roumelia 1877, pp 50–1, No. 7].

The Government of the day, in the early stages, never seemed to know what they really wanted. Their orders were ambiguous, and that ambiguity was carried through every department of the army, and resulted in half-measures – a desire to do what would suit two distinct lines of policy.

When disasters seemed to threaten, there followed an excited, feverish action, striving by lavish expenditure to recover lost time and make up for previous parsimony; this expenditure benefitted the army but slightly, while a host of civilians, vice-consuls and Levantines of all shades, fattened on it.

Urged by the Press and eager to do something, the War Office fell a prey to inventors – amateur soldiers, amateur engineers. The old and tried servants were put to one side, or compelled to carry out the whims and ideas of men whose notions of war were derived from the columns of 'our own correspondent'.

Reading the mass of papers connected with the Crimean War of a confidential nature that have passed through my hands in my official capacity, I have been perfectly astonished at the extraordinary proposals gravely made in England by these amateurs, and as gravely submitted to the chiefs of the army in the field for report.

Acknowledgements

We would like to acknowledge the very generous assistance and advice given by Dr Ian Mumford, and the excellent pioneering articles by Col. Mike Nolan RE (retd) on Gallipoli mapping which appeared in *The Gallipolian* in 1993–5[1] and have been extremely useful. The exhaustive work by the late Jim Tolson on sorting and listing the maps which were subsequently transferred to the Public Record Office (now the National Archives) should here be commemorated, and the thorough compilation of details of Gallipoli maps in the Australian War Memorial collection, undertaken by John Bullen, should also be recorded.

Particular thanks are accorded to the courteous and helpful staff of the National Archives (Public Record Office) at Kew, the source of a large number of the maps and documents consulted during the research for this book. Several of the photographs are reproduced with kind permission of the Trustees of the Royal Engineers' Museum, Chatham. Thanks are also given to the following for their various forms of assistance: the staff of the Imperial War Museum at Lambeth, the British Library, the Admiralty Library, RUSI Library, the Royal Engineers Institution Library and Museum at Chatham, HM Hydrographic Office at Taunton, Keith Atkinson MBE, Prof. H-K Meier, Dr Andrew Cook, Francis Herbert and David McNeill of the RGS Map Room, Peter Jones and the staff of the Defence Geographic Centre, DGIA, Anne-Marie de Villèle and Claude Ponou of the Service Historique de l'Armée de Terre at Vincennes (Paris), Nigel Steel, Peter Barton, Matthew Bennett, Sarah Nicholas, Adrian Webb, Jenny Wraight, Dave Parry, Kenan Celik and Bill Sellars. Thanks are also due to Gill Dowson for allowing us to reproduce in Appendix VII the hitherto unknown report by Ernest Dowson on his visit to Gallipoli in July 1915.

Notes

1. Nolan (1993–5).

Authors' Note

To avoid confusion, place names are those in use by the British (including Anzac) forces in 1915, and still in use in most of the anglophone literature today. To quote a well-known author on the Aegean: 'An unfamiliar spelling of a well-known name is apt to annoy the reader – or so it seems to me, as Socrates might say.'[2] There is nothing wrong with anglicised names; every country uses its own version (London, Londres, etc.) and it implies no disrespect. To the British and Australasians, Gallipoli rather than Gelibolu is the familiar style, and so is used here. In the same spirit, Constantinople is used rather than Istanbul; it was the form used by the Allies at the time. British sources used both Gaba Tepe and Kaba Tepe, and no attempt has been made to standardise these usages. Finally, it is correct to use 'Ottoman Empire', rather than Turkey, which was reborn under the leadership of Kemal Atatürk out of the ashes of the old empire following defeat in the First World War. Ottoman troops included many from Turkey itself, but also many ethnic groups from across Asia Minor and the Arabian Peninsula. However, we have used the two terms interchangeably throughout the text to ease its flow; we hope that this device is understood. Where the phrase 'the Peninsula' is used, it refers to the Gallipoli Peninsula. The Australian and New Zealand Army Corps (ANZAC) is here used as a proper noun, rather than an acronym, to aid the flow of the text. Also, where dates refer to Ottoman maps, they are not necessarily accurate, owing to faulty conversion in some sources from the Ottoman Calendar.[3] Finally, it should be pointed out that a one-inch map has a scale of 1 inch to the mile (1:63,360), that a nautical mile = 6,080 feet (2,026.67 yards, or 1.15 miles), and that a map scale of 3 inches to a nautical mile = 1:24,320.

Notes

2. Pentreath, Guy, *Hellenic Traveller*, London: Faber, 1971, p. 12.
3. Anon. (probably Col. Mehemmed Shevki Pasha), 'The Topographical Service in the Ottoman Empire and the Modern Turkish Cartography', in *L'Universo*, No. 1, pp. 127– 36. Typescript translation in MCE, RE, Ref. D30/H1/A5. MS note on MCE copy.

Introduction: The Issues

The Gallipoli Campaign of April–December 1915 – the Allied landings on the shores of Turkey – has been the subject of a vast literature, which has most unfortunately propagated a great untruth – that the War Office was unprepared for operations in the Dardanelles area, and had little or nothing in the way of maps and geographical intelligence to give to Sir Ian Hamilton, the commander of the Mediterranean Expeditionary Force (Medforce), and his Staff. First explored in Aspinall-Oglander's Official History,[1] this theme is developed in most one-volume histories that have followed, and has since passed into mythology.[2] Hamilton's most recent biographer repeated this canard, echoing Hamilton himself in claiming that he only received from the War Office 'a 1912 handbook on the Turkish Army, a sort of tourist guide to the area with a thoroughly defective map and the single sheet of general instructions from Kitchener', while his Staff officers 'were not given access to Callwell's 1906 report or to the valuable reports on the Dardanelles by the British military attaché.'[3] Yet the reality is somewhat different, and this book demonstrates that this myth, perpetrated by Hamilton himself among others, is a gross distortion of the truth. While there were problems in London with strategic policy and planning (or lack of it) at the highest level, the War Office (and the Admiralty) possessed a great deal of previously collected terrain information, maps and charts, covering the topography and defences of Gallipoli and the Dardanelles, *much of which was duly handed over* to Hamilton and his Staff, either before they left London or subsequently. Additional material was obtained from the Admiralty and Navy, and still more gathered in theatre, in the Aegean and the Levant before the landings.

Whether all this intelligence was properly processed, distributed and efficiently used is a different matter and this book, which incorporates much previously unpublished material, attempts to penetrate behind the veil of obfuscation to get to the truth of the matter. Intelligence has to be analysed, interpreted and evaluated, and then distributed and explained to commanders and their Staff, who must base their plans on it and not ignore it. All too often, politicians and commanders ignore intelligence, and indulge in wishful thinking by creating a false scenario in which they then believe. Very little has been written on the intelligence side of the Gallipoli Campaign, and it is typical that John Keegan's recent book *Intelligence in War*,[4] admittedly a selective case-study approach, omitted it. It hardly featured in two key studies of British 20th century intelligence work: Michael Occleshaw's *Armour Against Fate, British Military Intelligence in the First World War*,[5] or in Christopher Andrew's *Secret Service, The Making of the British Intelligence Community*.[6] While we should not overstate the importance of intelligence – that most eminent of cryptanalysts David Kahn called it a secondary factor in war[7] – it is undeniable that possession of desirable information gives a significant advantage and may occasionally tip the balance. We should also note, as Kahn did, that intelligence can only work through strength; the primary factor is force, and this is certainly true of the Dardanelles operations.

Briefly considering the types and sources of intelligence available before and during the Gallipoli Campaign, we will see that before the outbreak of war open-source intelligence, attachés' reports and clandestine reconnaissances were vital sources. Once hostilities with Turkey had started, given the paucity of signals intelligence at the time, human intelligence was a vital source of strategic, terrain, operational and tactical intelligence in the Dardanelles operations before the landings. Imagery intelligence also provided vital information about Turkish defences before and after the landings.

The lies and myths about a lack of geographical preparations began during the Gallipoli Campaign itself, and the Dardanelles Commission, set up to determine the causes of failure, became a battleground of accusation and counter-accusation. An extreme perpetrator of the myth was the journalist Ellis Ashmead-Bartlett, who stated, with complete untruth:

> There were undoubtedly no maps in existence at all… The main difficulty was the question of maps; nobody had maps. There were no maps in existence and it was almost impossible to fire from the ships without them. . . If the War Office engages in a war with a nation, you would think they would make preparations before the war starts.[8]

As this book demonstrates, there were many maps (though not many large-scale ones to start with), and also much supporting strategic, geographical, terrain and tactical intelligence, a huge amount of which was gathered in the immediate pre-war period.

What happened to all this material within MO2, a section of the Directorate of Military Operations (DMO, which included Intelligence) at the War Office, and within the Naval Intelligence Division at the Admiralty, forms an important part of this study, as does the way in which it was fed (or not, as the case may be) to the field commanders. The fact, and problem, of divided command was recognised as an issue by a few perceptive individuals at the time, and has been accepted, with the benefit of hindsight, as one of the contributory causes of failure.

Hamilton was no stranger to the concept of combined amphibious operations, as John Lee has recently shown. In the early 20th century, Britain experienced a collective hysteria relating to a predicted German descent upon her coastline. Henry Rawlinson had introduced his study to the Staff College in 1903, and his protégé, George Aston of the Royal Marines, led staff rides along the south coast of England to further their understanding. The analysis in 1905 by an Admiralty and War Office Committee of a botched 1904 joint manoeuvre led to a report which laid the foundations for the *Manual of Combined Naval and Military Operations* of 1911 (reprinted 1913).[9] This established the principles followed (as far as was possible) for the actual landings in 1915. In the pre-war period, naval officers lecturing at the Staff College assumed an unopposed landing; the firepower of modern weapons made an opposed landing unthinkable, while Aston himself had concluded that naval gunfire was powerless to overpower modern coast-defence forts.[10] While GOC Mediterranean in 1912 (just after the new *Manual* had appeared), Hamilton observed the work of the new Combined Operations Command in Cairo and attended combined operations exercises and debriefs. In the same year he also studied amphibious operations from the defenders' viewpoint. Churchill and Kitchener were also present at joint exercises in the Mediterranean.[11]

Combined operations always present a particular hazard because of the dangers and problems associated with divided intelligence, planning and command – the inevitable friction between army and navy jealous of their own capabilities and traditions. There have been many disasters due to these causes – Walcheren in 1809 during the Napoleonic Wars, the Crimea in 1854–5, Gallipoli in 1915. The American historian Theodore Ropp judged that 'British Army intelligence did very badly in World War I ... in amphibious operations [i.e. Gallipoli], where intelligence responsibilities were no clearer than they had been during the Crimea ...'[12]

Intelligence matters were not all well-ordered within the Admiralty and the War Office. In the 1860s, even after the lessons of the Crimea:

> British military intelligence lacked central direction and management. ... Weaknesses in Britain's intelligence system ... were generally not in the collection of information, but in two other major functional areas, processing-analysis and dissemination-reporting.[13]

Certain aspects improved in the 1870s with the establishment of an Intelligence Branch, but the Gallipoli tragedy was to demonstrate that all was not necessarily well in those functional areas.

A similar situation pertained apropos the mapping of potential operational areas. Despite repeated warnings of Boer unrest, and the experience of the First Boer War in 1880–1, the British Army began operations against the Boers in 1899 without any good mapping, and had to improvise half-inch scale cover in the field from farm surveys. This time the British learnt from experience, and preparations for operations in France and Belgium were accordingly much better; any deficiencies in the maps used by the BEF in 1914 were due to the tardy state of French national mapping (despite the experience of 1870) rather than to any inefficiency in the Geographical Section at the War Office. What is more, in the aftermath of the Akaba incident of 1906, a one-inch map of the Gallipoli Peninsula had been prepared, in two sheets. Much more will be said about this later, but at least a reasonable operations map was available in 1914–15. However, good, large-scale operations maps could not be improvised; they relied upon a pre-existing data-bank of geodetic and trigonometrical data, and for inaccessible areas, as this book will show, this presented a huge problem. But how inaccessible was the Gallipoli Peninsula? We will return to this question in Chapter 2.

In 1887 that splendid and efficient intelligence officer, Henry Brackenbury, instructed the young Charles Callwell, later one of the major players in the Gallipoli saga, in the proper duties of an intelligence officer:

> I shan't expect you to be able to answer every question . . . right off the reel; I shan't even expect the information necessarily to be actually available in the department. But I shall expect you not to be helpless, but to find means of getting that information somehow within a reasonable time. . . if you keep sucking information into the place, and if you see that [it] is properly registered and so made available when required, your particular section will in course of time become a real going concern. Its archives will enable you, or whoever succeeds you, to answer any question that I or any properly authorised person may desire to ask.[14]

Unfortunately, as the Dardanelles episode so graphically depicts, this advice was not always adhered to, and the 'lack of central direction and management' was the skeleton in the cupboard (or rather pigeonhole).

What of the putative intelligence target? The Gallipoli Peninsula had the reputation of being rugged, wild and inhospitable. The 1910 Macmillan *Guide to Greece, The Archipelago, Constantinople, The Coast of Asia Minor, Crete and Cyprus* (the Asia Minor part of which was revised by the geographer and archaeologist D G Hogarth, friend and mentor of T E Lawrence) noted of the Peninsula that leopards, lynxes, hyenas, brown bears, wolves, jackals and wild boars were occasionally encountered.[15] The *Guide*, besides giving the usual information about ancient Troy and the Hellespont, stated that the castles on either side of the Narrows at Chanak had recently been restored and armed with Krupp guns.[16] This was the period when the Admiralty Chart warned that vessels entering the Dardanelles during the hours of darkness would be fired on. Apart from this, no indication was given of its strategic importance.

This does not, however, give a true picture of public, as well as military and naval, awareness in Europe. The Dardanelles had been of importance in the Crimean and Turco–Russian Wars of the 1850s and 1870s, in both of which conflicts the Gallipoli Peninsula had been occupied by British and French troops, and more recently in London had been discussed at the highest level in 1906 during the Akaba Crisis, had been the subject of several joint naval and military appreciations between 1906 and 1912, and had again been involved in headline-grabbing conflicts in the Italo–Turkish War of 1911 and in the Balkan Wars of 1911–13, when the Bulgarians attacked the Bulair Lines defending the Peninsula and the Greeks were planning landings on it. The attention of the world had therefore been very much focused on the Dardanelles in the years just before the First World War, military and naval attachés had been sending back reports, intelligence officers had been gathering information, and naval and military staffs had been preparing appreciations and making outline plans. 1906 was a crucial year. Apart from the implications of war with Turkey following from the Akaba crisis, it saw the launch of the *Dreadnought*, precipitating the naval race with Germany which meant that the British were effectively forced to abandon the Mediterranean to the French, implicitly accepting in turn the task of defending the Atlantic coast of France. The year also saw the beginning of the Wilson–Foch military conversations which were to lead to the plan that the BEF would stand on the left of the French armies in the event of a German attack. Despite all this, Anglo–French strategic planning and naval coordination, apart from the agreement to send the BEF to France, were in a state of chaos on the eve of the war.[17]

In the decade before 1914, Turkey had been becoming more closely involved with Germany. If Turkey did become involved in a war on the German side, how much did those on the Allied side with a 'need to know' actually know about the terrain of the Gallipoli Peninsula, as opposed to its coast defences? And to what lengths did they go to find out? Today, knowledge of the world's terrain, photographed and remotely sensed from satellites, airliners, helicopters, and various other platforms, and viewed by the public from aeroplanes flying miles above remote and inaccessible parts of the globe, makes it difficult to comprehend the difficulties of acquisition of terrain intelligence only a hundred years ago when powered flight was but a few years old. From an aeroplane floating over the Aegean towards the historic Dardanelles, can be seen today, particularly when the sun is low, practically every significant feature of this epic and tragic landscape and seascape.

But things were very difficult in late 1914 and early 1915 when, following the outbreak of hostilities with Turkey, the British were thinking about the need for amphibious combined operations to capture the Gallipoli Peninsula and push the fleet through the Dardanelles and the Sea of Marmara to Constantinople, to deal Turkey such a body-blow that it would capitulate. This, it was assumed, if successful would so alter the strategic balance in south-east Europe and the Moslem world that it would knock the Central Powers off-balance and lead to a speedy Allied victory.

At this time, the Allies possessed a great deal of strategic, tactical and topographical intelligence, including a medium-scale (1:50,000 and its 1:63,360 derivative) map which, although based on a Crimean War reconnaissance survey, was contoured and good enough for swift operations. This was also the situation that obtained in France and Flanders, and on the Eastern Front. In no theatre of war did either side, in 1914–15, go to war with a large-scale artillery map, except in those localised operations where fortresses had to be besieged. What both sides were not prepared for, and this is strange in the light of recent operations such as the Russo–Japanese War and the Balkan Wars, was trench warfare, in which attacks were consistently held up by barbed wire and the concentrated fire of magazine rifles, machine guns and field artillery, and therefore they had not equipped themselves with what rapidly became essential for any such operations – the accurate, large-scale, artillery map, which could be used as a base for overprinting trenches and other tactical detail, thus creating the trench map with which the First World War, on almost every front, is practically synonymous.[18] Such a map could not at that time be constructed for inaccessible terrain; it had to be based on an existing national precision survey. If this was not available, and in the absence of modern photogrammetric techniques and equipment, no accurate map could be made.

The prerequisites for such an amphibious operation, apart from the availability of trained men and sufficient *matériel*, were surprise and good intelligence. Well-known principles of war (decide on aim and pursue it remorselessly, act offensively, concentrate at the decisive point, be mobile, achieve surprise, cooperate, security of base and communications, economy of force, etc.) were, as always, relevant; it is instructive to see how many were ignored in the Dardanelles operations. Speed was essential, as Admiral 'Jacky' Fisher pointed out in January 1915, quoting Napoleon: 'CELERITY – without it FAILURE,'[19] and also strength; as Stonewall Jackson observed, you had to 'get there fustest with the mostest men'.[20] You also, as a Polish officer said during the Second World War, with feeling, from bitter experience, had to be stronger.[21] But first, intelligence was needed, and lots of it. It is important to 'know your enemy', both in terms of his military forces, dispositions, capabilities and intentions but also in terms of that equally important enemy – the terrain.

The Gallipoli Campaign includes a large number of 'firsts'; airfield reconnaissance, beach photography from the air, map supply by air, air reconnaissance and photography of underwater obstacles (mines). These are all documented here. As an example of successful landings, followed by a failure to break out of the bridgeheads, it deserves extremely careful study to determine to what extent this success and failure were linked to the quality of geographical and tactical intelligence. Inevitably it demands comparison with the successful NEPTUNE and OVERLORD (D-Day) and subsequent operations of 1944. The similarities are obvious, but bear careful scrutiny. Both involved amphibious combined operations, cooperation with allies, deception, technology advanced for its time (e.g. indirect naval gunnery, aircraft and aerial photography, etc.). But on another level there was a world of difference between Gallipoli and the D-Day operations. In the case of D-Day there was a clear strategic priority and aim, well-defined political control and leadership, joint staff, planning and intelligence, a long planning period, genuine combined amphibious operations, vast resources, and a huge amount of intelligence available and well-processed (by a specially created Allied joint-staff Theatre Intelligence Section), and intelligence and operational support from the indigenous resistance movement. As has been pointed out on many occasions, the Dardanelles operations benefited from none of these.

The planners of the D-Day landings in June 1944 had a great advantage – from the time that the German invasion threat receded, at the time of Hitler's invasion of Russia (1941), they had almost three years to prepare, and the call went out for holiday photographs of French beaches and coastal resorts; ten million were eventually received.[22] Gallipoli was very different – from the start of hostilities with Turkey at the beginning of November 1914, there were almost six months to the landings on 25 April 1915, in which it must be said much planning and preparation could have been done. Without such crucial groundwork, a disaster was a certainty. And so it proved. On 16 February 1915 the War Cabinet decided that troops might be required, and decided to send them from Egypt and Britain and set up a base on the island of Lemnos. From the time that a firm decision was made to commit large ground forces on 19 March, only five weeks remained until the landings. Even at the time of Kitchener's appointment of Sir Ian Hamilton, on 12 March, to the command of the ill-fated Constantinople Expeditionary Force (hurriedly, but too late, renamed Mediterranean Expeditionary Force for security reasons), no such firm decision had been taken.

Planning for the eventuality could and should been undertaken earlier. Such an operation had been mooted for decades, and both the Army and the Navy had studied the problems and prepared joint appreciations and reports. They had gathered much information, and could have obtained a great deal more. Any operation has to be based on organised and focused intelligence; intelligence is the handmaid of operations; it should not be vague or haphazard. Planners and commanders have to consider what information they need. Information needs have to be identified; intelligence has to be acquired by various methods, both overt and covert; it has to be processed – i.e. analysed, interpreted and evaluated; it needs to be distributed to all those with a need to know; and often it needs to be explained to those who receive it. Finally, commanders must base their plans on it, and not ignore it.

This book charts the interplay between intelligence, strategy, planning and operations; unfortunately the strategy, such as it was, was formulated without paying much attention at all to the intelligence (though the in-theatre planning took intelligence very seriously indeed), and ghastly mistakes were made as a consequence. While many in London, and almost all those on the spot, opposed the idea of 'Navy only' operations, and also large-scale military operations, both of these went ahead. It examines the intelligence about the Gallipoli Peninsula, and the methods by which it was acquired, both before and during the operations. In so doing it demolishes the myth, encountered in so much of the Gallipoli literature and sedulously fostered by Sir Ian Hamilton himself, that the Allies were ignorant of the terrain and were not prepared for the realities of what they encountered. Indeed, General Callwell, the Director of Military Operations in 1914–15, was so incensed by Hamilton's deliberately misleading statements to the Dardanelles Commission, that he asked to be able to give further evidence to the Commission, and publicised this in a post-war book.

It is demonstrated here that the British were in fact well-prepared with topographical and tactical intelligence, not least from a book published in 1914 by a German ordnance officer who had served in Gallipoli, that they possessed key details of a pre-war Anglo–Greek plan, formulated by Admiral Kerr with the encouragement of King Constantine of Greece, to capture the Peninsula, and that they were well-placed to conduct a successful operation if a sufficiently long planning period had been available and surprise had not been lost. Even with a very short time for planning and preparation, an amphibious operation as envisaged by Birdwood could have been successful if it had been carried out immediately, with sufficient trained forces, without prior bombardments by the fleet which took away the last elements of surprise. It is also clear that there was systematic lying to, and collusion against, the Dardanelles Commission, by Winston Churchill, Sir Ian Hamilton, and other key players, an episode well documented by Tim Travers and Jenny Macleod.[23]

One of the crucial questions is the extent to which the strategic, geographical, and tactical information which had been accumulating in the War Office and Admiralty was actually made available to the political, military and naval decision-makers, and to the field commander – Hamilton – and his Staff. While various pieces of evidence point to much more having been used in the field than Hamilton claimed, it is undeniable that certain appreciations – for example the 1906 joint report and Frederick Cunliffe Owen's 1914 reports – had a very limited circulation and were apparently not seen by Hamilton; indeed, most copies of the 1906 report had been destroyed. The surviving archival material is not always as helpful as might be expected in this respect. Even if they had not seen certain reports, Hamilton and Braithwaite were probably familiar with their main outlines and tenor.

The alleged lack of a British operational plan for the Dardanelles Campaign has long exercised many commentators. Here it is revealed that an important reason for this is that a plan did in fact exist – the Anglo–Greek plan – which, according to Churchill's evidence to the Dardanelles Commission, he could not remember whether he was aware of or not. In fact, he was the prime instigator of this plan, instructing Admiral Kerr (Commander-in-Chief of the Greek Navy) at the beginning of September 1914 to create such a plan in conjunction with the Greek General Staff. As we shall see, this plan involved the strengthening of the Greek fleet by the British Navy and landings by the Greek Army to capture the Gallipoli Peninsula before the fleet went through the Dardanelles to Constantinople. As will be made clear, this plan was well-known to several British officers apart from Kerr, including Admiral Limpus, in charge of the British Naval Mission at Constantinople, and Frederick Cunliffe Owen, the military attaché.

The Gallipoli Campaign was launched too late, as Admiral Kerr realised. After the realisation of lost surprise, the only valid reason for launching it was to take pressure off the Russian Caucasus front. When it was launched, it failed on the first day, after which it should have been abandoned. The land campaign, the tragic and glorious development of the military operations from April 1915 to January 1916, was an irrelevance. Its only useful purpose was, briefly, to divert Turkish attention from other fronts. Unlike the Western Front, where a series of attrition battles gradually wore down the Germans, the Gallipoli Campaign could never hope to achieve anything other than through surprise.

It was perhaps a brilliant strategic idea which could only have succeeded if all factors had worked in its favour. It depended upon that concatenation of circumstances which rarely arises: good planning, sensible and prolonged preparation, superior and trained forces, capable commanders, enemy caught off-balance and looking in the wrong direction – and (Napoleon's crucial ingredient) luck.

It could have succeeded in February 1915 but not, after prolonged naval bombardment and landings, in April. Key figures may have been playing duplicitous games; Kitchener, on 1 March, was urging Maxwell in Egypt to conceal the small size of Birdwood's force in order that the population of the Levant and Middle East might envisage something altogether more powerful – against Alexandretta, rather than against Gallipoli. Far from surprise being lost by accident, Kitchener was actually proposing a deliberate policy of encouraging a view in the Moslem world of certainty of large-scale operations, but against Alexandretta, not against the Dardanelles. The relevant telegram read:

> From Lord K. London. To Sir J. Maxwell, Cairo. Rec'd 1.3.15. 3341 Cipher. Private and Secret. Do not allow numbers and destination of troops you are sending to Lemnos be made public, as it might be advantageous if the impression in the Levant that a larger force had been sent.[24]

This deception attempt may have backfired on the expedition, as by this time the Turks were becoming thoroughly alarmed over the threat to the Dardanelles.

Peter Chasseaud
Peter Doyle
September 2005

Notes

1. Aspinall-Oglander, Brig.-Gen. C F, *History of the Great War, Military Operations, Gallipoli*, Vol. I, London: Heinemann, 1929, p. 90.
2. See for example, Moorhead, Rhodes James, etc. That the 'myth' of the maps is carried forward into popular culture is seen in an American comic book (World War Stories, Gallipoli, 1965), which pictures British intelligence officers combing the bazaars in Alexandria for intelligence. This was indeed done, but for two reasons: firstly, to gather material relating to the Ottoman domains generally, and secondly, as a deception scheme.
3. Lee, John, *A Soldier's Life. General Sir Ian Hamilton 1853–1947*, London: Pan, 2001, p. 146.
4. Keegan, John, *Intelligence in War. Knowledge of the Enemy from Napoleon to Al-Qaeda*, London: Pimlico, 2004.
5. Occleshaw, Michael, *Armour Against Fate. British Military Intelligence in the First World War*, London: Columbus, 1989.
6. Andrew, Christopher, *Secret Service. The Making of the British Intelligence Community*, London: Heinemann, 1985.
7. Kahn, David, *Seizing the Enigma. The Race to Break the German U-Boat Code 1939 – 43*, Boston MA: Houghton Mifflin, 1991.
8. Minutes of Evidence to the Dardanelles Commission, pp. 1403–1405, The National Archives (PRO) CAB 19/33.
9. War Office, *Manual of Combined Naval & Military Operations*, London: 1911 (reprinted 1913).
10. Lee, op. cit., pp. 102–3.
11. Ibid, p. 115.
12. Ropp, Theodore, in Foreword to Fergusson, Thomas G, *British Military Intelligence 1870–1914. The Development of a Modern Intelligence Organization*, London: Arms & Armour Press, 1984, p. xii. See also Ropp, *War in the Modern World*, New York: Collier, 1962.
13. Fergusson, op. cit., pp. 3, 12.
14. Callwell, Maj.-Gen. Sir Charles E, *Stray Recollections*, Vol. I, London: Edward Arnold, 1923, p. 305.
15. *Guide to Greece, the Archipelago, Constantinople, the Coast of Asia Minor, Crete and Cyprus*, 3rd edn, London: Macmillan, 1910, p. xviii.
16. Ibid, pp. 174–5.
17. Miller, Geoffrey, *The Millstone. British Naval Policy in the Mediterranean 1900–1914: The Commitment to France and British Intervention in the War* (Vol. III of the *Straits* trilogy), University of Hull Press, 1999.
18. The development of trench maps, artillery surveys and related matters is studied exhaustively in Chasseaud, Peter, *Artillery's Astrologers – A History of British Survey and Mapping on the Western Front 1914–1918*, Lewes: Mapbooks, 1999.
19. Rhodes James, Robert, *Gallipoli*, London: Pimlico, 1999, p. 27.
20. Quoted in Masters, John, *The Road Past Mandalay*, London: Michael Joseph, 1961.
21. Bidwell, Brig. Shelford, *Gunners at War*, London: Arrow, 1972, p. 241.
22. Collier, Richard, *D-Day, June 6, 1944. The Normandy Landings*, London: Cassell, 1999, p. 105.
23. Travers, Tim, *Gallipoli 1915*, Stroud: Tempus, 2001; Macleod, Jenny, *Reconsidering Gallipoli*, Manchester University Press, 2004.
24. Kitchener to Maxwell, in TNA(PRO) WO 158/574, Dardanelles Operations – Copies of Telegrams 1915 (GOC-in-C, Egypt).

CHAPTER 1

The Gallipoli Peninsula

The Gallipoli Peninsula is a small slither of land jutting defiantly out into the Aegean Sea. Adjacent to mainland Greece – Thrace – the region has seen conflict for centuries, part of the European legacy of the Ottoman Empire. Geologically, the Balkans and the Aegean Sea are complex, a function of major earth movements when, resulting from continental drift, the subcontinent of India impacted into the continent of Asia some 60 million years ago. The creation of the Dardanelles, the Sea of Marmara (so called because of the proximity of reserves of pure white marble) and the Bosphorus, waterways which have seen much intrigue and conflict, date from this continental collision, but continue to be modified today by movement along an active fault zone – the North Anatolian Fault – that periodically brings with it earthquakes, and resulting human tragedy.[1] This fault system has also created the offsets and constrictions that are such a feature of the Dardanelles, and have been influential in the formation of the Gallipoli Peninsula itself, which like most of the landscape, is still being shaped today.

The landscape of Gallipoli is hauntingly beautiful – a fact not lost on the young men who fought there, and the poets who followed.[2] Fragrant, green, teeming with wildlife and with the blue waters of the Aegean lapping its shores, it is no wonder that today tourists from Istanbul come to bathe in the quiet waters and take in the grandeur of the landscape. One hundred years ago it was somewhat different. The same landscape had a key role in the outcome of the battles there, in 1915. This is recorded in numerous histories and personal reminiscences of the Gallipoli Campaign which detail the local inadequacy of water supplies, the steepness of slopes, the incision of ravines, the precipitous nature of the cliffs, and the density of vegetation.[3]

With the benefit of today's memorialised, protected and revered landscape it is possible to do what was impossible for the Allies in 1915. Walking the landscape, examining its intricacies and points of detail, one may see how difficult it was to assault the beaches and climb the slopes – of varying angles – that characterise the Gallipoli Peninsula and its associated coastlines. It is also possible, not least from well-logs taken by the

British after the war,[4] to examine the potential for ground water supply for the invading troops, and to examine geological and botanical details of the valleys, ravines, hills and slopes, all of which could play a significant factor in any military campaign, if it were carried out in the region today. But was it not possible to collect this data from the field when the campaign was committed? It can be demonstrated that terrain materially affected the prosecution of the campaign from landings to evacuation,[5] and as such it can be argued that it was incumbent upon the General Staff to at least go some way in accumulating information on all these factors, prior to landing.

In this chapter we set the scene for the Gallipoli Campaign by examining the ground from first principles. Although couched in modern language, the techniques used are no different from those available to the men on the ground, on the sea, or in the air in 1915. It is an exercise on what might have been possible from ship, aircraft and small-scale landings, and in this way, sets the scene for our understanding of the level of terrain intelligence needed in planning an operation like that of Gallipoli in 1915.

Terrain evaluation for military purposes

Many modern writers have discussed the importance of terrain in determining the outcome of military campaigns, demonstrating that most successful campaigns draw upon the discriminating use of terrain by commanders.[6] Most successful commanders can see the advantage of the wise use of terrain, using it as an additional munition of war to magnify the efforts of the defender; as a force multiplier, terrain is of paramount importance, and perhaps nowhere so well demonstrated as at the Dardanelles. The informed gathering of terrain intelligence, and its use in the prosecution of battle is of paramount importance. We must judge the Gallipoli Campaign from this perspective. Aspects of terrain are considered at two scales: in strategic planning, usually reflecting the gross spatial distribution of major elements such as seas and mountains, and at the tactical (and operational) level during action, making the best use of ground in the furtherance of the strategic aims of the campaign. Not surprisingly, strategic aspects are of greatest importance at the inception of a campaign, and involve specific decisions about the deployment of troops and the provision of resources. Tactical considerations are made in order to fulfil the strategic aims on the ground.

Typically, there are five types of problem in tactical assessments of terrain:[7]

1. Position, that is in the provision of vantage points, and of refuge from those vantage points held by the enemy;

2. Mobility, most especially with respect to the existence of natural terrain barriers such as rivers and impassable slopes, and the ability of surfaces – the 'going' surfaces – to sustain the movement of troops, machinery and animals;

3. Ground conditions, and particularly their impact on the construction of entrenchments, permanent emplacements, tunnels and defensive positions;

4. Resource provision, particularly potable water supplies and building materials for roads, and defensive works; and

5. Hazard mitigation, particularly in the prevention of prevailing winds for chemical weapons, and the prevention of floods and mass movements which could threaten the lives and infrastructure of the troops.

Today, military assessments of terrain have attained a high degree of sophistication thanks to an ability to fingerprint the characteristics of certain terrain types across the world in order to predict the resource needs and to direct the tactical aspects of a battle.[8] Most conflicts are highly mobile, simply because of the increase in the efficacy of military vehicles and air power. However, the strategists of the First World War were hampered by poor communications, limited knowledge of terrain, outdated combat techniques, and a defensive ethos hard learnt on the Western Front. All these factors, it can be argued, militated against the favourable outcome of a campaign such as that fought in Gallipoli, where the terrain is complex. Some of this could, at the very least, have been mitigated with adequate intelligence, again the subject matter of this book.

This chapter outlines the role of gross terrain characteristics of the Gallipoli Peninsula in order to provide an appropriate context for the battleground of 1915. To express this, a simple system of compartmenting the terrain into specific areas with similar attributes – called 'land systems' by today's military analysts – is used. Although complex-sounding, this does not demand something of the order of 'rocket science' to understand, as it represents a simple comparison of pieces of ground, like-for-like. In fact, it is a geographical tool that was developed for the British military in planning for another war – the expected onslaught from the east across the battlefields of Germany during the Cold War.[9] Typical terrain units, the land systems, are characterised in terms of their geology, geomorphology, surface 'going' characteristics, vegetation and hydrogeology – all of which influenced the tactical use of ground. An overview of the terrain characteristics of the Gallipoli Peninsula is given below, an essential component of any understanding of the prosecution of the battles in 1915,[10] and a precursor to our discussion of the adequacy of terrain intelligence in preparation for these battles.

Climate and vegetation of the Peninsula

The climate of the region is typically Mediterranean, with mild winters, the mean January air temperature being normally between 7 and 9°C, and hot summers, with average air temperatures exceeding 25°C in July and August. Despite this norm, winter on the Peninsula can be hard, with dramatic fluctuation in temperature which means that it can be very cold indeed. There is a marked summer drought, although annual precipitation is normally between 600 and 700mm at sea level, rising to in excess of 1000 mm in mountain regions.[11] Heavy rainfall can lead to flash floods, with the otherwise dry valleys filled with raging torrents. In winter months it is not unheard of for the Peninsula to be blanketed with snow. Offshore, the weather conditions affecting the Mediterranean and Aegean were a material consideration in planning the campaign, as for just five months out of twelve the sea is calm, the rest of the time, from May to October, there is the likelihood of storms and strong winds.[12]

The vegetation on the Peninsula reflects the Mediterranean climate, developed by human clearance from the original mixed woodland, and comprises low herbaceous and aromatic shrubs of *garrigue* type, often dense and hostile to the passage of people.[13] Periodic fires, now often created by human activity, but a natural process nonetheless, mean that the level of vegetation can vary on the dry upland slopes. There are few naturally wooded areas, and trees of evergreen oak and pine are usually isolated and scattered, particularly where exposed. Elsewhere, active cultivation has tamed the landscape, particularly in the southern Peninsula and within the sheltered confines of Suvla Bay.

Geology

The Gallipoli Peninsula forms part of the Alpine Pontide range, formed during the great interval of earth movements that created the Alps, Himalayas, Karakoram and Atlas mountains. The Pontides have a strong east-west orientation – what geologists call their 'structural grain' – and are made up of more ancient crystalline rocks developed in Anatolia, and younger, softer but still folded sedimentary rocks in Thrace and the margins of Anatolia. This grain defines the shape and form of the Gallipoli Peninsula and its associated waterways, and is a significant feature of the 'bigger picture'. The oldest and hardest rocks seen on the Peninsula are crystalline rocks north-east of Bulair, at the point where it is at its narrowest. The geologically youngest rocks are the sediments found infilling the valleys and bays of the Peninsula; these are still soft and, in some cases, water-saturated.

A dominant feature in the Dardanelles is the North Anatolian Fault Zone, an important geological fracture that separates the European and

Anatolian tectonic plates, and an actual and symbolic separation of Europe from Asia. The fault zone itself runs under the Sea of Marmara and crosses the Peninsula to the Gulf of Saros (Xeros), forming the strongly rectilinear northern margin of the Peninsula and separating it from the rest of Thrace.[14] This fracture is complex, as it branches; its tributaries have formed the Dardanelles and the Sea of Marmara. It is still active today.[15] Movement of the fault produced the Sea of Marmara between 15 and 20 million years ago, with a maximum depth of 1000 metres, and led to the deposition of the thick sedimentary rocks on either side of the Dardanelles.[16]

The Gallipoli Peninsula is therefore mostly composed of relatively simple strata of sedimentary rocks, mostly limestones and sandstones.[17] On top of these are still younger sedimentary rocks formed as rivers spread out over the surface of the Peninsula, and at the foot of the older Anatolian uplands on what was called in 1915 the 'Asiatic Shore.' These comprise rocks formed some 4 million years ago, simple sands and silts, and these too have been subjected to earth movements along the fault zone, creating the plateaux and escarpments that are such a dominant feature of the topography of the Peninsula.

Relief

The relief of the Gallipoli Peninsula is relatively subdued, the dominant topographic elements being a series of ridges in the north and north-east–south-west trending plateaux, especially dominant in the south.[18] The northern ridges, narrow 'hog's backs' that border the northern margin of the Peninsula, are composed of mostly coarse-grained, folded sandstones and limestones. These hard rocks are steeply tilted from the horizontal, which creates prominent east–west trending headlands such as Nibrunesi Point, which continue to the coast at Bulair. The hardest of these rocks define a series of small, sheltered, but steep bays at the northern margin of the great expanse of Suvla Bay.

The hard ridges forming the northern coast contrast with the plateaux that characterise the upland areas of the rest of the Peninsula, which are formed from much softer rocks, with some notable exceptions. These exceptions were to be of great significance in the battles ahead in 1915. The plateaux of the southern Peninsula are made up of fine sands, fine silts and clays which sit upon the harder, bedded limestones which make up the coast of the Peninsula from south of Gaba Tepe around to Maidos – present-day Eceabat.

One of the most prominent topographic features of the southern Peninsula is the heavily dissected Sari Bair range – the highest hills in the fighting zone of 1915, and a plateau composed of a steep north facing cliff, created by the movement of geological faults, throwing up the cliff and

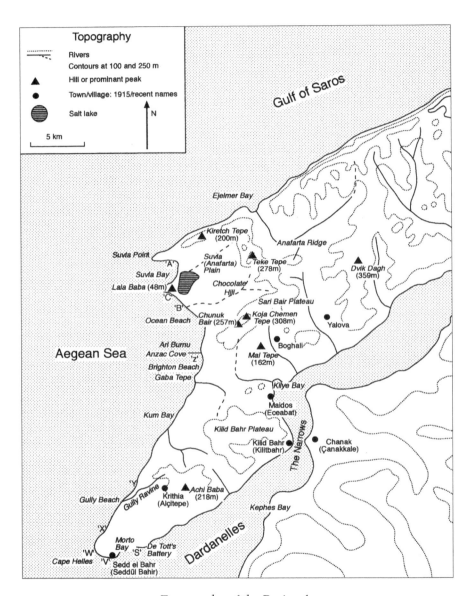

Topography of the Peninsula

creating a natural barrier. Heavily gullied by the action of periodic heavy rainfall on otherwise barren slopes, the steepness, and the action of weathering and erosion means that vegetation has a difficult time establishing a foothold, creating a 'badland' topography. This means that the margins of this plateau are heavily dissected, forming a complex network of sharp-crested ridges – the military term for which would be 'broken ground', in this case not an exaggeration.

Here and there, harder rock bands create more resistant features, such as 'The Sphinx', a feature named for its resemblance to the Egyptian monument, adjacent to which Anzac soldiers had camped and exercised. As was apparent to the men on the ground, the Sari Bair Plateau is dissected by three major gullies which run down to the sea, part of a drainage pattern in which water defines its own, parallel path from the peaks. This creates the amphitheatric form of the Anzac battlefield, supplied by the major gullies, the three intervening ridges being important strongholds and observation platforms. Famously, the first of those loses its broad character to become 'The Razor's Edge', created by the erosion of a hard cap to the ridge, the softer sediments forming a sharp, blade-like, unvegetated crest.

In the south-eastern part of the Peninsula, the Kilid Bahr Massif forms a counterpart to the Sari Bair Plateau, divided from it by a belt of low ground exploited by rivers and man which passes from Gaba Tepe across the Peninsula to the shore of the Dardanelles, just north of Maidos (Eceabat) which shelters under the steep cliffs of the Kilid Bahr Plateau. Formed from the same rocks and sediments as its counterparts, the boundaries of this mountain are more subdued than that of the Sari Bair range. Nevertheless, its northern boundary, the scarp slope, glowers down on the low ground crossing the Peninsula from Gaba Tepe, and is sharply incised by two valleys running down to the Dardanelles, the second of which, Saghani Dere, separates the Kilid Bahr escarpment from the Achi Baba (Alci Tepe) Plateau. The strongly fortified Kilid Bahr fortress, commanding the Narrows and facing similar forts at Chanak (present Cannakale), is completely protected by the steep cliffs of the massif that bears its name.

Achi Baba – actually Alci Tepe[19] – is in fact a continuation of the Kilid Bahr escarpment, separated by the incised valley of the Saghani Dere. A true plateau, its flat top is surmounted by the small, almost rectangular peak of Achi Baba itself, almost a classic 'Kopje' – a feature that must have chimed with Hamilton and other veterans of the South African veldt – and its slopes are incised by ephemeral streams that flow north-east and south-west, controlled by the strong structure imposed over the rest of the Peninsula. These streams, particularly those heading for the tip of the Peninsula are strongly gullied, in some cases forming deep ravines – Zighin Dere (Gully Ravine), Kanli Dere and Kereves Dere, all of which serve to break up the Peninsula into separate broad spurs. These ravines exploit the structural grain of the Peninsula, to give a parallel-alignment to the drainage of the southern Peninsula. This large area of the southern Peninsula gives the impression of a long, low-angled glacis, a tantalising vision for the military planners of 1915, entertaining the possibility of low trajectory naval guns sweeping its low angled slopes.

Hydrology

The majority of rivers within the Gallipoli Peninsula are seasonal, and most valleys are dry for much of the year. Exceptions occur in the northern part of the study area, on the margins of the Suvla Plain, where there are some perennial streams. All the major rock strata forming the Peninsula have potential as aquifers – those natural water containers. Few detailed hydrological studies have been carried out in the Gallipoli Peninsula itself, as it is relatively unpopulated, and most studies have concentrated upon the Ergene Basin to the north, strategically important for the supply of water to Istanbul.[20] However, it is clear from studies of sediments on the southern margin of the Dardanelles[21] that the main aquifer potential lies with the limestones that form the cliff lines, and within the much younger sand and gravel deposits that fill the valleys.[22]

Terrain classification

Given the factors discussed above, it is possible to divide the terrain of the Gallipoli Peninsula into a series of sectors, land systems, which have in common aspects of landscape, geology, available water and vegetation characteristics, and that may be distinguished from each other. In turn, these 'land systems' should enable us, 100 years on, to make some judgements about the key issues that would have had a material effect on the campaign, as it unfolded.

Taking all the available evidence, six types of landscape, six land systems, may be recognised, all of them dependent largely on the underlying geology – the 'structural grain' – of the Gallipoli Peninsula.[23] These land systems are described below.

Plateaux. North-east–south-west trending, flat-topped escarpments and plateaux which are dissected by deeply incised valleys are a major component of the landscape. These landforms have been created on a bedrock of soft layers of clays and sandstones, which overlie harder limestones beneath (see below). These plateaux form the dominant topographical features of the Peninsula, but are usually set back from the coast, with coastal cliffs formed by harder limestone rocks found beneath the softer materials, with the notable exception of the Anzac sector. The surfaces of this land system are relatively firm and dry 'going' surface, although disturbed, finer-grained sediments are prone to wind transport during the summer months. The softer rocks can be dug easily – particularly important to both defender and attacker.

In most cases, the plateaux are vegetated by relatively dense, low growing *garrigue* shrubs typical of the Mediterranean coastal areas – this is a disadvantage to the attacker, as the shrubs, with their spikes and barbs, are hostile and dense enough to shelter snipers. Water availability in this landscape is locally variable, and is dependent on the disposition of locally porous and impervious strata, and ground water is found only at great depth, usually within the underlying limestone aquifers. Surface ground water is scarce, although it may occur here and there where water has perched on thin clay strata that have impeded the downwards movement of water from periodic rainfall.

At Anzac, this land system is heavily dissected, with dense, closely spaced and dry valleys separated by a complex network of sharp-crested ridges. Vegetation is typically dense consisting of low ground cover shrubs, but this falls away to bare surfaces where the slopes are steep and unstable. Trees are sparse and widely spaced. A steep, north-west-facing scarp which trends south-west–north-east defines the northern boundary of the Sari Bair Plateau, and this is no doubt the action of a geological fault. The lower slopes of this scarp are heavily gullied, and typical slope angles range from 20 to 40° on the valley sides. The plateau top is dissected by north-east–south-west trending valleys – gullies like Shrapnel Gully, which were to become an important lifeline during the campaign. High points tend to form along ridges, typified by the peaks of Chunuk Bair and Koja Chemen Tepe, with elevations of 261 and 308 metres respectively. To the south-west of the plateau area there is an undulating dip slope (5–10°), deeply incised by a network of dry stream beds, the valley sides of which are covered in dense scrub.

The Kilid Bahr and Achi Baba plateaux, with a mean elevation of 150 metres, have much broader plateau surfaces dissected by deep, steep sided river valleys. These valleys exploit the underlying structural grain of the Peninsula, and between them are broad, flat-topped elongate spurs oriented north-east–south-west. Farther east, towards the Gulf of Saros, the same dissected plateaux can be observed forming the spine of the Peninsula. Heavily dissected steep slopes are typical of the Chinar Dagh and Karaman Dagh between Suvla Bay and the Gallipoli Straits, the opening to the Sea of Marmara. Most celebrated are the low plateaux west of Bulair, at the neck of the Peninsula, heavily fortified since the Crimea, defending the remainder of the Peninsula, dominating the Narrows, from attack.

Limestone cliffs. This landscape is formed by the layering of harder limestone layers over softer rocks, and it typifies the cliffs that are seen all around the coast of the southern part of the Peninsula, from Kum Tepe to

Maidos (Eceabat). In fact, these rocks form the basement for the hills and mountains of the plateaux, and some of the gentler, cultivated slopes from Cape Helles to Krithia (Alcitepe) are formed by the same combination of limestones. These slopes have relatively gentle slope angles and are usually dissected to a varying degree by a number of prominent dry valleys, with broad undulations between. These slopes provide satisfactory 'going' surfaces which are mostly dry and firm, especially were there is insubstantial soil development, and particularly in the coastal areas. Most slopes are cultivated, and have been for centuries, but where slopes are too steep for cultivation, they are covered with the same dense, low *garrigue* scrub that is characteristic of the more upland sectors of the battlefields. Water is present as ground waters in the limestones, and spring lines, found at the junction of the permeable limestone with impermeable clays, are seen around the coast.

River beds. Low lying, flat or gently undulating valley floors filled with alluvium are an important component of the landscape; few if any have flowing rivers or streams. The majority of these valleys are cultivated and have been cleared of dense vegetation. The valley floors provide variable 'going' surfaces; although in dry valleys the surface may be relatively firm, it may be prone to lifting by wind where exposed. As such, the valleys have been important communication ways, in the southern Peninsula between Gaba Tepe and Maidos (Eceabat); from Ejelmer Bay east of Suvla on the Gulf of Saros to the villages east of the Anafarta mountains; the stream beds down to the Dardanelles at Karakova; and, most notably, at the town of Gallipoli (Gelibolu) itself, also on this coast.

In all the river beds, the possible presence of potable ground waters is tempting to the military mind; but it is dependent on the underlying geology and the thickness of the alluvium. The river alluvium itself – sands and gravels – may also be a useful aquifer, although close to coastal areas, groundwater is seasonally contaminated by sea water.[24]

Coastal plain. This system consists of a low lying coastal plain, typified by the Suvla (Anafarta) Plain, with gentle slopes and areas of inland drainage. In the Suvla Plain, water flow is highly seasonal and is impounded by a system of coastal sand dunes, and an area of elevated terrain at Lala Baba, to form a salt lake. Low lying areas close to the lake may retain water and are usually marshy. The alluvial plain associated with the lake is mostly cultivated, with few trees, although uncultivated areas may be covered by dense *garrigue* scrub. Where this coastal plain is traversed by perennially flowing rivers, the river corridor/valley is densely vegetated. The Salt Lake is known to dry out completely during high summer (August), but is today kept wet through a permanent connection to the sea. The coastal plain 'going' surfaces are variable, as they are usually soft and water saturated close to the lake, although in 1915 seasonal desiccation produced a surface traversable by foot in August. In the inland areas, the 'going' surfaces are passable in most cases. The Salt Lake is too saline to provide potable water, due primarily to seasonal evaporation, and is used in the production of salt. Ground water is present in the alluvium, although close to the sea it may be contaminated by salt.

The most celebrated area of coastal plain is that close to the small settlement of Bulair. The low, cultivated, and heavily fortified hills west of Bulair give way to an area of coastal plain adjacent to potential landing beaches at Bakla Liman.[25] Marshy in places, defended by sand spits and dunes, this area of coastal plain played on the mind of both attacker and defender alike.

Linear ridges. Linear ridges trending approximately east–west and north-east–south-west define the northern margin of the Peninsula almost to its neck at Bulair, with elevations typically up to 200 metres. There are two principal linear hills within this system: the Anafarta Ridge to the south-east; and the Karakol Ridge to the north-west, running parallel to the north-east coast, between Suvla Point and Ejelmer Bay. Both ridges are associated with the North Anatolian Fault system, as is the coast of the Gulf of Saros in the north. The ridges are made of hard rocks, a factor not lost on the soldiers of the day.[26] Typically, the sharp, thinly bedded and steeply tilted coarse sandstones break into slabs, and this helps create a coastline at the northern part of Suvla Bay that is highly indented, providing ample opportunity for the creation of small, natural harbours, harbours which are still used today for small-scale fishing operations.

The orientation of the ridges points to the strong east–west oriented structural control of the region. Both major ridges have an asymmetrical cross section, with gentler slopes to the south-east, and steeper slopes to the north-west. North-west slopes are dissected by shallow, parallel-aligned valleys, most marked in the main Karakol Ridge. The gentler dip slopes are only dissected to a minor degree by stream networks that feed low-lying areas. The two ridges are linked by a series of flat topped hills, with elevations of up to 250 metres, which trend north-west–south-east, and also show some limited dissection. In general, the slopes are broad and open, although usually covered by dense *garrigue* scrub vegetation. 'Going' surfaces are mostly firm and dry.

Military implications of the land system analysis

The subdivision of the beautiful landscape of the Gallipoli Peninsula into workmanlike packages – the land systems – serves to indicate what might have been known to the military observer standing on the deck of one of His Majesty's vessels off the shores of Gallipoli in 1915. Certainly, although pigeonholing of landscape in this way is a late 20th century phenomenon, all of its components would have been well known in 1915 and are picked out on the maps used in the planning stages, and in the contemporary reconnaissance panoramic sketches.[27] The hills, valleys and slopes, at the very least, would have been visible from the sea. What our retrospective analysis achieves is the highlighting of a number of terrain aspects that were to assume great importance in the Gallipoli Campaign of 1915: vantage points; ground conditions for trenches and fortifications; the traversability by men and animals of the ground surface, beach width and water supply. All of these factors, intimately associated with the terrain, were to grow in importance as the campaign unfolded, and are of importance in the prosecution of military campaigns throughout history. They were, surely, on the minds of Hamilton and his Staff in 1915.

Vantage/refuge points. The highest areas with the best vantage points are provided by the plateaux and ridges. Particularly important is the scarp line of the Sari Bair Range which provides a direct line of sight from the subsidiary peaks of Koja Chemen Tepe and Chunuk Bair to the Suvla Plain below. Little refuge is available for troops at the base of this slope, especially in the numerous deeply incised valleys and broad surfaces below. The south-east facing plateaux slopes have a gentler gradient and vantage is gained from the flat peaks such as Achi Baba with a good field of observation, although this has been challenged.[28] However, where deeply incised, the parallel valley systems provide good opportunity for refuge. The Karakol and Anafarta ridges also provide significant vantage potential, particularly with respect to observation of the Suvla Plain and valley bottoms, although the east–west orientation of the ridges is a complication that would require careful positioning for defensive positions. The Bulair Lines, heavily defended, provide vantage for defenders against seaborne invasion, the attackers rising up from open beaches.

Ground conditions for defensive works. Ground conditions for defensive works and 'going' surfaces for the movement of men and animals are variable. The softer sedimentary rocks of the plateau tops provide suitable ground conditions for trench, dugout and tunnel construction, especially where, as at Sari Bair, there are hard bands that could be, and were, used to give support to the roofs of offensive tunnels later in the campaign. Problems arise for trench construction through the density of vegetation cover and consequent root system penetration. The coastal cliff regions and harder ridges are composed of harder rocks which require heavier tools and more intensive excavation works, and this would be especially true of the long standing defensive works in the geologically older and harder rocks of the Bulair lines. On the southern part of the Peninsula, in

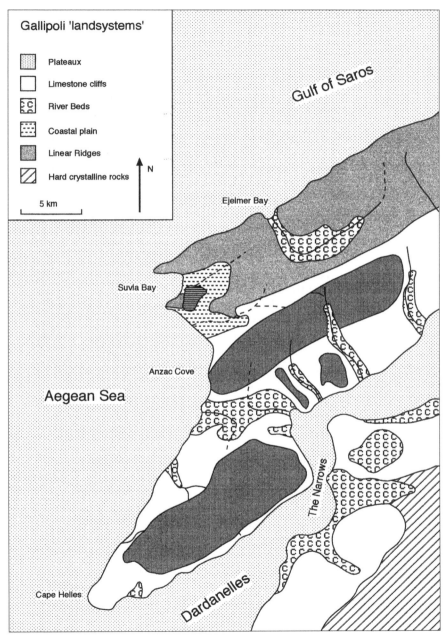

Gallipoli 'landsystems'

some cases, the slabby and blocky nature of the rocks provides the possibility of the construction of breastworks and outposts out of stone blocks, as occurred at Y Ravine on Gully Spur in Helles, and at Jephson's Post on the Karakol Ridge. Entrenchment of low-lying areas in valleys and plains would be possible, due to the ease of working – but floods, which were to occur in the later part of 1915, would cause a problem.

Traversability and 'going' surfaces. In all cases, with the possible exception of the low lying areas of valley and plain, slopes are difficult to traverse. In particular, the dissected slopes of the plateaux of Sari Bair, Kilid Bahr and Achi Baba are especially problematical. The steep, gullied, arid 'badland' topography of the north-western slopes of the Sari Bair Range is particularly so, as the depth of valley incision creates a broken terrain in which it is easy for attacking troops to lose contact and for communications to break down. Continuity of terrain features, difficult to assess remotely, is also a problem, and was especially to be so when the attacking Anzac troops found that there was no easy route from Plugge's Plateau up to the heights of Sari Bair – the Razor's Edge having been formed from the erosion of harder rocks capping what was thought in all pre-campaign intelligence to be a continuous ridge.

Finally, the steeply-incised, narrow and flat-bottomed valleys and steep coastal cliffs of Cape Helles are a significant barrier to mass troop movements and landings, something that would have been self evident in the reconnaissance, and which was indicated in the maps issued prior to the landing.[29] Given the overall aridity of the landscape, suitably firm 'going' surfaces are provided with the exception of seasonally wet land areas of valleys, coastal plains and the Salt Lake, with the most suitable for heavy traffic being the limestone cliffs and slopes of the southern Peninsula. In all cases, roads were poor, requiring the attention of engineers from their arrival in 1915.[30]

Beach width. The most suitable landing beaches, in the sense of width and the possibility of accommodating large numbers of men, are those associated with river valleys as they reach the coast, and the broad expanse of the coastal plain. These provide wide stretches of beach with a relatively gentle gradient which are not directly associated with coastal cliffs and other height and slope disadvantages. Suvla Bay is typical of this, but other, less expansive examples are seen either side of the Gaba Tepe promontory, and in Morto Bay. Bakla Liman, behind the Bulair Lines, was another possibility, with a broad, sheltered beach, albeit overlooked by the prominent central ridge of Kuru Tepe to the east. Beach development at the foot of the plateaux and limestone cliffs is mostly unsatisfactory, forming either narrow beaches with steep sea cliffs, or, in the case of the steep limestone cliffs, narrow beaches associated with steep, incised and easily enfiladed valleys, typical of the beaches at Cape Helles.

Water supply. The Gallipoli Peninsula is a mostly green and pleasant land in which cultivation, particularly of the low slopes of the southern part of the Peninsula, is entirely possible. This would have been observable from the sea and the air, as would the arid, badland topography of the Anzac area. Seasonal rivers flow when rainfall is heaviest in the winter months, and ground waters are recharged, particularly in the limestone strata of the coastal areas and the sands and gravels of the river valleys. Beach sediments also hold some water supply potential, although contamination from salt water is a problem.[31] The poorest opportunities for ground waters are in the higher plateaux, as surface ground-waters are present only locally, the rest being at depths beyond the capability of Royal Engineer drilling.

Summary. The land system analysis highlights two major points which would have needed to be considered in planning an invasion, but which were not necessarily to hand in the planning of the 1915 campaign. Firstly, there are few satisfactory landing beaches associated with the steep coastal limestone cliffs of the southern part of the Peninsula; yet those associated with broader coastal settings, such as that of Suvla and at Bulair, are wider and more suitable to mass deployment of troops – although, as in the case of Suvla Bay, overlooked by a range of hills, that required capture at the earliest opportunity.[32] Secondly, with the exception of the high ground surrounding the Suvla Plain (Karakol and Anafarta ridges), the remainder formed a distinct land system which, although suitable for the construction of defensive positions, has limited ground-water for the supply of troops. Clearly then capture of the high ground was of the greatest importance, and in normal circumstances, was to be executed rapidly to prevent stagnation into static warfare.

In a paper read to the Royal Geographical Society on 26 April 1915, the noted archaeologist and expert on the Near East, D G Hogarth, outlined the geography of the war with Turkey. This paper, read a day after the landing had been made and undoubtedly in ignorance of the land-based assault, made the following conclusion:

> All the western end of the Gallipoli Peninsula is of broken hilly character, which combines with lack of water and consequent lack of population and roads to render it an unfavourable area for military operations. No general, if he had the choice, would land a considerable force upon it at any spot below the narrows.[33]

Clearly, this was a view which upheld the need for a landing at Bulair. Yet despite the view of an expert – later to be attached to the Admiralty – and given that the strategic aims of the campaign were to simply support the naval operation through the capture of the high ground, and removal of the threat of shore batteries, a landing in the south-western part of the Peninsula was necessary, with a consequently limited range of options available to the Allied commander-in-chief. How he gathered information, and used this, will be a major preoccupation of the remainder of this book.

Notes

1. Outlined in technical terms by Perincek, D, *American Association of Petroleum Geologists Bulletin*, 75, pp. 241–57; and Sengor, A M C and Yilmaz, Y, *Tectonophysics*, 75, pp. 181–241.
2. Masefield, John, *Gallipoli*, New York: Macmillan, 1916; although a work of propaganda (see Macleod, Jenny, *Reconsidering Gallipoli*), the words of the Poet Laureate well express the beauty of the landscape.
3. These aspects of the terrain are well discussed in Aspinall-Oglander's official history (1929), as well as in most one-volume accounts, the most important of which remains Rhodes James (1965). The contemporary, propaganda-influenced account by John Masefield (1916) describes the landscape well, as does Nevinson (1919). Surprising detail about the geology of the region is contained in Hargrave, John, *The Suvla Bay Landing* (1964).
4. Preserved in the British Geological Survey at Wallingford are logs taken on the Peninsula during the period of post-war British occupation. These provide information not readily available, to the Allies at least, during the war.
5. Doyle, P and Bennett, M, 'Military Geography: The Influence of Terrain in the Outcome of the Gallipoli Campaign 1915', in *Geographical Journal*, 165, March 1999, pp. 12–36.
6. For example, Mitchell, C W, *Terrain Evaluation*, 2nd edn, Harlow: Longman, 1991; Mitchell, C W and Gavish, D, 'Land on which battles are lost or won', in *Geographical Magazine*, 52, 1980, pp. 838–40; Parry, J T, 'Terrain evaluation: military purposes', in Finkl, C W (ed.), *The Encyclopedia of Applied Geology* (*Encyclopedia of Earth Sciences*, Vol. 13), New York: Van Nostrand Reinhold, 1984.
7. Parry, op. cit.; Mitchell, op. cit.
8. Ibid, and Patrick, D M and Hatheway, A W, 'Engineering geology and military operations: an overview with examples of current missions', in *Bulletin of the Association of English Geologists*, 26, 1989, pp. 265–76.
9. Mitchell, op. cit.
10. Doyle and Bennett, op. cit. have discussed this in some detail. A summary and explanation are given here.
11. United Nations (1982).
12. Callwell, Maj.-Gen. C E, *The Dardanelles*, London: Constable, 1919 (2nd edn 1924). p. 31.
13. von Sanders, Gen. Liman, *The Dardanelles Campaign* (trans. and with comments by Col. E H Schulz), US Army Corps of Engineers, 1931, p. 8.
14. Sengor and Yilmaz, op. cit.
15. Crampin, S and Evans, R, 'Neotectonics of the Marmara Sea region of Turkey', in *Journal of the Geological Society of London*, 143, 1986, pp. 343–8.
16. Ibid, and Perincek, op. cit.

17. Sengor and Yilmaz, op. cit.; Ternek, Z; Erentöz, C; Pamir, H N and Akyürek, B, *1:500,000 Ölçekli Türkiye Jeoloji Haritasi. Explanatory Text of the Geological Map of Turkey, Istanbul*, Ankara: Maden Tetkik ve Arama Genel Müdürlügü Vayinlarindan, 1987.
18. von Sanders, op. cit., p. 8.
19. Named Achi Baba on all British maps since at least 1908 (GSGS 2285).
20. Karatekin, N, 'Hydrological Research in the Middle East', in *Reviews of Research on Arid Zone Hydrology*, UNESCO, 1953, pp. 78 –95; Pamir, H M, 'Hydrogeological research in the basin of the Ergene, in *Proceedings of the Ankara Symposium on Arid Zone Hydrology*, UNESCO, 1953 pp. 224–31; *Groundwater in the Eastern Mediterranean and western Asia*, Natural Resources/Water Series No. 9, New York: UN, 1982.
21. Well-logs in the possession of the British Geological Survey at Wallingford, drilled by the British as occupying power in the 1920s, also confirm this.
22. Beeby-Thompson, A, *Emergency water supplies for military, agricultural and colonial purposes*, London: Crosby Lockwood & Son, 1924; UN (1982), op. cit.
23. For a full account, see Doyle and Bennett, op. cit.
24. Beeby-Thompson, op. cit.
25. And noted as such on British military maps (GSGS 2285, 1908).
26. Hargrave, J, op. cit. Hargrave was a boy scout, and may well have been *au fait* with elementary geological principles; he certainly makes references to 'sandstones and schists', both hard rock types that define the northern ridges.
27. GSGS 2285 (1908), for all its shortcomings, refers to the state of vegetation ('low scrub' or 'cultivated slopes'); it clearly denotes cliffs, and the 'steep sandy bluffs' of Anzac, as well as the valleys and steep slopes of the Suvla area. The panoramas, drawn some time in the immediate run-up to the landings, also clearly define these features.
28. Ekins, Ashley, 'A ridge too far: military objectives and the dominance of terrain in the Gallipoli Campaign', in Celik, Kenan and Koc, Ceyhan (eds), *The Gallipoli Campaign International Perspectives 85 years on*, Turkey: Cannakale Onsekiz Mart University, 2001, p. 11.
29. The 1:40,000 maps issued, based on the 1908 maps, indicate the steepness of the limestone cliffs that surround the cape, and highlight the narrowness of the landing beaches in this area.
30. War Diary, 2nd Lowland Field Company RE, in The National Archives TNA (PRO) WO 95/4309 & 4319; Anon., ['GLC'], 1997. 'Engineers at Gallipoli, 1915', *Royal Engineers Journal*, 111, pp. 31–9.
31. Beeby-Thompson, op. cit.
32. Suvla Bay is dismissed by most authors due to the problem of high ground, but suggestions that it provided a viable alternative are given by the near contemporary accounts of H W Nevinson in *The Dardanelles Campaign* (1918) and Maj.-Gen. C E Callwell in *The Dardanelles* (1924).
33. Hogarth, D G, 'Geography of the war theatre in the Near East', in *Geographical Journal*, 65, pp. 457–471 (p. 461).

CHAPTER 2

Genesis of the Gallipoli Campaign

The Dardanelles, that strategic waterway connecting the Aegean Sea and Mediterranean with the Sea of Marmara and ultimately, connecting through the Bosphorus, the Black Sea, has been a point of interest to military minds for centuries. Constantinople, the modern city of Istanbul, sits astride the Bosphorus and guards the entrance to the Black Sea thereby controlling entry to the winter ports of Russia. Because of this and a myriad of other reasons, Constantinople, the seat of the *Sublime Porte*, the name commonly used for the Ottoman Court and the Turkish Government, has long been coveted, particularly by Greece and Russia.

At the other end of the Marmara lies the Dardanelles, a narrow passageway between European and Asian Turkey, a tightly constrained waterway created by geological faulting over millennia. In European Turkey, the shores of the Dardanelles are guarded by the Gallipoli Peninsula, a narrow finger of land named after its principal settlement. Opposing this is the Asiatic Shore, the Aegean expression of the great Anatolian Peninsula, the greater part of modern Turkey, and the heart of the ailing Ottoman Empire in 1915. Fortified for centuries, the idea of squeezing a fleet of ships between the beetling brows of the shores of the Dardanelles has continually exercised the mind of the military of many nations, particularly so in the complex diplomacies of two centuries before the Gallipoli landings of 1915.

It is not possible to examine the relationship between operational planning on the one hand, and geographical intelligence on the other, without taking account of the political decision-making process, and of the extent to which the military and naval authorities were admitted to this decision-making in wartime. It is therefore necessary to look at the prolonged period during which Britain's strategic gaze, not to mention that of other European nations, was drawn to 'The Sick Man of Europe', and during which the consequent 'Eastern Question' was one of the dominant issues of political and public debate. Conflict with Russia over her approach towards India, or with Turkey over Egypt and the Suez Canal, inexorably raised the question of operations in the Dardanelles on several occasions, and on each of these occasions led to surveys, reconnaissances and intelligence-gathering initiatives which added to the data bank of available information.

What stands out from an examination of these issues during the century before the Gallipoli expedition of 1915 is the very large number of studies, naval, military and amphibious, which were made of the 'Dardanelles problem', and particularly those of 1854–5, 1876–80, 1904, 1906, 1908 and 1911–14. Despite this, when the time actually came to launch the 1915 operation, confusion still reigned and, despite the efforts of successive military attachés and vice-consuls, insufficient attention was focused by the General Staff on the difficult terrain of the Gallipoli Peninsula itself. In the immediate pre-war period, according to one of its intelligence officers, the Directorate of Military Operations was instructed to put most of its intelligence-gathering efforts as far as the Ottoman Empire was concerned into the frontier zones of Syria, Mesopotamia and Egypt. Gallipoli did not feature to any great extent in its concerns.[1]

International tensions

As international tension grew in the approach to the First World War, Turkey slipped remorselessly into the German camp. For much of the 19th century Britain had viewed Russia as the main enemy in Asia, largely because of the perceived threat to India, and therefore supported Turkey against Russia, notably in the Crimean War of 1854–6, but in 1876–8, British public opinion, led by Gladstone, shifted away from Turkey following Turkish atrocities against the Bulgarians.

An extreme British pamphlet of 1876 was entitled *The Dardanelles for England: the true solution of the Eastern Question*.[2] Captain John Ardagh RE studied the Dardanelles defences and wrote a *Report on the Defences of the Dardanelles* in 1877,[3] at a time of tension (followed by war) between Turkey and Russia. During the same prolonged crisis, in 1878, Admiral Hornby wrote a report on the problem of forcing the Dardanelles,[4] while in 1880 Ardagh advocated the seizure of the Dardanelles to forestall Russia. Matters became more complex in 1882, when British relations with the Sultan further deteriorated following trouble in Egypt; the subsequent effective British occupation of Egypt led to worsening relations with the *Sublime Porte*, which later erupted into a serious incident – almost leading to war – in the Akaba incident of 1906.

In 1896 Ardagh (now Colonel), very familiar with the topography and defences of the Gallipoli Peninsula and the Dardanelles, noted that an earlier study of the question of forcing the Dardanelles in the context of a possible war with France and Russia in 1888–9 had led to the conclusion that solely naval operations would be 'both dangerous and ineffective', and that if surprise were lost a whole army corps would be required in a combined operation.[5] In the 1890s Lord Salisbury, the Prime Minister, almost sent the fleet through the Dardanelles, and British opinion was again alienated by Turkish massacres of Armenians in 1896.

If Britain was increasingly alienated from Turkey, the Sultan, desperate for an ally in his dealings with Russia, sought the assistance of Bismarck's 'dynamic new Germany, with its formidable military machine and no apparent designs on Abdul Hamid's domains'.[6] The Germans seized the opportunity to court the Sultan. Kaiser Wilhelm II was keen to develop friendly relations with the Ottoman Empire as part of a strategic policy focused on the east, and linked this firmly with the German-inspired and engineered Berlin–Baghdad railway. German diplomatic and commercial initiatives increased, and in 1898 Wilhelm II paid a state visit to the Ottoman cities of Constantinople, Jerusalem and Damascus, an event viewed with alarm in London, Paris and St Petersburg. Between 1883 and 1895, and again between 1908 and 1911, a German military mission under General Kolmar von der Goltz was sent to Constantinople, and Germany assisted in developing the Dardanelles defences. Von der Goltz's reorganisation of the Turkish Army did not prevent German prestige taking a bad knock in Turkey when the German-trained Army did badly in the Balkan Wars.[7] The German Ambassador from 1897 to 1912, Baron Marschall von Bieberstein, and his successor Wangenheim, did much to consolidate German influence, particularly with Enver, the leader of the Young Turks' 'Committee of Union and Progress', and a new German Military Mission under General Liman von Sanders, though not popular with the German diplomats as it unsettled the Russians, arrived in December 1913.[8]

French influence in the Ottoman Empire was considerable during the 19th century, but although it was on the decline by the turn of the century, the Germans did not have it all their own way. Turkish officers were trained at the *Ecole de Guerre* and the *Service Géographique de l'Armée* in Paris, returning to Constantinople in 1892, and the French helped the Turkish General Staff to set up their Military Mapping Department in 1895. In 1893 the French and Russians signed an *entente*, leading to a further distancing of France from Turkey. The Anglo–Russian Convention of 1907, effectively creating the triple entente, pushed Turkey further into the German camp. Despite waning British prestige in Turkey, a British naval mission was sent to Constantinople under Admiral Limpus, and this was still there at the outbreak of war with Germany in 1914.

In the early 20th century, in the atmosphere of growing tension between Britain and Germany which arose as a consequence of the German naval challenge to British maritime and imperial supremacy, the defensive alliance between France and Russia, seen by Germany as 'encirclement' and committing Germany to a war on two fronts, naturally led to Russia being perceived in Britain as more of an ally against Germany than an enemy. While Germany focused all her diplomatic energy on fostering the Turkish connection, a crucial component of German ambitions in the Middle East, and without which the Berlin–Baghdad Railway could not have been envisaged, the British lost influence with Constantinople.

The 'Dardanelles Problem'

Against a backdrop of diplomacy and political manoeuvring, the Dardanelles provided a focus of attention. John ('Jacky') Fisher (who had commanded a battleship under Admiral Hornby in 1878, following the Russo–Turkish War, when the British Fleet sailed through the Dardanelles to the Sea of Marmara) had a further opportunity to make an on-the-spot study of the problem of forcing the Dardanelles while commanding the Mediterranean Fleet from 1901 to 1904. One of the periodic early 20th century crises led Fisher, now the new First Sea Lord, to decide that even with a military landing force to neutralise the coast defences, such an operation would be 'mighty hazardous'. While war was avoided, the strategic gaze of the British government, War Office and Admiralty was trained, not for the first time, on the Dardanelles. With Russia as a potential ally, the opening and maintenance of a direct sea route was bound to exercise British and French minds in the event of war with Germany.

Like that of the British, the German view of forcing the Dardanelles changed over time. In 1836 General von Moltke prophesied that: 'When the artillery-material in the Dardanelles has been properly organised, I believe that no fleet of any country would dare to sail through the Straits.'[9] This view was echoed by Churchill in a Cabinet Memorandum of 1911,[10] but he soon changed his tune. Following the Crimean and Russo–Turkish Wars, and bearing in mind the technological developments in ironclads, guns and munitions, many commentators had changed their view. In 1894 Captain Stenzel put forward the opposite view in his booklet *Der kürzeste Weg nach Konstantinopel. Ein Beispiel für das Zusammenwirken von Flotte und Heer* (*The Shortest Route to Constantinople. A Case Study for Combined Fleet and Army Operations*).[11]

Tension flared up again in the Akaba Crisis over the Egyptian–Turkish boundary, which followed the 'Tabah Incident' of early 1906, and almost led to hostilities between Britain and Turkey. The Committee of Imperial Defence (CID) was told by the General Staff that it opposed any naval or military action there,[12] but yet again attention was focused on possible operations at the Dardanelles as a way of bringing pressure to bear on Turkey.

Captain Grant Duff wrote a memorandum for the CID, dated 11 July, entitled *Military Policy in a War with Turkey*,[14] which emphasised that 'our overwhelming naval preponderance cannot be brought to bear on any vital point [of the Ottoman Empire] unless the fleet is prepared to take the risk of attempting to force the Dardanelles.' After examining purely naval operations, he concluded that:

The only remaining alternative is a joint naval and military attack on the Dardanelles defences, with the view of clearing the way for the fleet to Constantinople. Such an expedition would be suitable to our fighting forces, it would be a short operation and if successful would be immediately decisive.

He felt justified in saying this, because the field defences of the Gallipoli Peninsula against landings were then almost non-existent.

At this time (July 1906), Captain Ottley, the Director of Naval Intelligence, circulated a further paper to the CID. At its meeting of 26 July it concluded[15] that:

.. circumstances might arise in which the forcing of the Dardanelles, with or without an expeditionary force, would become the most certain and expeditious way of bringing a war with Turkey to a conclusion. In such a case the operation might have to be undertaken even if it entailed considerable losses. The whole question should, therefore, be thoroughly investigated by the Admiralty and the War Office and a Report should be prepared for the consideration of the Committee. The same procedure should be followed as regards the question on the seizure of Haifa and Acre, and operations directed to cut the Turkish lines of communications through Syria.

At a critical meeting of the CID in July 1906, General 'Jimmy' Grierson, the DMO, gave his view that if forcing the Dardanelles should prove necessary, the best method, even though potentially costly in terms of casualties, was to land troops on the Gallipoli Peninsula to attack the forts on the European side of the Dardanelles in the rear. This contradicted Sir Charles Hardinge of the Foreign Office who, having studied the forts from the Straits and from the Asiatic coast, was of the opinion that the fort commanding Besika Bay on the Asiatic Shore should be reduced by naval fire, following which a force should be landed to capture from the rear the forts on the Asiatic side of the Dardanelles. The meeting concluded that the best way to defeat the Turks might be either a purely naval attack on the Dardanelles, or one accompanied by an expeditionary force, even if considerable losses were incurred thereby.[16]

This was followed by a 'Very Secret' report, dated 8 August 1906, entitled *The Forcing of the Dardanelles (The Naval Aspects of the Question)*[17] and submitted to the CID on 10 August. Ottley concluded that his considerations:

. . . make it plain that from the naval point of view any attempt to send the fleet to Constantinople as an operation of war against Turkey without first destroying the forts in the Dardanelles, is greatly to be deprecated.

Hence, if the emergency should arise, we are driven back upon *the well-known and matured plan* [emphasis added] for a combined naval and military expedition to seize and hold the isthmus [sic] of Gallipoli with the forts on the northern shore of the Dardanelles.

The report examined the amphibious operations which would be required, including capturing and holding the Bulair Lines at the narrowest part of the Peninsula using some 'less valuable ships',[18] a phrase which reappears in the December 1906 report. In the final draft of this report, Ottley concluded that 'Such an operation is believed to be perfectly feasible. It would be desirable as time and opportunity offers to frequently practise the joint naval and military operation of embarking and disembarking the troops', without giving away the intended destination. He emphasised that surprise was essential, and it was imperative to 'conceal any locality to be represented'.[19]

By the next meeting of the CID in November, Grierson had been replaced (for instigating unauthorised staff talks with the French) by Major-General Sir John Ewart, who advocated a surprise attack by troops rapidly and secretly transported from Malta, supported by fleet landing parties. Fisher stated that German control of Turkey implied that the Turks could no longer be bribed to allow the passage of the fleet, and he 'hoped that no attack on the Dardanelles would ever be undertaken in any form'. Esher wanted any naval attack to be supported by the military, while Haldane was concerned about Britain's loss of face in the Moslem world in the event of failure, and also about the possible loss of ships. He therefore favoured an alternative such as capturing Aegean islands. The failure on this occasion to arrive at a clear preference for one of the three possible alternatives outlined by the Prime Minister, Campbell-Bannerman – a purely naval attack, a naval attack supported by military landings, or a genuinely amphibious attack jointly by the fleet and a large expeditionary force[20] – was to be echoed in 1914–15. An important result of this meeting was that the conclusion of the previous meeting – that the best way to defeat the Turks might be either a purely naval attack on the Dardanelles, or one accompanied by an expeditionary force – was deleted.

As a result of this impasse, Campbell-Bannerman, for the CID, instructed the General Staff at the War Office, in conjunction with the Admiralty, to prepare a paper on 'The Possibility of a Joint Naval and Military Attack upon the Dardanelles, with a Note by the Director of Naval Intelligence.'[21] This was duly prepared at the War Office by Colonel Charles Callwell,[22] dated 20 December 1906, and printed as a secret document in February 1907. The General Staff at the War Office and the Director of Naval Intelligence at the Admiralty showed their appreciation of the 'great risks' of a joint naval and military operation to take the Gallipoli Peninsula. While the military were pessimistic about the prospects for success of such an operation, the Naval Intelligence Division, in view of developments in the power of modern naval guns, took a more optimistic view. It concluded: 'Military opinion, looking at the question from the point of view of coast defence, will be in entire agreement with the naval view that unaided action by the Fleet, bearing in mind the risks involved, is much to be deprecated',[23] leaving open the possibility of military landings to aid the navy. This memorandum was written by Charles Callwell, though it was printed under the name of General Sir Neville Lyttleton, the Chief of the General Staff. Being considered too sensitive, the report was withdrawn from circulation shortly after being issued.

Ominous information that the Turks were strengthening their forts and reinforcing garrisons in the Sea of Marmara was received by Haldane late in 1906, and would therefore be more resistant to pressure via the Dardanelles should another crisis occur.[24] It was agreed at a CID meeting on 28 February 1907 that the Dardanelles should only be tackled if there was no alternative, and that a sub-committee should be formed to look at other ways of applying military force to Turkey than via the Dardanelles.[25] This decision had far-reaching results, leading to the recall of all copies of the joint General Staff and NID memoranda. These were not therefore available at the War Office in 1914–15 when the question was reopened.[26] Not only that, but the decision had implications for intelligence acquisition, as it suggested downgrading (at least for the time being) the Dardanelles as an intelligence target.

Paradoxically, 1907 and 1908 were years in which the War Office and Admiralty gave great attention to the Dardanelles. A 1908 General Staff study of the Dardanelles problem concluded that if the whole operation could be cloaked in secrecy, a simultaneous action by a 20,000-strong military force landing south of Gaba Tepe and attacking the Kilid Bahr Plateau from the west, with the fleet shooting its way through the Narrows, could achieve success (the Ewart view). Yet another War Office review in 1911 confirmed the 1906 judgement, concluding that it was impossible to achieve surprise and that the operation was therefore too risky.[27]

Thus, at a critical stage of British relations with Turkey in the run-up to the First World War, the amphibious possibilities had been examined without any clear conclusion being reached. This lack of a clear operational vision, while it may well have been the result of a lack of precedent, technological unknowns, and a fine balance of probable outcomes, implied that whatever approach was endorsed would be a 'leap in the dark'. Another implication was that it would be less likely that a serious joint-service plan would be commissioned by the CID.

The Balkan Wars: the Gallipoli Peninsula is fortified

Between 1911 and 1914, while no further dedicated staff study of the Dardanelles problem was made, intelligence continued to be gathered. Meanwhile the Turkish war with Italy in 1911–12 (the Italians bombarded the Dardanelles forts in April 1912 but did not attempt to enter the mined waters of the Narrows), and the Balkan Wars of 1912–13, continued to focus London's attention on that theatre. It is important to realise the extent to which the Dardanelles, and the Gallipoli Peninsula, were being prepared against invasion in the years before the First World War. Against the background of the Balkan Wars, Italy and Greece island-hopped across the Aegean. In April and May 1912 Italy occupied Stampalia, Rhodes and the rest of the Dodecanese islands, while in November the Greeks occupied Lemnos, Imbros, Mitylene, Chios and the remaining Aegean islands, advancing to within a few miles of the Gallipoli Peninsula and generating such a spirit of 'revanche' that the Turks immediately ordered two new battleships from British shipyards.[28] Henceforth it would be even easier for Greece to gather military, topographic and hydrographic intelligence for future operations. On 21 January 1913 the Greeks defeated the Turks in a naval action off Lemnos. The Treaty of London of 30 May 1913 confirmed Greece in her possession of Chios and Mitylene, a clear threat to Smyrna, where half the population was Greek. In fact practically the whole population of the coast of Asia Minor was Greek.[29] In 1913 the Turks dug trenches on the Peninsula, mostly on the Kilid Bahr plateau, anticipating a possible Greek landing attack and, following the Bulgarian capture of Adrianople, actually repulsed a Bulgarian attack on the Bulair Lines defending the Peninsula from the north.

Following the Treaty of London, however, the Turks sent troops across the Enos–Midia armistice line and retook Adrianople, claiming that they needed to save the population from massacre and that they had to establish a suitable frontier to defend Constantinople and the Dardanelles. The new position was consolidated by the Peace of Bucharest on 7 August 1913, leading the ambassadors of the 'six powers' to ask that Turkey respect the Treaty of London and evacuate Adrianople, in return for possible strategic compensations. At the end of 1913 the powers agreed that Greece should keep the islands provided she evacuated southern Albania; the Turks only accepted this 'with regret', and made it clear that they would 'seek satisfaction'. At the same time the Italians remained in possession of Rhodes and neighbouring islands, and egged the Turks on to confront Greece. In the summer of 1914 war almost broke out between Turkey and Greece over attacks by Turkish immigrants from Macedonia on the Greek population of Ionia.[30] The whole of the Aegean was an armed camp; like the Balkans, of which it was an extension, it was a 'powder keg'.

The view in the War Office from 1910, and even earlier, was that, in the event of a general European war, Turkey would join the German camp. The British view was that the Greeks should hold all the islands other than Tenedos and Imbros, and in the early months of 1914, at a time when the Russians might get too involved in the question of control of the Dardanelles, the British Ambassador in Constantinople, Sir Louis Mallet, and the Foreign Office, were seriously discussing the use of force by Britain against the Ottoman Empire. The island situation became so tense that the Turks were actively preparing against a Greek invasion, and remained serious right up to the outbreak of war.[31] Two points arise from all this. Firstly, Turkey was fully alive to the dangers and had already put the Dardanelles and Gallipoli Peninsula into a state of defence. Secondly, decades of British interest in operations against the Dardanelles and the Peninsula had not weakened the British military and naval attention focused on this area. Despite these two factors, no strong intelligence attack or operational planning was started in London. HMS *Inflexible*, flagship of Admiral Milne, the C-in-C Mediterranean Fleet, sailed through the Dardanelles in June 1914, arriving at Constantinople for an official visit on the 26th.[32] No doubt British intelligence officers took the opportunity to make a close study of the defences.

In Greece, Rear Admiral Mark Kerr (Chief of the British Naval Mission to Greece and Commander-in-Chief of the Greek fleet) was assisting the Greeks to organise their defence plans. Kerr noted that, as a continuation of the Balkan Wars, at the beginning of 1914 it seemed likely that Turkey and Bulgaria would declare war on Greece. When Admiral Condouriotis told King Constantine that the Greek fleet could sail up the Dardanelles, Constantine asked the naval minister to pass this opinion to Kerr, and asked for his view. Kerr replied that the British Navy, even if supported by all other navies, could not pass the Dardanelles until the minefields were cleared, but these could not be swept until the forts overlooking them had been captured. This could not happen until the Gallipoli Peninsula, followed by the Asiatic Shore, was captured by a large military force. Following this, other places would have to be garrisoned to prevent Turkish reinforcements recapturing the shores of the Straits. Constantine, agreeing with Kerr, ordered him to prepare a scheme, and directed the army staff to work out the military requirements.

Kerr's scheme was for 20,000 men to capture Alexandretta, through which the railway from the south (Syria) passed, for another 30,000 to land at Aivaili in the Gulf of Adrymati, to prevent the Smyrna Army Corps from going north, and for two regiments to land behind the Kum Kale fort on the Asiatic side of the entrance to the Dardanelles and, capturing this, to turn the guns on to Sedd-el-Bahr fort on the Gallipoli side. A further 30,000 men would then, under cover of naval guns, capture the Bulair Lines, and 80,000 men would land between Gabe Tepe and Cape Helles, and capture the Kilid Bahr forts from the rear.[33] This plan, formulated in early 1914, was revived in September.

The military attaché in Athens from 1 March 1915, Lieut.-Col. Sir Thomas Montgomery Cunninghame, who conferred with Colonel Metaxas on 3 March 1915 and subsequently, told the Dardanelles Commission that the Greeks had in fact worked out several successive plans:[34]

1. Towards the close of the 1912 Balkan War, when the Turks were defending the Gallipoli Peninsula against the Bulgarians at the Bulair Lines;
2. In June 1914 Col. Metaxas's Anafarta (Suvla) plan which, combined with independent operations against Cape Helles and Kum Kale, stated that the scheme was impossible if not carried out as a *coup de main;*
3. Instructions given by the Admiralty on 3 September 1914 to Rear Admiral Kerr to work out a plan of descent on the Peninsula in concert with the Greeks; this was approved by King Constantine on 5 September, and
4. Col. Metaxas's plan for co-operation against Turkey by a direct march by Greece on Constantinople, making provision for possible hostility of Bulgaria, on which the Greek offer of co-operation against Turkey was made on 14 April 1915. This plan did not include an attack on the Gallipoli Peninsula.

Sir Basil Thomson noted that the Greek 'detailed scheme' of 1912 was given to Kerr by King Constantine, and that the 1914 plan, drawn up by Colonel Metaxas, was 'substantially the same as the Anafarta scheme adopted by Hamilton in August 1915' – i.e. the Suvla Bay landing scheme. He also stated that the Greeks refused to take part in the 'Dardanelles adventure' because they were convinced it would fail. Constantine and his General Staff held the view that the only way to force the Dardanelles was by simultaneous attack by a fleet and strong land forces supported by the heaviest artillery.[35]

In 1911 the remarkable figure of Winston Churchill appeared on the stage, when Asquith promoted him from Home Secretary to be First Lord of the Admiralty. Without this fateful decision the whole Gallipoli Campaign, that brilliant strategic conception which soared like a rocket before fizzling to extinction, might not have occurred. The collapse of the campaign brought Churchill crashing down. He was forced to resign from the Cabinet, and was only re-admitted to government after a spell cooling his heels as a battalion commander on the Western Front.

War with Germany, August 1914

But this is to anticipate. When war with Germany was declared on 4 August 1914, the Ottoman Empire remained neutral. Germany was determined to force Turkey into hostilities against the Allies in order to close the Dardanelles, blocking their southern route to Russia. This

Germany succeeded in doing by applying massive leverage via her diplomatic and military representatives in Constantinople and the Dardanelles. The separate but related incidents of the British impounding (on 3 August) two almost completed Turkish warships in British shipyards (for which the Turkish peasantry had paid large contributions), and the illegal passage on 10 August of the German warships *Goeben* and *Breslau* through the Dardanelles to Constantinople, where they became symbolic substitutes for the ships 'stolen' by the British, both played their part in tipping Turkey in favour of Germany. On 15 August the British Naval Mission at Constantinople, under Vice-Admiral A H Limpus, was deprived of its executive command, and the German Admiral Souchon was soon appointed to the command of the Turkish Navy.[36]

On 19 August Mr Erskine, the British *chargé d'affaires* in Athens, telegraphed to Sir Edward Grey at the Foreign Office that Venizelos, on behalf of the Greek government, had placed all its naval and military resources at the disposal of the Entente powers.[37] On the same day, Sir Louis Mallett, the British Ambassador at Constantinople, suggested that a possible forcing of the Dardanelles might help to win the war; however, he qualified this a week later by emphasising that the operation could only succeed if troops were also used. It should be emphasised that, despite this talk of operations, the Allies at this stage wanted to keep Turkey neutral, and to avoid a further Balkan war, within the context of a neutral *bloc* created from Rumania and the Balkan states. If the Allies accepted Greece's offer, their scheme for such a neutral zone would collapse, and the action might tip Turkey into Germany's willing arms.

On 29 August Sir Francis Elliot, the British Minister at Athens, informed the Foreign Office that the Russian minister there had asked the Greek king if he would consider providing an expeditionary force to assist an attack on the Dardanelles. The prospect of Constantinople was dazzling for Greece, which ever aspired to recreate Byzantium, if not Alexander's empire. The king replied in the affirmative, but later inserted the condition that the neutrality of Bulgaria (which threatened Greece's flank) must first be guaranteed.

So far, the Allies had chosen to ignore what they considered Turkey's flagrant breaches of neutrality but they were faced with a bewildering set of possible 'rational strategy' scenarios. Given their belief that it was not a question of 'if' but 'when' Turkey joined the Central Powers, they could not ignore the fact that there were great strategic and military advantages to be gained from a pre-emptive strike, either to force Turkey to throw off Germany's 'evil counsellors' and maintain its neutrality, or to attack before Turkish mobilisation was complete. War at a time of British choosing might be better than allowing Germany to impose her will. A credible threat against the Dardanelles might lead to a coup in which Enver's pro-German 'Young Turk' government would be replaced by a pro-peace party. Even if the Turkish coastal defences and minefields opposed the passage of an Allied fleet, the Gallipoli Peninsula might still be captured by a Greek amphibious force with small loss while its defences were still in a low state of preparedness. Combined with this, a successful joint naval and military operation could lead to the immediate surrender of Turkey, removing the threat to Egypt and the Canal. With so many momentous 'ifs' hanging in the balance, and possibilities impossible to distinguish from probabilities, the whole question of a Dardanelles operation clearly demanded consideration at the highest level.

On 31 August, while the British Expeditionary Force (BEF) was still retreating from Mons towards the Marne, the Dardanelles issue was discussed by Churchill and Kitchener. The latter was called away to Paris on the following day, to force Sir John French to cooperate with the French instead of insisting on pulling the BEF out of the line to refit but, at this time of great crisis in France, Churchill, in view of the imminent risk of Turkey declaring war, asked Sir Archibald Murray, the Chief of the Imperial General Staff (CIGS), to task two officers to examine and work out, with two officers from the Admiralty, a 'plan for the seizure of the Gallipoli Peninsula, by means of a Greek army of adequate strength, with a view to admitting a British fleet to the sea of Marmara'. Churchill later claimed to be ignorant, at this stage, of the existing Greek plan to capture the Peninsula, the outline of which was communicated in September. He emphasised that this was 'Urgent, as Turkey may make war on us at any moment.' The Official Historian took the view that, at this stage, no naval operation was contemplated (all the fighting would be done by the Greeks, who would merely 'admit the British fleet to the Marmara'), and there was no idea of precipitating hostilities.[38] On the face of it this seems a most disingenuous assumption.

On 1 September the Director of Military Operations, Major-General Charles Callwell (who had drawn up the 1906 memorandum), recalled to the War Office from retirement to replace Sir Henry Wilson who had gone to France with the BEF, gave his view that the operation was too dangerous (see Chapter 4), and two days later, pressured by Churchill, restated the General Staff view that an attack on the Peninsula would be extremely difficult. The land defences had been elaborated during the war of 1911–12, and also in 1913, and were now strong enough to resist a surprise attack. The peacetime garrison of 27,000 men had probably been considerably strengthened. A Turkish corps on the Asiatic side could be rapidly brought across the Straits to reinforce. The operation was not assured of success unless it was executed with at least 60,000 men supported by strong siege artillery (i.e. high-trajectory howitzers).[39] This view was not as pessimistic as the 1906 memorandum, which had concluded that the General Staff 'were not prepared to recommend its being attempted' owing to the risk involved, which was more or less what Callwell had repeated on 1 September.[40]

A key player now reappears on the stage. This was Rear-Admiral Kerr in Greece, who was on very good terms with King Constantine, the Prime Minister (Venizelos), and the Greek General Staff and naval authorities. To him, the Foreign Secretary and Churchill expressed 'in our most secret cypher' (in which Kerr also replied) the new British view that, in the event of hostilities with Turkey, a blow should be struck at Constantinople in cooperation with the Greeks and Russians. On 4 September Sir Edward Grey telegraphed to Athens that the British government wanted to avoid war with Turkey, but would cooperate with Greece if that proved impossible because of Turkish aggression. Kerr was therefore given instructions to discuss, in strict secrecy, details of such cooperation with the Greek naval and military staffs if the Turks forced a war. It was to be understood that Greece should not give any provocation to Turkey.[41]

These instructions were contained in a 'most secret' telegram sent by Churchill to Kerr almost simultaneously on the same day. The gist of this was that the Admiralty considered it necessary, as a staff precaution, to discuss with the Greek general and naval staff the appropriate strategy to pursue if Britain and Greece became allied in a war against Turkey. Churchill authorised Kerr, if so approached by the Greeks, to begin discussions on behalf of the Admiralty, and stated that the Amiralty proposed to reinforce the Greek Fleet sufficiently to give 'decisive and unquestionable superiority' over Turkish and German ships it might encounter, and that Kerr should command the combined British and Greek fleets from the British battle-cruiser *Indomitable*. The Admiralty would also provide any reinforcements that might prove necessary. Churchill stated that 'the right and obvious method of attacking Turkey is to strike immediately at the heart', and this entailed a Greek army capturing the Gallipoli Peninsula under the guns of the fleet, thus allowing the combined fleet through the Dardanelles to the Sea of Marmara. The final stage, in cooperation with the Russian Black Sea Fleet and Russian military forces, would be to place such force at Constantinople that 'the whole situation can be dominated'. Churchill asked Kerr to hold immediate talks along these lines with the Greeks, and to obtain their views. In particular, Churchill wanted to know the size of the military force the Greeks thought necessary assuming that the British Navy guaranteed safe transit, and whether the Greeks could provide the necessary transports, or would these have to be found by the British?[42]

Kerr replied via Sir Francis Elliott on 9 September that he had carried out consultations with the Greek General Staff, and agreed with them that Greece could make a sufficient force available to capture the Gallipoli Peninsula if Bulgaria did not attack Greece. He stressed that it was not sufficient for Bulgaria to undertake to remain neutral, as the Greeks would not trust her unless she also turned all her forces to attacking Turkey. Kerr declared that the plan, originally worked out by the Greek General Staff and himself without outside assistance, to capture the Dardanelles was ready, given the conditions about Bulgaria, and that Greece could provide sufficient transports for the troops. He also gave details of the size and composition of the required British naval force – two battle-cruisers, one armoured cruiser, three light cruisers and a flotilla of destroyers and mine-sweepers. However, Kerr noted that as Turkey had now mobilised and obtained the *Goeben* and *Breslau*, the required operation had become greater in scale. He also revealed that the Greek General Staff had an alternative plan to capture the Baghdad railway from Mesopotamia at Alexandretta, the block to be garrisoned by a large force, but this would need financing by Britain. This would cut off the supply of cereals sent to Germany.[43]

In fact the situation was already lost by the time this last telegram (to which no reply was made) was sent, for Constantine had changed his mind, saying that Greece would not attack Turkey unless attacked by her first.[44] The Alexandretta operation, here mentioned for the first time, and for which T E Lawrence later pressed (he had reconnoitred this region earlier in 1914), was to cast a baleful influence on preparations for an attack on the Dardanelles.

Thus, although the British later claimed that they were never given a full copy of the Greek plan,[45] it was in fact an Anglo–Greek plan, with Kerr providing key elements; the British were therefore in possession of all its important details. This is made clear by Kerr himself in post-war correspondence with the Committee of Imperial Defence's Historical Section. As the plan was the property of the Greek General Staff, Kerr had to ask Constantine's permission before sending details to London on 9 September. Kerr stated that Constantine was extremely well-disposed to the Allies, and at once agreed to the British being given the plan. He also telephoned to the General Staff to update it, and tell Kerr when it was ready. This accounted for the three days' delay in answering the Admiralty telegram.

Kerr again emphasised that the Greek General Staff stressed that Bulgarian neutrality was not a sufficient condition for carrying out the plan, and that the Greeks had to maintain a sufficient force to attack them if they entered the war, before any expeditionary force could leave Greece. The Greek Army possessed only 180,000 men with modern equipment, and insufficient ammunition for more than a month of war, which implied that the Allies would have to provide a large military force to carry out the plan, given that the Bulgarian Army amounted to 350,000 men, with another 150,000 available to be mobilised. It would clearly be foolish to send the Greek Army to Gallipoli and replace them in Greece with Allied forces.

Kerr noted that Constantine and his government were fully aware of the Bulgarian understanding with Germany, and that they were obliged to enter the war at Germany's request. Further, Serbia had declared that she could not cooperate with the Greek General Staff as her new Russian allies required all their forces on their northern frontier with Germany and

Austria-Hungary, and could not therefore help Greece to defend the eastern frontier of Serbia and the Greek northern frontier with Bulgaria. Nor did Serbia believe that Bulgaria posed a threat. Despite this, Kerr claimed that the Allies ignored the Greek plan and tried a purely naval attack to force the Dardanelles; the Greek plan was for an essentially military operation with naval support, while the Allies attempted a naval operation without even military support. Finally, Kerr recalled that he was in the Greek Ministry of Marine when news arrived on 3 November that the Allied fleet was bombarding the Dardanelles forts. Reading the telegram, he realised immediately the implications of the loss of surprise, and commented to his Greek flag-lieutenant: 'That is the end of the Dardanelles expedition.'[46] To summarise, the Anglo–Greek plan was based on Kerr's correct appreciation that:[47]

1. No fleet could enter the Marmara until the mines had been swept;
2. The mines could not be swept until the forts protecting them had been captured;
3. The forts could not be captured without extensive landing operations on both sides of the Straits, and
4. After the fall of the forts, other distant points, notably the Bulair Lines, would have to be taken and held to prevent the arrival of troops to recapture the Straits.

Meanwhile the Germans continued to assist the Turks in fortifying the Dardanelles. Towards the end of October, Churchill, in view of Turkey's imminent 'rupture' again discussed the matter with Callwell, the DMO, who restated his view that the capture of the Straits was mainly a military rather than a naval task, and stressed its extreme difficulty.[48]

Hostilities with Turkey, the Dardanelles reconsidered

On 29 October the *Goeben* and *Breslau*, now 'sold' to Turkey and under the command of the German Admiral Souchon, bombarded Odessa, Sebastopol and other Russian Black Sea ports, forcing Turkey at last into the war. On 3 November 1914, while the First Battle of Ypres was raging in Flanders and the Channel Ports were still threatened, to Germany's great satisfaction hostilities commenced between Turkey and the Allies. The British blockading squadron bombarded the outer forts of the Dardanelles. Germany had not yet achieved hegemony of the Balkans, as Greece, Bulgaria and Rumania for the time being remained neutral, but the ensnarement of Turkey was a huge triumph for her. By threatening the Suez Canal and British oil interests in the Persian Gulf, Turkey could create valuable diversions and tie up large numbers of British troops. The same was true of Turkish action against Russia in the Caucasus, which served to relieve Russian pressure on their front with Germany and Austria-Hungary.

In London, the closing of the Dardanelles did not lead to any immediate decision concerning an attack on Turkey; the prime concern in the Middle East was the security of Egypt and the Suez Canal, which the Turkish advance across Sinai threatened. Around 24 November, at the first meeting of the new War Council, Churchill suggested that the best way to protect Egypt and the Suez Canal was to capture the Gallipoli Peninsula. However, he repeated Callwell's words of 3 September in saying that it would be very difficult and involve large military forces.[49] Churchill later changed his tune, claiming it could be done as a purely naval operation – the view he (incredibly) persuaded the War Council to endorse on 13 January 1915.

Then, towards the end of the year, faced with continuing stalemate on the Western Front as French attacks against the deepening German trench system broke down in bloody failure (a portent of what was to happen in Gallipoli), the British government began to reconsider the policy of concentrating resources on the Western Front. The situation in Serbia was insecure. If the Austrian–German forces defeated Serbia, Bulgaria would join them, opening a route for German assistance to Turkey should the latter attack the Suez Canal.

'Jackie' Fisher, the new First Sea Lord, who took over from Prince Louis of Battenberg in October 1914, had previously commanded the Mediterranean Fleet and had long exercised his mind with the problem of forcing the Dardanelles. He expounded his views to his new political master and Churchill, fired by Fisher's eccentric enthusiasm, decided to push matters further. On 2 January 1915 the British Ambassador at St Petersburg cabled that the Russians were asking Kitchener for a British naval or military demonstration against Turkey to relieve pressure in the Caucasus. That day Kitchener discussed a purely naval operation with Churchill, and cabled the Russians, with the agreement of the Foreign Office, that a demonstration would be made, suggesting to Churchill that the Dardanelles was the only spot where Turkish reserves might be pinned down. He was only contemplating a naval demonstration, making it clear that no troops were available and that, in any case, 'we shall not be ready for anything big for some months'. In fact the Turkish surrender at Sarikamish in the Caucasus had by 3 January obviated the necessity for such diversionary action but the British Government, not knowing this, pressed ahead.[50]

On 3 January Fisher, who was in the picture, wrote to Churchill strongly supporting an immediate Allied attack on Turkey – British forces to land at Besika Bay, on the Asiatic coast south of the Dardanelles, with diversions at Haifa and Alexandretta, the Greeks to land on the Gallipoli Peninsula, the Bulgarians to attack Adrianople, and the Rumanians, Russians and Serbs to attack Austria. Simultaneously, the Navy should force the Dardanelles. 'Celerity – without it Failure.' Unfortunately the diplomatic situation rendered this magnificent plan nugatory. However, it was not completely stillborn. Churchill seized on the naval part of the plan; if it could be achieved without committing troops, a concept totally at variance with his earlier ideas, he thought it should be taken further.

The Admiralty therefore, on 3 January 1915, signalled to Admiral Carden, commanding the Eastern Mediterranean Squadron, whether he thought it feasible to attempt to force the Dardanelles, which it was known was now mined as well as protected by shore batteries and torpedoes, using obsolete battleships. Carden replied, hedging his bets, on 5 January: 'I do not consider Dardanelles can be rushed. They might be forced by extended operations with large numbers of ships.' The following day the Admiralty asked him to expand on this curt answer, but, strangely, the idea was not even mentioned at War Council meetings on 7 and 8 January, though on the latter occasion Kitchener suggested that the Dardanelles might make the most suitable objective for the New Armies then forming in the United Kingdom, as such an operation, involving 150,000 men, could be made in cooperation with the fleet. He suggested a minor operation in the form of a landing at Alexandretta as a stop-gap. At present, however, no troops were available, and Kitchener would make no judgement until a clearer study had been made.[51] No such study was made at the War Office, and no combined staff was created to assess the feasibility of such an operation.

Carden replied to the Admiralty's request for a development of his ideas on the 11th, providing a detailed four-stage plan involving reducing the forts at Sedd-el-Bahr and Kum Kale at the mouth to the Dardanelles, destroying the inside defences up to Kephez at the entrance to the Narrows, reducing the forts at the Narrows and, finally, clearing the minefield, reducing the defences above the Narrows and advancing into the Marmara. He reckoned this would all, given the prevailing weather conditions in this season, take a month. The feeling at the Admiralty was that a combined operation was to be preferred to a purely naval attempt, and that troops would be needed to follow up a naval success and clinch the matter; the Gallipoli Peninsula and Constantinople would have to be occupied. The Admiralty War Staff accepted Kitchener's dictum that no troops were available, but considered that it would not do much harm to carry out a purely naval attempt. Only a demonstration had been called for by the Russians, and this could be called off if it proved futile. It was not, therefore, envisaged at this stage that any military landing force would have to be used.[52]

This was the context of that extraordinary War Council meeting on 13 January when Churchill, seizing on Carden's cautiously worded reply and ignoring the evidence of earlier studies, flung a bombshell in the face of the Council by proposing a purely naval attack on the Dardanelles. He explained Carden's scheme (Lord Fisher and Sir Arthur Wilson remaining silent), and the Council, knowing that no troops were available, came to the bizarre decision that: 'The Admiralty should prepare for a naval expedition in February to bombard and take [!] the Gallipoli Peninsula with Constantinople as its objective.'[53] How the navy could capture the Peninsula on its own was not explained. On 19 January Churchill went further, in assuring the Russians that the government intended to 'press the matter to a conclusion'.[54] This was no mere 'demonstration' to help the Russians.

Preparations went further when a 'Special Service Force' of two battalions of Royal Marines of the Royal Naval Division was warned for Dardanelles service on 29 January and sent out to the island of Lemnos on 6 February to be used as demolition parties against forts and batteries.[55]

Diversions and landings

In January and February 1915 the possibility of landing troops at Alexandretta – the Greek alternative plan – was being discussed in London, partly as a diversion while the Navy forced the Dardanelles. A landing at this point, as T E Lawrence and others were feverishly pointing out, would cut Turkey's strategic railway communications with Palestine, Arabia and Mesopotamia. Sir William Birdwood, at that time commanding the Anzac Corps in Egypt, recalled that at this time Maxwell (GOC Egypt) told him that he had received a message from Kitchener asking if Birdwood could send 5,000 of his Australians to Alexandretta. This was before any intimation had been received that the Anzacs might be required for Dardanelles operations. Birdwood replied in the affirmative, but was shown no intelligence reports or documents of any sort relating to Alexandretta or Asia Minor; he was training his Corps for France, and was completely 'in the dark' as to other theatres. In any case he thought his whole Corps, not just a brigade or two, might be necessary for the Alexandretta operation. Kitchener told him that he would be supported by some 20,000 Armenians, whom Birdwood would supply with rifles. As a result of this directive from Kitchener, Birdwood and his staff prepared all the details of the landing, including the planning of operations to seize and hold the Bailan Pass.[56] Such a diversion of planning effort from the Dardanelles was to contribute to the failure of the Gallipoli operation.

On 16 February a crucial informal meeting of most of the War Council (including Asquith, Churchill, Fisher and Kitchener) decided that the Dardanelles should be forced, that troops should be committed to the operation, and that the 29th Division and Birdwood's two Anzac divisions should be sent to Lemnos. On the same day, Kitchener sought the opinion of Captain Wyndham Deedes, an intelligence officer at the War

Office who had served with the Turkish Army, about a purely naval attack, but refused to listen when Deedes told him it was fundamentally unsound.[57] Yet the feeling of the meeting was that troops were necessary. Kitchener, however, reversed his decision to use the 29th Division three days later. He instructed Maxwell, GOC Egypt, to coordinate operations with Carden. The naval attack on the outer forts began on 19 February.

It was decided that the Admiralty should arrange transports for 50,000 men, and Rear-Admiral Wemyss would be sent to Mudros, as Governor of the Island of Lemnos, as a first step towards establishing an Allied base there. On 22 February a Base General Staff (A and Q Branches) for the new Constantinople Expeditionary Force (as it was first called, with an alarming disregard for security) was mobilised at the Tower of London. One of the GSOs was Major Plunkett. The embryonic base organisation sailed from Avonmouth in the *Dunluce Castle* on 27 February, arriving at Lemnos on 10 March.[58] It was followed a few days later by the Royal Naval Division. The facilities, including the lack of a suitable harbour, proved so inadequate that the base was temporarily moved to Alexandria. *Dunluce Castle* therefore sailed from Lemnos on 25 March, arriving at Alexandria on the 27th. GHQ MEF (less its A and Q echelon) returned to Lemnos on 10 April. According to Lady Hamilton, Churchill wanted the Navy to get the kudos for the successful and potentially war-winning operation of forcing the Dardanelles, bringing Turkey to her knees and swinging the Balkans behind the Allies, and was reluctant to share the laurels with the Army. Kitchener, on the other hand, was anxious to send troops in before the naval attack had sacrificed all surprise.[59]

On the 19th the Allied fleet under Carden began its ill-advised bombardment of the Dardanelles forts,[60] the Navy finding that seaplanes were not effective at observing and reporting ships' fire during the bombardment.[61] The Turks were now under no illusions as to what was coming. In Egypt, Ronald Storrs wrote that 'After the first naval assault we had so advertised our military intention as to convince some of my neutral friends (but alas none of the enemy) that we must be feinting for Alexandretta.'[62] This illusion may have been strengthened within the Ottoman camp by the arrival of the battleship *Bacchante* off Alexandretta on 14 February.

At all costs

The War Council, with Churchill providing much of the driving force, now reached a crucial decision. On 24 February it decided that a withdrawal in the event of naval failure at the Dardanelles would involve too great a loss of prestige, and serious strategic disadvantage in the Balkans. The operation must be carried out at all costs. Kitchener agreed that the Army must help if necessary, and that operations should be pressed forward.

However, the size of the required force and the nature of its task were not discussed. The government was waiting to hear on these points from Carden, who in turn expected to receive instructions from London.

On the same day (24 February), Kitchener outlined his reasoning in a further telegram to Maxwell, speaking of Birdwood 'concerting operations', with the forcing of the Dardanelles by the Navy to be immediately followed by the retirement of the Turkish garrison and the subsequent occupation of the Peninsula by British troops. He did not envisage a 'landing in force' in the presence of the assumed Turkish garrison of 40,000 men, stating that 'To land with 10,000 in the face of 40,000 seems extremely hazardous', but went on to allow that:

> If it can be done without seriously compromising the troops landing for the purpose, there would be no objection to the employment of troops to secure forts or positions already gained or dominated by naval fire, and to deny their reoccupation by the enemy.[63]

In other words, he wanted the military to take the minimum of risks; it was an application of the French doctrine developing on the Western Front: 'Artillery conquers, infantry occupies.' This was essentially the War Office view that prevailed up to the failure of the great naval attack on the Narrows on 18 March, following which the logic was suddenly reversed – the army must now clear the way for the navy. Also on 24 February Maxwell telegraphed Kitchener, passing on Maucorps' view that the Peninsula had been heavily fortified, was 'practically a fort', and that heavy guns, on land, were necessary to the success of such an operation.

Birdwood's preparations for the Alexandretta operation were made before he had received any suggestion that his force might be required for the Dardanelles. Thus at a critical period Birdwood, Maxwell and their staffs were using valuable time and intelligence effort in preparing for the Alexandretta operation rather than landings on the Gallipoli Peninsula. That said, Birdwood admitted that in the period January–March 1915 the weather would have made it absolutely impossible to land troops, stores and ammunition on the Peninsula. As there were no harbours, any men landed would have been cut off.[64]

Despite all the deliberation in London, there was still no General Staff preliminary plan for the landing of military forces on the Gallipoli Peninsula, and this omission was later remarked upon by the Dardanelles Commission. In effect, the General Staff had adopted the Greek plan, or an Anglo–Greek variant as envisaged by Kerr. Although the CIGS, Lieut.-Gen. Sir James Wolfe Murray, attended all War Council meetings, he did not participate in them to the extent of speaking, and when he returned to the War Office after each meeting he failed to issue any instructions to Callwell (the DMO) or to any other officer of the General Staff.[65] Nor did Callwell, although he was asked to prepare staff appreciations on the Dardanelles in September 1914 and February 1915, take it upon himself to instigate such work. We do not know whether he suggested this to Wolfe Murray or Kitchener, but presumably if he had done so he would have made this clear in his evidence to the Dardanelles Commission and in his memoirs. Until 11 March, therefore, the General Staff were to some extent in the dark; they were not officially informed that the War Council was considering large-scale military operations in the Dardanelles. Thus the whole purpose of a General Staff – to prepare contingency plans for future operations – was negated.

The influence of Callwell, who also had responsibility for Intelligence, which was a sub-division of his Directorate, on Kitchener and the campaign is highly significant. He blew cold in September 1914, then warmer in February 1915 when, according to Aspinall-Oglander, his very optimistic memorandum influenced Kitchener in his later decision to go ahead with the land operations.[66]

Though there may have been agreement on a clear strategic aim, the same could not be said at an operational level. There was no shared view of operational objectives and priorities, and it was unclear at this time whether a true combined operation was intended. Indeed, there was a divergence of views. This arose because the problems had not yet been fully appreciated, and without such an appreciation there could be no plan. It was felt in London that only those on the spot could make such an appreciation, and therefore in turn two sailors and two soldiers – Carden, Birdwood, de Robeck and finally Hamilton – made their reconnaissances and gave their opinions.

Naval opinion was very much in favour of certain land operations, and as naval operations progressed (or rather failed to make much progress), the belief that land forces should be employed became firm. On 15 February Sir Henry Jackson advised the early seizure of shore spotting stations to overcome the difficulties of the operation, emphasising that in the Russo–Japanese War, the capture of the Port Arthur Peninsula by the Japanese depended on the taking of 203-Metre Hill, a vital observing station which Admiral Togo stressed was the decisive primary objective for the army.[67] Achi Baba, the commanding hill in the Helles sector of the Peninsula, came to have the same significance at Gallipoli, to the point of obsession.

Birdwood and the Anzacs

On 20 February Kitchener cabled Maxwell (3180 Cipher), informing him that the fleet had begun an attack on the Dardanelles, and warning him to prepare to send a force of two divisions (30,000 troops) of the Australian and New Zealand Army Corps (ANZAC, or Anzac) under Birdwood, to be ready to sail from Egypt on about 9 March. An advanced force as large as could be accommodated in the available transports should be sent to Lemnos immediately, in case Carden needed troops at once. Birdwood's task was 'To assist the navy . . . to give any co-operation that may be required, and to occupy any captured forts.'[68] Clearly no serious opposition from the Turkish garrison of Gallipoli and the Dardanelles was expected. Maxwell replied on the same day: '621E. Your 3180 Cipher. We have no maps available here. Please supply.'[69]

The War Office duly arranged for the forces sailing from England to bring stocks of the 1908 one-inch map (overprinted with red 'artillery squares') with them. A decision was made by Maxwell and Birdwood, perhaps in consultation with the navy who were to land the troops and support them with covering fire, that this one-inch map should be enlarged to 1:40,000; this was done in Egypt during March.

Birdwood, commanding the Anzacs, was also charged with the local direction of the 'Special Mission,' 'Detached Force' or 'L Scheme' (for Lemnos?), as the Anzac Staff knew it. Colonel E G Sinclair-MacLagen, Yorkshire Regiment, commander of 3rd Australian Infantry Brigade, was OC 'Special Mission' landing force, and was later to command the Anzac covering force on 25 April. The Special Mission force sailed from Egypt on 2 March for Mudros, arriving on the 4th, where they trained in landing operations. While at sea the force officers were lectured by Mr Hough, an interpreter, on Turkey and the Turkish Army.[70] The cover destination for this force was Alexandretta.

It was appreciated in London that Turkish forces on the Gallipoli Peninsula numbered some 40,000 (a figure supplied by Colonel Maucorps, of the French Mission in Egypt), so the landing of only 10,000 men was an alarming prospect. Maxwell and Birdwood wanted to be able to control the uses to which their troops were put, and needed much more information about the situation.[71] By 23 February Maxwell had enough transports to carry a brigade, but the Anzac Corps as a whole still lacked much in the way of equipment and stores, which all had to come from England, before it could take the field. On the same day, Kitchener ordered Birdwood to clarify the situation by making an immediate reconnaissance of the Dardanelles and producing, together with Carden, a joint appreciation:

Proceed to meet Admiral Carden at the earliest possible opportunity and consult him as to the nature of the combined operations which the forcing of the Dardanelles is to involve. Report the result to me. You should learn, from local observation and information the numbers of the Turkish garrison on the peninsula, and whether the Admiral thinks it will be necessary to take the forts in reverse; if so what force will be required, and generally in what manner it is proposed to use the troops. Will the Bulair lines have to be held, and will operations on the Asiatic side be necessary or advisable.[72]

Carden was waiting for instructions from England before formulating his requirements for military forces, but the government was waiting on him. On 23 February he told Maxwell:

> I have been directed to make preparations for landing a force of 10,000 men, if such a step is found necessary; at present my instructions go no further. If such a force is sent, I would propose landing it at Sedd el Bahr with the object of occupying the Gallipoli peninsula as far east as the Soghanli Dere – Chanav Ova.[73]

This was a line across the Peninsula at the foot of the south-western slopes of the Kilid Bahr Plateau, thus including the Achi Baba heights but excluding the crucial Kilid Bahr Plateau itself, the importance of which was stressed in pre-war reports.

Apart from making his reconnaissance and appreciation on the Dardanelles combined operation, Birdwood was also asked to inform Kitchener at the same time how he thought additional troops should be employed 'for a further enterprise after the Straits have been forced', a clear reference to an advance eastwards towards Constantinople. On 25 February Carden signalled to the Admiralty that it might be necessary, to protect the fleet from concealed guns, to land a force at Sedd-el-Bahr to occupy the tail of the Peninsula as far as the Soghanli Dere line. This area included Achi Baba. However, as unsettled weather put the maintenance of such a force at risk, he was not going to attempt the landing unless it was essential.[74] The next day Maxwell passed on a report by Colonel Maucorps, former French Military Attaché at Constantinople and now leading the French Military Mission in Cairo, stating that a landing on the Peninsula with its garrison of 40,000 men (and another 30,000 on the Asiatic Shore) would be extremely hazardous, that the Bulair Lines had been rearmed, and that the Turkish commander was excellent and energetic.[75]

Birdwood and Carden make their appreciation

Birdwood and Lt-Col. Skeen, his senior staff officer (GSO1), embarked in the *Swiftsure* on 24 February, and while at sea received a message telling them to make for Imbros. *Swiftsure* arrived in the lee of this island on 28 February, and Birdwood met Carden the next day, 1 March, before transferring to the *Irresistible* on 2 March to make his reconnaissance.

Following this he conferred with Carden and Rear Admiral Wemyss (1st Naval Squadron). At this conference at Lemnos, the nature of the joint operations was fully discussed, including the possible course of further operations towards Constantinople in the event of success. Carden stated baldly that troops had to land to deal with the mobile batteries, following which the fleet's minesweepers could clear the mines and the fleet could go through.[76] Following the conference, Birdwood replied to Kitchener's earlier questions on 3 March (relayed by Maxwell to London on the 4th):

> I anticipate that if required to land by Navy, in taking concealed guns or howitzers it would not in any way be possible to restrict movements to minor operations, as any guns are sure to be in strong position, abounding everywhere and being covered by strongly entrenched Infantry who in places would doubtless be able to command coast fort guns which might have been reduced by Navy. . . . [Regarding the Asiatic side] from personal observations I know the country is big and difficult and even a whole division would soon lose itself; so you can rely on my avoiding it if possible.[77]

Birdwood's reconnaissance of the Straits led him to conclude that the immediate landing of troops was needed as the hidden Turkish batteries putting down a barrage on the waters in which the fleet was operating were the real problem as they prevented minesweeping and therefore impeded the progress of the fleet; as these were in dead ground to the guns of the fleet they could not be located. The Turks were using terrain skilfully, and as air power was practically non-existent (only a few under-powered seaplanes were available at this stage), these guns could not be located or neutralised from the air, or by air-directed naval gunfire. It was therefore necessary to neutralise them by landing troops to occupy the ground from which they were firing.

Birdwood wanted to land a strong force at Helles, covered by a feint at Bulair. The Helles force, having secured a bridgehead, would then fight forward to the line Gaba Tepe–Kilid Bahr. This was the line of heights just short of the Narrows, from which position the main forts on the European side of the Dardanelles could be taken in reverse and the hidden batteries on both shores dealt with (though it was not explained how the hidden batteries on the Asiatic side could be neutralised). Kitchener, at the War Office, had not yet embraced this plan to help the Navy to take the forts by direct combined operations. Could Achi Baba be permanently held? The naval view was affirmative; they believed it was possible to capture and hold Achi Baba, if not the Soghanli Dere line.[78]

As far as operations east of Bulair towards Constantinople were concerned, Birdwood stated that:

> … at present I have no information to guide me in advising as to operations after the Gallipoli peninsula has been taken, and I have as yet no maps of the country [east of the peninsula, towards Constantinople]. A man-lifting kite or a captive balloon would be of great use to the Navy.

He recommended the despatch of one or the other for locating concealed batteries and artillery-spotting.[79]

On 26 February Kitchener told Maxwell that only minor operations were envisaged, and instructed Birdwood to practise his troops in rapid opposed beach landings. In London, in Egypt and at Lemnos, confusion and puzzlement reigned. On 23 and again on 28 February Maxwell confessed himself 'in the dark about the intentions and objects of the fleet in forcing the Dardanelles', wondered who was directing the operation, and asked if he might have a copy of the pre-war combined staff appreciation and plan for the forcing of the Dardanelles (he received a negative reply to this on the 26th), and Birdwood was under the impression that he was the Commander-in-Chief designate. His staff had latterly been planning the Alexandretta operation, and was now working on possible Gallipoli landings.

On 3 March Maxwell, alarmed by Maucorps' reports and what he had heard from Birdwood, sent his views on the expedition to Kitchener's military secretary, Fitzgerald, to the effect that the navy was too sanguine about the prospects and that he advised leaving the Gallipoli Peninsula 'severely alone'.[80] The following day, Kitchener informed Maxwell that troops would not be used to capture the Peninsula, but they might be used for the follow-up operations towards Constantinople, and the next day telegraphed to Maxwell for Birdwood in much the same sense: 'The Concentration of Troops at the entrance to the Dardanelles therefore is not so much for operations on the Gallipoli Peninsula as for operations to be undertaken in the neighbourhood of Constantinople.'[81] On 8 March Maxwell again wrote to Fitzgerald asking 'who is co-ordinating and directing this great combine?'[82] As a result of this lethal hiatus and muddle at the highest level, no serious planning was being done, although Birdwood's Anzac staff were doing their best; the landings took place only seven weeks later.

Apart from the Anglo–Greek scheme, no preliminary plan for a Dardanelles operation had been prepared by the General Staff in London. The reason for this was simple, and unbelievable: it was only on 11 March that the General Staff were told that large-scale military operations were being considered, despite the fact that Wolfe Murray, the CIGS, had been present at all War Council meetings.[83]

The Navy's progress and Achi Baba

Admiral de Robeck intended to land a demolition party on 3 March at Sedd-el-Bahr, but was prevented by bad weather. Landings took place the next day, but little success was achieved. Demolition, survey and beach parties were landed from *Inflexible* and *Ocean* under Lieut. Commander Giffard. A covering company of the Plymouth Battalion under Major Palmer of the Royal Marines was to move forward to a line from Morto

Bay to the 'fountain' north of Tekke Burnu, which it would hold for three hours while the demolition and survey parties did their work. In fact seaplanes had located old trenches behind the Old Castle at Sedd-el-Bahr, from which Turkish fire prevented the covering force from advancing, so the operation was aborted.[84] On 5 March the Navy planned to use a cairn on the summit of Haji Monorlo Dagh as an aiming point for *Queen Elizabeth* to lay her fire over the Peninsula at targets in the Narrows.[85]

On 8 March Captain Fitzmaurice of the *Triumph*, after observing the naval bombardment from Morto Bay, stated his view that 'no real progress could be made without the assistance of land forces to supplement and make good the work done by the fleet'. He considered that Achi Baba, the commanding feature of the southern Peninsula, was essential as an artillery spotting station for the Navy. This judgement was based on his experience at Tsingtau, where naval bombardment had proved ineffective until an observing station was established on Prinz Heinrich Berg. In addition, he thought that guns might be taken ashore.[86] Clearly the accumulation of these naval views, and particularly their emphasis on the importance of Achi Baba, later carried much weight with Sir Ian Hamilton. On the other hand, the Naval Official Historian commented that the 'high authorities of both services' ignored the lessons of Port Arthur and Tsingtau: 'Owing to our imperfect machinery for bringing together the naval and military staffs for intimate study of combined problems, such failures in council were inevitable.'[87] By 8 March, although it was clear that observation of naval gunfire and the location of concealed batteries was the key to the situation, Kitchener gave no suggestion in his instructions to Birdwood that troops should be used to remedy the situation.

The importance of Achi Baba as an artillery observation post was emphasised by many of the Army and Navy staff involved in planning the initial operations. Surgeon Rear-Admiral Jeans later repeated the discussions he had heard, possibly on board *Euryalus*, between Hamilton's HQ and de Robeck about capturing Achi Baba in order to emplace heavy artillery behind it to bombard the defences of the Narrows:

> Its summit commanded the whole system of gun positions on both sides of the Dardanelles at Kilid Bahr and Chanak, and once the 15-inch howitzer already at Mudros with its tractor and railway lines, could be mounted there and brought to bear on that system its destruction was anticipated in a few days.[88]

Witnesses to the Dardanelles Commission, including Lieut.-Col. Hore-Ruthven and Lieut-Col. T H B Forster, confirmed the existence of this massive howitzer at Mudros; apparently it was never unloaded from its ship.[89]

The high-trajectory 15-inch howitzer, a new design rather than merely a scaled-up version of the new 9.2-inch and 12-inch models, had been ordered by Churchill in 1914 for the Royal Marine Artillery, but the prototype ('Granny') went to France and took part in the Battle of Neuve Chapelle in March 1915. Twelve such howitzers were under construction in early 1915, and on proof firing a range of 11,000 yards was attained.[90] On 14 May 1915, the landings at Gallipoli having been made but only slow progress achieved towards Achi Baba, Churchill minuted: 'The fifth 15-inch howitzer, with fifty rounds of ammunition, should go to the Dardanelles with the least possible delay, being sent by special train across France and re-embarked at Marseilles. . . .'

He also proposed to send 9.2-inch guns, to be mounted on land or on monitors as occasion demanded, and several monitors.[91] So Churchill secretly sent a howitzer and ammunition out to Mudros. However, the distance from the summit of Achi Baba to Kilid Bahr was 13,000 yards (12km), so the range from heavy artillery positions behind Achi Baba was much greater than the maximum range of the 15-inch howitzer. It would therefore have been necessary to advance the howitzer to the forward slopes, unacceptable as it would expose it to enemy fire. Reports by British artillery commanders at Gallipoli do not mention this addition to their arsenal, for the simple reason that it was never landed on the Peninsula.

The destruction of the defending coast batteries would enable the fleet to push through the Straits and the Bulair Lines to be captured. Undoubtedly there was considerable naval and Army agreement on the importance of Achi Baba for such a purpose, but it was based on a misconception; the summit did not in fact give a direct view of the Narrows defences, which were defiladed by intervening high ground and the steep scarp edge of the Kilid Bahr Plateau. This suggests that key figures on the staff could not read the one-inch map, and did not understand the elementary concept of intervisibility; the map gave perfectly good information on this point.

Command passes from Birdwood to Hamilton

Birdwood had been led to understand by Kitchener that he would be given command of the expanded 'Constantinople Expeditionary Force'. The addition of the Royal Naval Division, the 29th Division and d'Amade's French contingent led Kitchener to appoint Sir Ian Hamilton, a General of more experience and greater reputation. Birdwood started planning landings, in cooperation with the Navy, at his Egyptian HQ. He had presumably been provided with an outline copy of what was known of the Greek plan by way of Admiral Kerr in Athens. Frederick Cunliffe Owen, who had gone from Constantinople to Egypt via Athens, was also familiar with the Greek plan, and probably imparted it to Clayton and Maxwell. Following Hamilton's arrival at Mudros, and later in Egypt, he took over from Birdwood the planning material thus far accumulated, and also the Anzac Printing Section (including both hand-litho and letterpress capability) which Ernest Dowson,

Director General of the Survey of Egypt, had formed in early March for Birdwood when he first heard of impending operations at the Dardanelles. From this point on, the tragedy unfolds with relentless inevitability.

Notes

1. Lt-Col. F Cunliffe Owen to The Secretary, Army Council, 27-9-1927, in Imperial War Museum Department of Documents.
2. Anon. (1876), *The Dardanelles for England: the true solution of the Eastern Question*, 28pp., 8vo., War Office Library Catalogue, 1912, Part III.
3. *Reports and Memoranda relative to Defence of Constantinople and other positions in Turkey . . .* (1877), pp. 135–46, in TNA(PRO) WO 33/29.
4. *The Dardanelles Commission*, in *The World War I Collection* (Uncovered Editions), London: The Stationery Office, 2001, p. 32.
5. Ardagh, *The Eastern Question in 1896*, Ardagh Papers, October 1896, pp. 32–4, TNA(PRO) 30/40/14/1.
6. Hopkirk, Peter, *On Secret Service East of Constantinople*, London: John Murray, 1994, p. 13.
7. Aspinall-Oglander, Brig.-Gen. C F, *History of the Great War, Military Operations, Gallipoli*, Vol. I, London: Heinemann, 1929, p. 5.
8. Ibid, pp. 5–8.
9. Quoted in Rohde, Lt G H, Die *Operationen an den Dardanellen im Balkankrieg, 1912/13*, Früher Ordonnanz-Offizier im Stabe des Oberkommandos auf Gallipoli, Mit 9 Abbildungen auf 8 Tafeln and 3 Kartenbeleigen. 8vo. vi + 136pp, Berlin: R Eisenschmidt (BL Shelfmark: 9136.dd.21), p. 97.
10. Rhodes James, Robert, *Gallipoli*, London: Pimlico, 1999, pp. 3–4.
11. Stenzel, Kapn A, *Der kürzeste Weg nach Konstantinopel. Ein Beispiel für das Zusammenwirken von Flotte and Heer*, 1894, 73pp. Map. 8vo.
12. *The Dardanelles Commission*, op. cit., p. 90.
13. *Military Policy in a War with Turkey*, memo by Captain Grant Duff, 11 July 1906. TNA(PRO) WO 106/42, Envelope C3, 21a.
14. *War with Turkey. The Forcing of the Dardanelles. 10 August 1906. Secret.* Capt. Ottley's submission. Papers and various drafts. TNA(PRO) ADM 1/8884.
15. Minutes of 92nd meeting of Committee of Imperial Defence, 26 July 1906. TNA(PRO) CAB 38/12/46.
16. TNA(PRO) ADM 1/8884 op. cit. *Very Secret. The Forcing of the Dardanelles (The Naval Aspects of the Question).* Capt. C L Ottley, Director of Naval Intelligence. E44942. 12.-8/06. Pk. E&S. A. 12pp., final (third) and earlier drafts.
17. Ottley (1906), op. cit., final draft, p. 11.
18. Ibid, first and second drafts.
19. Minutes of 93rd meeting of Committee of Imperial Defence, 13 November 1906. TNA(PRO) CAB 38/12/55.
20. *The Possibility of a Joint Naval and Military Attack upon the Dardanelles. Secret. 92B. Printed for the Committee of Imperial Defence. 2 Whitehall Gardens. December 20, 1906. I Memorandum by the General Staff. N.G.L. December 19, 1906. [4pp.] II Note by the Director of Naval Intelligence [1p.]. February 1907. Printed at the Foreign Office by J W Harrison, 14/2/1907.* Foolscap. Cover + 5pp. TNA(PRO) CAB 17/184.

21. Aspinall-Oglander, op. cit., p. 41.
22. *The Dardanelles Commission*, op. cit., p. 32.
23. Haldane to Knollys, 10 December 1906, Royal Archives: RA W27/51.
24. 96th meeting of the CID. TNA(PRO) CAB 2/2/1.
25. Gooch, J, *The Plans of War. The General Staff and British Military Strategy c1900– 1916*, London: Routledge, 1974, p. 262.
26. Aspinall-Oglander, op. cit., p. 29.
27. Ibid, p. 11.
28. Morgenthau, Henry, *Secrets of the Bosphorus*, London: Hutchinson, 1918, p. 30.
29. Graves, Philip, *Briton and Turk*, London: Hutchinson, 1941, pp. 179, 184–7.
30. Heller, Joseph, *British Policy Towards the Ottoman Empire*, London: Cass, 1983, pp. 116–23.
31. Ibid, p. 131.
32. Kerr to Inglefield (CID, Historical Section), 27 March 1922, in TNA(PRO) ADM 137/4178, 1915–22, Greece, papers relating to economic and strategic position in Balkans and Dardanelles campaign – letters from Admiral Mark Kerr.
33. Cunninghame's evidence to Dardanelles Commission, TNA(PRO) CAB 19/33.
34. Thomson, Sir Basil, *The Allied Secret Service in Greece*, London: Hutchinson, 1931, pp. 50–1.
35. Aspinall-Oglander, op. cit., p. 14.
36. Gaselee (Foreign Office) to Daniel (CID, Historical Section), 17 April 1925, in TNA(PRO) ADM 137/4178, op. cit.
37. Aspinall-Oglander, op. cit., pp. 40–1.
38. Ibid, p. 41.
39. Ibid, p. 29.
40. Grey to British Minister, Athens, 4 September 1914, in TNA(PRO) ADM 137/4178, op. cit. Gaselee states: 'see Greek White Book (original and supplement) in our [Foreign Office] Printed Library, Quarto 1854. The document of which I have just spoken is the only one of its contents which bears directly on this particular crisis.'
44. Aspinall-Oglander, op. cit., p. 42 & fn.
45. Kerr to Inglefield (CID, Historical Section), 27 March 1922, in TNA(PRO) ADM 137/4178, op. cit.
46. Aspinall-Oglander, op. cit., p. 42.
47. Ibid, p. 43.
48. Ibid, p. 44.
49. Ibid, pp. 52–3.
50. Ibid, pp. 55–6.
51. Ibid, p. 57.
52. *The Dardanelles Commission*, op. cit., p. 95.
53. Aspinall-Oglander, op. cit., p. 44.
54. Ibid, p. 67 & fn.
55. Birdwood to Ellison, 13 April 1924, TNA(PRO) WO 161/84.
56. Rhodes James, op. cit., pp. 40–1.
57. GHQ MEF War Diary, TNA(PRO) WO 95/4263.
58. Lady Hamilton's Diary, Hamilton Papers, Liddell Hart Archive, King's College London.
59. Fitzherbert, M, *The Man who was Greenmantle. A Biography of Aubrey Herbert*, London: OUP, 1985, pp. 149–50.

60. Corbett, Sir Julian S, *History of the Great War, Naval Operations*, Vol. II, London: Longmans Green, 1921, pp. 147, 173.
61. Storrs, R, *Orientations*, Definitive Edn, London: Nicholson & Watson, 1945, p. 198.
62. Aspinall-Oglander, op. cit. pp. 74–5.
63. Birdwood to Ellison, 13 April 1924, TNA(PRO) WO 161/84.
64. Aspinall-Oglander, op. cit., p. 69fn.
65. Ibid, Vol. II, p. 417fn.
66. Corbett, op. cit., p. 174fn.
67. ANZAC Corps General Staff (Special Mission) War Diary, TNA(PRO) WO 95/4280.
68. Ibid.
69. Ibid. War Diary of Major N P Hancock DAA & QMG ANZAC, TNA(PRO) WO 95/4280.
70. Aspinall-Oglander, op. cit., pp. 73–4.
71. Kitchener to Birdwood via Maxwell, in ibid, p. 74.
72. Ibid, pp. 73–4.
73. Corbett, op. cit., p. 174.
74. Aspinall-Oglander, op. cit., p. 76.
75. Wemyss, Admiral, *The Navy in the Dardanelles Campaign*, London: Hodder & Stoughton, 1924, p. 27.
76. Birdwood to Kitchener, rec'd Cairo 4.3.15, in TNA(PRO) WO 158/574, Dardanelles Operations – Copies of Telegrams 1915 (GOC-in-C, Egypt).
77. Corbett, op. cit., p. 176.
78. Birdwood to Kitchener via Maxwell, TNA(PRO) CAB 63/17 p. 81.
79. Maxwell to Fitzgerald, in Kitchener Papers, TNA(PRO) 30/57/61.
80. Kitchener to Maxwell for Birdwood, rec'd 5.3.15, in TNA(PRO) WO 158/574, Dardanelles Operations – Copies of Telegrams 1915 (GOC-in-C, Egypt).
81. Maxwell to Fitzgerald, in Kitchener Papers, TNA(PRO) 30/57/61.
82. Aspinall-Oglander, op. cit., p. 69fn.
83. Corbett, op, cit., p. 176.
84. Ibid.
85. Ibid, p. 174.
86. Ibid, p. 175.
87. Jeans, Surgeon Rear-Admiral T T, *Reminiscences of a Naval Surgeon*, London: Sampson, Low & Marston, 1927, p. 248.
88. Minutes of Evidence to the Dardanelles Commission, pp. 741, 753–4, TNA(PRO) CAB 19/33.
89. Edmonds, Brig.-Gen. Sir James, *Military Operations, France and Flanders*, Vol. I, London: Macmillan, 1927, p. 83.
90. Minute by First Lord of the Admiralty [Churchill], 14 May 1915 to Secretary, I.S.L. [First Sea Lord], C.O.S. [Chief of Staff], in TNA(PRO) CAB 19/28.

CHAPTER 3

Pre-War Geographical Intelligence

Intelligence . . . must be timely, accurate, relevant and verifiable. It must answer a question and it must engender proactive, actionable decision making even if that decision is not to act.[1]

While we are clearly in a position to assess whether available 'open source' intelligence was in fact collected and used in the run-up to the Gallipoli operations, we will never, given the nature of this particular animal, know very much about the clandestine intelligence-gathering prior to those operations. Published histories of intelligence services are rather obviously full of *lacunae,* and histories (and biographies) of military and naval operations and their participants likewise omit crucial aspects of this vital preliminary function. There is a sense in which we will never know the true history of any event, given that crucial elements of the equation remain locked away in secret files, or have long-since been shredded or gone to the grave with the actors concerned. Nevertheless, certain pieces of information survive in the archives or in the literature, and we can state with confidence that various intelligence agencies were supplying strategic, topographical, operational and tactical intelligence; in fact a great deal was available in various forms and in various departments. Whether it was properly used is a different matter. The mounting of the Gallipoli landing operations was a classic example of intelligence being available in various forms but not being correctly collated, analysed, evaluated, distributed or used operationally. There was no 'Theatre Intelligence Section' before the Gallipoli landings as there was before D-Day.

Military and naval studies of the Dardanelles to 1906

Regarded as the geographical key to 'the Eastern Question', the Dardanelles area had long been considered of strategic importance by the British, and many studies of various kinds had been made of its defences, terrain and possible landing places. These studies were carried out over several centuries prior to the inception of the Gallipoli Campaign of 1915.

In their early development, the British Army and Navy each developed their own Intelligence departments which drew on a variety of sources. The Lords of the Admiralty were keenly interested, and the National Archives contain papers relating to the Admiralty's 'Secret Branch', including documents from the 1796–1826 period: 'internal memoranda, correspondence, intelligence reports and papers or operational or political questions of particular delicacy, or special interest to the First Lord and the members of the Admiralty Board. They include Duckworth's passage of the Dardanelles'[2] in 1807.

In 1799, following the French seizure of Egypt, a British military mission (including three Royal Engineer officers) under Brig.-Gen. Koehler RA, was sent to Constantinople to advise and assist the Sultan.[3] Major M Hope, Commanding Royal Artillery, and Major Charles Holloway, Commanding Royal Engineers, were ordered to 'visit and examine' the castles, defences, batteries, magazines, etc., at the Dardanelles, and submit a report. This they did, concluding that the defences were totally inadequate, would not prevent an enemy fleet from forcing a passage to Constantinople, and should be augmented, re-sited where necessary and re-armed. Hope raised a significant point when he noted that 'it is not to be supposed that these Castles will at any time be attacked by sea and land together'; he gave no reason for this supposition.[4]

In the early 19th century the eastern Mediterranean and the Aegean were very poorly charted; in 1832 Midshipman Thomas Spratt began his career as a naval hydrographic surveyor under the tutelage of Commander Thomas Graves who had been directed to the Greek Archipelago (the 'Arches') by Captain Francis Beaufort, the Hydrographer of the Navy, and in 1833 the Gulf of Saros (Xeros), lying to the north of the Gallipoli Peninsula, was surveyed by Commander Copeland. Tom Spratt was one of the hydrographers, under Graves, responsible for a crucial survey which resulted in the definitive Admiralty Chart (one-inch to a nautical mile, or 1:72,960) No. 2429, *The Dardanelles (Ancient Hellespont), From the West Entrance to Cape Nagara*, published in 1871. This chart was compiled from an 1840 survey by Graves, and a specific survey by Commander Spratt and others in the paddle steamer HMS *Spitfire* in 1855, covering *The Narrows*; the latter portion was separately incorporated as a larger-scale (1:29,136) inset.[5] The Gulf of Saros portion had been surveyed by Copeland in 1833, and 'The remainder from various documents in the Hydrographic Office.'

Spratt and *Spitfire* became 'a sort of intelligence headquarters' in the Black Sea during the Crimean War of 1854–6 in which Britain and France supported Turkey against Russia. He surveyed the Bay of Balaclava and the positions of ships of the Allied Fleet for the bombardment of Sevastopol, prefiguring in a remarkable way the activities of naval hydrographers at Gallipoli in 1915. Following this, he surveyed large parts of the Russian Black Sea coast. The war ended, Spratt, now promoted to Captain, resumed his Mediterranean surveys.[6] This episode demonstrates the great contribution of the Navy's hydrographers to intelligence gathering, to land mapping and to operations. The Navy continued its silent (and often forgotten) service in the Mediterranean and the 'Arches' up to 1914, as did the Consular Service. British yachtsmen, including the military attaché Frederick Cunliffe Owen and others such as Pirie Gordon who later became RNVR intelligence officers, explored the islands and inlets of the Aegean, the Dardanelles itself, and the Sea of Marmara.

The Calvert brothers were key figures in the Consular Service in the mid-19th century. Frederick Calvert was one of three British brothers living and trading at Chanak (modern Cannakale) on the Asiatic side of the Narrows, all antiquarians fascinated by the problem of finding the precise location of ancient Troy. He had long been associated with the Dardanelles, and was British Consul there during the Crimean War. James was the American Consul, and handed this job on to Frank, who lived closer to the mouth of the Dardanelles at In Tepe on the Asiatic Shore. Frank occupied the British and American Consulships for several decades in the second half of the 19th century, and was obsessed with finding Troy, going to the lengths of buying a field at Hissarlik from a local farmer. Here he succeeded in excavating sufficient remains to confirm Troy's location. He and Frederick passed their knowledge on to Heinrich Schliemann who later took all the credit. In fact Frank had shown a site to Tom Spratt as early as 1839, and Spratt had duly entered it on the beautifully drawn Admiralty chart of the Troad and the Dardanelles, which was engraved and sold in England.[7] To call this a chart is to understate Spratt's land-mapping contribution, which extended to the Gallipoli Peninsula. On this map he entered many antiquities, including the name '*Ilium Novum*?' at Hissarlik. We can see this as the origin of the 'chart-map' concept which underwent further development in 1915 at Gallipoli and in 1944 for D-Day.

The Allies were concerned to secure their sea-route to the Black Sea during the Crimean War and to this end in 1854–5 they occupied the town of Gallipoli, the French making an excellent 1:50,000 scale contoured reconnaissance survey, based on a triangulation, of the whole Peninsula (see Chapter 6). The Bulair Lines were created by the French and British in 1855 to defend the Peninsula from a possible Russian land attack from the north, and a report on the Lines, including a large-scale contoured map, was written in 1877 during another Russian war scare.[8]

Maps and reports, 1872–80

In 1872 the stretch of the Dardanelles from Nagara to Gallipoli port was surveyed by Commander W J L Wharton and others in HMS *Shearwater* (see Chapter 8). This new survey was duly added to the 1871 chart, and proved extremely useful a few years later, when the Balkan crisis of 1875–6, triggered by revolts against Ottoman rule in Bosnia and Serbia, followed by the Turks' 'Bulgarian atrocities' in 1876, led to growing tension between Turkey and Russia, which erupted in April 1877 when Russia formally started hostilities, capturing Plevna in December. The Foreign Office was vitally interested and, in October 1876, the War Office ordered Lt-Col. Home and Captain Fraser, both Royal Engineers, to Constantinople to study the military situation, and conduct surveys (assisted by various other RE officers). They were to report on the defences of the Gallipoli Peninsula against attack from the west and prepare plans for holding the Peninsula so that the fleet could pass through the Dardanelles. The result was a 'Strictly Confidential' volume printed at the War Office in 1877: *Reports and Memoranda relative to Defence of Constantinople and other positions in Turkey. Also on Routes in Roumelia*, which contained a large number of specially surveyed maps and plans, including many of the Gallipoli Peninsula;[9] these are described in Chapter 6. Though Britain was falling out of sympathy with the Ottoman Empire, the Foreign Office was still determined to support the *Sublime Porte* against Russian expansionism.

In February 1876 Captain G E Grover RE, who in 1862 had pioneered air observation using balloons,[10] executed a rapid reconnaissance survey of a route from the coast near Gaba Tepe to the Kilid Bahr Plateau, which he drew at a scale of four inches to the mile (1:15,840) in three sheets, soon lithographed at the Intelligence Branch in London. This map described the coast north of what in 1915 became Anzac Cove as 'Steep Sandy Cliffs. Impassable', and north of Gaba Tepe as 'Sandy Precipitous Cliffs (Impassable)'. A 'Coast Track Over Beach' was shown north of Gaba Tepe, but this disappeared in the area of Anzac Cove, to reappear farther north.[11] Grover included this map in a report he wrote in January 1877 on a 'proposed landing place for troops south of Hanafart (Anafarta Lim)'.[12] This included a map at the scale of 1:50,286, 'From a French map of Gallipoli', showing the Peninsula between Kilid Bahr and the Gulf of Edjelmar (Ece Lim), printed by the Ordnance Survey in 1877.

Grover's covering letter from Maïdos, written on 31 January 1877, makes fascinating reading in the light of the 1915 plan for the landing at what became known as 'Brighton Beach' (the original destination for the Anzac Corps):

I have the honour to forward herewith sketch sheets (with general map *Carte de la Presqu'Ile de Gallipoli . . . 1854. Photozincographed at the Ordnance Survey Office . . . 1876*) on the scale of 4 inches to a mile, prepared, in accordance with your directions, to show the portion of the coast between Kaba Tépé [Gaba Tepe] and Suwla [Suvla] Bay, on the west side of the Gallipoli Peninsula, opposite Maïdos, which seems suitable for the landing of a force to attack, in rear, the batteries of Kilid Bahr and

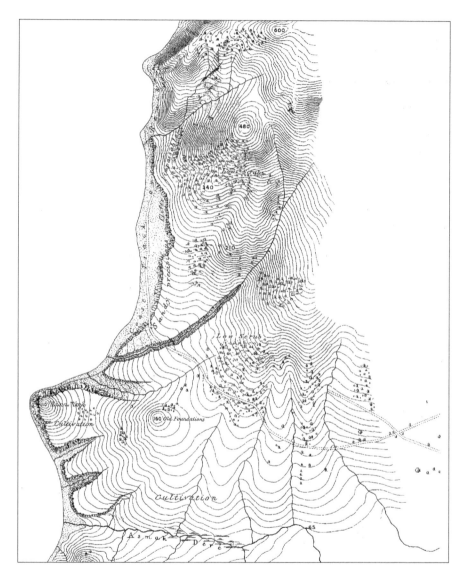

Extract from Grover's 4-inches to the mile reconnaissance map 1876, 'Sketch of Portion of the West Coast of the Gallipoli Peninsula,' showing the area between Gaba Tepe and Anzac Cove

Boukali, as a means of land – co-operation with a naval effort to force the passage of the Dardanelles.

The selected coast is low, and affords easy access to the interior, for an extent of nearly two miles, on the west of the villages of Böjök Anafarta. It is here protected from the prevalent north-east winds, and the Admiralty Chart appears to show sufficient depth of water, and good anchorage, for the proposed operation.[13]

British editions of the French 1854 1:50,000 map of the Peninsula were printed in 1876 and 1880. Captain John C Ardagh RE wrote his *Report on the Defences of the Dardanelles,*[14] which contained plans of the forts surveyed by him, in Constantinople in December 1877, and this utilised the 1876 printing. Odoni, the British vice-consul at Gallipoli, also sent despatches on the Gallipoli Defences in 1877.[15] A survey was also ordered of the Bulair area, which was printed as *Survey of Defensive Position near Bulair shewing the lines constructed by the Anglo-French Army in 1855. Sketched December 1876 by Lieut. Cockburn RE and Lieut. Chermside RE. 1:15,840 or 4 miles to 1 inch.* This excellent map was close-contoured (or form-lined), with spot-heights. This map was included in a *Report on the Defences of the Gallipoli Peninsula at Bulair,* by Captain T Fraser RE.[16]

At the same time a one-inch map was made of the area north-west of Constantinople: *Reconnaissance of the Chatalja Lines between the Sea of Marmora [sic] and Black Sea covering Constantinople from the westward, sketched October and November 1876 under direction of Lt Col R. Home CB, RE, by Capt. Ardagh DAQMG RE, Lieut. Cockburn RE and Lieut. Chermside RE. Shewing also works proposed by Capt. T. Fraser RE.*[17] The Chatalja Lines, defending Constantinople, ran across the isthmus north of the city. In January and February 1877, as part of this general survey, the road on the Asiatic side of the Dardanelles from Chanak to Kum Kale was reconnoitred (in a north-easterly gale and snow) by Home and Lieutenant Hare RE, as was the coast in the Bulair region by Captain T H Anstey RE.

Passage through the Dardanelles

In 1877 Admiral Sir Geoffrey Hornby concentrated the British Mediterranean Fleet in Besika Bay, ready to sail through the Straits to Constantinople to demonstrate British commitment to Turkey. However, Hornby protested that the safety of his fleet would be endangered by lack of possession of the Gallipoli Peninsula, which the Russians might well occupy, cutting off his line of retreat. He proposed the landing of a British force to strengthen the Turks holding the Bulair Lines. In August 1877 his appreciation correctly identified the great problem the Navy was to face in 1915 – that though the Fleet could force the Dardanelles, the passage could not be kept open because the enemy would deploy mobile batteries on the shore of the Peninsula, which the Navy would find it 'most difficult' to silence.[18] He finally took the Fleet through to the Marmara in a snowstorm on 13 February 1878, after an armistice between the Turks and the Russians. One of his captains on this occasion was 'Jackie' Fisher, later to become First Sea Lord. Fisher, with his first-hand experience of the Dardanelles, became convinced of the impossibility of any purely naval attack. The situation was resolved for the time being by the Treaty of San Stefano and the Congress of Berlin in that year. The passage of the Fleet was an opportunity for further hydrographic survey work in the Dardanelles.

John Ardagh, now a major and staff officer (DAQMG), wrote on 2 September 1880 a *Memorandum on passage of Dardanelles*, which outlined landing operations, and was accompanied by a new printing of the French 1854 map, together with many others. This map carried a red overprint, prepared at the Intelligence Branch in the Quarter-Master General's Department at the Horse Guards, on the 1876 base map showing Turkish defences at Chanak Kale and on the Kilid Bahr Plateau, the Bulair Lines, a fleet anchorage off Suvla Bay, the main landing place south of Nibrunesi Point, the line of advance southwards to the Kilid Bahr Plateau, and diversionary landings on the east coast and south of Gaba Tepe. The armament of Turkish forts and batteries was also given.[19] This memorandum was part of a broader 1880 paper, *Seizure of the Dardanelles as a means of coercing the Porte.*[20]

After 1880, British attention, while still keeping one eye on the 'Eastern Question' and on Russia's expansion towards India, gradually became more and more focused on the growing German threat. German and Austrian cartographers became increasingly interested in the area. Kiepert produced a 1: 400,000 *Karte von Kleinasien*, covering the Dardanelles and the Troad, and Philippson followed this up with his 1:300,000 *Topographische Karte des westlichen Kleinasien*, based on Kiepert's map. War with Turkey again threatened in 1882 over Egypt, and the unstable situation in the Balkans, coupled with British concern about Russian designs on India, combined to keep the Dardanelles at the forefront of British minds. A German Military Mission under von der Goltz appeared in Constantinople in 1883, and from 1885 the Turks reorganised their coast defence batteries and rearmed them with Krupp guns. Von der Goltz stayed until 1895, and led a further German Mission in 1908–11. The activities of the Germans were closely watched by British military attachés. The rearming of the Narrows batteries with modern, high-velocity, breech-loading rifled guns, which at the short ranges involved could punch straight through a ship's armour, led the Admiralty to realise that a naval attack was now not a practicable proposition. Further, both services viewed with increasing pessimism the possibilities of even a combined naval and military operation.[21]

Shortly after joining the Intelligence Branch of the War Office in 1887, Captain Charles Callwell sailed through the Dardanelles on his way to

Constantinople, visiting Chanak, from which vantage point he studied through binoculars, at close range across the narrows, the high ground of the Kilid Bahr Plateau which 'with the numerous batteries which nestled at its foot', struck him as being the 'Key of the Dardanelles'.[22] Careful not to offend the Turks, he did not set foot on the Gallipoli Peninsula. Nevertheless, this first-hand knowledge later proved of great value when, as a pre-war staff officer in the Directorate of Military Operations, and in 1914–15 in the same capacity, he made studies of proposed operations and eventually, in March 1915, briefed Hamilton and Braithwaite.

In 1904 Lt-Col. Thomas English, late RE, a Fellow of the Geological Society of London, conducted privately a geological survey of the Dardanelles and Aegean coast, and published a paper in the Society's Journal in 1905.[23] Intended as a reconnaissance survey of potential economic resources (Spratt had discovered coal at Erekli on the coast of Asia Minor[24]), this was clearly a vital source of terrain intelligence, including water supply, but appears to have been ignored in 1914–15, despite the fact that English offered his services to the War Office.[25] English visited the Gallipoli Peninsula again in 1912, executing a prismatic compass survey with Lieutenant F G Hill.[26]

Lt-Col. Maunsell, military attaché

In 1903 a further War Office volume, *Reports on the Defences of Constantinople*, which did not cover the Dardanelles or the Gallipoli Peninsula but concentrated on the immediate defences of the Bosphorus and the Chatalja Lines, was prepared by Lt-Col. Francis Richard Maunsell RA (military attaché, Constantinople),[27] who undertook much topographical work on the ground, and who subsequently extended his area of study to include the Dardanelles and the Gallipoli Peninsula. He drew further panoramic sketches which were included in the 1909 *Report on the Defences of Constantinople*, misleadingly given a name almost identical to that of the 1903 report, and probably also took some of the panoramic terrain photographs included in that *Report*.

Maunsell was consul at Van, in southern Armenia near the border with Persia, before going to Constantinople as military attaché in 1901–5, but fell out of favour and was exiled to the Macedonian Gendarmerie, retiring in 1906. He undertook a great deal of reconnaissance in the Gallipoli and Dardanelles region, as well as in the area closer to Constantinople, and revised the 1876 *Reconnaissance of the Chatalja Lines* one-inch map, which was reprinted in 1903.[28] Presumably Maunsell himself undertook the corrections in 1905. He also drew two panoramic sketches in March 1904 which were added to the foot of a new edition of Cockburn and Chermside's 1876 Bulair map (now designated TSGS 2052), which was corrected to June 1905. This map was appended to the Confidential 1905 *Military Report on Eastern Turkey in Europe*,[29] written by Maunsell, which contained a chapter on the Gallipoli Peninsula (see Appendix I), and to the Secret 1909 *Report on the Defences of Constantinople* (see below), which contained a great deal about Gallipoli and the Dardanelles defences.

As military attaché, Maunsell was clearly on good terms with the Turkish authorities as he had good access to the Constantinople hinterland, to the Dardanelles and to the Gallipoli Peninsula. He was able, openly, to make maps and panoramas, and take photographs. In his introduction (dated 7 April) to the 1903 *Report*, he speaks of the 'notes and sketches of the Chatalja Lines and Black Sea Coast, which I was permitted to visit last November and again a few days ago, by the Minister of War'. However, it may have been this zealous pursuit of intelligence that led to his departure from Constantinople to the wilds of Macedonia.

Like other military attachés, Maunsell sent his reports, after they had been vetted by the Ambassador, by diplomatic bag to the Foreign Office in London, who then forwarded them to the War Office and the Admiralty War Staff, who incorporated the information into their intelligence reports. He was a close friend of Mark Sykes, an honorary attaché at the Constantinople Embassy in Pera, and they agreed on the defence capabilities of the Turkish army, the forces they could set against any Russian invasion, and standing against the increasing German domination of Turkish policy. Following Maunsell's retirement, Sykes was for a while made responsible for writing the intelligence reports. However, further military attachés were posted to Constantinople, and continued to supply vital intelligence.

Colonel Herbert C Surtees was appointed military attaché from 1 July 1905, being followed on 4 December 1909 by Major Gerald Ernest Tyrell. Maunsell, Tyrell and Surtees were all accredited to Athens as well as Constantinople, so they had their work cut out. During the Balkan War, two temporary military attaché appointments were made – Lt-Col. Frederick Cunliffe Owen RA on 9 November 1912 to Athens, and Lt-Col. Hamilton L Reed VC on 24 November 1912 to Constantinople. Reed seems to have been the victim of an entrapment by a blackmailing adventurer, Captain Jorge Nelcken y Waldberg, in the pay of the Turkish secret police and possibly of the Germans as an *agent provocateur*, who managed to get him embroiled with the military opposition to Mahmud Shevket Pasha who was assassinated on 11 June 1913. The net result of this was to discredit Britain further, and to lead to the recall of Reed, who was replaced in Constantinople by Cunliffe Owen on 26 November 1913. Captain Arthur Fitzheary Townshend was briefly Consul for the Vilayet of Adrianople from 13 April 1905 to 2 February 1906.[30] He was followed at Adrianople by Major L L R Samson, later to conduct a clandestine reconnaissance of Gallipoli landing places and play a key role in British secret intelligence in the Mediterranean and Aegean during the war.

Britain did not do well with its ambassadors to the *Sublime Porte*. Sir Nicholas R O'Conor was an ineffectual diplomat wedded to the old Liberal position of regarding the Turks with distaste and had, by his stance, alienated the *Sublime Porte* and assisted the German policy of increasing penetration. He was replaced by Sir Gerald Lowther, who in turn was succeeded in July 1913 by the ineffectual Sir Louis Mallett, an ex-'Soul', who was encumbered by little diplomatic experience and no knowledge of Turkish. His report for 1913 contained his assessment that Turkish policy was unlikely to take a revolutionary course, and that British influence was strong and was not under threat.[31]

Gathering intelligence

The Consular Service also provided a vital source of information. The British Consulate at Constantinople was in Galata, as was the British Post Office under Frank Ferguson. Mr. C E S Palmer, the vice-consul at the Dardanelles, lived at Chanak, on the Narrows, while another British vice-consul William Grech, lived on the European side of the Straits at Gallipoli port. The Austrians, French, Russians and Germans also had their own post offices at Constantinople. The German Embassy, built in 1875–7, was in Fundukli. In 1898, as part of his policy of cultivating good relations with Turkey, and increasing German influence and penetration in the Near and Middle East, the Kaiser paid two state visits to the Sultan and his domains. He later claimed to be a secret Moslem, to be the protector of all the Moslem peoples, and on one of his visits rode through a specially created gateway in the wall of Jerusalem, in full field marshal's regalia, on a black charger.[32]

William Thompson was Harbour Master and Inspector of Police, and appears to have played a murky role. A further interesting sidelight on the Foreign Office's clandestine activities in Constantinople is provided by surviving correspondence relating to the Constantinople Quays Company. One letter of 1907 from the Foreign Office to Sir William Garstin, asking if he would be interested in becoming a director, declared:

> The F.O. are very greatly interested in the welfare of the Constantinople Quays Co. I do not for the present intend to enter into the details as to the scope or workings of this Co, as this can be done later . . . this is not an ordinary sort of Co, but one in which the F.O. has a very special interests [sic]. . . May I ask you to reply by the Agency bag?[33]

Further such correspondence makes it very clear that in the period 1905-7 officers and agents were engaged on duties for 'His Majesty's Secret Service', in many theatres ranging from the Baltic to the Ottoman Empire to China.[34]

Much of the intelligence work was in the hands of the amateur 'honorary attachés', usually aristocrats with good education and linguistic capability (including George Lloyd and Aubrey Herbert; they were to be reunited after the outbreak of war in the Intelligence Department at GHQ Egypt, and later the Arab Bureau) who intended to make the Foreign Office and Diplomatic Service their career. They had no intelligence training, and did not necessarily receive instructions from military or naval intelligence as to what types of information to seek. It does not appear that Sykes, or any of the Embassy staff, tried to get an agent into the Turkish Survey Department to obtain copies of the new maps but, even if it had occurred to them to try, such an action would probably have been ruled out by the Embassy as being ungentlemanly and undiplomatic. It was a matter for secret service. As Callwell knew, gold would buy anything in Turkey, but apart from being expensive it was an extremely dangerous business. Such an agent could easily disappear; his body might be found floating in the Golden Horn. Whatever the fact of the matter, none of the crucial results of the new Turkish survey of the Gallipoli Peninsula found their way into British (or Allied) hands before the landings in April 1915.

Multicultural and cosmopolitan, Constantinople was particularly fertile ground for espionage. Moslems, Christians (Catholic, Protestant, Greek and Russian Orthodox), Jews, Turks, Greeks, Europeans, Asians, Levant traders, diplomats, consuls, attachés, members of military and naval missions, businessmen, scholars and archaeologists all rubbed shoulders. Bribery of underpaid officials was commonplace. English sovereigns and French Napoleons were freely circulated. There was a large expatriate community, with two daily Anglo-French newspapers, the *Levant Herald* and the *Oriental Advertiser*, English, French and German bookshops, French, German and Russian hospitals and a British seamen's hospital. However, the easy multiculturalism of earlier decades was, before the war, giving way to increasing polarisation between Christians and Moslems. From 1907 the Constantinople mosques were closed to Christians; henceforth special permission had to be sought in advance through diplomatic channels. Macmillan's *Guide*, later to be echoed by John Buchan in *Greenmantle*, noted that:

Stamboul . . . is a meeting-place for men of all races and religions. Costumes and dialects of every variety are to be seen and heard in the streets, where Armenian porters, Levantine sailors, Greek merchants, Turkish soldiers, priests of various confessions, mullahs, and dervishes, jostle each other all day long.[35]

The strategic position of Constantinople, on the cusp of west and east, north and south, on trade and shipping routes from Europe and the Mediterranean to the Middle East, the Black Sea, the Danube, and Russia (Britain's arch-enemy in the 'Great Game') made it a natural magnet for espionage. The British watched Russian activity in the Caucasus, and the German construction of the Berlin–Baghdad and Hedjaz Railways, with great interest. A vast tonnage of shipping flowed ceaselessly through the Bosphorus, the Sea of Marmara and the Dardanelles, and the masters of ships continually reported on the evolving defences, as did British lighthouse keepers, coal merchants, salvage operators, lawyers and traders. On the Black Sea coast, the life-saving stations of Kilia and Riva were under British captains, as was the lightship fifteen miles from the eastern mouth of the Bosphorus, marking the approaches.[36]

The military attachés and 'military consuls' at Constantinople and Adrianople supplied vital information to London. They had various sources, some of them clandestine, and were anxious to protect these sources which their reports, even if they survive in the archives, do not specify. In his evidence to the Dardanelles Commission, Colonel Hankey was asked about the reports of Colonel Frederick Cunliffe Owen, military attaché at Constantinople from December 1913 until the outbreak of war: 'Were not the reports of the various Military Attachés from Constantinople and elsewhere communicated to the Imperial Defence Committee, and subsequently to the War Council, or were they kept at the Foreign Office?' Hankey replied that: 'They come to the Foreign Office, who practically use themselves as a post office to send them on to the War Office.'[37] Cunliffe Owen, whose leisure activities as an enthusiastic yachtsman provided him with convenient access to the waters and shores of the Dardanelles, supplied important reports on the eve of, and after the outbreak of, the war. Compton Mackenzie was more forthright about the activities of military attachés in the Balkans, stating that 'they are really War Office spies in the Embassies and Legations to which they are posted; but few of them have the courage to admit this to themselves.'[38]

Naval intelligence up to 1914

The Navy had not only been gathering hydrographic and other intelligence but had, as was seen in Chapter 2, studied the problem of forcing the Dardanelles on several occasions, but most recently in the aftermath of the 1906 Akaba crisis. The Naval Intelligence Department (it became a division of the newly formed Naval Staff in 1912) printed two reports on *Turkey, Coast Defences* (including the Dardanelles) around the turn of the century: *NID 458, December 1896* and *NID 458a, June 1901*. These were superseded by *NID 838, May 1908*.[39]

The final draft of Ottley's 1906 report made it clear that naval intelligence was considered very efficient at this time, noting about the defences that: 'We have reliable secret information in regard to these points of armaments and mines.'[40] Further, the good intelligence extended to landing places:

The character of the beaches selected for the landings [on the north shore, in the area of the Gulf of Saros] is entirely satisfactory, and accurate and recent information is in our hands as to the nature of roads for the march across the peninsula.[41]

However, Ottley explained that the halcyon days of easy intelligence gathering in the Ottoman Empire were now a thing of the past; the veil was coming down. In his first and second drafts, Ottley had made the point that increasing religious sentiment among the Turks was making bribery less possible, and intelligence about Turkish defences more difficult to gather. Citing the claim of the Sultan to be Khalif of all Islam, he stated that 'it is now no longer possible to buy even the most venal of Moslem pashas with a view to secure the inaction of the batteries in the Dardanelles', and 'the loyalty of the pashas in charge of [the forts] was, until very recently, believed with reason to be not proof against bribery.' They could no longer be paid to abstain from firing as the fleet passed through the Straits! In the same context, 'our secret agents at the Dardanelles' were now finding their task almost impossible. German political influence and German gunner instructors were also important factors. Intelligence would still be forthcoming, however, from attachés, consuls, ships' masters and the indigenous Greek population.

After 1906, both services went ahead with the gathering, collating and printing of voluminous reports on the defences of the Dardanelles and the Turkish coast generally. The Akaba crisis, Ottley's paper and subsequent studies led to the NID amplifying and updating their earlier report on Turkey's coast defences. The new version, *Naval Intelligence Department: N.I.D. 838, Turkey. Coast Defences and Resources; Coast Defence Ordnance and Arsenals, May 1908*,[42] gave a very full description of the defences of the Dardanelles (including a description of the Peninsula, its land defences, and the Bulair Lines), including many maps, plans, charts and plates (see Appendix II). The War Office also produced a new *Report on the Defences of Constantinople* (1909). Both of these important documents were printed as secret or confidential books, with many maps, charts and plates, and were to prove a vital source of tactical and topographical intelligence when war broke out in 1914. They were periodically supplemented by updated intelligence reports, and were continually referred to by the CID, the War Council (after the outbreak of war in 1914), the War Office and the Admiralty. Copies were also issued to naval and military commanders in the Mediterranean theatre, where the Navy in particular had a well-developed intelligence service.

Apart from the armaments question, the Navy does not seem to have given the Gallipoli Peninsula and Dardanelles a high intelligence priority. While attempts to gather hydrographic and other intelligence were made by NID at points on the German coast, Lieutenant Brandon (Admiralty

Hydrographic Department) and Captain Trench (Royal Marines) being arrested and convicted by the Germans in 1910 for spying on North Sea coastal defences,[43] no such efforts apart from the normal hydrographic surveys already discussed have come to light in the Dardanelles area as far as the specific, detailed hydrographic intelligence it needed for landings was concerned, and in 1915 the Navy complained that it suffered from lack of such information. It had, therefore, to acquire it during the operations themselves.

While Haldane's reorganisation at the War Office had created an efficient, modern General Staff, at the Admiralty there was no such staff in 1911 when the Agadir Crisis focused attention on the appalling lack of preparedness should Germany launch a sudden attack. As a result of the naval issues highlighted by the Agadir Crisis, Asquith appointed Churchill as First Lord in 1911, specifically tasking him to make such preparations. Churchill set up an Admiralty War Staff for this purpose in 1912. The Naval Intelligence Division (NID) was formerly the Foreign Intelligence Committee (formed 1882), which became the Naval Intelligence Department, created in 1887 under 'Blinker' Hall's father, Captain W H Hall. NID was incorporated by Churchill into the new Admiralty War Staff.

In 1912 the Admiralty also created its Air Department, which (under Churchill's overall leadership) was to prove vital for making the decisions enabling the RNAS to provide aircraft, crew and photographic equipment for the Dardanelles in 1915. There was a certain amount of general, and occasionally specific, liaison between the War Office, Admiralty and Foreign Office before the war, while the CID provided an efficient working framework. There was, however, no joint intelligence committee and no joint chiefs of staff committee as there was in the Second World War. On a planning as well as operational level, the Army and Navy were jealous of their traditions and spheres of action, and cooperation did not come naturally in an atmosphere of competition and rivalry. The naval race had seen the Army very concerned for the safety of its annual estimates, as the cost of building new dreadnoughts and super-dreadnoughts gobbled up large chunks of the budget.

The Turks had long prepared the Dardanelles against naval attack by constructing forts and batteries, supplemented before the war, following the advice of the British Admiral Limpus, by torpedoes and plans for minefields. They also constructed certain fieldworks on the Peninsula, commanding the landing places, in 1897,[44] and again during the war with Italy in 1911–12 and the Balkan Wars of 1912–13. The reports and maps of the period after 1906 were prepared as the result of appreciations made by the Military Operations Directorate at the War Office and the Naval Intelligence Department at the Admiralty following the increased tension with Turkey associated with the 1906 Akaba Incident. With a Naval Mission in place, and British merchant shipping passing through the

Straits daily, the British were perfectly positioned to gather intelligence on the Dardanelles.

In fact the Dardanelles fixed defences and topography were extremely well-documented by both the British Navy and the Army, drawing on information supplied by their own intelligence departments, through diplomatic and consular channels, by secret service agents and above all by military attachés in foreign capitals; each service, in cooperation, produced its own copiously illustrated report on them, containing printed descriptions, maps and plans, photographs and panoramic sketches.

These crucial reports, details of which have already been given, were *Naval Intelligence Department: N.I.D. 838, Turkey. Coast Defences and Resources; Coast Defence Ordnance and Arsenals, May 1908* (see Appendix II), and *General Staff, War Office: Report on the Defences of Constantinople, 1909, Secret* (see Appendix III), which also gave a full description of the Dardanelles defences, as well as much vital topographical information, including landing places, 'going' and water supply, useful to a force landing on the Peninsula. It was accompanied by a folder of associated maps, plans, panoramic photos and topographical sketches, including a panoramic sketch of Suvla Bay from the sea and full details of the Bulair Lines. A crucial component of this Report was the one-inch to the mile (1:63,360) *Map of the Gallipoli Peninsula* (GSGS 2285) in two sheets. A secret edition of this map showed the Dardanelles Defences and the Bulair Lines in red.

There is abundant evidence of extremely close cooperation between Admiralty and War Office in both reports. They contained much the same material on the Dardanelles coast defences, though *NID 838* was much more detailed; Part II of *NID 838*, focusing on the 'Dardanelles, Coast Defences and Resources', specifically noted: 'Much of the information used to bring this Report up to date has been supplied by the Military operations Directorate' at the War Office, while among the supporting maps were the two secret edition sheets of the War Office one-inch map (GSGS 2285) used in the 1909 Report. *NID 838* also noted that 'In this description the spelling of the names of places in the Gallipoli Peninsula has been made to conform with the spelling on the M[ilitary]. O[perations]. D[irectorate]. Map (Map 3A) accompanying this report.' This was the secret one-inch map. The reports were periodically brought up-to-date by intelligence reports before and during the war.

The British and French had appreciated in the years before the war that Turkey was likely to join the Central Powers in the event of a European War, and this was certainly the British General Staff view from 1910. While there was close cooperation between the British War Office and Admiralty in this period, there was no joint intelligence committee or joint planning staff. It was not until 19 March 1915 that the Secretary to the War Council (formerly to the CID), Colonel Maurice Hankey, as a former Royal Marine officer extremely aware of the hazards of amphibious operations, tried to remedy this situation by recommending to the War Council the setting up of a joint technical committee, but nothing came of this prescient move.[45]

The military intelligence situation from 1906 to the First World War

The aftermath of the Boer War, and Haldane's subsequent reforms and reorganisations at the War Office had created an efficient, modern General Staff for the specific purpose of planning, organising and collecting intelligence for war. The Directorate of Military Operations from 1907 to 1914 comprised the following sections:[46]

MO1 Strategical Section
MO2 Foreign Intelligence – European Section (Sub-Section B included Balkans and Ottoman Empire in the Near East)
MO3 Foreign Intelligence – Asiatic Section
MO4 Geographical Section (GSGS); Topographical Section (TSGS) until 1907
MO5 Special Section (Section A included Wireless Telegraphy and Ciphers; Section B was the General Staff Library); in 1909 the Special Intelligence Bureau was added, for Counterintelligence; in 1912 the Special Intelligence Section was created to coordinate British covert intelligence operations abroad
MO6 Medical & Sanitary information re Foreign Armies

In the decade from 1904 to 1914, hardly a year went by without British geographers and officers setting foot on both shores of the Dardanelles for reconnaissance purposes. Much of this reconnaissance was directly instigated by the War Office, but some was more nebulously associated. During Charles Close's time as Chief of the Topographical/Geographical Section (1905–11), serious preparations began to be made for war against Germany and it became obvious that plans would have to be made and maps printed to meet all possible contingencies. This was the function of a General Staff. Close, and later Hedley, was responsible for the preparation of maps of all possible theatres of war including the Dardanelles, not just of France and Belgium, under the instructions of the DMO. This meant that the meagre resources of the Geographical Section had to be spread rather thinly. From 1906 onwards, the War Office and Ordnance Survey printed many maps and diagrams of the possible area of operations, covering the topography, communications, telegraphs, army corps districts and headquarters of Belgium, France, the Netherlands, Denmark and Germany. Preparations were thorough for this potential theatre of war, except for the lack of large-scale sheets suitable for directing artillery fire. Maps of other possible theatres of war were also prepared, including the two one-inch

Gallipoli Peninsula sheets of 1908 with their secret defence overprints.[47] No further maps of the Peninsula were prepared or printed before the war, apart from small-scale (1:250,000) sheets.

The Intelligence Branch at the War Office had developed a formidable reputation in the 19th century, enhanced by the renown of its counterpart in Simla. In the early 20th century the Branch had been downgraded and subsumed into the Directorate of Military Operations; it relied primarily on attachés' reports, which were often of great value. As international tension rose in the early years of the new century, it became apparent to many that plans would have to be made and maps printed to meet all possible contingencies. As Kaiser Wilhelm II flexed his imperial muscles and expanded his navy, serious preparations began to be made for war against Germany. Treaty obligations towards Belgium would have to be honoured in the event of a German invasion of France through Belgium, and this might involve the landing of an expeditionary force. There was, however, no specific undertaking to land such a force. Pre-war Staff 'conversations' with the French, originating with the *Entente Cordiale* of 1904, were based on this eventuality.

In 1906 Major-General Grierson, Director of Military Operations from 1904 to 1906, began serious conversations with the French, which resulted from 1911 in a detailed scheme to land an expeditionary force in France and concentrate it in the Maubeuge–Le Cateau–Hirson area. His successors, Spencer Ewart (DMO 1906–10) and Henry Wilson (DMO from August 1910 to the outbreak of war), pursued studies of the British scheme of operations.[48] Major General Sir Henry Wilson was the co-architect of the 'Wilson–Foch' scheme for Anglo-British cooperation in the west, and General French's Chief of Staff designate for the BEF's coming campaign. For the western theatre there was certainly no shortage of topographical information, and in any case Wilson spent many pre-war summers cycling around the Franco-Belgian frontier and the BEF's intended Concentration Area.

For other, less predictable, theatres it was a very different story, though the British attachés in Constantinople supplied a stream of first class information on the Dardanelles defences and the terrain of the Gallipoli Peninsula. Wilson seems to have been understandably obsessed with the French theatre, to the practical exclusion of others, including the Dardanelles, and he took a dim view of Turkish capabilities. During a visit to Constantinople in October 1913, he formed the opinion that the Turkish Army was neither serious nor modern, was unadapted to western thoughts and methods, and was badly commanded, badly officered and badly equipped.[49] While this was perhaps understandable in view of the mixed performance of the Turkish Army in the Balkan Wars, the experience of its fighting powers in 1915–18 was to prove how wrong he was.

Staff officers from MO2 and MO3 (Foreign Intelligence Sections) were encouraged to travel abroad to gather intelligence; they had rather more freedom of action than the accredited military attachés.[50] Colonel Gleichen made a 'little spy journey' to Holland with the Royal Marine George Aston of NID in 1907, going on to Denmark and Sweden. In 1908 he visited Spain, Morocco and France, and in 1909 travelled via Vienna, Belgrade, the Danube through Rumania and Bulgaria, and the Black Sea, to Constantinople where he spent ten days cultivating Turkish notables and 'trying to acquire as much information as I could'. It was obvious to Gleichen that in Turkey 'our British star was sinking and the German one beginning to shine brightly'.[51]

From 1902 to 1911 the Special Duties Section at the War Office was so small that it could only recruit and direct secret agents overseas on a very limited basis. During this period it therefore financed, from its very limited budget, the travels of MO2 and MO3 officers. The expenses of 'Secret Service' conducted by the War Office (and perhaps also by the Admiralty) were carried on the Foreign Office budget.[52] The War Office Special Intelligence Section (part of MO5) was created in 1912 to coordinate covert intelligence operations overseas,[53] and presumably had a larger budget. It does not appear to have directed many resources against the Dardanelles, which may well have been considered more of an Admiralty (NID) matter but, as we have seen, Wilson was not particularly bothered with that area.

Lieutenant H Charles Woods, an officer of the Coldstream Guards from 1900 to 1907, undertook unpaid clandestine intelligence work in 1905 and 1906 on behalf of Colonel Surtees, the military attaché in Constantinople. This involved not only road and military resource reconnaissances in the Balkans, reports on which were sent to the War Office complete with sketch maps and photographs, but also, in late 1906, a clandestine reconnaissance of the south-western tip of the Gallipoli Peninsula. His instructions from Surtees were:[54]

1. To ascertain the exact locality from which the forts defending the narrows, particularly the Yildiz/Tepeh fort south-west of Kilid Bahr, could be best attacked by surprise and commanded from the rear;
2. To find out the most suitable landing places on the north-west coast of the Peninsula, and
3. To reconnoitre the ground between these beaches and the hills overlooking the forts.

His first step was to obtain a *teskereh*, or ordinary permission to travel, to pay a visit by sea to William Grech, the British vice-consul at the port and town of Gallipoli who, without attempting to obtain further permission, arranged a secret trip in a small sailing boat across the Narrows to Chanak, on the Asiatic Shore, where they landed unnoticed after hiding in a tug, and met the British vice-consul with whom Woods stayed. The venture was helped by the facts that Grech was associated with the tug company of that name which had facilities at Chanak, and that his house at Chanak fronted the water. Such devious methods were necessary as Woods could not obtain a visa for Chanak without attracting suspicion, particularly in the aftermath of the Akaba incident when tension between Britain and Turkey was still high and the British Cabinet and military and naval authorities were seriously considering the question of forcing the Dardanelles. The Turks were understandably wary of the British at this time, and Grech and the Chanak vice-consul impressed upon Woods that all strangers landing on the south-western part of the Peninsula were under very close surveillance. The Peninsula was not normally accessible to foreigners because of the strategic importance of its coastal forts and batteries, and the three decided to use the cover of a hastily improvised shooting party to enable Woods to get a view of the terrain.

Early the following morning Woods re-crossed the Dardanelles, sailing, again secretly, for the Greek-populated village of Maidos in a boat normally used for carrying water and, on landing, headed for a mile northwest up onto the high ground in rear of the forts – the Kilid Bahr Plateau – before turning south over rough country towards the fort. Describing the going, he provided crucial terrain intelligence: 'The whole of this area is made up of irregular, almost rocky hills and steep sided valleys covered with prickly bushes and scrub, which made it necessary at times to go on hands and knees.' Reaching the Kilid Bahr Plateau after a couple of hours, he found a good vantage point from where he could look down at the rear of Yildiz Fort, containing some twelve large guns, about a mile away to the south-east and some forty feet lower. The fort was open at the rear, and completely undefended. He immediately decided, as Grover had done thirty years before, and 'knowing that the all-important forts defending the Narrows are located in the immediate neighbourhood of Kilid Bahr', that an attacking force should be landed at a point to the west, across the narrowest part of this end of the Peninsula, only five miles from the forts. This pointed to beaches in the vicinity of Gaba Tepe, preferably to the north-east (Brighton Beach, south-west of Anzac Cove). Landings here would have the advantage of using the grain of the country rather than fighting against it; the valleys ran roughly west–east, favouring rapid movement along them, whereas a force landing at Cape Helles, twelve miles away from the forts, would have to cross the valleys and their intervening ridges to reach the Kilid Bahr Plateau.[55] He reckoned that, despite the rough country, a landing force with artillery could reach the forts in a few hours. This scheme was also that recommended by General Callwell, the DMO, in 1914–15.[56]

Woods discovered that the water supply to the forts was carried from the high ground by aqueducts and pipes, and that Kilid Bahr was connected to Sedd-el-Bahr by telegraph lines. He also headed across the Peninsula towards the north-west coast, where he reconnoitred landing places from Suvla southwards, and discovered a new look-out station at Gaba Tepe which compromised his favoured landing area. A surprise attack, he considered, could have dealt with this. He immediately wrote a report on the Peninsula which he sent via the Constantinople Embassy to the War Office. A key point of this report, which was supported by a sketch map, was that landings could only succeed if they were surprise attacks and the Turks had no time to entrench the hills defending the forts. The report was received in January 1907 by Major G D Symonds of the Intelligence Department at the War Office (MO2b), and in February Woods was asked to go the Admiralty to brief Captain Charles Ottley, Director of Naval Intelligence, and other naval officers.

Following the outbreak of war in 1914, Woods reminded Naval intelligence about the report but, possibly because the War Office could not find it, NID could not get a view of it. Yet Ottley must have seen it in 1907. Luckily, Woods was able to supply a rough copy.[57] In essence, such was the logic of the terrain that he was repeating what Grover and the other British soldier-surveyors had decided three decades earlier. In 1908 Woods published his first book, based on his experiences.[58] He visited the Dardanelles again in 1909, while gathering information for his second book, and this time reconnoitred the military road from Uzun Kupru to Gallipoli, which was currently being reconstructed and improved, and the Bulair Lines. The book was published in 1911,[59] in which year a French edition also appeared.[60]

Only a year later, September 1910 saw yet another close reconnaissance of the Peninsula, focusing like those of Grover and Woods on the Gaba Tepe–Kilid Bahr area, this time by Major L L R Samson, the 'military consul' in Adrianople and an officer of considerable standing within the intelligence community. His report, completed on 28 September and forwarded to the War Office, was entitled *Report on Landing Places at Kaba Tepe (Gallipoli Peninsula) with two roads leading therefrom to Maidos and the Kilid Bahr Plateau. Road Traversed 8th to 10th Sep. 1910*[61] (see Appendix IV). Samson, later to head the British military intelligence station in Athens during the war, was an acute observer, and provided a remarkably detailed report on the beaches and their exits, the inland terrain, and the nature of the going along roads and tracks, particularly with an eye to landing and moving artillery.

In April and May 1911 the historical geographer Dr Walter Leaf, who was researching for a book on the Troad, took a set of panoramic photographs from the land and sea of the shores of the Dardanelles, including Sedd-el-Bahr, Kilid Bahr, the Narrows, Morto Bay, Sestos, Chanak, Kum Kale, the island of Tenedos and many other places on the Asia Minor side, during a five-week reconnaissance with F W Hasluck, the acting Director of the British School at Athens, escorted by an armed Turkish gendarme. Apart from taking some 400 excellent terrain photos, showing in detail the estuaries, harbours (such as they were), beaches, cliffs, hills, tracks, vegetation, scrub and tree cover of the localities, and checking and correcting the Troad areas of Admiralty charts and Philippson's and Kiepert's maps,[62] he also took 142 aneroid observations to check heights, and ascertained the state of recent Turkish survey activity in the area.

An article by Leaf – 'Notes on the Troad' – which contained some of the photographs and a wealth of terrain information, including the state of repair of the roads and tracks, was published in *The Geographical Journal* in 1912,[63] accompanied by a hill-shaded 1:600,000 map. Leaf's book, entitled *Troy, A study in Homeric Geography*, was published by Macmillan in 1912.[64] Strangely, a further article was published in *Country Life* on 17 April 1915, only eight days before the Allied landings on the Peninsula and at Kum Kale. After correspondence with Hinks and Reeves, officers of the Royal Geographical Society (RGS), in July 1915, copies of some of the photographs were ordered for the Society, being accessioned on 27 August 1915.[65] It did not apparently occur to anyone at the War Office or Admiralty to contact Leaf to obtain photographs or information following the outbreak of war.

The period of the Balkan Wars focused international attention on the Dardanelles and the Gallipoli Peninsula, and war conditions, together with the presence of many military attachés, journalists and adventurers, made intelligence-gathering relatively easy. In March 1912 Colonel English returned to the Gallipoli Peninsula with Lt F G Hill, and executed a prismatic compass survey which was plotted on a trace of the War Office 1:250,000 sheet (series TSGS 2097) covering the Peninsula. This drawing was given to the Royal Geographical Society Map Room on 1 July 1912.[66] In early 1912 Justus Perthes of Gotha published a 1:100,000 map of the Dardanelles defences, *Die Befestigung des Westlichen Dardanellen-Eingangs*, by D A Janke. This prime example of 'open source' intelligence was acquired by the RGS on 11 March 1912.[67]

The journalist Ellis Ashmead-Bartlett later told the Dardanelles Commission that during the Balkan Wars, when he was in Constantinople, the Turks had maps of the Peninsula, and that he obtained a set of these – 'which were not the best' – which Sir Ian Hamilton, also in Turkey at the time, asked him to send to England. However, it is clear that Ashmead-Bartlett knew little if anything about Turkish large-scale mapping; he dwelt on the fact that the 'Turks chiefly relied on the great Austrian Staff map, which was a very fine map which they were in course of preparing in the Balkans. It was not completed at the time of the Balkan Wars. Whether it was completed when this war broke out I am not sure.'[68] This Austrian Staff map was not at all the same thing as the Turks' own large-scale military surveys of the Dardanelles area. Ashmead-Bartlett was not a reliable witness when it came to maps.

Lt-Col. Frederick Cunliffe Owen RA, a General Staff Officer (GSO2) of MO2 (2b) until the beginning of October 1912 (and later the military attaché at Constantinople), gave a crucial insight into War Office strategic thinking and planning intentions, or lack of them, when he stated that his sub-section's instructions regarding Turkey, given by the DMO (Henry Wilson) and the section's GSO1, were 'to concentrate upon Syrian, Mesopotamian and Egyptian frontier zones. . . . No instructions envisaged any particular study of military operations in the neighbourhood of the Straits.' He recalled that in the period of the Balkan Wars, the British 'military vice-consul' at Adrianople (Captain Townshend was followed there by Major L L R Samson) 'carried out a reconnaissance about 1912 of the country, as far as I can remember south and west of Bulair and Maidos, and made sketch maps'.[69] He may have had Samson's 1910 reconnaissance in mind, or that of English and Hill in 1912. Whichever it was, the report and maps would have been sent back to the War Office.

Cunliffe Owen went to Constantinople as military attaché in December 1913, and in the spring of 1914, using his cover of amateur yachtsman, 'made his own tour down to Chanak, Gallipoli and the entrance to the Straits'.[70] In March 1914 he warned London that there were at least forty-seven German officers in the German Military Mission; many were holding important positions, being given 'executive functions' in Constantinople and other Ottoman centres.[71] As the situation in the Balkans worsened, he redoubled his efforts:

> From . . . July onwards, I made frequent reports as to any activities in the region of the Dardanelles and as the situation became more intense, I reported at considerable length about troops, movements and installations in regard to armaments, location or setting up of mine fields, collection of shipping and appreciations.[72]

Much, if not all, of this intelligence was passed on by the War Office to the Naval Intelligence Division.

Thus, to our certain knowledge, apart from providing information about the Turkish Army and defences, and political and strategic intelligence, British army officers had conducted surveys and reconnaissances on the Gallipoli Peninsula in 1854–5, 1876–7, 1904, 1905, 1906, 1909, 1910, 1912 and 1914, and possibly on other occasions, while the 'Homeric Geographer' Walter Leaf conducted his own in 1911. No one at the War Office or elsewhere could subsequently legitimately complain of lack of opportunity or information. Many British explorers had travelled through near and distant parts of the Ottoman Empire, and a remarkable body of knowledge was shared among the members of such bodies as the Royal Geographical Society and the Palestine Exploration Fund. It is unsurprising that Colonel Hedley, the Chief of the Geographical Section of the General Staff (MO4), was a member of both. No doubt the Greeks, Russians, French and others were also conducting their own reconnaissances.

The Director of Military Operations' obsession with the security of Egypt and the Canal led to an extraordinary survey being made in Ottoman territory on the eve of the war. Major Stewart Francis Newcombe RE executed, with Lieutenant J P S Greig RE, a topographical survey of southern Palestine (a continuation of a post-Akabar-Crisis survey of Sinai) in the early months of 1914, using T E Lawrence and Leonard Woolley as archaeological cover. They returned to England via Carchemish in Syria, where they called on Lawrence and Woolley, and then via the Taurus Mountains where the Germans were directing the boring of the tunnels of the Berlin–Baghdad railway. This 'tourism' was as thinly veiled as the earlier survey, and both had direct application in the event of war. Newcombe and Greig encouraged Lawrence and Woolley to follow them on this route, and to take photographs of the railway works. Naturally all four passed through Constantinople, where they may have met Cunliffe Owen, whence the Orient Express whisked them on to Paris and London.

The December 1914 issue of the *Geographical Journal* carried a four-page report by Newcombe and Greig, illustrated with a map and photographs (possibly taken by Lawrence) on 'The Baghdad Railway'.[73] Specifically, this dealt with the Taurus Mountains tunnels section between Dorak and Karapunar reconnoitred on horseback and on foot in the second half of May 1914. This must have been submitted for publication before war broke out between Britain and Turkey. Woolley later remarked that this was 'the only piece of spying that I ever did before the War'.[74] The southern Palestine survey had annoyed the Turks, as no doubt had the Taurus reconnaissances.

The Dardanelles had, as Cunliffe Owen pointed out, a mysteriously low priority. The idealistic Liberal government, while not averse to taking measures to defend imperial frontiers, appeared to be very much opposed to the Army and Navy making plans to attack Constantinople via the Dardanelles. General Staff feasibility studies were one thing, but serious, coordinated intelligence-gathering and planning was quite another.

British intelligence to 1914

The dispersion of many of the existing General Staff from the War Office in August 1914, their replacement by 'dug-out' officers, and the subsequent hiatus created by Kitchener's arbitrary rule, does not excuse any pre-war intelligence failures. There was hardly a pre-war failure of topographical intelligence collection and processing inasmuch as the good War Office and Admiralty reports on the Turkish defences and the topography of the Gallipoli Peninsula and Dardanelles, well-illustrated with maps, plans, panorama sketches and photographs, had been prepared and printed, as a direct result of the Akaba crisis, in 1908 and 1909. The War Office report, and the one-inch map (in two sheets), were prepared under Spencer Ewart

(Director of Military Operations August 1906–August 1910). The one-inch map, which was not a bad map in itself, was based on the old French 1:50,000 map, and had been prepared as a possible operations map.

The crucial point here is that it was not possible to prepare any more accurate map as no other compilation material was in the possession of the War Office – the Turks themselves only had a 1:50,000 scale map, and had only just begun to make their large-scale (1:20,000 and 1:25,000) regular surveys of the Dardanelles area immediately before the war, in 1912–13 (though more localised large-scale surveys had been made previously – see Chapter 6). Given that the possibility of operations in the Dardanelles had been discussed at high level since 1906 (and for a century before), this was a serious, but not insurmountable, drawback. Such maps could possibly have been compiled from various sources – clandestinely acquired Turkish maps (the Turkish 1:25,000 sheets were still in process of survey and reproduction, but earlier 1:20,000 surveys had been done), reports and surveys by agents, reports by military attachés, and close study of air photographs. A considerable pre-war intelligence attack on the Turkish target would have been necessary to acquire the information needed, and this at a time when the Allied governments were trying not to offend the Turks. It is significant that the foreign section (later MI6/SIS) of the new Secret Service Bureau (SSB, set up around October 1909 at a time of German invasion scares) in London, under Commander Mansfield Cumming was, from 1910 to 1914, responsible to its main customer, the Admiralty, although it also supplied intelligence to MO5 at the War Office.[75] Moreover, shortage of funds meant that 'its restricted energies were almost entirely directed against Germany',[76] in particular aimed at the acquisition of intelligence relating to (non-existent) German planning for a surprise attack on England. Thus there appears to have been no direction of 'energies' by the SSB (foreign section) against Turkey. The prime concern in England was with the German naval and invasion threats. The NID was, of course, collecting intelligence on the Dardanelles defences, and the military attachés on these and other aspects, such as topography and land defences, of the area.

The most likely alternative sources of information about the Gallipoli Peninsula itself were the Greek naval and military staffs in Athens, and the indigenous Greek population of the Dardanelles area, some of whom were presumably already supplying information to Greek intelligence. In the absence of acquired Turkish large-scale mapping a possible, though unrealistic, solution would have been to conduct a clandestine topographical survey, a difficult proposition in such a strategically sensitive area, but not totally impossible. It would have required a small corps of trained clandestine topographers, along the lines of the *pundits* used by the Survey of India to execute trans-frontier surveys – the sort of operation that was everyday work for Kipling's Colonel Creighton in *Kim*. This corps could have operated on either shore of the Dardanelles to create an accurate large-scale map, sustained by the local Greek population, but it is hardly likely that such survey operations could have been conducted in the relatively settled agricultural conditions of the Gallipoli Peninsula under continuous Turkish scrutiny.

The German intelligence dimension

From their intimate involvement with the Turkish Army and government, notably over the Dardanelles defences, the Germans had drawn a huge amount of defence and topographical information. The Turco-Italian and Balkan Wars in the immediate pre-1914 period, which saw the Dardanelles and the Gallipoli Peninsula directly threatened – and in the Second Balkan War actually attacked at Bulair by the advancing Bulgarians – also enabled the Germans (and military attachés of other states) to observe closely the defensive dispositions of the Turks. A remarkable book by a German Officer, Leutnant Georg Hans Rohde, entitled *Die Operationen an den Dardanellen im Balkankriege, 1912/13,*[77] was published in 1914 and immediately bought by the British Museum Library (stamp: *3 Ju 1914*) and the War Office Library. The book, which had two chapters on the Battle at Bulair, and one each on further events up to the armistice, the Gallipoli Peninsula and the Bulair Lines, supply and medical services on the Peninsula, and lessons and conclusions, included several maps, photographs and tables of Turkish Army organisation. Some of the photographs gave a good indication of the terrain variations.

Rohde had been an Ordnance Officer on the Staff of the Gallipoli Commander, and knew all about the coastal defences and the dispositions made by the Turks to meet amphibious attacks or attacks on the Peninsula via the Bulair Lines. A 1:50,000 sketch map of the Bulair Lines area in the book showed trenches, barbed wire, forts, and Turkish and Bulgarian positions in February–May 1913, while a 1:200,000 map of the whole Peninsula showed the deployment of the Turkish infantry divisions, regiments and battalions, artillery, command posts, cavalry, coastal batteries and forts. It also showed an entrenched, horseshoe-shaped 'Second Position' running across practically the whole Peninsula, creating an entrenched camp around the town and port of Gallipoli; this meant that even if the Helles area or the Bulair Lines were captured, the Peninsula could still be reinforced from the Asiatic side via this port. He gave details of the development of the coast defences, the bombardment by the Italian fleet on 13 April 1912, the calibre, range and numbers of coast guns, towns, their populations and forts, minefields, the Bulair Lines, the further development of the land and sea defences during the war with Italy and the Balkan Wars, including works in rear of Kilid Bahr, and applied the concepts of the famous Belgian fortress engineer General Henri Brialmont and his idea of the double bridgehead. Trenches and strong wire entanglements had been erected, machine guns emplaced, and telephone exchanges installed. During the Second Balkan War, Mal Tepe (Hill 95) near Bulair was renamed by the Turks 'Mitrailleuse [Machine Gun] Tepe'. Aeroplanes were also used for reconnaissance and artillery spotting.

Rohde revealed that the Greeks and Bulgarians had, during the Second Balkan War, developed a plan to attack the Gallipoli Peninsula, and it was this threat that led Turkey to make peace. He also examined the various possible ways in which such an attack might develop, including systematic land and sea combined operations. Landing places were given as Gaba (or Kaba) Tepe and (on the Asiatic side) Besika Bay. As far as the Peninsula itself was concerned:

> As landing-points on the Gallipoli Peninsula the first that should be considered are the areas at Kaba Tepe, the bays of Anafarta [Suvla] and Murmidia [Ejelmar] as well as the area north of Jenikoj [Yeni Keui; west of Bulair].

The possession of this Turkish defence scheme may not have been much further use to the German General Staff, but it was an invaluable addition to the stream of information about the Dardanelles arriving in London (and Paris). It could be assumed that, apart from strengthening their defences in detail, the Turks, and their German advisers, would not greatly alter their defensive dispositions, which had been tested in war. Readers of Rohde's book would be in no doubt as to the nature of modern warfare and the power of the defensive, particularly of artillery, machine guns, trenches and barbed wire.

In 1914 a second Edition of Karl Baedecker's Guide to *Konstantinopel . . . Kleinasien* etc. appeared, with its full complement of maps and plans.[78] Copies of this were acquired for the British War Office, Foreign Office, etc.

The Greek dimension

The Greeks had invaded the Turkish islands of Imbros, Lemnos and Mitylene in 1912, thus acquiring advanced bases and intelligence facilities for an attack on the Gallipoli Peninsula. If any Allied attack on the Peninsula was under consideration the Greeks, who understood its terrain 'better than any other nation',[79] were therefore the right people to consult and involve. They had long coveted European Turkey, and as the key to its acquisition, the Gallipoli Peninsula. Their army had, during the Balkan Wars of 1911–13, prepared plans for such an attack. Rear-Admiral Kerr, the leader of the British Naval Mission to Greece, had been involved with such planning since the start of 1914, and was in possession of considerable details of the Greek plan in September 1914,[80] when for a short while it looked as though the Greeks would be prepared to cooperate in joint operations against Turkey.

The British, through Kerr, knew about these plans in a fair amount of detail but, so far as is known, no full copy of the Greek plan ever found its way to Britain. The Greeks certainly passed on a considerable amount of detail about their plans. The British Military Attaché at Athens, Colonel Cunninghame, not to mention Major Samson, the Secret Service head-of-station in Athens, may have known a great deal, and it is perhaps significant that Cunninghame offered his services to Sir Ian Hamilton before the landings. Hamilton rebuffed him. Captain Frederick Cunliffe Owen, returning from his military attaché post at Constantinople in early November 1914:

> … stopped at Athens on the way. Here I took the opportunity of discussing with the Greek general staff (with whom I had been closely associated during the two Balkan wars) the question of operations at the Straits and acquainted myself with the projects and views on record with them and which they had closely studied.[81]

The Greeks do not appear to have had a better map of the Gallipoli Peninsula than that in the possession of the Allies, or if they did, it was not handed over. Had such a map been available to the British, it would undoubtedly have been used to prepare a better operations map.

In August 1914 the Russians had asked for Greek help in an attack on the Dardanelles. The Greeks, although neutral, expressed interest and, on 1 September Churchill asked the British Army and Navy to plan a joint operation involving capture of the Peninsula by the Greek Army, while simultaneously the British Navy ran through the Dardanelles to cow Constantinople. Callwell was unenthusiastic, and delivered an outline plan which he intended to be 'dissuasive'.[82] Churchill was insistent, and asked the Greeks for more details of their plan, which turned out to include landings on both sides of Gaba Tepe at the western end of the Peninsula and at Kum Kale on the Asiatic Shore, followed by further landings at the neck of the Peninsula at Bulair, and also at Alexandretta and near Smyrna.[83] It is unclear how much of the Greek plan was seen by the British, though Kerr and Cunliffe Owen knew a great deal about it. The Naval Official Historian stated that the Greeks planned to land between Fishermen's Huts, north of Ari Burnu, as far as the cliffs running northeast from Tekke Burnu, all of which 'excellent beach' the Turks had heavily wired and entrenched;[84] this includes a three-mile stretch (Brighton Beach) north of Gaba Tepe, the designated location of the later Anzac landing.

There is little about the Greek plan in the Dardanelles Commission report; Callwell stated that no full copy of the Greek plan was received in Britain, while Churchill dishonestly stated that he could not remember anything about it. Admiral Kerr later spilled the beans, when in 1922 he wrote to Captain V E Inglefield, of the Historical Section of the CID:

... most people will have forgotten that Mr. Winston Churchill, giving evidence to the Dardanelles Commission enquiry, stated that he did not know that a Greek plan had ever been asked for or offered. There are no copies of these telegrams to be found in the F[oreign] O[ffice] or in the Legation at Athens. Mr. Churchill asked me for my copies some time ago, but I wrote to the FO as I did not want to part with mine. It was then that I found out that the FO copies had vanished. I have refrained from publishing these telegrams for fear of stirring up trouble which would not assist our country or empire, but probably would have the opposite effect. If by publishing them we could repair the incalculable damage done by the infernal mess made of the Gallipoli expedition, I would welcome sandwich [board] men walking up and down with them all over the Empire.[85]

For reasons of diplomacy and internal politics the Greeks lost interest in the plan. Churchill, however, on 3 November 1914, foolishly gave the Turks the alarm by ordering the Navy to bombard the outer defence forts. Henceforth the Turks, assisted by the Germans, worked feverishly to render the Peninsula impregnable.

The Greeks, being antagonistic to the Turks, made natural clandestine agents, and it is inconceivable that the Greek General Staff, Navy, or both, did not have good intelligence networks operating into the Peninsula and Asia Minor. The Aegean coast, with its many inlets and fishing villages, was a perfect scene for small boat operations before and during the war. As we shall see, much of the population of the Gallipoli Peninsula and the Dardanelles area generally was Greek, and a great deal of valuable intelligence was obtained from them. The important 1909 War Office Report stated that 'the population of the Peninsula is principally Greek, but at the southern end there are several Turkish villages'.[86] This was later echoed in a secret War Council paper of March 1915 entitled *After the Dardanelles – The Next Steps* in which Hankey noted that the greater part of the population on both sides of the Dardanelles was Greek, and that Greek information regarding garrisons was usually reliable.[87] As the risk of Allied action increased, the Turks began to remove the Greek population from the threatened zones, as it posed a clear security risk.

The mixed population and ease of movement by caique in the Aegean may possibly also have worked against the Allies; Aspinall-Oglander noted that:

The Turks had other means, too [apart from air reconnaissance] of learning the course of events at Mudros. The island was under British governorship, but it was impossible to control the whole civilian population, or to guard against any leakage of information by means of the small local craft trading between the islands of the Aegean.[88]

The Turks after the war told British Intelligence officers that they had no agents on Imbros. They had other, very effective, forms of intelligence-gathering: the British seaplanes could not reach sufficient altitude to intercept the Turkish reconnaissance intruders, which overflew Mudros harbour almost daily from 11 April 1915.[89]

The Russian dimension

The Russian had long had designs on Constantinople and the Dardanelles, the latter representing an ice-free trade-route to the southern Russian ports. The Russians were in direct conflict with Turkey in the Caucasus, and were happy to provide any information to the Allies which would create a diversion. An attack on the Dardanelles was eminently suitable for this purpose, so they duly supplied intelligence on the Dardanelles forts and defences. In early 1915 a Russian report on the Defences of the Dardanelles was received by Admiral Carden from the British Minister at Athens; this included photographs and tracings of plans of the forts. Carden reported to the Admiralty on 11 February 1915 that his War Staff Officer had compared the Russian report with the British Official Report (*NID No. 838, Turkey Coast Defences, May 1908*); this officer's comparative report (*Turkey Coast Defences*) went into great detail, including lines of mines.[90] Dealing with the 'Principal Differences between Russian and British plans,' Carden's Intelligence Officer noted that the 'latest additions to defences given in Russian plans are very similar to the tracing sent to Intelligence Division of War Staff [London] in my letter of 26 December 1914'.[91] At an early stage, the Russians were keen to participate in an attack on Constantinople and the Dardanelles, but they later declined to commit forces. Not only were they short of manpower at a critical juncture, but they were reluctant to see the Greeks in, or even near, Constantinople which they coveted for themselves.

The availability of intelligence

Applying the tests suggested in the quotation opening this chapter, the following questions should be asked of the intelligence available before the landings:

- Was it timely? The nature of the political decision-making, and the attitude of Kitchener and Churchill in particular, meant that insufficient time was available to perform the intelligence function properly. That said, and given the shortage of aircraft and cameras, a remarkable amount of topographical, hydrographic and operational intelligence was gathered in a few weeks.

- Was it accurate? Much of the operational and tactical intelligence collected in the two decades before the outbreak of war was remarkably accurate. The terrain intelligence was mostly good, but it is doubtful if it was properly studied and understood at command level, and disseminated, as there is no evidence to suggest it was consulted widely.
- Was it relevant? Clearly, if troops were to land on a hostile shore.
- Was it verifiable? Intelligence relies on cross-checking from as many independent sources as possible. To some extent this was possible – reports from agents, consuls and attachés might be verified by naval or air observation – but not always.
- Did it answer a question? What were the questions? Were the politician and commanders asking the right questions? For example, were efforts made by agents to obtain the most up-to-date Turkish maps? There is evidence that the questions were not sufficiently focused, and that the targets were not sufficiently specific. Some of this lack of focus may be due to the low priority afforded to the Gallipoli Peninsula by Henry Wilson, the pre-war Director of Military Operations (DMO).
- Did it engender 'proactive actionable' decision-making? There is a huge problem here. As the landings drew closer, the intelligence picture was turning Hamilton's staff officers and divisional commanders against the operation, but the message coming from London was that the operation had to be carried out. In this case, with hindsight, we can see that the field commanders (except for Hamilton) were right and the politicians wrong.

The following chapters consider the nature of the terrain and the British Intelligence effort as it gathered momentum from August 1914.

Table 1: Summary of Geographical etc. Handbooks available for the Dardanelles area in 1914

1905 Confidential	*Military Report on Eastern Turkey in Europe* [with three maps]
1906	Extracts from Military Reports on Western Turkey in Europe
1908	*NID 838, Turkey Coast Defences* [Part II on Gallipoli Peninsula & Dardanelles Defences], with charts, maps, plans & photos
1909 Secret	*Report on the Defences of Constantinople* [including Gallipoli Peninsula]; with separate folder of plates – maps, plans, panoramas & photos
1909 Confidential	*Military Report on Eastern Turkey in Europe and the Ismid Peninsula*, 2nd Edn; with separate folder of plates – maps, plans & photos.

1909 Secret	*Report on Certain Landing Places in Turkey in Europe* [not Gallipoli]
1912	*Handbook of the Turkish Army*
1913	*Manual of Combined Naval and Military Operations* [& 1911]
	Military Report on Western Anatolia, by Captain G S Pitcairn
	Military Report on Asia Minor
	Handbook on Western Turkey in Europe

Notes

1. Gibson, Stevyn, 'Open Source Intelligence: An Intelligence Lifeline', *RUSI Journal*, 149 (1), February 2004, pp. 18–22.
2. Secret Branch: 1796–1826. TNA(PRO) ADM 1.
3. Porter, Maj.-Gen. W, *History of the Corps of Royal Engineers*, Vol. I, Chatham: Institution of Royal Engineers, 1889, p. 229.
4. Hope, Maj. M, 'The Defence of Dardanelles, A Report written in 1799', *Royal Engineers Journal*, September 1918, pp. 118–23.
5. British Library Map Library, Maps SEC. 5 (2429).
6. Ritchie, Rear-Admiral G S, *The Admiralty Chart*, London: Hollis & Carter, 1967, pp. 269–73.
7. Wood, M, *In Search of the Trojan War*, London: BBC Books, 1985, pp. 42–6.
8. *Survey of Defensive Position near Bulair shewing the Lines constructed by the Anglo-French Army in 1855 . . . 1877.* TNA(PRO) MPH 1/871/2.
9. *Reports and Memoranda relative to Defence of Constantinople and other positions in Turkey. Also on Routes in Roumelia, Strictly Confidential, printed at the War Office by Harrison & Sons 1877.* [0631] 103 WO. TNA(PRO) FO 358/1; FO 881/3676; WO 33/29.
10. Mead, Peter, *The Eye in the Air. History of Air Observation and Reconnaissance for the Army 1785–1945*, London: HMSO, 1983, pp. 17–19.
11. *Sketch of Portion of West Coast of the Gallipoli Peninsula N.W. of Maidos.* G E Grover, Capt. RE, 8 February 1876. Lithd. At the Intelligence Branch, Qr Mr Genl's Department under the direction of Lt Col. R Home CB RE, April 1877. [1:15,840]. Stamp: Rec'd TSGS Map Room 7 Jan 1888. British Library Map Library, pressmark Maps 43335 (94).
12. Three maps of Gallipoli Peninsula from report of 31-1-1877 by G E Grover Capt. RE about proposed landing places for troops south of Hanafart (Anafarta Lim). TNA(PRO) MPH 1/871/5–7.
13. *Reports and Memoranda . . .*, op. cit., pp. 147–8.
14. Ibid, pp. 135–46.
15. Turkey: Despatches. Defences of Gallipoli (Vice-Consul Odoni). TNA(PRO) FO 881/3288.
16. *Reports and Memoranda . . .*, op. cit., pp. 103–9.
17. Reprinted by OSO Southampton, 1903. In: *Reports on the Defences of Constantinople by Lieut.-Colonel F. R. Maunsell, R.A. (Military Attaché, Constantinople.) 1903.* TNA(PRO) WO 33/284.
18. Aspinall-Oglander, Brig.-Gen. C F, *History of the Great War, Military Operations, Gallipoli*, Vol. I, London: Heinemann, 1929, pp. 26–7.

19. *Carte de la Presqu'Ile de Gallipoli* – 2 sheets, 1876–80. TNA(PRO) MPH 1/803/2–3 from WO 33/35.
20. Paper No. 797, *Seizure of the Dardanelles as a means of coercing the Porte*, War Office, 1880, in TNA(PRO) WO 33/35.
21. Aspinall-Oglander, op. cit., p. 27.
22. Callwell, Maj.-Gen. Sir Charles E, *Stray Recollections*, Vol. I, London: Edward Arnold, 1923, pp. 39, 344–7.
23. English, Lt-Col. T, late RE, 'Eocene and Later Formations Surrounding the Dardanelles, *Quarterly Journal of the Geological Society of London*, 60 (1905), pp. 243– 77.
24. Ritchie, op. cit., p. 270.
25. Information from RE Corps Library, Chatham.
26. Map bearing results of this survey in RGS Map Room.
27. *Reports on the Defences of Constantinople by Lieut.-Colonel F. R. Maunsell R. A. (Military Attaché, Constantinople). 1903. Secret. [A 826] 9/1903 – (B 157) – 209 WO. Intelligence Department, War Office, 12th September 1903. 50 pp.* TNA(PRO) FO 881/9666X, also WO 33/284.
28. *Reconnaissance of the Chatalja Lines [1876], IDWO 1736 (Secret), Heliozincographed at the Ordnance Survey Office, Southampton, 1903. Corrections up to date. Signed F. R. Maunsell Lieut.-Col., 15th March 1903, Military Attaché.*
29. *Military Report on Eastern Turkey in Europe, 1905, Prepared by the General Staff, War Office. Confidential. A 1027. I 38535. 150.-11/05. Fk. 728. E.&S. A2.* Small 8vo. [Chapter VI (pp. 53–72) is on the Gallipoli Peninsula.]
30. Foreign Office Lists, 1902–13, Public Record Office, open shelves.
31. Graves, Philip, *Briton or Turk*, London: Hutchinson, 1941, pp. 180–1.
32. Brandenburg, Erich, *From Bismarck to the World War. A History of German Foreign Policy 1870–1914*, London: OUP, 1933.
33. Foreign Office correspondence relating to Secret Service: Errington (FO) to Sir William Garstin, 31-10-1907, in TNA(PRO) HD 3/135.
34. Ibid.
35. *Guide to Greece, The Archipelago, Constantinople, The Coast of Asia Minor, Crete and Cyprus*, 3rd edn, London: Macmillan, 1910, pp. 110–11, 122.
36. Ibid, p. 158.
37. Hankey's evidence to Dardanelles Commission, TNA(PRO) CAB 63/18 (microfilm), sheet 146.
38. Mackenzie, Compton, *Gallipoli Memories*, London, Cassell, 1929, p. 86.
39. PRO ADM 231/49, NID 838. Turkey. Coast Defences, &c. May 1908. The earlier reports are elsewhere in ADM 231.
40. Ottley, *The Forcing of the Dardanelles*, op. cit., final draft, p. 8.
41. Ibid, p. 10.
42. A copy of the text of NID 838, Turkey. Coast defences, &c., Parts I, II and III, is at TNA(PRO) ADM 231/49, but the maps, charts, plates, etc., although listed in the contents, are lacking. Several of these may be found in PRO WO 301 Gallipoli Campaign maps, and in TNA(PRO) CAB 19, Minutes of Evidence to the Dardanelles Commission.
43. *The Times*, 22 & 23 December 1910.
44. TNA(PRO) CAB 17/184, sheets 248–53. *The Possibility of a Joint Naval and Military Attack Upon the Dardanelles, I. Memorandum by the General Staff. N.G.L. December 19 1906. II Note by the Director of Naval Intelligence. December 20 1906. 92 B. Secret. Printed for the Committee of Imperial Defence. February 1907.*

45. Rhodes James, Robert, *Gallipoli*, London: Pimlico, 1999, p. 94; Travers, Tim, *Gallipoli 1915*, Stroud: Tempus, 2001, p. 35.
46. Fergusson, Thomas G, *British Military Intelligence, 1870 –1914. The Development of a Modern Intelligence Organization*, London: Arms & Armour Press, 1984, Chart 10, p. 252.
47. GSGS Register, MCE, RE, MRLG, Tolworth. Copies in TNA(PRO) WO 301.
48. Edmonds, Brig.-Gen. Sir J, *History of the Great War, Military Operations, France and Flanders 1914*, Vol. I, 3rd edn, London: Macmillan, 1933, pp. 13–14.
49. Gooch, J, *The Plans of War. The General Staff and British Military Strategy c1900 –1916*, London: Routledge, 1974, p. 271.
50. Fergusson, op. cit.
51. Gleichen, Maj.-Gen. Lord E, *A Guardsman's Memoirs*, London: Blackwood, 1932, pp. 314–16, 330–2.
52. Foreign Office correspondence relating to Secret Service, TNA(PRO) HD 3/135.
53. Fergusson, op. cit., p 221.
54. H Charles Woods, Evidence to the Dardanelles Commission, pp. 853–60, in TNA(PRO) CAB 19/33.
55. Ibid.
56. Callwell's Summary of Proposed Evidence to the Dardanelles Commission, in TNA(PRO) CAB 19/28.
57. Minutes of Evidence to the Dardanelles Commission, pp. 853–60, in TNA(PRO) CAB 19/33.
58. Woods, H Charles, *Washed by Four Seas – An English Officer's Travels in the Near East*, London: T Fisher Unwin, 1908.
59. Woods, H Charles, *The Danger Zone of Europe – Changes and Problems in the Near East*, London: T Fisher Unwin, 1911.
60. Woods, H Charles, *La Turquie et ses Voisins*, Paris: E. Guilmoto, Librairie orientale et Americaine, 1911.
61. Samson, Maj. L L R, *Report on Landing Places at Kaba Tepe (Gallipoli Peninsula) with two roads leading therefrom to Maidos and the Kilid Bahr Plateau*, Adrianople 28.9.1910. 10pp. duplicated typescript. TNA(PRO) WO 106/1534.
62. Philippson: 1:300,000 *Topographische Karte des westlichen Kleinasien*, based on Kiepert: 1:400,000 *Karte von Kleinasien*.
63. Leaf, Walter, 'Notes on the Troad', *The Geographical Journal*, July 1912, 40(1), pp. 25–44.
64. Leaf, Walter, *Troy, a study in Homeric Geography*, London: Macmillan, 1912.
65. Acquisition date in RGS Picture Library Catalogue.
66. RGS Catalogue Ref: MR Turkey S/S. 36.
67. RGS Catalogue Ref: MR Turkey S/S 15.
68. Minutes of Evidence to the Dardanelles Commission, p. 1404, TNA(PRO) CAB 19/33.
69. F Cunliffe Owen to The Secretary, Army Council, 17-9-1927, in IWM Department of Documents.
70. Ibid.
71. F Cunliffe Owen to Mallet 23-3-14, in Mallet to Grey 24-3-14, N. 201; Minute by Russell 30-3-14. TNA(PRO) FO 371/1847.
72. F Cunliffe Owen to The Secretary, Army Council, 27-9-1927, in IWM Department of Documents.

73. Newcombe, Capt. S F RE and Greig, Lt J P S RE, 'The Baghdad Railway', *Geographical Journal*, December 1914, 44(6), pp. 577–80.
74. Woolley, C L, *As I Seem to Remember*, London: Allen & Unwin, 1962, p. 93.
75. Hinsley, F H et al, *British Intelligence in the Second World War*, Vol. I, London: HMSO, 1979, p. 16.
76. 'Reduction of Estimates for Secret Services', Cabinet Memorandum 19-3-1920, House of Lords Record Office, Lloyd George MSS F/9/2/16.
77. Rohde, Lt G H, *Die Operationen an den Dardanellen im Balkankriege*, 1914.
78. Baedecker, Karl, Guide to *Konstantinopel . . . Kleinasien*, etc., 2te Auflage, Leipzig, 1914.
79. Carlyon, L A, *Gallipoli*, London: Doubleday, 2002, p. 50.
80. Aspinall-Oglander, op. cit., p. 42fn.
81. F Cunliffe Owen to The Secretary, Army Council, 27-9-1927, in IWM Department of Documents.
82. Rhodes James, op. cit. p. 10; Carlyon, op. cit., p. 50.
83. Aspinall-Oglander, op. cit., pp. 42–3.
84. Corbett, Sir Julian S, *History of the Great War, Naval Operations*, Vol. II, London: Longmans, Green, 1921, p. 306.
85. Greece, 1915–1922, papers relating to economic and strategic position in Balkans and Dardanelles Campaign – letters from Admiral Mark Kerr, TNA(PRO) ADM 137/4178.
86. *Report on the Defences of Constantinople. General Staff. Secret. 1909. War Office. [A 1311]. [(B 369) 100 2/09 H & S 400WO].* Copy No. 3 D.M.O. Hard buff covers, portrait format, c4.5 x 6.5 inches. xii + 151 pp. TNA(PRO) WO 33/2333. pp. 3–5.
87. *After the Dardanelles. The Next Steps. Secret. Notes by the Secretary to the Committee for Imperial Defence, dated March 1st 1915.* TNA(PRO)CAB 63/17 (microfilm), sheet 137.
88. Aspinall-Oglander, op. cit. p. 139fn.
89. Ibid, p. 139 & fn.
90. TNA(PRO) ADM 137/1089, Dardanelles 1915 Jan–April (H.S. 1089), item 120.
91. *The Dardanelles Inquiry. Proof. Notes for Evidence . . . Part II – The Origin and Initiation of the Joint Naval and Military Attack on the Dardanelles, April 25.* Sheet 350. TNA(PRO) CAB 17/184.

CHAPTER 4

Terrain Intelligence at the Outbreak of War

This chapter deals with the intelligence processes from the outbreak of war with Germany, through the period of the commencement of hostilities with Turkey, and considers the intelligence-gathering activities in the Aegean and the Levant, particularly by the Navy. It looks critically at the accounts of Kitchener's briefing of Hamilton and Braithwaite at the War Office in March 1915, the briefing that was to initiate the land campaign, and set the scene for one of the most controversial military expeditions in history.

The General Staff and the Directorate of Military Operations in 1914–15

Many of the intelligence and operational planning problems in the early months of the war may be traced to the dispersion of the General Staff, and its Division and Branch officers, following mobilisation; most experienced officers joined the BEF by a decision of the Army Council, and their replacements, if any, were retired officers with little up-to-date knowledge, dominated by Kitchener.[1] This autocrat, who appeared incapable of delegation, by-passed his General Staff, preferring to maintain direct contact with the commanders in the field. One historian has gone so far as to claim that during the first year of war Hankey, the Secretary to the War Council, effectively took over the strategic-direction role of the General Staff: '. . . his written papers were exceptionally able and distinct and represented precisely the work which the General Staff should have produced.'[2]

Thus an appalling situation obtained at the War Office from August 1914 to December 1915, when Sir William Robertson, as the new CIGS, took over responsibility for military strategy. At the same time (the end of 1915) the Intelligence Branch, which hitherto had been part of the Directorate of Military Operations, was made into a separate Directorate of Military Intelligence under George Macdonogh. Robertson wrote that hitherto 'a more deplorable state of affairs can never have existed in the conduct of any war'.[3] While Kitchener tried to be his own Chief of Staff, the creation of well-considered and evaluated strategy and plans was not going to occur. His weak and fearful Staff, under the 'notoriously incompetent' Sir James Wolfe-Murray,[4] appointed by Kitchener but not taken into his confidence, were never going to become the strong, efficient General Staff required for effective strategic coordination and direction. This was to strangle the Dardanelles operation in its cradle.

To assist in planning any operation, relevant intelligence should have been forthcoming at various stages from the European Section of MO2 under Col. B T Buckley, who had succeeded Col. Dallas in late 1914, covert or semi-covert collection operations of the Special Intelligence Section (SIS) of MO5, and various embassy, military attaché and consular reports to the Foreign Office, the Naval Intelligence Division at the Admiralty, and the Intelligence Branch at GHQ in Egypt (later also the 'Arab Bureau', set up at the beginning 1916, which was an offshoot of this) and the Survey of Egypt. Major L L R Samson, already introduced as a 'military consul' at Adrianople before the war, was head of the British Secret Service in Athens in 1914, and provided an extremely useful channel; he also opened an office in Egypt. Compton Mackenzie worked for him from 1916. The French Deuxième Bureau, the Greeks and the Russians also supplied information.

What happened in the Geographical Section of the General Staff (GSGS, MO4) on mobilisation may be regarded as typical. All officers immediately departed for duty except Colonel Hedley and Captain W V Nugent RA, and the latter left on 15 November, being replaced by Lt-Col. P J Gordon, formerly of the Survey of India.[5] Nugent, who went to Gallipoli with the 29th Division, later took command of the 2nd Ranging & Survey Section RE when it was sent to Gallipoli in June 1915. Hedley soon found himself with no other officers, and thirty-one other staff, including civilian trades, to look after. Later more civilians were employed. At the same time, the volume of work increased enormously, not just for the Western Front but all other theatres of war as well.[6]

A temporary member of GSGS in the autumn of 1914 was T E Lawrence, who had already spent some years in the Middle East, and who in January and February 1914 had spent six weeks with Leonard Woolley, providing the archaeological cover for Captain S F Newcombe's topographical survey of southern Palestine; it has also been suggested that Newcombe was conducting a clandestine reconnaissance of tracks and water holes in the Sinai desert (the Negev) in order to determine the likely route of a Turkish advance towards Egypt. Newcombe later commanded the 4th Field Company RE of 2nd Australian Division at Gallipoli, and was responsible for the mapping of the Anzac area.

Lawrence returned to England in June 1914, visited GSGS at the War Office in that month in connection with a map of Sinai – he was writing-up, with Woolley, the archaeological part of the Southern Palestine survey, to be published the following year by the Palestine Exploration

Fund as *The Wilderness of Zin* – and when war broke out tried to join the OTC in Oxford. He was not accepted, and neither was he accepted in London because the flood of volunteers had been so great, so, after trying in vain to get a war job through Newcombe, he wrote to the archaeologist D G Hogarth, Keeper of the Ashmolean and a member of the Royal Geographical Society – as we have seen he was to speak on Gallipoli to this learned society at the time of the landing.[7] Hogarth had, in 1910, fixed Lawrence up with a job on a British Museum dig at Carchemish on the Euphrates, and now, in 1914, he was instrumental in obtaining, as a special favour of Colonel Hedley, a week's trial for him in GSGS. Lawrence had been working there for three weeks when Hogarth asked Hedley if he had been any use; the latter replied that he was running the whole department. Under Hedley, Lawrence worked on a 1:125,000 map and handbook of Sinai, but also on maps of Belgium and France. Lawrence's desk at the War Office used to be pointed out to newcomers – Carrol Romer, who was with Hedley from 1916 to 1918, noted of Lawrence: 'He used to occupy the position I now occupy at the W.O. He had an astonishing memory but would take no notes. Hence his handing over was something of a debacle.'[8]

Early in December 1914, a month after the commencement of hostilities with Turkey, Kitchener, realising the value of their knowledge in planning Egypt's defence, sent the two archaeologists (Lawrence and Woolley) of the southern Palestine survey expedition to join General Maxwell's new Intelligence Department in Cairo. Second Lieutenant Lawrence and Captain Newcombe (who had been sent to France but was soon recalled) left together for Marseilles on 9 December, sailing to Port Said, and then on to Cairo.[9] At the same time George Lloyd MP, Aubrey Herbert MP and Captain Hay left London, also on their way to join the Military Intelligence Department in Cairo, and later the newly created Arab Bureau. Other members of the Bureau, under its chief, Colonel Gilbert Clayton, were Lawrence's mentor Commander Hogarth, Colonel K Cornwallis, Lt Wyman Bury RNVR, Sir Mark Sykes and Gertrude Bell.

Lawrence joined the Intelligence Department of GHQ Egypt as its Maps Officer, providing liaison with Ernest Dowson at the Survey of Egypt.[10] There he took over the job of Captain L B Weldon of the Egyptian Survey, who joined the 7,000-ton *Aenne Rickmers*, a seaplane carrier converted from a captured German cargo ship, which had brought the 'Nieuport Squadron' of seven or eight seaplanes to Egypt. The ship and squadron had concentrated at Nice in August 1914, moving to Bizerta in September to protect Allied shipping in the Mediterranean. From here she sailed to Malta, and on 1 December arrived at Port Said, having been placed under Maxwell's command to help the defence of Egypt and the Suez Canal.

Weldon arrived at Port Said on 16 January 1915, to join Clayton's Intelligence Service and performed a vital role in the *Aenne Rickmers* (equipped with two seaplanes) determining the Turkish order-of-battle at Gallipoli and in Syria and Mesopotamia. Apart from commanding five bluejackets and six marines, his task was a combination of liaison and intelligence work – in particular to infiltrate spies, or 'agents' as they were more politely known, behind the Turkish lines. He landed these agents on the Palestinian and Syria coasts and collected them when they had gathered information on enemy troop movements, etc. from the many people in those territories who were willing to help.[11] Weldon was later engaged in reconnaissance work and clandestine operations in the Red Sea.

The *Aenne* was part of an operation contributing a huge amount of vital intelligence about the Turkish Army and its movements to Maxwell, Birdwood and Hamilton. In March she was torpedoed, wounding several men, but stayed afloat. Weldon was then given temporary command of the transport *Euryalus* and carried the Lancashire Fusiliers from Mudros to Gallipoli. He later worked with Lawrence and Feisal, and in February 1917 was given the *Managem*, a 160-ton steam yacht, and continued to do 'spy work' for the Army, rather than the Navy. In early 1918 he was made Intelligence Officer, Port Said, a post he held until the end of the war.[12]

Despite the departure of many officers from MO4 and the rest of the War Office to the Western Front, there should have been no difficulty in supplying maps and geographical information to Hamilton and Braithwaite. The loss of staff applied to MO4 and the MO5 Library to a lesser extent; Hedley, Chilcott and Hudleston, the Geographical Section Librarian, had all remained in place, were totally familiar with the resources of the Section and Libraries, and were able to point to key topographical and other intelligence resources. The GSGS Map Room was well-organised, and maps of 'Turkey in Europe', which included Gallipoli, were kept together. Colonel Hedley noted after the war that:

> ... the burden of map supply in Gallipoli fell on the Survey of Egypt [he had arranged this with Dowson, Director General of the Egyptian Survey, shortly after the outbreak of war], but the original supply of [one-inch and 1:250,000] maps and the printing plates for all small scale maps came from the War Office.[13]

Intelligence after the outbreak of war

The flow of intelligence from Constantinople and the Dardanelles continued after the outbreak of war with Germany in August 1914, and before the outbreak of hostilities with Turkey at the beginning of November. As early as the period August–October 1914, the Royal Navy was including in its intelligence reports information about defensive activity against landings on the Peninsula. Cunliffe Owen, the military attaché at Constantinople from the end of 1913 to the outbreak of war, who made a thorough reconnaissance of the Dardanelles area in the spring of 1914, sent to the War Office a continual flow of data about new or projected armaments, changes in the locations of batteries and minefields, and related matters, as well as vital topographical information about the Peninsula and the Asiatic Shore. From July 1914 he:

> ... made frequent reports as to any activities in the region of the Dardanelles and as the situation became more intense, I reported at considerable length about troops, movements and installations in regard to armaments, location or setting up of mine fields, collection of shipping and appreciations.[14]

In the gathering of this intelligence, he was aided by Mr C E S Palmer, the vice-consul at the Dardanelles, who lived at Chanak, and was later captured by the Turks when serving as an intelligence officer in the submarine E15. It may well have been Palmer who reported on the approximate position of a minefield laid by the *Selanik* on 4 and 5 August 1914.[15] On 15 August Palmer sent a letter from Chanak to the Senior Naval Officer at Malta about the Dardanelles defences, giving information about mines, guns, batteries, troops, etc., and stated that in future he would be using coded messages. His word-code was very simple: 'Feeling better' meant that the *Goeben* was at Ismid and still flying the German flag; 'Boy born' meant that the Turks would probably assist the enemy; 'Mary better' meant that the German ships were sold.[16]

In the same month the master of a British merchant ship and his wife counted the mines set out in long lines on the decks of Turkish transports in the Dardanelles, before they were laid in the water. Many British merchant ships were being prevented from leaving Constantinople, but nine managed to get through to the Aegean in August and September bringing vital information.[17] The French military attaché in Constantinople, Colonel Maucorps, also provided intelligence via the Deuxième Bureau and, after the commencement of hostilities with Turkey, through the French Military Mission in Cairo.

On 1 September 1914, when the question of the feasibility of capturing the Gallipoli Peninsula was raised in London, Colonel Talbot of the Directorate of Military Operations prepared a paper simply entitled *The Gallipoli Peninsula* for Callwell (DMO) to brief the CIGS. From this date the interplay between intelligence and operational planning becomes crucial. A new file was now opened. Talbot's memorandum comprised a description of the Peninsula and its defences, including the point that the Bulair Lines 'successfully kept out the Bulgarians'. He looked back to 1906, when he noted that:

> ... a scheme was prepared for the capture of this Peninsula. It included the use of 4 divisions, each of 3 brigades. The general plan was to land them on the south west end of the peninsula and take in rear the forts commanding the Dardanelles.[18]

He then drew attention to the recent enhancement of the defences:

> Since the date of this scheme the fortifications have been much strength-
> ened: and it is believed that an attempt to capture the peninsula would
> be a much more serious operation now, than it was before the Turko-
> Bulgarian war.[19]

At this stage, still on 1 September, Colonel A G Dallas hastily looked
through the 1906 scheme and prepared a memorandum entitled *The
Dardanelles and Gallipoli Peninsula*,[20] to which a 1:250,000 outline map was
attached showing the coastal batteries and forts and also the Bulair Lines,
possible landing places, bridgeheads and route from the Gaba Tepe area to
Kilid Bahr. After providing details of the Turkish garrison of the Peninsula
and Asian and European Turkey, Dallas wrote a brief strategic appreciation in the light of the continual flow of fresh intelligence, and referred to
possible Greek involvement:

> A map is attached to show the armament as it existed before the last
> Balkan war. Since then additional modern guns have been mounted and
> it is possible that some of the armament reported to have been brought
> [from Germany] to Constantinople through Roumania during the last
> week may have been sent to the Gallipoli Peninsula. The extreme width
> of the Bulair Peninsula [i.e. isthmus] is some 5,200 yards. In 1912 the
> Turks easily held it against a serious military operation in force under-
> taken by the Bulgarians. It is believed that German officers and a propor-
> tion [of] German personnel are in charge of the Dardanelles defences. It
> might be possible to induce Greece to undertake the military part of an
> offensive directed against the Gallipoli Peninsula but this would most
> probably lead to a Bulgarian incursion into Macedonia. The pressure
> now being exerted by Servia [Serbia] on Austria would then at once be
> removed. Servia is nervous of her rear and of any proposal or threat
> against Macedonia from which she has drawn a part of her army and is
> drawing supplies.

Callwell having been briefed with this material, he and Talbot crossed
Whitehall to the Admiralty where, at 6pm on 1 September, they met Captain
C F Lambert (Fourth Sea Lord), Mr Thomson (Director of Transport), and
Captain H W Richmond (Assistant DOD). These Admiralty representatives, warmer to the proposed operation than the outnumbered War Office
contingent, stated that, given six weeks' warning, they could assemble
sufficient ships to carry 40,000 or 50,000 men (Greek, not British) to the
selected landing places, while warships could also be provided to give
covering fire; significantly, the Navy were thinking at this stage of a combined operation. Callwell stated bluntly that, considering the strength of

the Turkish garrison and the large force already mobilised in European Turkey, he did not regard it as a feasible military operation; he capped this by saying that he believed this to be the War Office view.[21]

As this was not what Churchill in particular wanted to hear, the initial meeting of subordinates was immediately followed up a day or two later by a top-level conference at the Admiralty, dominated by Churchill and the First Sea Lord (Prince Louis of Battenberg), and attended by Callwell and Captains Lambert and Richmond. Strangely, the CIGS was not present. Talbot noted that 'the matter was thrashed out again, with the result that the DMO put his views on [enclosure] D'.[22] This appreciation by Callwell, dated 3 September, and written under pressure from Churchill, is a crucial and prescient document which is worth studying, if only for its emphasis on the vital putative Greek contribution. Callwell did not mention this meeting in his evidence to the Dardanelles Commission, merely stating that it was only about the end of October that 'Mr Churchill asked me to go over to him from the War Office to discuss the possibility of an attack on the Dardanelles', and that 'early in September, at the suggestion of Mr. Churchill, I drafted a memorandum, based on the assumption that Greece would be prepared to despatch a military force to co-operate with our Navy'.[23] This memorandum, in which Callwell adjusted his judgement of the operation from his early 'not a feasible military operation' to 'extremely difficult', stated:

It ought to be clearly understood that an attack upon the Gallipoli Peninsula from the sea side (outside the Straits) is likely to prove an extremely difficult operation of war. The subject has often been considered before by the General Staff and it was examined by the Committee of Imperial Defence in 1906: it was then decided that such an operation could not be regarded as feasible with the British Troops that might at short notice be collected for the purpose at that time. Since then the garrison has been greatly augmented, and as a consequence of threats on the part of Greeks and Bulgarians during the first Balkan War, and of the attack made upon the Lines of Bulair, the protection of the rear of the various batteries and works dominating the Straits was taken in hand. It is understood that what was then done renders them secure against anything in the nature of a surprise attack.

The garrison of the Peninsula now normally consists of an Army Corps which may be taken at 27,000 men with 136 guns. But under existing conditions this garrison will almost certainly have been strengthened considerably, and it would be unsafe to assume that the attacking side would only have the above number to deal with. In any case it would not seem justifiable to undertake an operation of this kind with an army of less than 60,000 men against the Ottoman Forces likely to be encountered. These 60,000 might, however, cross the sea in two echelons, admitting of the transports returning to Greece after disembarking the first echelon.

The Expeditionary Force could dispense almost entirely, if not entirely, with cavalry, and its mobile artillery might well be composed mainly of mountain batteries. It ought, however, to be accompanied by a strong contingent of siege pieces, especially howitzers, for attacking the batteries and forts bearing on the straits, which are the real objective; but unfortunately the Greeks do not seem to have any howitzers and very few siege guns.

It has to be remembered that there is nothing to prevent the Turks bringing strong reinforcements to the Gallipoli Peninsula from Constantinople, Panderma and elsewhere across the Sea of Marmara, until such time as it becomes impracticable for them to disembark such troops within the Peninsula. There is a division – say 6,000 men – normally stationed on the Asiatic side of the Straits which could be got across at the very start if there were a few steamers and launches available at Chanak. Moreover a report just to hand says that there is now an army corps assembled on the Asiatic side.

As a rough outline of the plan of attack it is suggested that in the first instance 30,000 men should be landed, should gain as much ground as possible, and should prepare landing stages while the transports return for the other 30,000 and the siege ordnance. The first 30,000 would have to be prepared to hold their own for about a week [the 1906 scheme stated that the whole operation should be finished within three days], allowing for the time taken on the voyage and in getting the transports loaded up afresh at the port of embarkation. But the actual details would of course have to be worked out by the General appointed to command the Expeditionary Force [not by the General Staff]. It is not unlikely that the Greek War Office and Admiralty are in possession of later information as to the conditions of the land defences of the Gallipoli Peninsula than we are.[24]

No less striking than the emphasis on the necessity for the Greek military contingent, carried in British transports, is Callwell's remark that the details would have to be worked out by the force commander, rather than the General Staff whose task it properly was. And so it turned out in March 1915, when Hamilton was appointed to command just such an Expeditionary Force, but with British, Anzac and French rather than Greek troops.

On the same day (3 September), two staff officers of MO2(b) – Major F W Gossett RA and Captain F W L S H Cavendish, 9th Lancers, p.s.c. (passed staff college), prepared short statements on the strengths and compositions of the Greek Army and 'Present dispositions and strength of Turkish Army Corps exclusive of those in Eastern Asia Minor, Lower Syria and the Yemen' respectively.[25]

On 6 September 1914 Frederick Cunliffe Owen sent from Constantinople to Callwell a copy of a five-page feasibility report on operations in the

Dardanelles – entitled *Question of Passage of the Straits* – which he had prepared a week earlier for Mallet, with a covering letter,[26] in which he assessed the complex strategic situation and the strength of the defences and stressed the rate at which the Germans were working to improve them. He advised against a Dardanelles operation, preferring the Persian Gulf, Red Sea and Syria if Turkey joined the Central Powers, but said that if an attempt to force the Dardanelles was made, a combined operation was to be preferred to a purely naval one. To facilitate the passage of the fleet through the Narrows and to keep the Straits permanently open, military force was necessary in the Besika Bay and Kilid Bahr areas. He was in close touch with the Greeks who, he said, believed they could succeed in this. According to the annotations on its cover, this copy of the report did not go outside the Military Operations Directorate, though Callwell may have discussed it with Kitchener and others. Mallet, of course, passed on his views to London, so Churchill and Fisher were familiar with them. As there was no intention of landing British troops at this early stage, any Dardanelles operation may have been considered primarily a naval and Greek matter, and therefore have aroused less interest than it should at the War Office.

Cunliffe Owen later stated that on his return from Constantinople (November–December 1914), after going via Athens (to liaise with the Greek General Staff) and Egypt, where he presumably put Maxwell and Clayton in the picture, he made himself available in London to give advice but was not consulted at any stage of the preliminary deliberations and was subsequently ignored. After training a 'New Army' field artillery brigade in England, he finally got his way and arrived at Hamilton's GHQ at the end of June 1915, where he was told they already had too many 'experts'.[27] It is difficult to exonerate the War Office from culpability in this matter. Just as Limpus was exiled to Malta (where he became a key figure in intelligence gathering and dissemination) by the Admiralty, for fear of offending Turkish susceptibilities before hostilities with Turkey began, and subsequently, so Cunliffe Owen was kept in England. Although it could be argued there was a serious shortage of experienced regular officers who were needed to train the New Armies, his presence at Hamilton's headquarters would have added invaluable local knowledge and intelligence expertise, and could have tipped the balance against the launching of the landing operations.

Much has been made by historians of the supposition, based on Hamilton's claims, that he was not shown Cunliffe Owen's report, or indeed the 1906–7 (in fact 19 December 1906) joint assessment, before going to the Dardanelles. Given that the contents of both reports had permeated Naval Intelligence Department (NID) and Directorate of Military Operations (DMO) consciousness, and that the tactical details of the 1914 report were incorporated into NID intelligence summaries, and given the over-hasty nature of his briefing and departure, there is no particular reason why they should have been. They were essentially of a strategic nature, for the guidance of policy-makers in London, although they had clear operational implications. Kitchener had given Hamilton the outline of the Greek plan. Things had moved on. Churchill's idea of a purely naval operation took over, even if the War Council and Kitchener realised that troops would be necessary. Nor, apparently, did Braithwaite see any of Cunliffe Owen's Dardanelles reports at the War Office before sailing for the Mediterranean, or know of the 1906–7 joint-staff enquiry and report.[28] Nor, apparently, did they see a review by the War Office in 1908, and another in 1911, though Callwell, who knew the content of all these, imparted their gist at the briefing. Both would, however, also have become aware of the conclusions of the joint report 'in theatre' via the Navy.

Naval intelligence

In the early months of the war, naval intelligence was particularly forth-coming. Two British steamships, the *Thistleban* and *Wallace*, passed through the Dardanelles in September, and reported to the Navy on the mine-fields, marker buoys and other defences. Tracings or charts showing their information in manuscript were prepared by the Eastern Mediterranean Squadron, and forwarded to the Admiralty. Admiralty Charts Nos 1198 and 2429 were used as a base to show drawings and information from HMS *Itchen*, obtained from the master of the SS *Wallace* which navi-gated the Dardanelles on 24 September. The zig-zag tracks through the clear, buoyed channels of the Bosphorus and Dardanelles minefields were shown. The Admiralty thereupon proposed that the Hydrographer should 'collate this information with what we possess already and build up a new chart. Make 2 copies. Send one to V[ice] A[dmiral] Mediterranean, and one to Russian Naval Attaché. Propose in sending to V.A. Med. To desire him to consider the feasibility of a submarine attack upon Turkish fleet.'[29] These copies were duly made.[30]

A note, dated 14 November 1914 and signed by J F Parry, Hydrographer, on a similarly augmented chart, stated:[31]

> The information concerning the Dardanelles was obtained principally from reports made by two British steamships, the *Thistleban* and the *Wallace*, which passed through in September, but it must be noted that Sir L[ouis] Mallet [the Ambassador], telegraphed from Constantinople on October 3rd and 4th, saying it was presumed that [the] Germans had mined the Straits still more effectively.

> Chart No. 2429 shows:-
> (1) In red, track taken by SS *Wallace*, and buoys reported.
> (2) In blue, the report by SS *Thistleban*.

(3) In green, approximate position of mine field laid by Turkish vessel *Selanik*, 4th and 5th August 1914.

(4) Lights reported extinguished by Turkish Govt, dated 7th August.

Note. This is all the information received in the Hydrographic Department; it is not known if mines are laid in other areas, although it would appear probable.

The Navy continued to watch the land for signs of Turkish defensive activity, and on 26 September a naval intelligence report[32] stated that trenches and wire had appeared at Cape Helles. The Turks were fearful of a landing attempt, whether by the Greeks, the British or indeed any interested party.

A remarkable coup occurred on 13 October 1914, when Churchill and the First Sea Lord (Prince Louis of Battenberg) were handed the German Navy cipher and signal books which had been retrieved by the Russians from the wreck of the light cruiser *Magdeburg*. This was the beginning of a successful attack on German ciphers. This advantage was amplified on 30 November when a British trawler hauled up a chest from a sunken German destroyer containing, in addition to squared German naval charts of the North Sea, a copy of the crucial *Verkehrsbuch* (traffic book), and by 3 December this was at the Admiralty,[33] where cryptologists in Room 40 could now decipher all German naval signals between Constantinople and the Dardanelles on the one hand, and Berlin on the other. This was to prove a useful source of intelligence on munitions flows, ammunition shortages, etc. The Turks and Germans were, however, capable of intercepting and decrypting British naval wireless traffic.

According to Callwell, it was around the end of October that he again conferred at the Admiralty with Churchill, Prince Louis and Commodore Lambert (Fourth Sea Lord). This meeting took place in Churchill's room 'where there were maps and charts available', and 'appears to have been almost the only occasion – if it was not actually the only occasion – when a representative of the General Staff in a responsible position was afforded an opportunity of discussing the problem of an attack on the Dardanelles with high Admiralty officials'. He appears to have forgotten the earlier meetings. Callwell wanted the Dardanelles Commission to know that 'I did my best to throw cold water on the scheme as a whole.'[34] Soon after this, Kitchener asked Callwell to investigate the feasibility of a landing at Alexandretta, using troops from Maxwell's command in Egypt. 'This project was fully considered by the General Staff and it was discussed with Sir H. Jackson and other Admiralty officers.' The War Office view was that this was a feasible operation which would entail minimum use of troops, and was the best way, coupled with 'threats' against the Dardanelles, of dealing with Turkey.[35] At this time, therefore, the War Office was clearly against landings on the Gallipoli Peninsula. Its attention was also diverted from the Dardanelles by the Alexandretta proposal. The other serious claims on its attention at this time – the critical situation on the Western Front during the period of the First Battle of Ypres (October–November 1914), and the Turkish threat to Egypt and the Canal, should also be borne in mind.

In the War Office in London, Colonel B T Buckley, Northumberland Fusiliers, took over MO2 from Colonel Dallas. Changes of key personnel at this critical time were not conducive to continuity in corporate memory or a proper handling of intelligence, the flow of which continued after the outbreak of hostilities with Turkey at the end of October, following the bombardment of Odessa, Sebastopol and other Russian ports by Admiral Souchon's Germano-Turkish squadron, which was successfully designed to force Turkey's hand. On 2 November the Admiralty signalled:

> … latest for information of Vice Admiral [Carden, who had been appointed to command the Dardanelles Squadron in September 1914] *Indefatigable* only:- latest information about guns herewith, begins:- Dardanelles modification to Chart 3, N.I.D. Report 838 [Turkey Coast Defences] of May 1908.

This signal went on to give important intelligence about new batteries, modifications to defences, etc.[36]

Palmer was still at Chanak on 3 November,[37] the day the British naval squadron blockading the Dardanelles bombarded the outer forts, continuing to supply intelligence, but had to evacuate as a result of the commencement of hostilities at this time, so this direct source soon dried up. By the beginning of March 1915 Palmer had found his way, now with a temporary commission as an RNVR lieutenant,[38] to Athens where he provided information on the Turkish coast batteries covering the Straits.[39] He was permitted to join the submarine E15 as an intelligence officer, and on 28 March was captured by the Turks and interrogated; he managed, however, to avoid giving away any information that specifically compromised the landings on 25 April.[40]

Information was still forthcoming from neutral consular agents, and of course various intelligence agents in the area, particularly Greeks. A trickle of foreign residents managed to get out of Constantinople, bringing with them important information. Sir Edwin Pears, a shipping lawyer who was also President of the European Bar at Constantinople, author of *The Destruction of the Greek Empire*, a friend of Aubrey Herbert, a *Daily News* correspondent, and had vast local knowledge through having been closely involved with the Dardanelles for decades, left Constantinople on 9 December, claiming that:

> It has been my lot as a lawyer for forty years out there to have to deal with certainly not less than from seventy to one hundred collisions or strandings in the Dardanelles or immediate neighbourhood, so that you would have some difficulty in puzzling me as to the depth of water and topography of the hills in these straits or in the Bosphorus.[41]

What is more, he received a letter from Constantinople 'by underground post' on 24 April 1915, the day before the Allied landings. His son-in-law, Thompson, who spoke good Turkish, worked in Clayton's Intelligence Department in Cairo with Lawrence in December 1914.[42]

Following the outbreak of hostilities with Turkey, intelligence from within the Ottoman Empire naturally became harder, but not impossible, to acquire. Lawrence wrote to Hogarth from Cairo on 20 December 1914 that Turkey had 'forbidden ingress & egress for people, merchandise and mails'. However, the Syrian Protestant College, under American auspices, was still in wireless contact with Washington.[43]

The Navy kept the Dardanelles under continuous surveillance, watching among other things for the emergence of the *Goeben* and *Breslau*. New information was immediately passed to the Admiralty. Captain Godfrey (Royal Marines) of the *Indefatigable* submitted on 14 December a duplicated sketch map of the tip of the Gallipoli Peninsula, covering the Dardanelles from the mouth to the Narrows, traced from Chart 2429 (one inch to a nautical mile or 1:72,960, *The Dardanelles (Ancient Hellespont) 1871*). It stated: 'Defences placed in position since 4th August 1914 shown in RED.' Six lines of mines, designated A to F, were shown, and in addition '45 mines have been laid inshore and to close channel making total of 199 of which 4 exploded whilst being laid'. Also shown were field guns and howitzers, small guns, machine guns, one 6-inch or 8-inch gun at Cape Tekke, camps on both sides of the Narrows, a hangar for hydroplanes north of Chanak, etc. Ships shown were the *Lily Rickmers* in Dardan Bay north of Chanak, and the *Ssudiyeh* moored in Sari Siglar Bay.[44] The Navy also watched closely the progress of Turkish work on land defences.

Other intelligence sources

Certain other naval personnel were well-positioned in terms of experience and location to supply information and appreciations. Admiral A H Limpus had formerly commanded the British Naval Mission in Constantinople, and had intimate knowledge of the Turkish Navy, to which he was an adviser, and of the Dardanelles defences – he had been responsible for the siting of some of the torpedo tubes. On 22 January 1915 he signalled from Malta where, in addition to commanding the dockyard, he was in charge of the Naval Intelligence office, to Admiral Carden that he had received a telegram from Athens. This concerned the venerable Frederick Calvert, who was expelled from the Dardanelles on 22 December, left Constantinople on 12 January, and gave a report to Limpus about the Dardanelles forts, their manning by Germans, hills being entrenched on European and Asian sides, etc.[45]

A further signal from Limpus to Carden, on 25 February 1915, specifically mentioned an intelligence agent. This contained details about the:

German Admiral and the staff of the Dardanelles on the west side
of Nagara side of Calvert's Park [the Calvert family had been British
Consuls at the Dardanelles since before the Crimean War], the house of
Godfrey Whittall ... it is suggested by our agent that torpedo tubes may
have been placed on the hulk [of the *Messudye*]. Some of the Christian
population still remain in town of Dardanelles [Chanak]. Village of
Erenkeui has been cleared of the Greeks. On Gallipoli side of Straits all
Greeks have been collected at Maidos ...[46]

which in any case had a predominantly Greek population. One of
Hamilton's staff officers, Aspinall, noted that two intelligence officers
(Doughty Wylie and Deedes), sent out from the War Office in London just
before Hamilton and his Staff arrived in March, provided vague information about Turkish troop numbers and dispositions, but as the district
had been cleared of civilians they had not been able to get any agents into
it.[47]

On 10 March 1915 Limpus, who was extremely familiar with the
Dardanelles defences, wrote an important document, *Notes on Method
of Forcing the Dardanelles*,[48] which although dealing primarily with naval
operations included recommended landing places, and four days later he
wrote from Malta to Rear-Admiral Phillimore at the Admiralty:

Seen from here, I consider the landing and seizure of the Gallipoli Peninsula
to be a necessary and very tough part of the operations. I studied the matter from the inside (Turkish) point of view when I was in Constantinople
and the Greeks were contemplating the same operation ...[49]

This document was studied closely by Kitchener. Like Kerr and Frederick
Cunliffe Owen, Limpus was clearly familiar with aspects of the Greek
plan.

Like the Calverts, the Whittall family were well established in business in the Levant; Sir James W Whittall controlled J W Whittall & Co.,
Lloyds Agents in Constantinople.[50] Edwin Whittall was associated with
an extraordinary attempt in the spring of 1915 by the Director of Naval
Intelligence, Admiral Sir Reginald ('Blinker') Hall, with the full knowledge
of Fisher, the First Sea Lord, to bribe the Turks to pull out of the war and
surrender the Dardanelles, with, of course, the mines removed; this failed
because the British were unable to promise the Turks that Constantinople
would remain in their hands – indeed the Allies had already promised
the city to the Russians. Assisted by Gerald Fitzmaurice, who had been
attached as Dragoman to the British Embassy to the *Porte* for several years,
Edwin Whittall and a contractor, George Eady, who was familiar with the
Levant, were secretly conducted to Dedeagach, in neutral Bulgaria on the
coast of Thrace, to meet leading members of the Turkish government. On

15 March 1915, however, Fisher ordered Hall to break off negotiations. The trigger for this was the interception and decrypting by Room 40 at the Admiralty of a signal to Constantinople from Berlin revealing the crucial fact that the Dardanelles forts were short of ammunition. On 17 March, therefore, Whittall and Eady left for Salonika.[51] A month later, on 16 April, Hamilton's GHQ recorded that 'Military Attaché Sofia and Mr Fitzmaurice left for Dedeagatch [sic] on HMS *Dublin*'.[52] Further negotiations were in train, but with Bulgaria rather than Turkey. They were in vain; Bulgaria signed a military convention with the Central Powers on 6 September 1915.

Pre-war reports

The pre-war War Office and Admiralty reports, particularly NID 838 (*Turkey, Coast Defences*) were periodically brought up-to-date by supplements and intelligence reports before and during the war. For example, NID squared charts numbers X93, X94 and X95, published in February 1915 specifically for the Dardanelles operation, contained a summary of all the intelligence available up to December 1914.[53] Copies of the reports and subsequent intelligence updates were closely studied by the CID before the war, and by the War Council (the Cabinet committee tasked with the higher direction of the war) following the outbreak of war, and were taken to the Aegean by Hamilton and his Staff. Copies of the naval report were in the possession of the Mediterranean Fleet. These reports provided much of the intelligence foundation on which the political decisions were made and the operations were based.

Charts X93, X94 and X95, studied in conjunction with the one-inch map, gave a good general picture of the terrain. These charts were enlargements of the 1871 Admiralty Chart which was at the scale of one nautical mile to the inch. This, like the one-inch map, drew on other sources for coastline and topography in addition to the 1854 survey of the Peninsula, particularly surveys by Graves, Spratt and other naval hydrographers (see Chapter 8). The Royal Marines 'Special Service Force', commanded by Brigadier-General Charles Trotman, issued orders from the *Braemar Castle* on 1 March 1915 which referred specifically to Charts 3 and 3a of *NID 838, May 1908*, but not to the new X-charts.[54] The Force's task was to complete the demolition of the forts at the entrance to the Dardanelles, and to:

> ... select suitable landing ground for use as a Base for aircraft. ... O.C. Plymouth B[attalio]n. [Lt-Col. G E Matthews RM] will detail 2 detachments of 1 Company each to cover demolition parties provided by H.M. Ships, and also the Air Base Reconnaissance Party. These covering forces will land simultaneously at Seddul-Bahr and Kum Kale ...[55]

This was the first time in history that such an airfield reconnaissance party landed under fire on hostile territory.

In the Directorate of Military Operations (DMO) at the War Office, Captain Wyndham Deedes, a regular who at one time had served in the Turkish Army and was now working in MO2 dealing with the Ottoman Empire, was called by Kitchener on 16 February to give his opinion on the prospects for success of a purely naval attack. Deedes echoed the conclusion of all earlier General Staff assessments that this was fundamentally unsound, at which Kitchener bawled him out. Deedes, who as we have seen was, with Doughty Wylie, trying to get agents into the Gallipoli Peninsula in March), later served at GHQ in Egypt and at Gallipoli, where Kitchener apologised on meeting him again.[56] The point of this story is that the Intelligence Staff at the War Office did not merely consist of 'dugouts'; officers like Deedes knew the Turkish Army well, and as Deedes went out before Hamilton's Staff, and soon joined it, he provided crucial intelligence continuity. In fact, it was hardly fair of Callwell to be self-disparaging in styling himself a 'dug-out', for he had been in harness up to 1913, and was very much *au fait* with Turkish affairs and the Dardanelles.

Four preliminary landings for demolitions and reconnaissance were made at the Sedd-el-Bahr camber, the last on 4 March. Matthews (who landed at Kum Kale on the 4th) and other officers of the landing parties gained invaluable information about the terrain and defences, which Hamilton, when he arrived, found invaluable if disturbing. This evidence demonstrated that the impression given to Hamilton and Braithwaite by Kitchener of the terrain south of Achi Baba was false; it was neither bare nor empty. It was in fact heavily fortified, and protected by barbed wire concealed in folds of the ground near the shore.[57] Landings, at first unopposed, and subsequently with only light opposition, had previously been made on 26 and 27 February and guns were destroyed. But as a result of these landings more surprise was lost, the Turks began to dig trenches and erect wire entanglements, and the 29th Division lost 3,000 men landing here on 25 April.[58]

The French, who had their own intelligence organisation in the Levant, were also carrying out intelligence work and preparations. The French battleship *Gaulois* prepared a report on landing places, which she lent to *Irresistible* who passed it on to *Ark Royal*; the last named returned it on 12 March.[59]

Hamilton's briefing – 12 March 1915

There is a great deal of uncertainty about the exact details of the initial briefing of the newly appointed commander and chief-of-staff of the Mediterranean Expeditionary Force. Hamilton had been aware of his impending appointment for some days,[60] but Braithwaite, Director of Staff Duties at the War Office, was only informed of his own appointment on the afternoon of

11 March. At the briefing, Callwell took Kitchener and Hamilton through the Anglo-Greek plan for attacking the 'Forts at the Dardanelles' by landing troops 'on the North-west coast of the Southern part of the Peninsula, opposite Kilid Bahr'.[61] Callwell later told the Dardanelles Commission that he had never seen the Greek plan, although he had tried to obtain details through the military attaché (in Athens); though he claimed he was unsuccessful in this, he was clearly in possession of at least an outline. A story was current in 1915–16 that the War Office had a copy of the Greek plan, but omitted to show it to Hamilton before he left England.[62] The evidence given by Kerr relating to this has already been cited; he knew a great deal about the plan, and had in fact drawn up the outline himself.

It is unknown whether Braithwaite sought out any information on the day he was informed of his appointment, but Hamilton made it clear that the following day, after their briefing by Kitchener and Callwell, Braithwaite at once investigated the resources of the Intelligence Branch. Hamilton claimed that here, Braithwaite found little in the pigeon holes 'beyond the ordinary text books' [i.e. the 1905 *Report on Eastern Turkey in Europe*, the crucial 1909 General Staff *Report on the Defences of Constantinople*, the 1913 *Combined Operations* handbook, handbooks on *Western Turkey*, perhaps the *1908 NID Turkey Coast defences* Report, etc.], and that 'The Dardanelles and Bosphorus might be in the moon for all the military information I have got to go upon. One text book and a book of travellers' tales don't take long to master'.[63] Either his memory was faulty or, as we shall see, he was deliberately playing down the intelligence material received to suit his agenda.

Callwell had drawn up staff appreciations of the Dardanelles problem from 1906, including one in September 1914. He therefore knew exactly what handbooks and other material were relevant to Hamilton's expedition. He later admitted that the 1906 report was considered so secret (in 1906 itself and for some years subsequently), because it contained very sensitive material relating to a possible attack upon Turkey, that it was improperly withheld, even in 1915 after hostilities with Turkey had commenced. To compound this omission, the Military Operations Directorate, confronted on 26 February 1915 with a request from Maxwell (GHQ Egypt), who had read Maucorps' alarming report and asked for topographical information and copies of General Staff studies of the Dardanelles problem at a time when it seemed that Birdwood and the Navy were to conduct imminent operations, stalled by replying that it was inconvenient to send this material and referred Maxwell to more generally available material:

> 3290 Cipher M.O. 177. Feby. 26th. Your 639 E. Difficult to send you resume of General Staff studies of Gallipoli. Suggest your consulting Admiralty reports of Turkey Coast defences [NID 838 May 1908], Part II, of which all war ships have copy. Ten copies of Military Report 1905 Eastern Turkey in Europe being sent you to-day by [diplomatic] bag.[64]

This obstructive approach was less than helpful; either the War Office could not be bothered, or it considered that strategy and high-level assessments of operational feasibility were none of Maxwell's business. No doubt there was also a reluctance to release the contents of classified documents. Maxwell probably already had the secret 1909 Report, which covered Gallipoli and the Dardanelles; a copy of this was held later, if not at the time, in the library of the Survey of Egypt.

Hamilton, describing the paucity of information given to him, commented that it was useless to plan operations 'unless there is some sort of material, political, naval, military or geographical to work upon.'[65] Again this was disingenuous.

Materials made available at the briefing

So what material was actually handed over at the time of the briefing? The Dardanelles Commission, having taken evidence from Hamilton, Braithwaite, Callwell, and many others, reported that Hamilton had taken:

1. 'The official handbooks' [i.e. the secret 1909 *Report on the Defences of Constantinople* and the 1913 *Manual of Combined Naval and Military Operations*. Aspinall stated that Hamilton also had with him the pre-war Admiralty report on the Dardanelles defences – this was *NID 838, Turkey Coast Defences, May 1908*];
2. The outline of a Greek General Staff plan for an attack on the Dardanelles [as gathered by Kerr, Cunliffe Owen and others, and expounded by Callwell to Kitchener and Hamilton on 12 March];
3. Kitchener's statement that the Kilid Bahr Plateau had been entrenched and would be 'sufficiently held' by the Turks, and that south of Achi Baba the point of the Peninsula would be 'so swept by the guns of the fleet that no enemy positions would be encountered in that quarter', and
4. The one-inch map of the *Peninsula of Gallipoli and Asiatic Shore of the Dardanelles* 1/63,360 (GSGS 2285), reduced in 1908 from the 1:50,000 French 1854 map, and revised, in two sheets, 1 & 2, the secret editions of which were overprinted with the Turkish defences in red. The Commission noted, following Aspinall, that this map 'afterwards proved inaccurate, and of little use'.[66]

Hamilton and Braithwaite were given a copy of the secret May 1909 War Office *Report on the Defences of Constantinople, Prepared for the General Staff* (its accompanying *Plates* (maps, plans, panorama sketches and photographs) volume, which also contained topographical panorama photographs, was dated 1908, but printed in 1909),[67] of which 100 copies were printed, and which contained a great deal of invaluable information on the topography and defences of the Gallipoli Peninsula and its possible landing places. Much of this information was similar to that printed in the Naval Intelligence Division handbook *NID 838 Turkey Coast Defences* of May 1908. Both reports were dealt with in Chapter 3, and extracts from them are given in Appendices II and III. Callwell made it clear, both in his evidence to the Dardanelles Commission and in his post-war books, that these 'secret reports' were either handed over to Hamilton and his staff before they left London, or sent out subsequently.[68]

Those who assume that Hamilton's expedition was ill-equipped with topographical and tactical information should look closely at the 1909 *Report* and its accompanying *Plates* folder of maps, plans, panorama sketches and photographs; their importance cannot be over-emphasised. They represented a very detailed and thorough topographical and tactical survey of the Gallipoli Peninsula, the whole Dardanelles area, and the close defences of Constantinople itself, well supported with visual material. It gave a clear idea of the difficulty of the terrain, including information on roads and tracks, water supply, possible beaches for landings, etc. The only thing missing was air photos, hardly surprising as the aeroplane had only just appeared on the scene, and no opportunity had been forthcoming for taking photos from balloons or airships. It could be argued that efforts should have been made to supplement the *Report* with air photos between 1909 and 1914, but this ignores the facts that no British bases were within flying distance, no aircraft carriers existed, no naval airships were in theatre, seaplanes could not attain the required altitude, and British air photography was in a primitive state.

Enough of the 1909 *Report* is given in Appendix III to show that Hamilton and his Staff were not bereft of information. Naturally they did not base their plans purely on the information on landing places given in the *Report*, but also took into account the results of their own reconnaissances, intelligence reports, air reconnaissance and air photographs, etc., particularly as far as Turkish defences and dispositions were concerned. We know from Callwell that Hamilton and Braithwaite took a copy of this 1909 *Report*, together with the associated maps and plates, when they left London on 13 March 1915.

The 1909 *Report on the Defences of Constantinople* was more or less contemporaneous with another secret June 1909 War Office *Report on Certain Landing Places in Turkey in Europe, Prepared for the General Staff*,[69] fifty copies of which were printed, which gave information on Rodosto, in the Sea of Marmara, as well as Dede Agach on the Aegean, Salonica and Valona. A *Report on Eastern Turkey-in-Europe* was also printed in the same year.

These pre-war reports focused on the infrastructure of existing Turkish coast defences, such as forts, gun batteries, mines, torpedoes, searchlights, telephone lines and cables, etc., and on man-made harbours and landing places, but they were written very much bearing in mind the possibility of opposed landings across natural beaches, and looked closely at the terrain problems that might be encountered in the beach areas and inland. The panorama sketches in particular were specifically marked with suitable landing places.

The *1913 Manual of Combined Naval and Military Operations*, was 'issued by command of the Army Council, and with the concurrence of the Lords Commissioners of the Admiralty. It is for the use of officers only. 2nd September, 1913'[70] (see Appendix V). This revision of the earlier 1911 manual was a most valuable guide to the principles and execution of such operations, and included a chapter on 'Reconnaissance'. It was studied by all the officers on Hamilton's Staff, and also by officers of the formations under his command. Its principles were followed as far as possible.

As far as maps were concerned, Hamilton's Staff first used the one-inch map of the Gallipoli Peninsula, the secret edition of which showed the Bulair Lines and other fixed defences at Sedd-el-Bahr and along the Straits.[71] This was supplemented in-theatre by up-to-date intelligence reports and maps. A 1:250,000 sheet *Gallipoli* (GSGS 2097) had also been printed at the War Office in October 1908; various other 1:250,000 sheets of the area were also sent with the expedition (see Chapter 6).

Reviewing the information

It is clear that, in their evidence to the Commission, Hamilton and Braithwaite tried to shift at least part of the blame onto the paucity of information supplied by the War Office:

> Sir Ian Hamilton, in the evidence which he gave before us, dwelt strongly on the total absence of information furnished to him by the War Office Staff. No preliminary scheme of operations had been drawn up. 'The Army Council had disappeared.' No arrangements had been made about water supply. There was 'a great want of staff preparation'.[72]

Much of this may have been true, but not the part about information. We have seen that Braithwaite also garnered information in the War Office. His evidence to the Commission told disingenuously of his obtaining 'such information as was available at the War Office, which was of a very meagre description'.[73] There was in fact a great deal of information at the War Office, which continued to generate a flow of information to Hamilton and Braithwaite after they left England, and Maxwell and Birdwood in Egypt had also been gathering intelligence. It should also be borne in mind that there was collusion between Hamilton, Braithwaite and other witnesses.[74]

In fact, the contemporary accounts are all contradictory. Hamilton stated that he and his Staff had, apart from the rough notes which Braithwaite had made, 'the text book on the Turkish Army, and two small guide books', and did not find these very illuminating.[75] He also claimed that 'there is no information at all about springs or wells ashore'.[76] According to Rhodes James, Braithwaite obtained from the Intelligence Branch at the War Office an out-of-date 'textbook' on the Turkish Army and two small 'guidebooks' on Western Turkey.[77] The handbook on the Turkish Army was largely irrelevant, as the Intelligence Department in Cairo was working hard at updating it and compiling an accurate Turkish order-of-battle.

Aspinall (later Aspinall-Oglander, the campaign's Official Historian), in a statement to the Dardanelles Commission, wrote, under the heading 'Information available on leaving London':

> A serious difficulty experienced by Sir Ian Hamilton and his Staff on leaving London, and when making arrangements for the landing was, that we had received little information as to the strength, dispositions and armament of the enemy and as to the topography of the country. The only map issued to us proved to be inaccurate.[78]

In his evidence, he described the map as out-of-date rather than inaccurate:

> I shall never forget the dismay and forebodings with which I learnt that apart from Lord Kitchener's very brief instructions, a pre-war Admiralty report [NID 838, May 1908] on the Dardanelles defences and an out-of-date map, Sir Ian Hamilton had been given practically no information whatever.[79]

Like Hamilton's own, this statement is disingenuous; Hamilton had a copy of the excellent 1909 War Office report (see below) on the Gallipoli Peninsula and its defences, the Admiralty report was being systematically updated from many sources, while the one-inch map, although based on an old survey, was the best available at the time. Maps are always out-of-date. What is important is how quickly and how accurately they are updated, or supplemented by the necessary additional information such as charts, visual reconnaissance and air photos. An experienced commander like Hamilton knew very well not to rely solely on the map, as he himself readily admitted. Nevertheless, as one of Hamilton's staff officers from the start, and therefore in a position to know, Aspinall's view must be taken seriously. He gave further examples of the inadequacy of the map in the Official History, and indeed in several respects it was inferior to the French original from which it was derived (see Chapter 6). Orlo Williams, Hamilton's cipher officer from the beginning, wrote in his diary of the whole staff having to study the 1913 *Combined Operations* handbook,[80] but made no mention of any other reports or maps.

T E Lawrence, who was in a position to know about maps having briefly worked at GSGS and then as 'Maps' Officer at Maxwell's GHQ providing liaison between Hamilton's Staff and the Survey of Egypt, did not mention the one-inch map of Gallipoli when he wrote to Hogarth from Cairo on 20 April 1915, stating (complaining about the dearth of maps of Asiatic Turkey and Syria, and not making a comment on the maps of Gallipoli) that 'The expedition came out with two copies of some ¼" [i.e. 1:250,000] maps of European-Turkey as their sole supply. I hope you get me some of Butler's [leader of the American Archaeological Expedition) N. Syrian maps. Tell him the 1905 ones are ROTTEN.'[81] This has often been misinterpreted, by those who have accepted uncritically the statements of Hamilton and others, to mean that no larger-scale maps of Gallipoli were available.

The truth comes out very emphatically in Callwell's evidence to the Dardanelles Commission, and in his post-war books, *The Dardanelles* (1919) and *Experiences of a Dug-Out* (1920). Not only did he make it clear that Hamilton deliberately misled the Commission, but he emphasised that Hamilton and his Staff took copies of the secret reports on the Dardanelles defences and Gallipoli Peninsula when they set out from London in March. He stated that:

> . . . the information contained in the secret official publications which the Mediterranean Expeditionary Force took out with it was by no means to be despised. All but one of the landing places actually utilised on the famous 25th April were, I think, designated in these booklets [emphasis added], and that one was unsuitable for landing anything but infantry. A great deal of the information proved to be perfectly correct, and a good deal more of it might have proved to be correct had the Expeditionary Force ever penetrated far enough into the interior of the Peninsula to test it.[82]

Callwell was in fact so incensed by Hamilton's dishonesty in disparaging the Directorate of Military Operations in this way that he asked to be allowed to give further evidence to the Dardanelles Commission, and when he appeared again in front of the members he actually brought copies of all the relevant documents that he had handed to Colonel Fuller, one of Hamilton's Staff, before he departed for the Dardanelles. He described these as: 'pamphlets and Reports... all compiled by the General Staff. It was all old stuff, I mean – it was not my own work at all; but these reports are kept up to date, and I think they were fairly well up to date as far as could be ascertained'. Callwell also stated that copies of the 1906 General Staff memorandum on forcing the Dardanelles had been destroyed (burnt) by order of Campbell-Bannerman, the Prime Minister, and that his own copy had been removed from his safe for that purpose.[83] This explains why Hamilton was not shown a copy, though other copies survived.

Callwell asked to give further evidence to the Commission, and restated it forcefully in his memoirs, in order to underline the point that 'no blame was fairly attributable to those who were responsible for information of some sort being available'.[84] As DMO, he was, of course, protecting his own reputation and that of his Directorate. From his position of inside knowledge about military intelligence work, he made the situation regarding the availability of information very clear:

> To have obtained full information as to the Gallipoli Peninsula and the region around the Dardanelles, but especially as to the peninsula, was a matter of money – and plenty of it. In no country in the world in pre-war days was spying on fortified areas of strategical importance without money a more unprofitable game than in the Ottoman dominions. There were, on the other hand, few countries where money, if you had enough of it, was more sure to procure you the information that you required. Ever since the late General Brackenbury was at the head of the Intelligence Department of the War Office in the eighties secret funds have been at its disposal, but they have not been large, and there have always been plenty of desirable objects to devote those funds to. Had the Committee of Imperial Defence in 1906 taken the line that, even admitting an attack upon the Straits to be a difficult business, its effect if successful was nevertheless likely to be so great that the matter was to be followed up, a pretty substantial share of the secret funds coming to hand in the Intelligence Department between 1906 and 1914 would surely have been devoted to this region. All kinds of topographical details concerning the immediate neighbourhood of the Dardanelles would thereby immediately have been got together, ready for use; it would somehow have been discovered in the environs of Stambul that the Gallipoli Peninsula had been surveyed and that good, large-scale maps of that region actually existed, and copies of those large-scale maps would have found their way into the War Office, where they would speedily have been reproduced.[85]

Apart from refuting Hamilton's assertions, Callwell was also concerned to rebut the claim by two members, representing Australia and New Zealand, of the Commission that 'there had been great neglect on the part of the War Office'. As far as Callwell's view of the correct military plan to follow is concerned, he later told the Dardanelles Commission that the 'right plan would be to effect a landing in strength on the west side of the Gallipoli Peninsula, where there was a long stretch of suitable beach (at, and north of, the point where the Anzacs actually landed), and to capture the high ground dominating the Narrows on that side'.[86] This was the old Grover plan of 1877.

Much has been made by various critics of the 'out-of-date' nature of some of the information provided (in fact a great deal was remarkably good), but little has been said about the serious, and successful, attempts to update it. Even if Hamilton and Braithwaite were not given, before they left London, copies of reports on the Dardanelles defences which had been sent to the War Office since 1911 by successive military attachés at Constantinople and vice-consuls at Chanak, they soon received this information in theatre. If they did not receive it at the briefing stage, we can only suppose that it was because the expedition was despatched in such a hurry. The information was certainly in the hands of the Navy, both in the Naval Intelligence Division at the Admiralty and in the Eastern Mediterranean (Dardanelles) Squadron under Carden and later de Robeck. The Naval Intelligence Officer at Malta also acted as a clearing house for all information coming into his hands relating to the Aegean and Levant.

The War Council in London was also fully informed. Hankey told the Dardanelles Commission that the Admiralty War Staff kept a book on the Dardanelles (presumably *NID 838: Turkey Coast Defences, May 1908*), and that he kept a copy of this and the 'General Staff book on the Dardanelles Defences' (the 1909 *Report on the Defences of Constantinople*) by his side at every meeting of the War Council in 1914–15. He constantly referred to these confidential books at every meeting, and gave out information from them to members of the Council.[87] Hankey also stated that the British fleet in the eastern Mediterranean in late 1914 and early 1915 had an intelligence officer who in February 1915 (and probably earlier) supplied the military with information, and that all intelligence available in the Admiralty and the War Office was sent automatically (to Hamilton).[88]

When asked whether the War Council was given any intelligence reports on Gallipoli, Hankey made the following statement:

> Yes, as I said, I always had these books [Admiralty War Staff book on the Dardanelles *NID 838*, and the War Office 1909 *Report*] in the room, and there were long extracts from them frequently read out. Of course, the Admiralty and the War Office had them all, and any member of the War Council who wished to could come to my office and see them. Mr Balfour frequently used to come in.[89]

He stated too that additional information from the Admiralty and the War Office was also given regularly to the War Council,[90] and that in peace-time Secret Service sources had been feeding information to the service Intelligence Departments.[91] In a secret paper for the War Council entitled *After the Dardanelles. The Next Steps* (dated 1 March 1915), Hankey noted that the greater part of the population on both sides of the Dardanelles was Greek, and that Greek information regarding garrisons was usually reliable.[92] As the risk of Allied action increased, the Turks took measures to remove the Greek population from the threatened zones, as it posed a clear security risk. The key village of Krithia, in the Helles sector, had been 'abandoned at the close of 1914 by the Greeks and actually taken possession of by the [Turkish] troops'.[93]

Concluding remarks

Undoubtedly the lack of a permanent joint naval and military combined operations planning staff played a big part in any intelligence hiatus in the run-up to the despatch of Hamilton's force. A continual flow of information was arriving in London via military attachés, the Naval Mission in Constantinople, consuls, allies, etc., and was not properly coordinated, analysed, evaluated or distributed. By comparison, the 1943–4 preparations for the D-Day landings had the advantage of a unified command and chief of staff, a combined joint staff, a Theatre Intelligence Section, a prolonged preparation period, vast resources, a proper recognition of the importance of air reconnaissance and survey, of beach and terrain intelligence, and so on.

Nevertheless, it is a gross libel on all the War Office staff to suppose that they did not supply the reports, handbooks, maps and other information, held in their departments or in the War Office Library, to Hamilton, Braithwaite, and the officers of the Mediterranean Expeditionary Force General Staff, and the 'A' and 'Q' Branch officers who followed as a second echelon. Callwell made it clear that all the available secret reports and handbooks were supplied. Hedley, of MO4 (GSGS), certainly did his bit by arranging with Dowson, the Survey of Egypt chief, in August 1914 to take responsibility for Middle East mapping and, in particular, to enlarge to 1:40,000 and reproduce the one-inch map when a decision to operate at the Dardanelles had been taken. Hudleston, in charge of the War Office Library, must also have played his part.

And it should also be remembered that there was a great Allied intelligence-collecting centre in Egypt. Maxwell's Intelligence Staff in Cairo, under Clayton, were gathering information on the Turkish order-of-battle, dispositions and other related matters, and were able to share this with Birdwood's Anzac, and later with Hamilton's 'Medforce' Staff. They also had the benefit of the French Military Mission in Egypt, one member of which was Colonel Maucorps, who for five years had been French military attaché in Constantinople.[94] The next chapter takes the developing intelligence picture up to the landings of 25 April.

Notes

1. Aspinall-Oglander, Brig.Gen. C F, *History of the Great War, Military Operations, Gallipoli*, Vol. I, London: Heinemann, 1929, pp. 46–7.
2. Gooch, J, *The Plans of War. The General Staff and British Military Strategy c1900– 1916*, London: Routledge, 1974.
3. Robertson, Gen. Sir W, *Soldiers and Statesmen*, Vol. I, London: Cassell, 1926, p. 160.
4. Magnus, Philip, *Kitchener*, London: John Murray, 1958.
5. Hedley typescript, para 2. In Defence Geographic Centre.

6. *History of RE*, Vol. 6, 113.
7. Hogarth, D G, 'Geography in the war theatre in the Near East', *Geographical Journal*, 65, 1915, pp. 457–51.
8. Romer Diary.
9. Garnett, David (ed.), *The Letters of T E Lawrence*, London: Spring Books, 1964, pp. 188–9; Newcombe, Col. S F, 'T E Lawrence. Personal Reminiscences', *PEF Quarterly*, July 1935, pp. 110–13.
10. Graves, Robert, *Lawrence and the Arabs*, London: Cape, 1927, pp. 81–2.
11. Weldon, L B, *'Hard Lying'. Eastern Mediterranean 1914–1919*, London: Herbert Jenkins, 1925.
12. Ibid.
13. Hedley typescript, para 11, subsection (a).
14. Cunliffe Owen to The Secretary, Army Council, 27-9-1927, in IWM Department of Documents.
15. Typescript note, signed by Parry (Hydrographer) and dated 14-11-1914, on chart in Dardanelles Charts relating to Eastern Mediterranean Squadron, 1914–1916. TNA(PRO) ADM 137/787.
16. 1914, Mediterranean War Records, Dardanelles, pp. 281–5. TNA(PRO) ADM 137/2165.
17. Pears, Sir Edwin, *Forty Years in Constantinople*, London: Herbert Jenkins, 1916, p. 343.
18. Talbot for Callwell, memorandum *The Gallipoli Peninsula*, signed 'Cal DMO 1/9/14', 'A', in TNA(PRO) WO 106/1463.
19. Ibid.
20. Dallas, memorandum *The Dardanelles and Gallipoli Peninsula*, dated 1.9.14, 'B', in TNA(PRO) WO 106/1463.
21. Covering minute by Talbot, dated 5.9.14, in TNA(PRO) WO 106/1463.
22. Ibid.
23. *Summary of Proposed Evidence of Major-General Charles Callwell*, Minutes of Evidence to the Dardanelles Commission. TNA(PRO) CAB 19/33, p. 107.
24. Untitled typescript memorandum signed 'Charles Callwell DMO 3/9/14', at 'D', in TNA(PRO) WO 106/1463.
25. Both at 'C' in TNA(PRO) WO 106/1463.
26. Cunliffe Owen, Lt-Col. F, file *Forcing of Dardanelles. Feasibility Report on Operations in the Dardanelles*, 1914, TNA(PRO) WO 106/1462.
27. Cunliffe Owen to The Secretary, Army Council, 27-9-1927, in IWM Department of Documents.
28. Rhodes James, Robert, *Gallipoli*, London: Pimlico, 1999, p. 80.
29. Portions of Charts Nos 1198 and 2429, bound in HS Vol. 901 Dardanelles, Charts relating to eastern Mediterranean Squadron, 1914–1916, as nos 12 & 13, TNA(PRO) ADM 137/787 and letter No. 215 in ADM 137/881.
30. Letter No. 216 in TNA(PRO) ADM 137/881.
31. Typescript note, signed by Parry, op. cit.
32. Dardanelles 1915 Jan–April (H.S. 1089), item 316. TNA(PRO) ADM 137/1089.
33. Andrew, Christopher, *Secret Service. The Making of the British Intelligence Community*, London: Heinemann, 1985, p. 89.
34. *Summary of Proposed Evidence . . . Callwell*, op. cit., p. 107.
35. Ibid.
36. 1914, Dardanelles, Mediterranean War Records, Dardanelles, p. 366. TNA(PRO) ADM 137/2165.

37. Dardanelles, 1914 Sept–Dec. TNA(PRO) ADM 137/881.
38. Admiralty files on Loss of Submarine E15 on 18-4-15. TNA(PRO) ADM 1/8418/90.
39. Signal from Malta to Vice Admiral, Eastern Mediterranean Squadron, 4-3-15; British Library: Keyes Papers, 5/11.
40. Keyes, R, The Naval Memoirs of Admiral of the Fleet Sir Roger Keyes, Vol. I, London: Butterworth, 1934, pp. 288–90.
41. Remarks after paper by D G Hogarth, given at the Royal Geographical Society on 26 April 1915: 'Geography of the War Theatre in the Near East', *Geographical Journal*, 45(6), June 1915, pp. 457–71.
42. Garnett, op. cit., p. 190.
43. Ibid.
44. Dardanelles. Tracing Admiralty Chart No. 2429, Defences since 4th August 1914, Enclosure No. 11 in Med. Letter No./34 dated 24-12-14, in TNA(PRO) ADM 137/787.
45. *The Dardanelles Inquiry. Proof. Notes for Evidence . . . Part II – The Origin and Initiation of the Joint Naval and Military Attack on the Dardanelles, April 25.* Sheet No. 353. No. 45. TNA(PRO) CAB/17/184.
46. Ibid.
47. Minutes of Evidence to the Dardanelles Commission, p. 725, TNA(PRO) CAB 19/33.
48. *Notes for Evidence . . .*, TNA(PRO) CAB/17/184, op. cit.
49. Dardanelles 1915 Jan–April (H.S. 1089), item 317. TNA(PRO) ADM 137/1089.
50. *Guide to Greece, The Archipelago, Constantinople, The Coast of Asia Minor, Crete and Cyprus*, 3rd edn, London: Macmillan, 1910, p. xiii.
51. See Allen, Capt. G R G, 'A Ghost from Gallipoli', *RUSI Journal*, May 1963, 108(630), pp. 137-8, and letter from Adm. W M James in *RUSI Journal*, November 1963, 108(632), pp. 374-5; also Rhodes James, op. cit., pp. 48–9.
52. GHQ MEF Intelligence Summary, Dardanelles, TNA(PRO) WO 157/647.
53. TNA(PRO) ADM 186/600, *C.B. 1550 Report of the Committee Appointed to Investigate the Attacks delivered on and the Enemy Defences of the Dardanelles Straits, 1919. Admiralty, Naval Staff, Gunnery Division, April 1921*, p. 3. Unsquared copies of these charts are at TNA(PRO) WO 301/619, 620 & 621.
54. Royal Naval Division, General Staff, War Diary, TNA(PRO) WO 95/4290.
55. Ibid.
56. Rhodes James, op. cit., p. 41.
57. Hamilton, Sir Ian, *Gallipoli Diary*, Vol. I, London: Edward Arnold, 1920, p. 73.
58. Aspinall-Oglander, op. cit., p. 79.
59. *Reports from HMS Ark Royal, Dardanelles Operations, Feb–May 1915.* TNA(PRO) AIR 1/2099/207/20/7.
60. Lee, John, *A Soldier's Life. General Sir Ian Hamilton 1853–1947*, London: Pan 2001, pp. 143–4.
61. Hamilton, op. cit., p. 6.
62. Aspinall-Oglander, op. cit., p. 88.
63. Hamilton, op. cit., pp. 13–14.
64. Dardanelles Operations – Copies of Telegrams 1915 (GOC-in-C, Egypt), TNA(PRO) 158/574.
65. Hamilton, op. cit., pp. 13–14.
66. *The Dardanelles Commission 1914–16*, London: The Stationery Office, 2001, p. 118.

67. *Report on the Defences of Constantinople. General Staff. Secret. 1909. War Office. [A 1311]. [(B 369) 100 2/09 H & S 400WO]. Copy No. 3 D.M.O.* xii + 151 pp. TNA(PRO) WO 33/2333. *Plates to accompany the Report on the Defences of Constantinople, General Staff, War Office, 1908. (B 369) 11 2/09 H & S 400-2 WO* containing 72 plates, including many folding plans, panorama sketches, photographs, etc. TNA(PRO) WO 33/2334.

68. See for example Callwell, p. 98, where he speaks of 'the secret official publications which the MEF took out with it'.

69. *Report on Certain Landing Places in Turkey in Europe, 1909. Prepared for the General Staff. War Office. (Secret). (B133) 50 6/09 H & S 158 WO.* vi + 56 pp. TNA(PRO) WO 33/478.

70. *Manual of Combined Naval and Military Operations, 1913. Confidential. 40/GEN. No./269 [A 1674] London: Printed for HMSO by Harrison & Sons, St Martin's Lane, Printers in ordinary to His Majesty. (B 156) 4000 9/13 H & S 194 WO.* 72 pp., c3.5 x 4 inches. hard buff covers. TNA(PRO) WO 33.644.

71. Copy in collection of Dr Peter Chasseaud.

72. *The Dardanelles Commission 1914–16*, op. cit., p. 68.

73. Ibid, p. 119.

74. Travers, Tim, *Gallipoli*, Stroud: Tempus, 2001.

75. Hamilton, op. cit., p. 16.

76. Ibid, p. 46.

77. Rhodes James, op. cit., p. 53.

78. Aspinall's written statement to the Dardanelles Commission, p. 59 in TNA(PRO) CAB 19/28.

79. Rhodes James, op. cit., p. 53.

80. Papers of Dr O C Williams (Private Diary, started March 13 1913, of O C Williams, Capt. GHQ, British Med. E. F.), IWM, Department of Documents, 69/78/1.

81. Garnett, op. cit., p. 197.

82. Callwell, Maj.-Gen. Sir C E, *Experiences of a Dug-Out*, London: Constable, 1920, p. 98.

83. Printed Minutes of Evidence to the Dardanelles Commission, pp. 1180–4, TNA(PRO) CAB 19/33.

84. Callwell, op. cit., pp. 96–7.

85. Ibid, p. 97.

86. Callwell's Summary, op. cit., in TNA(PRO) CAB 19/28.

87. Hankey's evidence to Dardanelles Commission, TNA(PRO) CAB 63/18 (microfilm), sheet 146.

88. Ibid, sheet 152.

89. Ibid, sheet 160.

90. Ibid.

91. Ibid, sheet 167.

92. *After the Dardanelles. The Next Steps. Secret. Notes by the Secretary to the Committee for Imperial Defence, dated March 1st 1915.* TNA(PRO) CAB 63/17 (microfilm). sheet 137.

93. 29th Division General Staff War Diary, Intelligence Summaries, in TNA(PRO) WO 95/4304.

94. *The Dardanelles Commission*, op. cit., p. 116.

CHAPTER 5

Intelligence from March 1915

With the arrival of Hamilton in the Aegean, it is time to consider the preparations which had already been made in Egypt, the Mediterranean and closer to the Dardanelles. In Egypt, in addition to their primary task of defending the Suez Canal and Egypt, and in Birdwood's case training the Anzac Corps (originally destined for France, but held in Egypt to help with its defence) as well, Generals Sir John ('Conkey') Maxwell and Birdwood did a great deal of intelligence-gathering and preliminary planning for their 'Special Mission' to the Dardanelles before Hamilton appeared on the scene. Clearly Hamilton had to see the situation for himself, which he did during the Fleet's bombardment on 18 March. It was then decided that Hamilton's Force needed to sail on to Egypt to reorganise; owing to a disastrous lack of clear strategic direction and planning in London, it had not been loaded for an opposed landing. This gave the Turks several more weeks to prepare for invasion.

Egypt as an intelligence centre

Following the outbreak of war, Maxwell, GOC Troops in Egypt, appointed Captain Gilbert Clayton as his Intelligence chief. In 1914 Clayton – the '"Bertie" of Khartum, of Cairo, of Palestine, of Mesopotamia' – was the Sudan government's Agent in Cairo, the Sirdar of the Sudan controlling the Sinai Peninsula and its frontier with Southern Palestine, and also the Egyptian Army's Director of Intelligence.[1] There was a gradual proliferation of intelligence agencies in Egypt, and within a year there was 'a variety of (sometimes conflicting) civil and military departments'.[2] Hamilton described Egypt as a 'no man's land in the region of responsibilities'.[3] Egypt's position was curious, as it was still nominally under the suzerainty of the Ottoman Sultan. Much of the population felt affection for Turkey and loyalty to Islam, and in November 1914 the proclamation of a British Protectorate rather than Annexation, as desired by Asquith's government, did much to stabilise the situation. It was naturally impossible to prevent the Turks from finding out what British forces were up to in Egypt, but the damage caused by any leakage was amplified by a general lack of security. The arrival of letters addressed to the Constantinople Expeditionary Force did not help.

In the autumn of 1914 Maxwell and Clayton recruited a team of highly talented 'special service' Arabic-speaking officers, several of whom had been involved in the recent Sinai and southern Palestine survey, for Clayton's Intelligence Department (from which the later Arab Bureau would evolve) in Cairo – T E Lawrence from GSGS and Major S F Newcombe RE, both of whom arrived on 14 December, were followed a few days later by George Lloyd, Aubrey Herbert (after recovering from a wound acquired at Mons) and Leonard Woolley.[4] Following his induction in the Geographical Section in London Lawrence, as 'Maps Officer', provided in-theatre liaison between the Survey of Egypt and the Mediterranean Expeditionary Force.

Herbert wrote from Shepherd's Hotel (GHQ) on 9 February 1915 that his colleagues in Clayton's Intelligence Department comprised members of parliament, engineers, archaeologists and still more members of parliament, and that all except the MPs were very keen on devising new policies. No doubt he had Lawrence's Alexandretta scheme in mind. Herbert thought his fellow officers were deluded enough to believe that the War Office and Foreign Office 'work lucidly in a sort of millennium with each other', and that Russia and France were 'sweetly reasonable'. Although a member of parliament, he wickedly started to develop a policy; his superiors reacted to this by tasking him with the Turkish order-of-battle. He had to learn the (revised) Turkish Army handbook by heart and mark up a giant map with Turkish troop movements. He delegated the map to his servant, Johny Allen.[5]

On 12 February Herbert was sent by Newcombe on an intelligence-gathering mission in the battleship *Bacchante*, to identify Turkish troop movements in the Levant. Any information on the dispositions of the Turkish Army would help to fill in the enemy-order-of-battle map, and would also help Maxwell and Kitchener to assess more accurately the Turkish garrison at the Dardanelles. *Bacchante* arrived at Alexandretta on the 14th after an eerily uneventful voyage via Haifa and Beyrout. All was thus quiet on the Levant front.

On 23 February, Maxwell had an interview with 'Colonel M_____', who vigorously drew a tiny but disturbing sketch map of the Dardanelles area, with Turkish troop deployments – 40,000 on the Peninsula, 50,000 in Thrace, 50,000 on the western Asiatic Coast facing the islands, and 30,000 on the Asiatic Shore of the Dardanelles.[6] This mystery Colonel was Maucorps, the former French military attaché in Constantinople, who was now in Cairo with the French Military Mission and who, like Frederick Cunliffe Owen, was pessimistic about the chances of success. Maucorps also submitted a report on the 26th, following which Maxwell cabled Kitchener that the Peninsula was 'practically a fort', being heavily fortified; any attack without heavy guns would be hazardous.[7] The key points of Maucorps' report telegraphed by Maxwell to Kitchener (though the figures had been toned down) were:[8]

1. It would be 'extremely hazardous to land on the Gallipoli Peninsula, as the peninsula is very strongly organised for defence';
2. It was garrisoned by 30,000 men; another 30,000 were on the Asiatic Shore;
3. The Bulair Lines had been rearmed, and
4. The Turkish commander of the Peninsula was an excellent and energetic officer

If anything, these communications from Maxwell reinforced Kitchener in his view that the Peninsula was 'a hornets' nest', and in his determination not to land large military forces.

Birdwood's reconnaissance

Meanwhile, on 24 February, Birdwood, with his senior staff officer Lt-Col. Skeen, sailed in the *Swiftsure* to meet Carden; while at sea they received a message telling them to make for Imbros, Hamilton's destination. *Swiftsure* arrived on 28 February and Birdwood met Carden on 1 March, before transferring to the *Irresistible* the next day to make his reconnaissance. *Irresistible* sailed to the Dardanelles, and Birdwood and Skeen:

> ... examined coast and interior from north-west of Tekke Burnu [Cape Tekke at Helles] over Krithia to Achi Babi Peak. General survey indicated possibility of fire of ships to cover or support movement. No coast suitable for landing. Then round to Tekke Burnu – Helles Burnu. A stretch of beach suitable but somewhat shallow – a very conspicuous trench runs down from Light House and seems commanded by a rise north of lighthouse. Would be useful as an additional beach if pressed for time. Beach between Cape Helles and Sedd el Bahr by no means as favourable as conveyed by Plan in N.I.D. *Report [NID 838, May 1908]*.[9]

The requirement for intelligence and operational information flows worked in both directions. On 26 February Kitchener wired to Maxwell for Birdwood: 'please keep me fully informed of your operations, referring to War Office Map GS[GS] 2285'.[10] This was the two-sheet, one-inch map of Gallipoli which, during March, was enlarged to 1:40,000 and reproduced at the Survey of Egypt. The Royal Naval and 29th Divisions were equipped with the one-inch map just two days before leaving England.

Also on 26 February the War Office (Military Operations) in London replied to Maxwell who, confused by the conflicting instructions he was receiving, had cabled, disingenuously or perhaps facetiously, or both, that he was:

> … considerably in the dark, as I have no knowledge of the deep study which must have been made of the whole question of the forcing of the Dardanelles by the Imperial General Staff and the Navy for many years, the result of which must be in the War Office and résumé of which I would much like.[11]

Maxwell was letting the cat out of the bag, and putting the War Office in a quandary; no single 'deep study' existed, but various short feasibility and intelligence reports did, and were probably, like the 1906 report, considered too sensitive, or negative in their conclusions, to release.

As already suggested, the War Office's reply of 26 February was a masterpiece of evasion, and is worth repeating here:

> Difficult to send you resume of General Staff studies of Gallipoli. Suggest your consulting Admiralty reports of Turkey Coast defences, Part II, of which all war ships have copy. Ten copies of Military Report 1905 Eastern Turkey in Europe being sent you to-day by bag.[12]

(Frequent King's Messengers and diplomatic bags were a prime means of sending such documents.) Maxwell was being told to mind his own business as far as strategy was concerned. But how could he formulate objectives and plans if he was not put in the strategic picture, and was not told whether it was to be a purely naval operation, a naval operation with limited assistance from the Army, or a fully combined amphibious operation? In the event, as carried out by de Robeck and Hamilton, it was a purely naval operation followed, after a month, by a fully military one with the navy putting the army ashore, but doing little else other than providing covering fire. No simultaneous attempt to force the Narrows was made.

New information about the Dardanelles defences, even if not given to Hamilton and Braithwaite at their War Office briefing, was available in theatre, and much was duly provided by the Fleet's Intelligence Officer. Hamilton's Intelligence Staff maintained liaison with Naval Intelligence as well as with Clayton in Cairo, and the MEF was well provided with many types of intelligence before the landings. The Army and Navy knew almost every fact about the coastal fixed defences, but of course much less about the mobile howitzer batteries and the dispositions and numbers of Turkish (and German) troops providing the garrison of the Peninsula.

On 10, 11 and 12 March sea and air reconnaissances of the Bulair Lines were carried out, a seaplane reporting four lines of traversed trenches and an entrenched camp with two redoubts.[13] All air reconnaissance at this time was visual, no cameras becoming available until April. Hamilton confirmed, following his own reconnaissance in the *Phaeton* on 18 March, that a landing at Bulair would be disastrous. On 15 March Limpus sent a report on the Dardanelles from his intelligence hub at Malta to Rear-Admiral Phillimore at the Admiralty (who received it on 19 March), stating that he had:

> ... studied the matter from the inside [Turkish] point of view when I was in Constantinople and the Greeks were contemplating the same opera-tion. Landing action was very much more necessary for them [as they did not have a fleet], but I still think it necessary for us; the more so since it is not the Turks, but the Germans, who are conducting the defence.[14]

Kitchener, after reading this report, signalled to Hamilton that it:

> ... seems to point to the advisability of effecting the main landing in the neighbourhood of Cape Helles and Morto Bay, while making a feint in considerable force north and south of Kaba Tepe with the possibility of landing and of commanding the ground of Sari Bair, so that the enemy on its southern slopes might be prevented from supporting those on the Kilid Bahr plateau. I presume that preparatory to destroying the forts at the Narrows, you will attack in force and occupy this plateau.[15]

This was essentially the plan adopted by Hamilton.

Aegean intelligence and the *Doris*

Much intelligence work was being done in the Aegean, particularly the interrogation of Greeks from the Dardanelles area. On 6 March Major Doughty Wylie, the former consul in Adis Ababa,[16] and Captain Wyndham Deedes arrived at Mudros from England 'as Intelligence Officers for deal-ing with ANZAC HQ'; it was hoped that they, with another (Captain J M Smith), would be able to provide Hamilton with crucial information when he arrived in theatre; they had been despatched from London on 26 February. On the 11th, Doughty Wylie, now Lt-Colonel, signalled to Birdwood from Mudros: 'Am detaching Deedes temporarily duty Smyrna stop. Propose going myself Tenedos if you approve. Vice Admiral has no objection.' This was approved.[17] As there was much small boat movement, vital intelligence about Turkish troop dispositions and movements could be picked up from Greek inhabitants and agents. According to Aspinall, they provided vague information about Turkish troop numbers and dispositions, but 'the district had been cleared of everybody except the soldiers and they had not been able to get any agents into it'.[18]

Birdwood, Major Wagstaff of his Staff, and Captain Mitchell RN, his naval liaison officer, sailed in the cruiser HMS *Doris* from Egypt on 16 March to meet Hamilton, due to arrive at Lemnos from Marseilles. Birdwood took with him much of the 'Special Mission' planning material his Staff had thus far accumulated:[19]

1. Set of papers re Dardanelles operations to date.
2. Large Map T[urkey] in E[urope].
3. 50 copies Squared map S[outh] end of Gallipoli.
4. 1 copy [indeciph.] sheet Gallipoli.
5. 12 copies of large scale Morto Bay [indeciph.]

Also statements showing (1) degree of preparation, (2) estimate of rate of disembarkation, (3) Draft orders to Colonel MacLagan.

This material was duly handed over to Hamilton's Staff. Sinclair-MacLagan commanded the 3rd Australian Infantry Brigade, designated as the covering force for any landing, and training for that purpose on Lemnos.

During the slow crossing in the *Doris*, Lieutenant Pirie Gordon RNVR, the *Doris*'s Intelligence Officer who had been active around the Syrian coast since November[20] (a party from *Doris* ripped up a Turkish railway and blew up locomotives at Alexandretta on 18 December[21]), briefed them on Gallipoli and the Asiatic Shore of the Dardanelles, which he had visited in 1908, probably while yachting, and also on the Greek plan which, he stated, involved main landings at Ejelmer Bay and west of Bulair, covered by demonstrations between these points. In 1908, he said, the Turkish defences all faced towards the Dardanelles, to oppose a landing from within the Straits.[22] Strangely, he did not mention the Greek planned main effort at Gaba Tepe, but then there were several versions of the plan. On 14 March a 'Greek General Staff summing up of the Gallipoli Peninsula' (garrison and troop movements) was received at GHQ and, on the 19th Major Samson (British Secret Service in Athens) sent a report about the Dardanelles, received at Anzac HQ the following day (parts of his 1910 report were incorporated into a GHQ report). Much Turkish order-of-battle material was also received, including information on Gallipoli and the Dardanelles on the 23rd. During March, intelligence bulletins were received regularly at Anzac HQ from the British and Egyptian War Offices.[23]

Following their briefing by Kitchener and Callwell, Hamilton, Braithwaite and their Staff arrived at Tenedos on 17 March, four days after leaving London, and conferred with de Robeck (Carden having fallen ill) and General d'Amade, commanding the French contingent, who had arrived at the same time. At this conference it was made clear that the Gallipoli Peninsula was being fortified, that trenches, redoubts and entanglements had been identified, and also that the British seaplanes were too heavy to rise out of rifle range.[24] All 'deplored the lack of aeroplanes', which effectively blinded their attack.[25] Intentions and reconnaissance were discussed. De Robeck wanted to know if Hamilton intended to land at Bulair, and received the reply that Hamilton believed in seeing things for himself, and would 'not come to any decision on the map if it were possible to come to it on the ground'. De Robeck said that, in any case, he could not land large forces at the Bulair neck itself, as there were no beaches.[26]

The following day Doughty Wylie, Deedes, and Captain Smith joined GHQ MEF at Lemnos for intelligence work;[27] the first two had been at Lemnos since the 6th, Deedes having visited the Smyrna area to gather information and organise agents, and Doughty Wylie, Tenedos.

On 18 March, during the big naval attack, Hamilton, a few of his Staff, and General d'Amade left Lemnos in the *Phaeton* to carry out their own reconnaissance of :

> ... the Gallipoli Peninsula, arriving about 12.30pm. She then proceeded along the North Bank of the Peninsula, and from 300 to 5000 yards distance from it to the Gulf of Saros, which was reached at 2.30pm. The natural landing places were noted, but it was observed that an elaborate network of trenches commanded all the landing places except that at Cape Helles.[28]

Hamilton noted: 'Here the Peninsula looks a tougher nut to crack than it did on Lord Kitchener's small and featureless map.'[29]

On the same day, de Robeck (Vice-admiral commanding Eastern Mediterranean squadron) wrote to Hamilton ('GOC Expeditionary Force to Turkey') from the *Queen Elizabeth*:

> Sir,
> [1] ... a telegram has been received from the British Minister at Athens to the effect that the ex-Russian Vice-consul of the Dardanelles is now at Athens at my disposal.
> 2. He further reports that the boatman's guild of the Piraeus offers ex-smugglers as guides to Gallipoli Peninsula.
> 3. Should you think the services of the persons mentioned might be of service to you please let me know, and also what action you wish taken in the matter.

No reply was recorded, and the letter was registered under 'Services of Diplomatic, Consular and Secret Agents'.[30] Clearly the smugglers were of great value, with their knowledge of the terrain, and Greeks were used as guides during operations. One guide, Athanasios Ballas, provided useful information on 16 April to Lieutenant Woods of Anzac Intelligence; this was forwarded to GHQ. Ballas was commended by the Anzacs: 'This man knows the Peninsula well.' On the allocation of guides by GHQ on 18 April, two were allotted to the Anzac Corps; they were 'said to be quite untrustworthy, though they dislike the Turks intensely'.[31] Presumably several also went to the 29th Division.

HMS *Doris*, with Birdwood and his small Staff, finally arrived at Mudros on the 21st, and they went on board *Franconia* to confer with Hamilton and his GHQ Staff. De Robeck was still under the impression that the main landing would be near Bulair, despite the fact that Hamilton had decided that a landing in force was only practicable at Cape Helles, between Tekke Burnu and Morto Bay.[32] De Robeck returned the next day, and it was immediately decided that Hamilton's force needed to go on to Egypt to reorganise, before returning to Mudros prepared for an opposed landing on Gallipoli. On the 23rd, as arranged the previous day, Wagstaff gave various 'maps and pamphlets' ('maps and other documents' in the message of the 22nd) to Colonel Sinclair-MacLagan,[33] commanding the Anzac 'Special Mission'.

Hamilton's requests

Hamilton was clearly worried about the lack of strategic and military intelligence. On 21 March he telegraphed from Lemnos to the War Office asking that 'arrangements be made for Diplomatic, Consular and Secret Agents to send all available information direct to him. News from Athens and Balkan States especially desirable.'[34] The following day London responded by telegraphing Maxwell:

> 3685 Cipher, MO5. Please send all information from Major Marsh, Tiflis [in Georgia], direct to Sir Ian Hamilton. All Diplomatic and Consular Agents have been instructed to communicate information direct to him. Major Samson [Secret Service chief] at Athens has also been instructed to do so.[35]

Marsh was particularly well placed to report Russian progress on the Caucasus front. At sea in the *Franconia* on the 25th, Hamilton received a reply from the War Office stating 'that they had arranged for all Foreign Office representatives to send C in C military intelligence direct in cipher, and that all other information would be sent from War Office'.[36]

In view of the planned landings, intelligence was desperately needed to make up the enemy order-of-battle and dispositions map, a task which had fallen to Aubrey Herbert (or rather Johny Allen) in Cairo. Doughty Wylie at Mudros telegraphed an urgent request to Maxwell for Clayton on 22 March: 'Please send information of Turkish forces in Syria and Mesopotamia. Important to know if any force has returned towards Dardanelles or date of possible arrival there. Ends'.[37]

At Malta on 24 March the Intelligence Staff of the outward bound 29th Division called at Limpus's intelligence office, and were given information about the Gallipoli Peninsula and the Turkish forces there, including a very detailed order-of-battle. The following day they were told that 'all the possible landing places in Gallipoli Peninsula were found by Naval Reconnaissance to be held and entrenched, generally with three lines of trenches, but not much wire was seen'. Arriving at Alexandria on 1 April, they compiled a report from verbal information giving details of Turkish troop totals and training, machine guns, artillery, strengths, transport, reserve formations, roads, water supply, inhabitants, defences, and opposition to be expected.[38]

Colonel Sir Thomas Cunninghame, the military attaché in Greece, wired on 26 March that he was leaving for Alexandria and wished to see Hamilton on the 28th. He arrived on 27 March, saw Braithwaite on the following two days, and left on the 31st. In fact he was urging avoidance of a landing on the Peninsula and, instead, recommending a landing at Salonika or elsewhere in Thrace where, presumably, the Greeks were willing to cooperate. He proposed a scheme to this effect on 3 April.[39] A telegram from the War Office received on 10 April stated that Cunninghame urged his appointment as Liaison Officer between Athens and the Mediterranean Expeditionary Force, but Hamilton replied that 'no necessity was seen for such an appointment'.[40] It is difficult to perceive the logic of this reply. Any arrangement which might have secured Greek assistance should have been welcome, but the Russians had vetoed Greek participation on 2 March.[41]

On 14 April a War Office telegram, forwarded by Maxwell, informed Hamilton ('GOC Medforce') that Captain C L Cobban, Indian Army, had been appointed Liaison Officer with Russian troops (who were planning to attack towards Constantinople from the Black Sea), and had left on the 12th.[42] Unfortunately the Russians were not prepared to commit their troops until German ships (*Goeben* and *Breslau*) were eliminated from the Black Sea, and this condition was not fulfilled.

Sketches and photographs

On 2 April, in Alexandria, Hamilton was informed by de Robeck, through Maxwell, that the 'Navy was making reconnaissances and sketches of all possible landing places, and asking for Staff Officer to be sent to assist arrangements for cooperation'. Hamilton replied 'that two trained aeroplane observers were being sent in the *Paros* today: also that Staff officer would be sent whenever he could be sent for'.[43] Considering the shortage of time, this lack of direct staff liaison was a serious matter. There was, however, a naval officer, Captain Mitchell, with Hamilton's Staff, who had worked with Birdwood on the plans for the Dardanelles operation before Hamilton arrived on the scene.

The Navy's reconnaissance sketches took the form of a set of drawn panoramas which were soon lithographed on tough, linen-backed paper by the GHQ Printing Section (see Chapter 8). These assault panoramas are evidence of the considerable thought, preparation and cooperation which were put by the Army and Navy into the brief, intense period before the landings. GHQ still needed further geographical information, and on 4 April Hamilton's Staff sent a telegram to the War Office regarding water supply on the Peninsula, a reply being received two days later about this, and also about firewood.[44] This was the type of information, included in the pre-war reports, which the military attachés could have supplemented before the war if so requested.

An important development in intelligence acquisition occurred early in April, following the arrival of Commander Samson's RNAS aeroplane squadron, capable of overflying the Peninsula at a safe height, something the Navy's seaplanes could not do. Lieutenant Butler of this squadron was an experienced air photographer and had brought his camera and processing equipment. The combination of a reasonable altitude (4,000 feet) and Butler's near-vertical photographs enabled Turkish trenches, batteries and other tactical features to be plotted with some precision on the new 1:40,000 (enlarged from the one-inch) map. Air photography and air survey are described in detail in Chapter 7 and in Appendix VI.

From 4 April the Anzac Corps was embarking in Egypt and receiving its new 1:40,000 maps from the Survey of Egypt, many being distributed at sea. On the 7th the Anzac General Staff handed over their file of papers relating to the aborted Alexandretta operation to Maxwell's GSO. On the same day, the Anzac Printing Section embarked on the *Arcadian* at Alexandria. This Section, formed for Birdwood's force by the Survey of Egypt, was handed over to Hamilton on the latter's arrival in Egypt, and was used for the lithographic printing of panoramas, sketch maps, diagrams and tactical intelligence maps before the landings, and topographical and trench maps afterwards (see Chapter 9). While at sea on 9 April, the Anzac General Staff explained the coming operations to the Australian Division Staff, and even to some members of the Corps HQ who were still in the dark.[45]

Following the arrival of Hamilton's GHQ, intelligence, much of it from Athens or Russian sources, continued to flow via Maxwell's HQ in Cairo; for example:

At Alexandria
21 March: Cairo reports following from Athens by Greek of good position who left Dardanelles March 9th [about German ship, Enver, guns, mines etc.]

	Agent of postal boat which left the Dardanelles on March 11th . . .
2 April	Greek engine driver who recently arrived Salonika from Constantinople . . .
6 April	Well informed man just arrived from Constantinople . . .

At Mudros

13 April	Important wire about Turkish troop numbers on Gallipoli, plus information about Smyrna, from Major Plunkett [Intelligence] in Alexandria. Informant an ex-officer of Greek Navy, now captain of SS *Indiana*.
15 April	Russian General Staff reports presence of 2nd Nizam Corps in Constantinople area.
16 April	Report by Greek [sea] Pilot who left Dardanelles March 8th ...

The Greek contribution is particularly important; the Greeks had very good intelligence sources in the Dardanelles area and elsewhere, and kept their material up-to-date. They had to be prepared to participate in operations if the right military, diplomatic and strategic circumstances arose. In particular, they were watching to see which way Bulgaria jumped, and were concerned about Russian designs on Constantinople and the Straits, which they intended to make their own.

Hamilton was also in regular contact with London through a weekly King's Messenger who travelled via Malta.[46] This was vital for material which could not be entrusted to wireless signals. Compton Mackenzie, who joined Hamilton's Intelligence Staff in May as a Royal Marine lieutenant, noted the existence of the 'V' or Special Intelligence Bureau for the Eastern Mediterranean, in Alexandria. Its chief was 'Major V' who reported to 'C' (Sir Mansfield Smith-Cumming) in London. After the division of Operations and Intelligence at the War Office at the end of 1915, Cumming headed MI1(c).[47] Mackenzie later joined the Alexandria Bureau, before transferring to Athens.[48] Lieutenant Thompson RNVR, a 'member of the British colony in Constantinople', was the Naval Intelligence Officer on Tenedos, where there were also two other Royal Marine lieutenants working as intelligence officers who had been with businesses in Constantinople. Major Eustace Fiennes was Intelligence Officer of the Royal Naval Division. Mackenzie also noted the large number of caiques and motor boats at Tenedos,[49] vital for clandestine operations to the Ottoman coast. Following the landings, GHQ was briefly established here before moving to Imbros.

Captain Nugent's Report on the topography
of the Gallipoli Peninsula

Captain Walter Vivian Nugent RA, a regular officer who had previously served with MO4 (GSGS), and later commanded the Ranging and Survey Section on the Gallipoli Peninsula, sailed from England with the 29th Division artillery, and on arrival in the theatre immediately began to gather topographical intelligence. By 5 April, in Alexandria, he had compiled sufficient information, some of it vitally important for the movement of artillery and other transport, to present a report to 29th Division HQ. His main points were:[50]

1. Many more villages exist than appear on the map, therefore more supplies and ox wagons.
2. All villages have cart tracks leading to them, suitable for supply wagons.
3. Field guns can be taken almost anywhere, country undulating.
4. Many roads made lately but country roads do not dry up for another month, and would now be impassable for heavy siege artillery, such as our 6-inch howitzer with narrow wheels.
5. At this time of year there is ample water, in fact many of the valleys are flooded and form lakes.
6. The colouring of the Peninsula is, at the present time, green. Khaki (Indian colour) will show up very much. Later it becomes quite brown or yellow.
7. Scrub covering hills is not sufficient to stop infantry progress. It is a kind of heather, about 3-feet high.

While it was substantially correct, this was inevitably a general report and could not cover every locality on the Peninsula. Clearly local conditions varied enormously, and it was most unfortunate that the landing forces at Anzac became entangled in country that did not fit Nugent's paradigm. That said, there was ample supplementary material on the Anzac zone from other sources.

GHQ intelligence reports on the Gallipoli Peninsula

Hamilton's GHQ Intelligence Staff was divided into I(a), responsible for acquiring information about the enemy and the theatre of operations, and I(b), responsible for counter-espionage. Given the initial lack of detailed knowledge of Turkish dispositions, and insufficiency of geographical information, I(a) had its work cut out to determine the Turkish defences and order-of-battle on the Peninsula, the Asiatic side, and in any other area which might be able to supply reinforcements, quite apart from the other huge problem of creating a realistic terrain-picture of the Peninsula from sea and land reconnaissance, pre-war reports and maps, and agents' reports. An air camera was not available until April, when it provided vital intelligence about the defence, and made it possible to correct the existing map and prepare a new intelligence map showing Turkish field defences.

Among the first reports issued by GHQ MEF were the following:[51]

1. *Extracts from Reports on Defences of Gallipoli Peninsula* (undated; 4 pages);
2. *Notes on Asiatic Coast, Gulf of Adramiti and Smyrna District* (undated; 2 pages) and
3. *Intelligence Report* dated 1 April (2 pages); 80,000 men on Gallipoli Peninsula.

During the period of preparation in Egypt, Hamilton's Intelligence Staff began an 8-page letterpress *Report on Gallipoli Peninsula*,[52] which was received by the Anzac Corps as early as 12 April, giving military and geographical information, some of which (on landing places in the Gaba Tepe area) was extracted verbatim from Samson's 1910 report. Further reports were soon issued, as the flow of information was unceasing. Some of the information in these was obtained from the pre-war reports, but much was the result of recently acquired intelligence, particularly that gleaned from local inhabitants. British intelligence officers were very active among the islands off the Dardanelles, and had agents on the mainland. Few in the expedition knew officially of its destination at this stage, and practically no one knew the Gallipoli Peninsula. They had to be briefed from cold, so a great deal of information had to be packed in. The report, distributed after the force arrived at Mudros, was in several sections; the first was:[53]

← Memorandum about Turkish defences on Gallipoli Peninsula (sent from GHQ on 15 April to Birdwood (Anzac Corps), Paris (Royal Naval Division) and General d'Amade (French contingent)).

On 15 April Anzac Intelligence noted: 'Information re-defences on Gallipoli Peninsula and re-water received from GHQ.' Further reports on aspects of the Gallipoli Peninsula were soon issued by GHQ to the attacking formations:[54]

1. *Report on Landing Places in Gallipoli Peninsula including results of reconnaissances* (received by Anzac Corps on 15 April).
2. *Water in Gallipoli Peninsula* (received by 29th Division on 16 April; much information, confirming good supplies, with map references).

3. *Report on Landing Facilities between Kaba Tepe and Cape Helles – Gallipoli Peninsula* (6 pages typescript, references to tracings and sketches, received by 29th Division on 19 April; also issued to Anzac Corps):

    General Description of country and coast line.

    Positions recommended for covering ships.

    Use of cavalry and field guns.

4. *Report on landing facilities and other remarks. Kaba Tepe to the Bulair Lines* (received by 29th Division on 19 April); both reports 9 pages in total.

5. *Local Names for Places on the Gallipoli Peninsula*; includes square references (4 pages; received by Anzac Corps on 16 April and 29th Division on 19 April).

6. *Information re Roads and Maidos* (received by Anzac Corps on 16 April); Maidos reports on roads, water, etc. by the Greek Speros 'whose home is at Maitos but who is now living at Portianos', and by Lt-Col. Eustace Fiennes, GSO3 RND; Speros also drew a rough plan of Maidos which was redrawn and reproduced).

7. *Aeroplane Reconnaissance, GHQ 14-4-15*; including a 'camera flight'; entrenchments seen; roads: 'An excellent road has been made from Sedd-el-Bahr to Krithia, and other roads not shown on map of Gallipoli have been constructed. A map of these roads is being sent from Tenedos, and will be forwarded when received.' (This and further air reports received by Anzac Corps on 15, 16, 17 April)

8. *Information on the Villages, Roads, and Water in the Gallipoli Peninsula* (6 pages; GHQ Stamp: GS Intelligence 16 April).

9. *Diagram showing position of supporting ships and arrangements for aerial observation and reconnaissance (Ops. Order No. 1 of 17-4-15. Para 13).* For Anzac Corps: covering area from just south of Nibrunesi Point to south of Gaba Tepe; Anzac Cove (then yet to be named) exactly in centre.

10. Further report (received by 29th Division on 20 April):

    Water Supply (includes note: 'it is reported that all wells and slow running streams have been poisoned').

    Landing Places (giving dimensions, shapes and slopes of beaches and exits of beaches).

    Land Mines.

    Movement (details of enemy troops seen).

11. Further report on enemy forces (received by 29th Division on 20 April):

    Distribution of Turkish forces; detailed breakdown given, including 34,000 on Gallipoli Peninsula and 44,000 on the Asiatic side of the Dardanelles. The positions of Turkish Divisions were reported.

    Reserve Divisions may be reckoned at about 1/3 in guns and machine guns of active Divisions.

    Gallipoli Peninsula is reported full of machine guns.

12. *Further Local names for Places* (received by Anzac Corps 21 April).
13. *Diagram of Enemy Positions up to 20 April* (received by Anzac Corps 22 April; lithographed sketch map – see below).
14. *Aeroplane Reports of 19 and 20 April* (received by Anzac Corps 23 April).

A 1:40,000 'Sketch map Square 177 Showing defences of Achi Baba correcting former reconnaissances on 13/4/15' was printed to update existing maps.[55] Successive editions of a 1:40,000 lithographed sketch map of the Turkish field defences, from 14 April in the Helles, and from the 18th in the Anzac, sectors, based on RNAS air photos and visual reconnaissance, were reproduced by the MEF GHQ Printing Section and distributed to the troops before the landings; these were dated 14, 18 and 20 April (see Chapters 6 and 7).[56] A separate, untitled 1:40,000 squared lithographed black sketch map of the Gaba Tepe–Anzac–Suvla–Maidos area, showing Turkish defences, was also produced before the landings by the GHQ Printing Section specifically for the Anzac Corps.[57] As this showed the area right across the Peninsula, it was clearly intended to be used for the Corps' main thrust to Mal Tepe, to cut off the Turkish forces in the Helles sector.

A section of the *Report on Landing Facilities between Kaba Tepe and Cape Helles* showed that the existence of gullies and dead ground had been appreciated, as had been the fact that the map did not show all the underfeatures:

> Aerial Reconnaissance: prior to a landing it appears most necessary especially to examine the ridges between Gaba Tepe and Helles already referred to. There is doubtless plenty of space here for enemy troops to take cover and to manoeuvre without being seen from seaward, and batteries do exist there, as HMS *Grampus* was fired upon when examining Chana Ovasi – the number and extent of ridges in this area it is impossible to know without walking over the ground or from an aeroplane reconnaissance.
>
> An examination of the trenches on the higher ridges and on Achi Baba, which are clearly visible from certain positions seaward would also appear desirable.
>
> Aeroplanes over Bulair are also considered necessary so as to support the enemy in the theory that a landing is to be made in that direction.

The report also referred to the Admiralty Chart F, which 'will give a very good idea of the [Gaba Tepe–Bulair] coast and topographical features.'

These GHQ reports were incorporated by Medforce's formations into their own reports and sketch maps, issued to officers for briefing purposes. Despite this high degree of preparation, however, there would inevitably be *lacunae*, both as far as specific geographical information was concerned, and in knowledge of the enemy's dispositions and plans.

Final preparations at Mudros

The image being formed by commanders and staff from the growing body of information at their disposal, and from sea and air reconnaissance, including air photography from about 11 / 12 April, was one of an ominous, dark, rugged, threatening, well-garrisoned and increasingly well-defended Peninsula, on which it would be folly to attempt to land their relatively small forces. Samson's RNAS Squadron flew forty-two reconnaissance and eighteen photographic sorties before the landings (see Chapter 7),[58] providing invaluable information, and all intelligence reports showed barbed wire, trenches and field batteries rapidly multiplying. It seemed increasingly likely that the landing forces would, even if they managed to get ashore, disappear into the hinterland and there be cut to pieces like an earlier British force in the similarly dangerous terrain of Afghanistan.

Hamilton's Intelligence Staff, like nearly everyone else who knew anything about the Dardanelles and the Turkish preparations, were pessimistic. Aubrey Herbert, who by now was with General Godley's New Zealand Staff as Liaison Officer and Interpreter, wrote soon after 12 April noting their profound depression, and giving the view of the Intelligence Staff that the landing forces would 'get a very bad knock'. It did not appear to him that the Intelligence Staff and Hamilton were in touch, while it seemed incredible that they were not better informed. For two more weeks the Staff fulminated, daily more convinced of vast incompetence and ignorance at GHQ and in London.[59] This horrifying situation confirms what the course of events later suggested – that the whole campaign was like Dr Johnson's leg of mutton, but rather than being 'ill-killed, ill-drest, ill-served, as bad as bad could be', it was ill-conceived, ill-planned and ill-led.

Hamilton's Staff received the confidential 'Orders for Combined Operations' dated *Queen Elizabeth* 12 April and issued under de Robeck's name, citing as references the report 'NID 838. Turkey Coast Defences', the 'Military Squared Map Scale 1:40,000', and 'Admiralty Charts Nos 1608, 2429 and 1004'.[60] On the same day the Anzac Corps Staff, which arrived at Mudros at 7 o'clock that morning from Egypt, was told that the Corps was to land near Gaba Tepe, and was given copies of the GHQ *Report on Gallipoli Peninsula*; these were 'issued to Divisions, and studied by all staff officers'.[61] A reconnaissance by sea was arranged for the Anzac Staff for the following day.

On the 13th General Hunter-Weston (29th Division) and his GSO2 sailed in the cruiser *Dartmouth* to Tenedos, where they conferred with Samson, studied the air reconnaissance and Butler's photo results, and arranged for a copy of the results to be sent to Divisional HQ the next day.[62] On the same day, Birdwood visited Hamilton, receiving an outline of the operations plan before sailing on the Anzac reconnaissance the next day.[63] In the absence of thorough air reconnaissance and good air photo coverage, visual reconnaissance from the sea, in any case important, was a vital last resort.

The Anzacs were as well-prepared as they could be, given the conditions; Brigadier-General C Cunliffe-Owen (the Anzac CRA, not to be confused with Frederick Cunliffe Owen, the former military attaché in Constantinople) with Birdwood's staff in Egypt, noted that 'General Birdwood and staff paid several visits to the Dardanelles in warships, and the Navy in their turn sent representatives to us, to arrange details for an expedition organised jointly by both services'.[64]

Visual reconnaissances

On 14 April sea and air reconnaissances were made of the two key sectors, Helles and Anzac. Hunter-Weston and the 29th Division Staff sailed in *Dartmouth* at daybreak for Helles:

> Cruised round Tekke Burnu, Cape Helles, Seddel Bahr and Morto Bay as far as Asski Hissarlik. During this no enemy was seen. Smoke from camps at various points – Chana Ovassi – behind North spur of Achi Baba – about Krithia and further South. The Southern end of the peninsula showed heavy entrenchments and much wire entanglement, especially round the three hills 114, 138 and 141. *Darmouth* returned via Tenedos to Mudros. GOC [Hunter-Weston] went to *Queen Elizabeth* to arrange principles of operation by the Fleet.[65]

The Anzac Staff left Lemnos in the *Queen* at 5pm on 13 April, for the reconnaissance the following day for which Birdwood's General Staff issued some guidance notes on 'what to look for'. The Anzac War Diary described this reconnaissance:

> *Queen* steamed down the Gallipoli coast from Bulair – went in close from Ejelmer Bay to Helles point. Landing places north of Kaba Tepe were carefully examined. Enemy trenches located, also gun positions. These agreed with information obtained from Intelligence Officer on *Queen* – for these see map [1:40,000 sketch map]. No men seen, and apparently no work in progress. . . The beach selected seemed excellent. The spur of the main hill [Sari Bair] (objective) which should form the primary objective was selected. No shots fired.[66]

C Cunliffe-Owen gave an account of the same reconnaissance in terms that left no doubt that the terrain of the Gallipoli Peninsula was seen as daunting:

The ANZAC Staff went on board the Flagship '*Queen*.' . . . we steamed up the coast for a preliminary reconnaissance, as far as Xeros Bay, and passing Gaba Tepe, our proposed landing place on the way back. The country was broken by huge ravines and mountains, rising from close to the sea. We could see very few roads, and practically no inhabitants. The country was dominated by high hills practically down to the coast. Many trenches were visible and a ship following us was fired on.[67]

As a result of this intensive reconnaissance effort, supplemented by the first air photos taken over the Peninsula, the Turkish defences identified were plotted on the first lithographed intelligence map issued by the GHQ Printing Company the following day, with defences to 14 April. Orlo Williams noted that these comprised a line facing the sea from Kaba Tepe to Tekke Burnu, an inner line running from Kalmaz Dagh to the north-west side of the Kilid Bahr plateau, thence to Maghram and Achi Baba, and then along the crest line to the Straits, and a third system of trenches at the south end of the Peninsula, Morto Bay, de Totts Battery, and the road to Krithia. About 100 mobile guns and howitzers had been identified.[68] The intelligence picture was regularly updated before the landings.

This offshore reconnaissance was invaluable, and together with an air reconnaissance from Tenedos on 14 April by Major Villiers Stuart of the Anzac Intelligence Staff,[69] enabled the Anzacs to create a terrain model used for briefing. C Cunliffe-Owen noted that after the reconnaissance a large plaster model was made of the proposed landing area, from which all officers studied the general terrain features.[70] He did not record whether air photos were used in the construction of this model; they were certainly available, even if in small numbers, but very few if any covered the crucial Anzac and Sari Bair area where the most difficult terrain would be encountered. Indeed the 1909 War Office *Report* – which drew on Grover's report of 1877 – had warned specifically about operations in this area, pointing out that although landing might be easy, the terrain was extremely difficult (emphasis added):

> From the head of Maidos Bay . . . to Kaba Tepe . . . a well-marked depression, slightly above sea level, runs across the Peninsula, dividing the Kilid Bahr plateau from the hills farther north. *North of this depression is the Saribair Hill, a steep, rugged ridge, which rises to 970 feet, and dominates very steeply the village of Biyuk Anafarta. It is seamed with many ravines, covered with brushwood, and generally difficult of access*, except on the southern spurs about Kojadere and Boghali, which are somewhat easier. . . . For 2 miles north of Kaba Tepe is a shelving beach, some 60 yards wide, *backed by steep, friable sandy cliffs from the Saribair, a very rough and difficult ridge which extends inland towards Biyuk Anafarta*. Landing for troops is easy, but they would have to march south on leaving the shore and join the

other troops in the Asmak Sere. A deep, sandy ravine occurs just north of Kaba Tepe, where ramps would probably have to be made to pass field guns. . . . The beach south of Nibrunesi Point, for a distance of 2 miles, as far as Fisherman's Hut, is wide and easy for landing, *but a belt of thick, low scrub, rather difficult to traverse, fringes the shore.* . . . A track runs along the beach to the landing place north of Kaba Tepe, but the cliffs have fallen and blocked it at some points, although it might be made passable with difficulty. *Between Fisherman's Hut and Kaba Tepe* [the actual ANZAC landing place], *where the hills approach the shore, the beach is generally narrow and lined with precipitous sandy cliffs.*

More of this document is given in Appendix III. The whole gist of this description was, as had been proposed in Grover's report, that troops landed in the vicinity of Gaba Tepe should then move south and then east towards Maidos, and not get entangled in the Sari Bair hills. In the event, through mistakes made during the landings which meant that the Anzacs landed a mile too far north, precisely the opposite took place, and the covering force became entangled in the very terrain the 1909 Report had warned about. As a result, it had to be reinforced by the main force, which was thus diverted from its strategic task of rushing across to the Straits.

Final preparations

The air camera with No. 3 Squadron only became available in the first two weeks of April, leaving a mere twenty days before the landings to create a good picture of the terrain and the Turkish defences. This was clearly a very difficult task with only one hand-held, folding camera. It was naturally suggested that air photos should be used for beach reconnaissance. On 16 April Hamilton, in the *Arcadian* at Lemnos, signalled asking de Robeck 'for further information as to length, breadth of Cape Helles beaches and preparations for defence from seaward of ravine in Sq. 184, S, T, X, Y [north of Krithia, running inland from coast]. Suggested photographs of beaches might be obtained from aeroplanes'.[71] The beach information was duly included in a GHQ report on 'Landing Places'. The remainder of Hamilton's GHQ Staff left Alexandria on the same day for Lemnos, arriving on the 18th; only four full days remained until the planned landings early on St George's Day (23 April), which bad weather later pushed back to the 25th.

On 18 April, key personnel of 29th Division made another sea reconnaissance of the Helles sector:

Personal reconnaissance by GOC [General Officer Commanding] with GOCRA [General Officer Commanding Royal Artillery], Infantry

Brigadiers, ADMS [Assistant Director of Medical Services], CRE [Commander, Royal Engineers] and OCs [Officers Commanding] of certain battalions which are to be first to land, proceeded to Tenedos in *Dublin*, thence to peninsula in *Swiftsure* and returned in evening.[72]

On the same day, Hamilton telegraphed to Kitchener an 'outline of enemy's defences as shown by aeroplane reconnaissance', essentially an updated version of that described by Orlo Williams four days earlier.

The following day Hamilton's Staff received the Naval Orders for the landing, and the naval plan for the control of the Dardanelles. A final up-to-date sketch map of the Turkish field defences in the area from Cape Helles to Achi Baba was being prepared with naval fire-control squaring, and this was lithographed on 20 April:

Gallipoli Peninsula. Z 2012A. Printing Section G.H.Q. Med. Ex. Force. Sketch Plan showing amended results of all Aerial Reconnaissances Corrected to 20th April 1915. Coastline taken from the 1/40,000 map supplied by War Office. Note. In all cases trenches appear to be well traversed. Where guns were noted it is so stated against emplacement.[73]

The reference (symbols) for this map showed fire trenches (square traversed), communication trenches (zig-zag), trees, gun emplacements with number of guns, paths and tents. Many long but isolated lengths of fire trench were shown, as well as many redoubts providing all-round defence on the hills protecting the beaches and on Achi Baba. A similar map was printed for the Anzac Corps, whose Intelligence Staff kept a detailed record of sea and air reconnaissances (including air photography) during April:[74]

13th HMS *Queen*; Turkish positions in Gallipoli Peninsula observed by aircraft (from Intelligence Officer, *Queen*). Information on sketch map.

14th Reconnaissance of West Coast of Gallipoli Peninsula in HMS *Queen*. Information on sketch map. Aeroplane reconnaissance carried out by Intelligence Officer, Anzac. Information entered on sketch map.

15th Aeroplane reports of 14th received from GHQ giving trenches and gun positions on Gallipoli Peninsula.

16th Aeroplane reports of 15th received from GHQ. Marked on map.

19th Air reports received giving further information of enemy's dispositions.

20th Map showing information gained by air reconnaissance up to 18th received from GHQ.

22nd Air reports of 19th and 20th received from GHQ and marked on map.

The importance of intelligence officers themselves going into the air, and of marking reconnaissance results on a master intelligence map, is clear; from this master map, continually updated, the Intelligence Staff prepared duplicated sketch maps which could be issued to the troops. Several problems remained. One was that, viewed from the air, much of the rugged nature of the terrain was lost – it seemed much flatter. Others were the poor quality and non-verticality of the air photos, the lack of accurate map detail against which to plot new information, and the lack of experience in interpreting air photos. All these improved immeasurably over the next few months.

Whatever Hamilton and others may have later claimed about lack of geographical information provided in London, claims refuted by Callwell, Hamilton was well-provided 'in theatre'. Indeed, as more and more topographical information came in from the RNAS and the Navy, it was certainly not the case, as perhaps it had been at an earlier stage, that an inadequate picture of the terrain had been acquired, and it may have been this, as much as the reports of Turkish numbers, defences and dispositions, that were turning Hamilton's formation commanders and intelligence officers, and Commander C R Samson of the RNAS who was regularly over-flying the Peninsula, against the very idea of landing.

Terrain analysis and engineer intelligence

A close examination of the 1877 Reports by Home, Ardagh, Grover, Hare and others would have revealed much about the terrain and resources of the Peninsula, important, as we have seen in Chapter 1, for any military commander. These reports had details of roads (going), water supply and firewood, and contained much information about streams, wells, and the animal and human populations supported by them. Grover's report on a landing on Gallipoli and an attack on the Kilid Bahr and Boukali batteries gave a very good picture of a rough and inhospitable country with bad roads. He made several mentions of streams, swampy meadows and inundations in winter to be encountered on the march upon the Boukali Battery. Seasonal variations were extremely important on the Peninsula; in the winter roads were sloughs; in the summer they gave hard, firm surfaces and the surface of the Salt Lake at Suvla dried out. Much of this information was repeated in the 1905 and 1909 reports.

Terrain. The terrain was well-described in the pre-war reports, maps and charts, and this information was amplified by attaché and consular reports, as well as by agents (Greeks). The 1908 NID (Naval Intelligence) and 1909 War Office Report on the Dardanelles defences, with their subsequent intelligence updates, gave a good appreciation of the difficult terrain and field fortifications. A post-war Naval report (Mitchell Report) giving extracts from these reports noted that: 'The configuration of the land from Nagara to the Entrance to the Straits, with its many hills, ridges and indentations, renders this portion of the Dardanelles particularly well adapted for defence. . .'[75] From late 1914, as we have seen, the Navy was gathering terrain information by visual reconnaissance, and from early 1915 an additional source of terrain intelligence was aerial reconnaissance by seaplane and in April by aerial photography.

Airfield Reconnaissance. An attempt at airfield reconnaissance was made by a landing party at Helles weeks before the main landings. This, and many other examples, show that the naval and military force commanders were well aware of the vital need for air support at all stages of the operations.

Roads, Going and Transport. Pre-war reports and reconnaissances gave a great deal of information about roads and their conditions. Yet General Maxwell told Kitchener about 7–9 March 1915 that there were no roads on the Peninsula, so the 29th Division would have to be supplied with pack animals. In fact there was one metalled road, and the rest were unmade roads and cart tracks, impassable in winter. All this was clearly stated in the 1909 Report which Braithwaite's Staff possessed. The Turks had, of course, been improving certain roads as the invasion threat increased. More up-to-date information was available in the reports of various military attachés, including those of Frederick Cunliffe Owen, and of vice-consuls and, in theatre, from Greek inhabitants. The Turks were improving the main route into the Peninsula, and before the landings the Force had good information on all aspects of roads and transport.

Water Supply. Water supply information was also given in the 1909 report, as it had been in the 1877 report. Even more information was forthcoming from Greek inhabitants. Despite this, it was claimed that little was known about water supply on the Peninsula. According to Hamilton and Aspinall, in March 1915 the War Office asked them, while they were at Alexandria, for such 'good and recent' information, as its only information was the 1905 *Report on Eastern Turkey in Europe* and a report from Admiral Jeffrey stating that village water supplies were 'scanty and polluted, and that the streams dried up quickly after rain'. Aspinall admitted that the 1905 handbook's statement that 'water is generally plentiful in the valleys' was correct and that the fears were groundless, except at Anzac where water supply was always a worry but thorough preparations had been made.[76] During the campaign, and following consultation with the Geological Survey of Great Britain under the direction of Sir Aubrey Strahan, preliminary information was gathered and then Survey geologists, already serving in the Army, were sent to the Dardanelles to study the water supply situation.[77] A great deal of information about water supply was forthcoming in theatre, and

GHQ was able to produce reports on this before the landings. There is, however, a good case for arguing, as Frederick Cunliffe Owen implied, that the CIGS should have instructed the Directorate of Military Operations to pay more attention to these and related points before the war.

The Turkish Land Defences. The post-war Mitchell report,[78] using extracts from the NID 838 and WO 1909 Reports, noted the following:

> Infantry defences in Connection with Coast Batteries.
>   Prepared Defences. . . extensive entrenchments had been prepared on the Kilid Bahr plateau during the war with Italy [1911] to protect the Narrows from land attacks from the west. These were repaired and added to during 1914–15 . . . Similarly the ridges east and south of Kum Kale were entrenched for a step-by-step defence against landing on the Asiatic Coast in the Besika Bay–Kum Kale area.
>   The southern extremity of the Gallipoli Peninsula was not considered favourable for landing attacks, and little had been done in that locality to prepare infantry defences for the protection of the coast batteries beyond the construction of a few fire trenches and small strong-points near possible landing places. Counter-attacks by mobile troops were relied on for local defence.

These comments were in line with those made by Hogarth on the eve of the landing in April 1915.[79]

Since the outbreak of hostilities, the Turks had re-utilised most of their Balkan War entrenchments, dug against the possibility of invasion over the beaches, and added significant new ones. Their plan was to defend the high ground, in particular the Kilid Bahr Plateau, and a discontinuous trench line, facing towards Helles, the Aegean coast (with Gaba Tepe at its centre) and the Maidos Plain, had been created. Amazingly, there were no fortifications across the Maidos Plain itself, a weak point and a major route across the Peninsula, so a force landing near Gaba Tepe could, in theory, rapidly push right across to the Dardanelles north of Maidos. Nor was Mal Tepe, the high point of a ridge east of the Maidos neck and a component of the Kilid Bahr Plateau, fortified. That said, any force landing at Helles or Gaba Tepe would come under fire from the infantry and artillery of the Turkish garrison holding this defended high ground, and would also be subject to attack by mobile forces which were kept back for just such counter-attacks. Trenches were also dug by the Turks to command the possible landing beaches, some of which were also covered by machine guns, pom-poms and mobile field artillery batteries.[80]

As we have seen, most of the trenches had been discovered by British sea and air reconnaissance (including air photography), and plotted on successively updated lithographed intelligence maps issued by GHQ and used by the Navy for fire control. However, poor communications and staff work prevented some information from getting to the troops concerned. Visual observation, communicated by *Queen Elizabeth* to GHQ on 23 April, determined that there was an unwired, though probably mined, sixty yard gap at the west end of W Beach (north of Cape Helles), and also the feasibility of a small number of boats landing men below the cliffs north-west of W Beach towards Cape Tekke. GHQ passed this information on the same day to 29th Division, but Brig.-General Hare's 86th Brigade, tasked with landing the covering force on the Helles beaches, never received it.[81]

The weather was an unknown quantity and, as on D-Day twenty-nine years later, threatened to disrupt or even wreck the landings. De Robeck, responsible for giving the word 'go', had to make this decision thirty-six hours before the landing date in order to allow time for the whole complex assault apparatus to function, and luckily read the weather correctly and gave the order on the morning of 23 April. The intelligence picture built up as regards roads, transport and water supply proved to be substantially correct,[82] but less was known about the dispositions of the Turkish divisions on the Peninsula and the Asiatic Shore, and nothing about the way in which those troops would be deployed and used when the landing forces assaulted the beaches. As commonly happens before contact is made with enemy land forces, the enemy's strengths and dispositions were hidden in the fog of war. The view prevailing in Medforce, based on a mass of accumulated intelligence, was that the Turks were too strong, but this did not prevent Hamilton and de Robeck from launching the assault on 25 April.

Hamilton's plan, operation orders and instructions for the 25 April landings

At the heart of the failure of the operations were three elements: numerical weakness, vague orders and, according to Aspinall, lack of initiative and leadership.[83] The first was the one that tipped the balance, the second might have led to failure even if the first had not applied, while the third meant that the successful landings at Helles were not exploited. The assault force was simply not strong enough to deal with a determined Turkish opposition; it should have been numerically stronger by a factor of two or three. As had been found on the Western Front, a well-entrenched enemy armed with magazine rifles could destroy a much larger force attacking across the open. It was not even necessary to have machine guns, although these would clearly help, as would barbed wire and other obstacles. The obverse of numerical weakness was the strength and leadership of the Turkish forces, and to these must be applied a 'terrain multiplier', the value of terrain in magnifying the efforts of the defender.

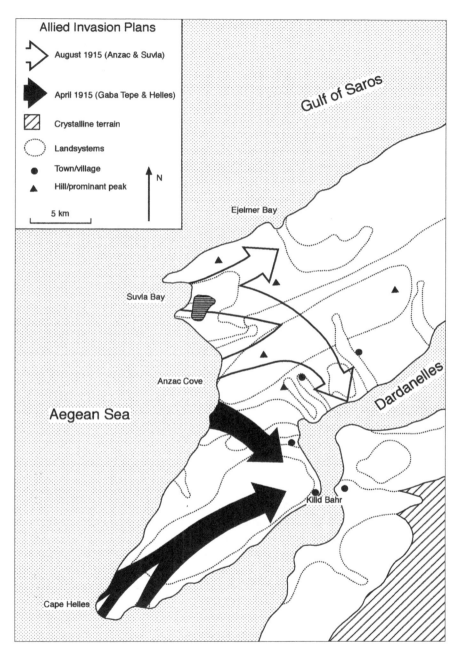

Allied invasion plans, 1915

Kitchener's instructions to Hamilton on 13 March made it clear that large-scale military operations were envisaged if the fleet failed to get through the Dardanelles aided by only minor operations. Kitchener saw the landings on the Peninsula as only the preliminary to large-scale operations in the Constantinople area in collaboration with the Russians, including the creation of an entrenched bridgehead on the Asian side of the Bosphorus. Although he stated that it was 'undesirable to land any permanent garrison or hold any lines on the Gallipoli Peninsula', in the next sentence he contradicted this by saying that: 'Probably an entrenched force will be required to retain the Turkish forces in the Peninsula and prevent reinforcements arriving at Bulair, and this force would naturally be supported on both flanks by gun-fire from the Fleet.'[84] Thus Kitchener appears either to have been suggesting the necessity of capturing and holding both the Kilid Bahr Plateau and the Bulair Lines, or at the least the latter. In his verbal instructions to Hamilton the previous day, he had emphasised the importance of capturing the Kilid Bahr Plateau and thus dominating the forts at the Narrows.

Hamilton's Force Order No.1 (dated 13 April 1915) for the landings made on the 25th was singularly lacking in both strategic and operational clarity, and little idea was given of the supreme importance of thrusting rapidly across the Peninsula from Gaba Tepe to Maidos in order to capture the Kilid Bahr Plateau (Grover's plan of 1877 and Ardagh's of 1880, and the main component of the Greek plan) and cut off the retreat of Turkish forces in the Helles area. After the war Hamilton admitted that he should have given much more weight to this crucial thrust, and landed troops on the good beaches south of Gaba Tepe.[85] In fact he regarded the push across the Peninsula to capture Mal Tepe as the easier of the two operations (the other being the Helles landing and push to Achi Baba), which is why he assigned it to the Anzacs. The only regular division he had, the 29th, was assigned to the Helles landings which Hamilton regarded as the crucial part of the whole operation.

By this time the idea of landings at Bulair had been abandoned, the area being too heavily defended, and he gave the aim ('object') of the Expedition as being 'to assist the fleet to force the Dardanelles by capturing the Kilid Bahr plateau, and dominating the forts at the Narrows'.[86] However, he did not concentrate his force to achieve this. Hamilton's command was scattered around the Peninsula from Kum Kale (French force) on the Asiatic Shore of the mouth of the Dardanelles to the north side of the Peninsula at Bulair (where the Royal Naval Division (RND) made an unconvincing feint). Concentration of force was not, therefore, achieved at the critical points of Helles (29th Division) and Gaba Tepe (Anzac Corps). While it was proper that diversions should be made, the form they took entailed a useless tying-up of manpower which would have tipped the balance elsewhere. Unfortunately it had been decided that the beaches at Helles were too restricted to land the RND simultaneously with the 29th Division. Had the RND been landed instead at Gaba Tepe or Suvla, simultaneously with the main landings, it could have joined forces with the Anzacs and together they could have cut across to Maidos.

Nor did the orders and instructions to the 29th Division and Anzac Corps emphasise the importance of capturing the Kilid Bahr Plateau. However, an Enclosure to 29th Division Operation Order No. 1 reiterated Hamilton's 'Object of the Expedition' given in Force Order No. 1 on 13 April, and clearly stated: 'The task of the 29th Division is the attack of the Kilid Bahr plateau from the south.' But in a concluding statement of 'the lines to be gained successively', the final line given ('the occupation and fortification of a line running east from Achi Baba to the sea about level 300, and west from Achi Baba via hill 472 to the sea') was one running from north-west to south-east across the Peninsula, with Achi Baba at its centre – miles short of the Kilid Bahr plateau.[87] A 'Secret Memorandum on Artillery Cooperation between HM Ships and 29th Division' gave the 'Final objective for 1st day – Line through Achi Baba Peak. Level 650 [in fact 600] – Halar – Achi Baba Peak – level 472. Flanks resting on sea.'[88] No mention was made in either of these instructions of pushing on to capture the Kilid Bahr Plateau. Thus formation and unit commanders could perhaps be forgiven for not clearly understanding this main imperative. There is evidence of poor staff work in the contradictory and incorrect map references provided. Again, orders were vague, despite the spot-heights and other features clearly shown and named on the 1:40,000 map.

Summary

To summarise, the Anzac Corps was directed to capture Mal Tepe, cutting off the Turkish defenders of the southern part of the Peninsula, including the Kilid Bahr Plateau, and denying them any reinforcements, but it was not ordered to push right across the Peninsula to the Straits. The 29th Division was initially to capture a line, with Achi Baba in its centre, across the Peninsula; the next stage would be to capture the Plateau and neutralise the forts so that the Navy could go through. The aim would, of course, have been made clear to General Hunter-Weston in the course of personal meetings with Hamilton and Braithwaite. Perhaps it was hoped that the success of the Anzac thrust, and the threat of the 29th Division's landing at Helles, would force a Turkish withdrawal, in which case it would not be necessary to storm the fortified Kilid Bahr Plateau. But would the Turks give up their 'fortress' so easily?

The objectives of the weak covering forces were given vaguely in the following terms; for the single brigade and RE field company of the Anzac Corps's covering force: 'At Gaba Tepe a covering position on the south-western spurs of the hill in squares 224-237-238 (WO Map Sari Bair)', and for the single brigade, plus a battalion and a field company, of the 29th Division: 'At Cape Helles the Achi Baba ridge'. Once the covering forces were ashore, the main bodies would land immediately. Hamilton also held the Plymouth Battalion of the Royal Marines ready to land at Y Beach, from where it could head across the Peninsula to cut any Turkish retreat from Helles and prevent reinforcements arriving from Krithia. Formations ashore would then assemble clear of the beaches, before moving to forming-up places and rendezvous designated by staff officers landed with the covering forces.

Beyond this, Hamilton's initial Force Order gave no further instructions regarding operations subsequent to the landings. It was almost as if the landings in themselves were considered sufficient. However, also on 13 April, GHQ issued the 'Instructions for Helles Covering Force' and 'Instructions to G.O.C. A. & N.Z. Army Corps.' The former were subsequently replaced by a new set of Instructions on 19 April. The 29th Division Covering Force was to be landed at Beaches S (Eski Hissarlik Point; De Tott's Battery), V (Sedd el Bahr – Cape Helles), W (Cape Helles – Tekke Burnu), X (Sq. 168Q.8 – just north of Tekke Burnu) and Y (point to be selected between Square 175.P. and Square 175.X – just north of the mouth of Gully Ravine), and was given the clear objective 'the ridge across the Peninsula, point 344 (Sq. 170.d.) [Tener Chift Knoll] – Achi Baba peak – 472 [Yazy Tepe] – coast line (Sq. 184) [Aegean coast].'[89] This line was less than halfway to the Kilid Bahr Plateau. No further instructions as to operations were given, but the implication was that once the main force was ashore it would advance to the final objective, which was not, however, clearly given.

The instructions to the Anzac Corps stated their objective as 'the ridge over which the Gallipoli–Maidos and Boghali–Kojadere roads run, especially Mal Tepe. Gaining such a position the Army Corps will threaten, and perhaps cut, the line of retreat of the enemy's forces on the Kilid Bahr plateau, and must, even by their preliminary operations, prevent the said plateau being reinforced, during the attack of the 29th Division, from Maidos, Gallipoli or Bulair.' Under the heading 'Topography,' the instructions stated:

> The first essential for the covering force will be to establish itself on the hill in Squares 224, 237 and 238 (Sari Bair on the War Office map) in order to protect the landing of the remainder of the Army Corps. From the ridge between squares 237.Z and 224.F spurs run north-west and south-west to the sea. This semicircular system of ridges seems to lend itself to the establishment of a strong covering position. Whether it will be necessary or not to include the crest of the mountain must be left to your discretion.

The 'General plan of operation of the Army Corps' was then to make a further crucial advance:

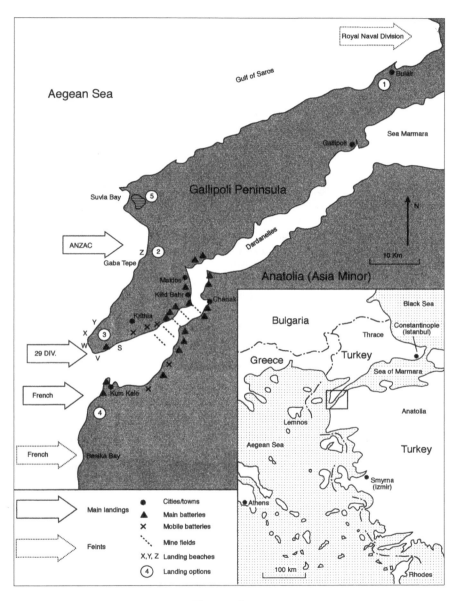

The Landings

Leaving the covering force to protect the northern flank of the landing place and line of communication, an effort will be made to storm Mal Tepe [four miles from the landing beach] which is the centre and key to the ridge over which the Gallipoli–Maidos and Boghali–Kojadere roads run. Should the A. & N.Z. Army Corps succeed in securing this ridge the results should be more vital and valuable than the capture of the Kilid Bahr plateau itself.[90]

In fact, the capture of Mal Tepe and a small further advance south to the Dardanelles north of Maidos would, provided the line could be held against attacks from both directions, automatically entail the cutting off of the Turkish forces in the Helles area and the capture of the Kilid Bahr Plateau. Again, the wording of the instructions was strangely lacking in imperative direction and clarity. Birdwood undoubtedly understood what was required of him, but simply did not have a large enough force to achieve it, particularly after landing too far to the north and getting too entangled in the tortuous ravines and gullies of the Sari Bair foothills. Had the Royal Naval Division also been available to land at Suvla or Gaba Tepe, it might have been a very different story. The terrain (see Chapter 1) lent itself greatly to a rapid push across the narrow part of the Peninsula running from Gaba Tepe to Maidos, as envisaged by Grover in 1877 and by the Greeks, and there seems no reason why, with determination and a clear plan, this could not have been achieved. This, after all, was the essence of the earlier Anglo-Greek plan.

Conclusion

Looking at the quantity and type of intelligence material in the hands of Hamilton's Force at the time of the landings, there can be no doubt that it was not bad maps or a lack of terrain intelligence which stymied the operation, but a poor plan and the sturdy fighting qualities of the Turkish soldiers. The British covering forces got ashore and, at Helles at least, initially defeated the opposition. Then a pall of exhaustion, uncertainty and inertia fell over the battlefield. Battle-shocked soldiers, their leaders having become casualties, went to ground when they should have been pushing forward. It was not the fault of the maps or lack of terrain intelligence.

Could more have been done to identify Turkish forces and dispositions? The British air survey effort in April 1915, though providing vital intelligence, was extremely rudimentary. It will be emphasised in Chapter 7 that the British lagged behind the Germans and Austrians in air survey; peacetime reconnaissance or survey flights had not been undertaken as no suitable air cameras had yet been developed by the British (despite decades of experiments), and no airships and few aeroplanes were in theatre. Air photo reconnaissance had only just been started in the RFC and RNAS in 1913–14, particularly by Victor Laws and the Watson camera in the Beta airship and later in an aeroplane. This prototype camera was most unfortunately badly damaged on the eve of the war when the aircraft in which it was mounted crashed on landing. With the primitive photographic equipment available in April 1915 at the Dardanelles, and even had Hamilton's force been equipped with more and better aeroplanes and with the new A-camera, it is extremely unlikely that, in such difficult terrain, Turkish troops and movements could have been identified, particularly as they were quite mobile and moved (often at night) in relatively small detachments. In France and Flanders, troop movements were identified in 1914 by long dark corps and divisional columns marching along dusty white roads, and by train movements. Neither of these applied to the Peninsula. Hidden among trees, olive groves, orchards and scrub, and in the shadow of ravines and gullies, companies, battalions and batteries could remain concealed and, except at times of emergency, move only under cover of darkness.

In the next chapter we look at the maps provided for the Allied forces in the run-up to the landings, and examine their sources and fitness-for-purpose.

Notes

1. Chasseaud, Peter, 'Mapping for D-Day: The Allied Landings in Normandy, 6 June 1944', *The Cartographic Journal*, London, 38(2), pp. 177–89.
2. Ibid.
3. Pritchard, Maj.-Gen. H L, *The History of the Corps of Royal Engineers*, Vol. VI, Chatham: Institution of Royal Engineers, 1952, p. 15.
4. Nasr, Seyyed Hossein, *Islamic Science*, London: World of Islam Festival Publishing Co., 1976, pp. 27–48.
5. War Office (1944), *Notes on Maps of the Balkans*, July 1944, Confidential, Directorate of Military Survey, London, p. 40.
6. Anon. (probably Col. Mehemmed Shevki Pasha), 'The Topographical Service in the Ottoman Empire and the Modern Turkish Cartography', *L'Universo*, No. 1, 1920, pp. 127–36.
7. Ibid.
8. Ibid.
9. *Planheft Südosteuropa, Südlicher Teil, 1 Juli 1943* (German Military Survey), Berlin, given in War Office (1944), *Notes on Maps . . .*, op. cit.
10. MI4 (1924), *Latitudes of the Turkish Mapping System*, typescript note by MI4, dated 8/8/1924, in MCE, RE.
11. *Plates to Accompany the Military report on Eastern Turkey in Europe and the Ismid Peninsula [General Staff, War Office, London] (Second Edition, 1909). (B414) 200 6/09 H & S 454-2WO.* Foolscap, buff thin card folder; maps, plans and photographs covering Constantinople, Central Plains (Adrianople, etc.), Istranja Balkan District, The Eastern Rhodope District. TNA(PRO) FO 881/9513X.
12. Col. Mike Nolan, in his unpublished notes '1907–1917 – The Golden Years in the Development of Cartography in the Ottoman Empire' (2000), states 'printed between 1910 and 1911 or 1913–1914'.

13. Dowson, E M, *Mapping from Aeroplane Photographs in Gallipoli*, Secret, duplicated typescript report with maps and photos, Survey of Egypt, *c*.Sep 1915, p. 3.
14. MI4, op. cit.
15. Anon, op. cit.
16. VA11 War Diary, Bayerisch Hauptstaatsarchiv, Kriegsarchiv, Munich.
17. See Chasseaud, Peter, *Artillery's Astrologers – A History of British Survey and Mapping on the Western Front 1914–1918*, Lewes: Mapbooks, 1999 for artillery survey in the period before and during the First World War.
18. Two copies are held in the Australian War Memorial collection.
19. Copy in Australian War Memorial; photograph of this in TNA(PRO) WO 153/1058.
20. Cunninghame, Minutes of Evidence to the Dardanelles Commission, p. 1155, TNA(PRO) CAB 19/33.
21. Sheets J8 (Kuchuk Keui), J10 (Hissarlar), K10 (Chamlija), L10 (Maltepe and Islands), in TNA(PRO) WO 301 pieces 171, 177, 187, 192, respectively.
22. F Cunliffe Owen to The Secretary, Army Council, 27-9-1927, in IWM Department of Documents.
23. A 1:100,000 contoured sheet in TNA(PRO) WO 153/1058 has no graticule; it carries a 1915 print date.
24. Anon., op. cit.
25. Nicholas to Hedley, TNA(PRO) WO 301/46.
26. In TNA(PRO) WO 153 and WO 301.
27. Anon., op, cit.
28. In *Report from Major R.H. Phillimore, R.E. (8th Field Survey Co., R.E.) on Turkish Staff Maps 1:25,000 and 1: 5,000 of Gallipoli and Chanak Kale, with list of Conventional Signs Employed. 20/2/1919. DGCD. 30, 3(4).*
29. Nicholas to Hedley, 8 May 1915, in TNA(PRO) WO 301/46.
30. TNA(PRO) WO 153/1055.
31. War Office (July 1944), *Notes on Maps of the Balkans*, op. cit.; *Planheft Südosteuropa*, op. cit., and other sources.
32. TNA(PRO) WO 153/1058.
33. MI4 (1924), op. cit.
34. *Carte de la Presqu'Ile de Gallipoli* (in two sheets); published in 1854 by the Dépôt de la Guerre, Paris, under the direction of Colonel Blondel (engraved by Erhard, 42 rue Bonaparte), printed Chez Kaeppelin, Quai Voltaire.
35. *Reports and Memoranda relative to Defence of Constantinople and other positions in Turkey. Also on Routes in Roumelia. Strictly Confidential, Printed at the War Office by Harrison & Sons. 1877. [0631] 103 WO.* TNA(PRO) FO 358/1; FO 881/3676; WO 33/29.
36. Memorandum on the Passage of the Dardanelles by Major J C Ardagh RE, in Paper No. 797, *Seizure of the Dardanelles as a means of coercing the Porte*, War Office, 1880, in TNA(PRO) WO 33/35.
37. *Reports and Memoranda*, op. cit.
38. *The Dardanelles Commission 1914–16*, London: The Stationery Office, 2001, p. 118.
39. Callwell, Maj.-Gen. Sir C E, *The Dardanelles*, London: Constable, 1919 (2nd edn 1924), pp. 47–8.
40. *Catalogue of Maps Published by the Geographical Section of the General Staff*, War Office, London, 1923, p. 7.
41. Gallipoli Campaign 1915, Maps, TNA(PRO) WO 301/473.

42. Close, Col. C F and Cox, Capt. E W, *Text Book of Topographical Surveying*, 2nd edn, London: HMSO, 1913, p. 183.
43. Ibid, p. 180.
44. Hamilton, Sir Ian, *A Staff Officer's Scrap Book During the Russo–Japanese War*, 2 vols, London: Edward Arnold, 1905.
45. Jones, H J, *The War in the Air*, Vol. II, London: OUP, 1928, p. 2.
46. Gallipoli Campaign maps in TNA(PRO) WO 153 and WO 301.
47. Bullen, John, List of Maps of Gallipoli Campaign, n.d., in the Australian War Memorial, Gallipoli, Vol. I, p. 8.
48. Travers, Tim, *Gallipoli 1915*, Stroud: Tempus, 2002, p. 68.
49. De Robeck to Churchill, 5 May 1915, 13/65, Chartwell Papers, Churchill College, Cambridge.
50. Diary and papers of General C Cunliffe Owen, p. 18. TNA(PRO) CAB 45/246.
51. Ibid, p. 19.
52. Ibid, Extracts from a lecture on Artillery at Anzac, given at the R.A. Institution by Brig. Gen. C. Cunliffe Owen, p. 1.
53. Dowson, E M, 'Further Notes on Aeroplane Photography in the Near East' *Geographical Journal*, 58, 1921, p. 359.
54. Moorhead, Alan, *Gallipoli*, London: Hamish Hamilton, Four Square edn, 1963, p. 108.
55. Author's study of Sheets 1, 2 and 3.
56. Ibid.
57. Dowson, 'Further Notes . . .', op. cit.
58. Royal Naval Division misc. correspondence & arrangements for embarkation 1915, p. 39, PRO ADM 137/3088A.
59. Anzac Corps General Staff War Diary, TNA(PRO) WO 95/4280.
60. Secretary, War Office, London to GOC-in-C, Egypt, rec'd 9/3/15, in TNA(PRO) WO 158/574.
61. Ibid.
62. Hickey, Michael, *Gallipoli*, London: John Murray, 1998, p. 58.
63. Diary of Brig.-Gen. S W Hare, GOC 86th Brigade, 29th Division.
64. Anzac Corps General Staff War Diary, op. cit., referring to 'Copy of W.O. Cablegram 4008 (recd 9th) – re maps'.
65. Anzac General Staff War Diary, op. cit.
66. Lt-Col. Ward, Mudros, Lemnos to Maps Officer, W.O. , recd 10/4/15, in TNA(PRO) WO 158/574.
67. Secretary, War Office, London to Director of Intelligence, Cairo, recd 10/4/15, in TNA(PRO) WO 158/574.
68. Col. Ward [GHQ Mudros] to Int. Dept Maps Section [Cairo], recd 13/4/15, in TNA(PRO) WO 158/574.
69. Secretary, War Office, London to Director of Intelligence [Cairo], recd 17/4/15, in TNA(PRO) WO 158/574.
70. Royal Naval Division, General Staff, War Diary, TNA(PRO) WO 95/4290.
71. Anzac Corps, Intelligence War Diary, TNA(PRO) WO 157/678, Appendix Z12.
72. TNA(PRO) WO 301/499-503, Gallipoli Campaign 1915, maps.
73. Anzac Corps, Intelligence War Diary, in TNA(PRO) WO 157/668 & 678.
74. Anzac Corps Intelligence War Diary, in TNA(PRO) WO 157/668.

75. [Mitchell Report] *C.B. 1550 Report of the Committee Appointed to Investigate the Attacks delivered on and the Enemy Defences of the Dardanelles Straits, 1919. Admiralty, Naval Staff, Gunnery Division, April 1921*, pp. 5–18. TNA(PRO) ADM 186/600.
76. Aspinall-Oglander, op. cit., pp. 121–2.
77. Strahan, A, *Summary of Progress of the Geological Survey and Museum for 1918*, HMSO, p. 3. The Survey geologists were C H Cunningham (Lt, Machine Gun Corps, died of wounds 1918), R W Pocock (Lt, Royal Garrison Artillery) and T H Whitehead (Capt., Suffolk Regiment).
78. Mitchell Report, op. cit.
79. Hogarth, D G, 'Geography of the War Theatre in the Near East', *Geographical Journal*, June 1915, 45(6), pp. 457–71.
80. Turkish historian Kenan Celik, on the basis of Turkish official accounts, holds that machine guns were not deployed in any great numbers on the beaches.
81. Aspinall-Oglander, op. cit., p. 142.
82. Ibid, pp. 121–2, 142, 149–50.
83. Ibid, p. 234.
84. Ibid, Maps & Appendices: Appendix 1.
85. Rhodes James, Robert, *Gallipoli*, London: Pimlico, 1999, p. 86.
86. Aspinall-Oglander, op. cit., Maps & Appendices: Appendix 3.
87. Ibid, Appendix 17.
88. 29th Division General Staff War Diary, op. cit.
89. Aspinall-Oglander, op. cit., Maps & Appendices: Appendix 4.
90. Anzac Corps General Staff War Diary, TNA(PRO) WO 95/4280; Aspinall-Oglander, op. cit., Maps & Appendices: Appendix 5.

CHAPTER 6

The First Operations Maps

Just as it has been generally accepted without query that the intelligence material supplied to Medforce was totally inadequate, it has been taken for granted in the literature on the Dardanelles Campaign that the maps were inaccurate and inadequate. In this chapter the mapping situation is examined, and it is suggested that the evidence is such that the War Office can at least be partly exonerated.

The maps, plans and operation orders for the first landings, April 1915

What was this map used at Gallipoli in 1915 which came in for so much criticism? The assault map, at the 1:40,000 scale (about 1¼ inches to the mile), was an enlargement of the 1908 one-inch War Office map produced by the Geographical Section of the General Staff (GSGS, or MO4) under the direction of Colonel Charles Close. This was derived from the French 1:50,000 survey of 1854. That much is incontrovertible, but why was this apparently unremarkable map the subject of so much ire? First and foremost, it was a scapegoat, blamed when the operations failed to make progress. Had the landing forces managed to overcome the opposition and rush forward those crucial four miles to Maidos and past Achi Baba, securing the Kilid Bahr Plateau and permitting the Fleet to at least attempt to pass the Narrows, little or nothing would have been heard of the inadequacies of the map (until the army was perhaps held up farther on). That much is clear.

Several points should be borne in mind. Most of Europe was already fairly well mapped, but Turkey was not. When the armies of Germany, France, Britain and Russia went to war in August 1914 they did so with small-scale maps. Their standard operations maps were copies of the national surveys of the countries in which they were planning to operate – the 1:80,000 map of France, 1:60,000 and 1:100,000 maps of Belgium, 1:100,000 maps of Russia, and so on. Many of these maps, particularly the French 1:80,000, were from old and relatively inaccurate surveys, and gave a poor impression of relief. In no case had they been revised from air photos, for the simple reason that air survey was in its infancy, and in fact had not yet emerged from its experimental stage. The resources and technology were not in place.

The British map of the Gallipoli Peninsula fell into this category, and in fact the French map on which it was based had been surveyed using techniques similar to those used for the French 1:80,000 General Staff map in the mid-19th century. No large-scale regular survey of the Peninsula was made until the eve of the war, and this by the Turks, the resulting maps only being issued to the troops just before operations began. They were, therefore, denied to the Allies until sheets were captured after the landings on 25 April 1915. The Allies cannot, therefore, be blamed for not possessing what was not yet available. Only an agent in place within the survey department in Constantinople would have been able to obtain the required material. We do not know whether the British, French, Russians or Greeks had such an agent, or whether attempts were made by military attachés or Secret Service bureaux to obtain such material. The Greeks would have been most likely to have obtained it, as their General Staff had been planning an attack on the Peninsula for several years.

When serious planning for the D-Day operations began in 1943, most of the intended area of operations was covered by an inaccurate, small-scale, out-of-date, map (the French 1:80,000 mentioned above), and a massive air survey effort, involving thousands of photographic sorties and the use of some of the most modern photogrammetric resources, had to be launched in order to provide the planners and invasion forces with an accurate, large-scale map suitable for fire-support, and for artillery work subsequent to the landing.[1]

The question of purpose is crucial when assessing whether a map is appropriate for its task. In 1944, as a result of the experience of Gallipoli and earlier Second World War amphibious operations, assault maps were prepared at the large scale of 1:12,500 covering the approaches to the beaches, the beaches themselves and the country inland, overprinted with detailed intelligence as to the enemy defences, and including information about beach gradients, underwater obstacles, going, and so forth. Similar maps were also prepared at 1:25,000, covering the whole operational area, and also gridded topographical maps at 1:50,000, 1:100,000 and 1:250,000.[2]

In early 1915, however, no preparations had been made for a large-scale opposed landing, as this had not been envisaged before the war. Although combined studies had been undertaken, reports written, and the subject included in the Staff College curriculum, there had been no combined amphibious operational planning or rehearsals; the War Office and Admiralty had simply not forseen the necessity for such a combined planning staff, although they cooperated closely when it came to intelligence gathering and dissemination, and in any case inter-service jealousies would have rendered it difficult to achieve. Nor was there any consideration of the potential of the embryonic techniques of aerial photogrammetry as aids to the preparation of assault mapping. This was not the case in other countries – the Austrians and Germans were notably ahead in their experiments with air survey, as we shall see in Chapter 7, the Germans even advocating a 'survey airship' of the Zeppelin type for colonial surveys. At the outbreak of war, aeroplanes were generally considered to generate too much vibration to be used as camera platforms. Effective dampening mountings were arrived at by experimentation during the early months of 1915. Until then, air cameras were normally hand-held.

Mapping for the Gallipoli Campaign has had a very bad press, though its reputation has more recently been at least partially salvaged by Colonel Mike Nolan RE, whose series of articles in the *Gallipolian* served as a much needed corrective but did not, unfortunately, reach a wide enough audience. The *History of the Corps of Royal Engineers*,[3] taking its cue from Aspinall-Oglander's Official History, stated: 'The only map of Gallipoli available for use during the attack was a one-inch [1:63,360] compilation made by the Geographical Section. From the nature of the case it was not reliable, and its inaccuracies caused many difficulties.' This chapter examines the maps available before the landings, and evaluates them in the light of contemporary and subsequent criticisms.

Existing Turkish maps and surveys

The mathematicians, astronomers, geodesists, navigators and instrument makers of the Islamic world were at one time world-leaders in their field.[4] However, a different pattern of technological and economic development from the European model meant that modern land survey techniques took longer to become established there. Theodolites first appeared on Ottoman territory in the hands of European explorers, map-makers and surveyors, and the arrival of the European railway companies in the 19th century – the railways from Salonika and Sofia to Constantinople were built and operated by German, Austrian, French and Belgian companies – created a further impetus for the use of modern survey methods, at least in great engineering works. The arrival on the scene of modern artillery in the late 19th century, together with continuing European encroachment on 'the sick man of Europe', meant that, like the European powers, the Ottoman Empire had to inaugurate a large-scale survey for defence purposes. No definitive history has yet been written of the Turkish Military Survey, and in the various sources available the facts and dates disagree.

The French Crimean War survey of the Gallipoli Peninsula, in two sheets dated 1854, remained the only large-scale survey of the whole

Peninsula up to the eve of the First World War. Austrian, Russian and Turkish small-scale General Staff maps of the Balkans, Dardanelles, Constantinople and Bosphorus areas were produced during the 19th and early 20th centuries. Russian surveys covered Turkey in Europe, including the Gallipoli Peninsula, and were used to produce various Russian maps at 1:42,000, 1:84,000 and 1:126,000;[5] although the ground surveys may have been executed at the larger scales, the final printed sheets covering the Peninsula appear to have been at 1:126,000. Smaller-scale maps were mainly German and Austrian productions; e.g. Kiepert's 1:400,000 *Karte von Kleinasien*, and Philippson's derived 1:300,000 *Topographische Karte des westlichen Kleinasien*.

The French helped the Turkish General Staff to set up their Military Mapping Department in 1895. Prior to this, Turkish officers had travelled to Paris for training at the École de Guerre and the Service Géographique de l'Armée, returning to Constantinople in 1892. The role of this new department was to initiate regular surveys and create maps covering the extensive Ottoman Empire.[6] The first regular survey was constructed on a base measured at Eski-Shehr in Anatolia, leading to a 1:50,000 map of the town and environs being completed by 1894.[7] Increasing German influence led to the French officers, General Defforges and Captain Barisien, who had been assisting the Turks to inaugurate their first regular survey, leaving the country around 1895,[8] although French influence in the Turkish survey appears to have continued for some time. The French therefore had access to a certain amount of Turkish survey data and cartographic products, some (subsequent to their 1854 survey) possibly relating to the Gallipoli Peninsula. Presumably, on the basis of their new knowledge and with German assistance, the Turks continued to make local defence surveys on a limited basis, and it is probable that part of the Dardanelles area was surveyed at this time. One German source gives 1902 as the year of the start of 1:25,000 mapping in Turkey, and describes it as 'Turkish survey (with French assistance)'.[9]

The training of a large Turkish cartographic staff started surprisingly late, in 1904, with the institution of a two-year course in map drawing, followed by training in topography, the latter to culminate in practical fieldwork exercises. Clearly no regular surveys could begin, and maps be drawn, by the Turks themselves as opposed to foreign officers and men, until the Turks had built up their own cadre of technical operatives. In 1906, after a period of little or no progress, and even regression, a fresh start was made under Colonel Mehemmed Shevki Pasha, one of those who had trained in Paris, using a Bonne projection whose central meridian ran through the crescent on the dome of the mosque of Ayia Sophia (the old Byzantine basilica of St Sofia) in Constantinople. This meridian was adopted for all Turkish mapping in 1909. In 1907 the drawing of the 1:25,000 map of the Constantinople area was begun. The intention was that European Turkey should be surveyed at 1:25,000, and Anatolia at

1:50,000; though both agreed on the central meridian, they adopted different latitudes, so the surveys could not initially be joined.[10]

A 1:25,000 contoured plan was made of Adrianople and its defences, which the British (who had a 'military consul' there – Captain Townshend in 1905) managed to obtain and reproduce in 1909 for their *Military Report on Eastern Turkey in Europe and the Ismid Peninsula*.[11] This date is rather earlier than those of 1910–11 or 1913–14 given by some authorities for the printing of the 1:25,000 sheets of the Adrianople area.[12] In six weeks in 1912 the Balkan League practically wiped out Turkey-in-Europe. The Greeks captured Salonika and the Serbs were victorious at Kumanova, while the Bulgarians defeated the Ottoman armies in Thrace (at Kirk-Kilisse and Lule Burgas) and pushed them back to the Chatalja Lines. Adrianople was captured by the Serbs and Bulgarians in renewed fighting during the London Peace Conference, and the Treaty of London (30 May 1913) restricted Turkey-in-Europe to little more than Constantinople and Gallipoli. In the Second Balkan War, Bulgaria attacked her recent allies, but was defeated by Serbia and Greece, assisted by Rumania, and Turkey took advantage of this situation to regain Adrianople (Treaty of Bucharest, August 1913). Clearly, in this chaotic military situation, Turkish surveys in the European part of the empire could not continue.

The 'Young Turk' revolution of 1908 may have given an impetus to Turkish surveys, but the direct threats of the Italian (1911) and Balkan (1912–13) Wars certainly seem to have accelerated their execution. German survey practice, rather than French, gradually became the model. In 1911 a new base, over three kilometres long, was measured 'to the east of the military hospital' at Chanak for a second 1:25,000 survey of the Straits. There was an earlier, independent, 1:25,000 survey, covering the west end of the Peninsula, apparently preceded by a 1:20,000 survey, so presumably at least one earlier base had been measured.

This new (second 1:25,000) survey of the Dardanelles, apparently executed in 1912 and 1913, covered the whole of the Gallipoli Peninsula and the Asiatic Shore although the disturbed conditions of the Balkan Wars, and later the First World War, rendered impossible the careful execution of a systematic geodetic survey; what was produced was more in the nature of a high-quality reconnaissance survey (based on a triangulation). The fear of invasion during the Balkan Wars caused an acceleration of the Straits survey, and eight sheets were completed of the south-west end of the Gallipoli Peninsula, the Narrows and Chanak and the Asiatic coast of the Aegean and Dardanelles. These were soon followed by others. The regular 1:25,000 survey of the Gallipoli Peninsula also formed the base for smaller-scale maps, being reduced by the Turks to 1:50,000 and 1:100,000 by 1915.[13]

According to Lt-Col. Wood, OC 8th Field Survey Company RE, who checked the sheets in 1918–19, the 1:25,000 survey was of the highest order. However, a British report dated 22 September 1915 noted that though 'the main outline . . . has proved to be very good . . . the contours are not up to much and the coastline is badly out in places'.[14] The map was only tested, however, within a small area. A British 1924 report stated that the sheets represented. 'a good reconnaissance survey, similar to the Ismid 1/50,000 but not of so high an order as the Constantinople and Chatalja 1/25,000. . . . The 1st Corps Survey Platoon in 1923, however, could find little in it to quarrel with.'[15]

In 1914 a map reproduction and printing office was set up in Constantinople, equipped with material acquired from Vienna and Berlin, and in 1914–15 two Turkish topographical officers were sent to these cities to learn the techniques of terrestrial stereophotogrammetry[16] (a survey technique which the British, notably Lt F V Thompson RE, had experimented with before the war, but which they did not use during the war) which the Germans and Austrians had pushed forward rapidly, being particularly suited to mountainous areas where plane-tabling was difficult. The German survey of the route of the Berlin–Baghdad Railway through the Taurus Mountains was made in this way. German photogrammetric technicians, experienced in plotting alpine terrain from co-planar photos, also travelled to Turkey; on 30 January 1916 two *Feldphotogrammeters* of Bavarian *Vermessungsabteilung* (Survey Company) 11, a unit with their 6th Army in France, were working in Constantinople.[17]

Turkish maps in Allied hands

A crucial – and unresolved – question is how long before the war large-scale maps of the Gallipoli Peninsula, the Dardanelles and the Asiatic Shore were surveyed, drawn and printed, and why copies were not acquired by the Allies? Given the rearming of some of the Straits' forts and batteries with modern Krupp guns in the early 20th century, it is probable that at least a local coast defence survey was executed to tie together guns, range-finders, searchlights, etc., for fire control purposes. A further reason, and one closely related to the development of fortress *plans directeurs*, artillery maps, and trench maps before and during the First World War, was that the mobile howitzer batteries defending the Straits' minefields were intended to fire 'indirect', i.e. to fire from defiladed positions, depending on survey for their line and range and on observation from a crest or flank for correction of fire. These batteries would have to shift position frequently to avoid being located and neutralised by air-directed naval gunfire (or by the fire of enemy artillery landed for the purpose), and depended on an accurate, large-scale map for determination of their position, the position of observation posts, and for target location.[18]

It is possible that a preliminary 1:25,000 'Southern Gallipoli' sheet (part of the first 1:25,000 survey of western Gallipoli) was specially surveyed and printed at this stage as such an artillery map. Such a map of the Helles–Krithia area, unnamed and undated, was captured by the British after the first landings in April 1915.[19] Another of the Helles–Kilid Bahr area, on sheetlines parallel to the graticule, was dated 1915 and allegedly used by Liman von Sanders.[20] Such surveys and maps of strategically sensitive areas were, of course, subject to security restrictions, and would have been particularly difficult for Allied agents to acquire. There seems to be a *prima facie* case for arguing that the Allies should, before the war, have made greater efforts to obtain copies of these recent Turkish surveys, but the Turks had only just made, or were still making, their own new large-scale regular survey, and issued some of the new sheets only just before the Allied attack.

The Greeks may well have obtained copies of the Turkish large-scale sheets. Greek villagers and farmers would certainly have been aware of the work of the Turkish surveyors on the Peninsula and the Asiatic Shore. Lt-Colonel Cunninghame, military attaché in Athens from 1 March 1915, was shown the Greek operations maps by Colonel Metaxas on 3 March (he gave no details of scale, etc.), but told the Dardanelles Commission that the earlier absence of a British military attaché, and poor diplomacy by the British minister in Athens, Sir Francis Elliott, placed difficulties in the way of obtaining copies of these. When asked whether it would have been possible for the British military authorities to have had access to these maps, he replied that a good deal of suspicion had been generated by the very strong line which the British representative in Athens had taken for Venizelos and against the Greek General Staff, and that there had not been an English military attaché there before he arrived. The French military attaché was not popular, while the Greeks were (naturally) extremely suspicious of the Russian military attaché. All this meant that 'it would have been very difficult for one to have got the maps'. The crux of the matter was the lack of British military representation. Asked whether he thought it would have been desirable to have had a military attaché at Athens from the beginning, he replied: 'Absolutely, and it probably would have been decisive and made the whole difference.'[21] An irony of this situation is that there was a British military attaché (including Frederick Cunliffe Owen) at Athens at various stages before war broke out. It was clearly unforgivable, given the situation in the Balkans and vis-à-vis Turkey, not to have had an officer in place from August 1914 to March 1915.

The British War Office did, however, manage to get hold of some Turkish 1:25,000 sheets of the Constantinople–Chatalja (Bosphorus) area in 1912–13 during the Balkan Wars[22] (possibly through Ashmead-Bartlett), but none of the Gallipoli Peninsula, despite reconnoitring visits in 1910 by Major L Samson, and about 1912 by the British military consul at Adrianople,[23] and subsequent visits by Cunliffe Owen in 1914. This omission could perhaps be counted an intelligence failure, particularly as several different surveys, made over several years, were involved.

After the winter of 1912–13 further efforts were made to complete the 1:25,000 survey of the fortified zone of the Straits, with detailed 1:5,000 plans 'of some areas of extreme military sensitivity near Anafarta and Sid-ül-bahr' (these were based on enlargements of the 1:25,000 surveys and do not appear to have been surveyed until after the British evacuation in January 1916). In February 1914 the trigonometrical and topographical sections restarted work on the north coast of the Gulf of Saros, north of the Bulair area.[24] As a result of the interrupted nature of these surveys, there was some overlapping and detail and contours from different surveys do not always agree. Lieutenant T C Nicholas, Hamilton's 'Maps' Officer, suggested in May 1915 to Hedley at GSGS that maps derived from at least three different Turkish surveys had been captured in April and May,[25] and this is confirmed by the examination of archive material.[26]

As suggested above, an area or block of 1:20,000 or 1:25,000 sheets, or both, appears to have been surveyed and printed before the regular Turkish 1:25,000 series; it differed in significant details from the later Turkish survey, and was on different sheetlines. It dated apparently from 1912, but may have been earlier, and coincided with the three sheets of the 1909 Turkish 1:50,000 map, except that sheet III (the southernmost) of the latter included a further row of 1:25,000 sheets surveyed in 1913. If this is the case, it is most unfortunate, given the time available, that the Allies did not obtain a copy before the campaign. The evidence for the existence of this earlier 1:25,000 survey and map is a Turkish index map dated 1917,[27] and captured maps (see Chapter 9). However, another index map of Turkish 1:25,000 sheets[28] gives 1912 dates for all sheets of the whole Gallipoli Peninsula except for sheet 44, immediately to the east of the Helles sheet (43), which was dated 1913. None of the Turkish index maps seen by the authors show the special large Helles–Krithia area sheet, and there remains the possibility that this was derived from an even earlier large-scale survey, particularly as some captured sheets provided evidence of different surveys of the same areas, and a few sheets were at 1:20,000 rather than 1:25,000.

Although Turkish sources only refer to the 1:25,000 survey of the Peninsula, the evidence of captured 1:20,000 and 1:25,000 maps makes it clear that there were several surveys, certainly of the south-western end of the Peninsula and the Straits, and that the 1:20,000 scale probably pre-dated the 1:25,000. This fits in with the transition from French to German survey influence in Constantinople. The use of the 1:25,000 scale was evidence of German influence, the French preferring the 1:20,000 scale for their *plans directeurs*. The use of the Bonne projection and grade graticule, however, was evidence of the strong initial French input.

Earlier 1:20,000 surveys were certainly made. On 8 May 1915 Lieutenant Nicholas described one of the first captured maps, to this scale, as of:

... the area around Maidos and Kilid Bahr, contoured every 10 metres and printed rather roughly, and hastily, in black. [Like the captured 1:25,000 map of the 'Gallipoli Peninsula from Cape Helles to a little south of Maidos'] it .. . looked very nice at first sight, but on comparing it with the other I found a difference of 30-40 metres in several of the heights; the topography differed considerably, and a test measurement of a length of about 4 km. showed a difference of 20%. One map is lying, and perhaps both.[29]

One British map of the Anzac area seemed to referred to another Turkish 1:20,000 survey; this was: 'Trench Map 1/1800 from Chatham's Post to Lone Pine (Provn.), Compiled from Photos and Traverses. Contours compared with enlargement of 1/20,000 Turkish Plan. Note any additions or corrections to be sent to Major Newcombe, 4th Field Coy., 2nd Austr. Div.'[30] However, this may refer to one of the British 1:20,000 maps based on captured 1:25,000 Turkish mapping.

In summary, the Turkish maps existing in the decade before the war were the following (there is considerable uncertainty about the dates of much of this Turkish mapping):[31]

Table 2:
Summary of Turkish (Ottoman) maps of Gallipoli and the Dardanelles

Scale	Remarks
1:5,000	Helles, Anzac, Suvla, etc. Based on enlargements of 1:25,000 sheets, but considerably more accurate. Limited coverage. Not printed until 1916.
1:20,000	One or more military surveys of part(s) of the Gallipoli Peninsula (1895–1910?).
1:25,000	Regular sheets of the Dardanelles area, and a large special sheet of the south-west end of the Gallipoli Peninsula, surveyed in 1912–14. Most sheets of Peninsula not apparently printed until 1915, though there is a suggestion that the printing date range is 1913–14. There was also the 1:25,000 plan of Adrianople and its defences, which the British reproduced in 1909.
1:50,000	1909 edition of Gallipoli Peninsula (in three sheets) existed, if date can be trusted. This possibly incorporated 1:20,000 or 1:25,000 survey. There was also a 1915 Turkish Staff Map, reduced from the new 1:25,000 survey; the three sheets were named: *Anafarta Sagir*, *Kilid-ul-Bahr* and *Sed-ul-Bahr*. Pre-war (1909) contoured 1:50,000 sheets of the Constantinople area were produced, but these were enlargements of von der Goltz's 1:100,000 map; the British pre-war one-inch sheets of the Constantinople and Bosphorus area were apparently derived from these.

1:100,000	*Gallipoli* sheet, of uncertain date, but as script is in French and Turkish this appears to be pre-war. 1:100,000 contoured sheet reduced from new 1:25,000 survey dated 1915.[32]
1:100,000	*Bosphorus* sheet 1908. Von der Goltz produced a 1:100,000 map of the Bosphorus and Environs in 1895.
1:120,000	*Les Dardanelles*. Apparently pre-war.
1:126,000	Pre-war Russian-Bulgarian series covering Balkans and European Turkey. 'Very old'.[33] The Russians described this as a 'contoured map of the Balkan Peninsula'.
1:200,000	Pre-war Austrian General Staff series. Turkish series produced from 1910.
1:210,000	Series produced in 1898 covering Imperial Turkey in Europe (southern Balkans and Greece).

Allied maps: the French *Carte de la Presqu'Ile de Gallipoli*, 1854

This map, in two 90 x 65 cm sheets,[34] was contoured (form-lined) at ten-metre vertical interval, and was a fine-looking map which gave a very good picture of the terrain. Particularly noteworthy was the way in which the confused, even chaotic, topography in the Sari Bair range (Anzac–Suvla Bay) was indicated. It also showed the spur between the coast and Gully Ravine covered with brush or scrub (*Broussailles*); this information was not shown on the British one-inch or 1:40,000 map, but was again picked up from reconnaissance before the landings.

The survey methods used by the officers who made this map were not stated on the original sheets, but presumably it was a typical military reconnaissance survey of the period, with a few points fixed by theodolite, sextant, plane-table or compass intersections, the details and form-lines sketched in (perhaps using a plane-table), and spot-heights obtained by taking vertical angles with a clinometer. Points marked on the map indicate that churches, mosques or shrines, windmills and other significant points were fixed, and used to control the map. To provide trig points in wild hilly country, temporary cairns or beacons were probably constructed. Either a cairn was erected on Achi Baba (*Atchi-baba* on the map), or an existing beacon was used; the map shows a sign for a trig point. Such constructions were a normal part of field triangulation. Azimuth would have been found from astronomical observations.

Sheets of the 1:80,000 General Staff map of France of this period were constructed in a similar way to the Gallipoli 1854 survey, though controlled by a good primary triangulation; the secondary and tertiary triangulations, however, left much to be desired. The Gallipoli map was not intended to act as a large-scale artillery map; there was no such concept at the time,

the nearest equivalent being a fortress survey. It was a good rapid topographical survey of its period and, as with all such maps, had to be supplemented by reconnaissance before an operation and eventually supplanted
by a larger-scale product if an assault involving modern weapons was
envisaged.

This French map was reproduced in England in 1876 by the Ordnance
Survey, at the time of tension before the war between Turkey and Russia
(1877), a scale in miles being added. It was incorporated in 1877, along with
many other plans and reconnaissance maps of the Gallipoli Peninsula,
into the 'Strictly Confidential' War Office *Reports and Memoranda relative to Defence of Constantinople and other positions in Turkey*.[35] In 1880 the
Intelligence Branch overprinted this 1876 background in red, showing a
fleet anchorage off Suvla Bay, a main landing place south of Nibrunesi
Point, a line of advance southward to the Kilid Bahr Plateau, Turkish
defences at Chanak and on the Kilid Bahr Plateau, and diversionary
landings on the east coast and south of Gaba Tepe. This accompanied a
Memorandum on the Passage of the Dardanelles by Major Ardagh.[36]

Early British surveys and maps

British medium-scale mapping of the Dardanelles area began with Tom
Spratt's impressive surveys, both land and hydrographic, from the late
1830s. These were augmented by the French 1854 map of the Peninsula,
and by further British surveys of the Bulair and Gaba Tepe–Kilid Bahr areas
made in 1877–8 before and during the Russo-Turkish War, when Britain
supported the Sultan. In 1877 the War Office ordered Lt-Colonel Home and
Captain Fraser, both of the Royal Engineers, to Constantinople to study
the military situation, conduct surveys (assisted by various other sapper
officers), and report back. The result was a 'Strictly Confidential' volume
printed at the War Office in 1877: *Reports and Memoranda relative to Defence of
Constantinople and other positions in Turkey. Also on Routes in Roumelia*, which
contained a large number of specially surveyed maps and plans, including
many of the Gallipoli Peninsula.[37] These have already been described in
Chapter 3. Maunsell revised the survey of the Bulair defences in 1905.

In the heightened tension of the period following the Akaba Crisis (1906),
the British one-inch map *The Peninsula of Gallipoli* (GSGS 2285, in two
sheets) was prepared in 1908 from the French 1854 map, when General
Spencer Ewart was DMO (1906–10). Colonel Charles Close, Chief of the
Geographical Section of the General Staff (MO4) from 1905 to 1911, was
directly responsible for its preparation. Detail and graticule were in black,
contours and spot-heights in brown, water in blue, scrub and forested areas
shown by green tree symbols, and sea in blue-green. Magnetic variation
was given for 1907, and the contour interval was stated in the margin as

100-feet. In addition, brief 'going' notes (*Steep sandy bluffs, Thick brushwood, Low scrub or occasional dense brushwood*, etc.) were added to the map face in black. A secret edition showed fixed defences (forts, batteries, etc.) in red. On the Asiatic Shore, only rough form-lines were used, as the French surveyors had not covered this area. No War Office specification survives but, although it may have been drawn and reproduced in a hurry in order to incorporate it into the 1909 *Report on the Defences of Constantinople*, its relatively large scale suggests that it was intended for possible operational use related to the contemporary War Office and Navy studies of forcing the Dardanelles.

The Dardanelles Commission, influenced by Aspinall and others, noted that the map (or rather the 1:40,000 map taken directly from it in 1915) 'afterwards proved inaccurate, and of little use'.[38] Was this true? Why did GSGS not supply more or better maps? Quite simply, there was little better material in Allied hands, apart from the French 1:50,000 survey from which it was derived, except for limited areas such as the Bulair Lines and the vicinity of the coast defence forts and batteries. There were, however, the large-scale reconnaissance sketch maps of the Suvla–Gabe Tepe–Maidos area made by Grover in 1877.

Callwell felt no need to apologise for the one-inch and 1:40,000 maps, stating correctly that 'in the absence of regular surveys, the maps supplied to the Expeditionary Force were necessarily untrustworthy in respect of the ground not actually visible from the sea'.[39] He was referring to the fact that the original French work was more in the nature of a reconnaissance survey, and to the need for visual reconnaissance to correct the map, and was very well aware that systematic air survey with the necessary large coverage was simply not an option at the time. Unfortunately no sheets of the Turkish 1:25,000 map came into Allied hands until after the landings of 25 April, so the one-inch and 1:40,000 maps were the only ones available. They were supported by a 1:250,000 sheet (*Gallipoli*, of the *Turkey in Europe* GSGS 2097 series: *Map of the Balkan States*, sheets published from 1908 onwards[40]), and various even smaller-scale sheets. There were no large-scale maps apart from Grover's sketch maps, and plans of the immediate areas of the forts made in 1877-80. There were also various Admiralty Charts (see Chapter 8).

The quarter-inch map

The British so-called quarter-inch to a mile sheet (entitled *Gallipoli*) of the Gallipoli Peninsula, first printed at the War Office under Charles Close in October 1908 (later copies were corrected to July 1915), was in fact one of a series (GSGS 2097) of 1:250,000 sheets covering Turkey, so it was not at the true quarter-inch scale (1:253,440) at all. Detail and spot-heights were black, hill-shading brown, and water blue. This small scale was in 1914 considered to be the 'strategical' rather than 'tactical' scale, and was only of any use in operations when nothing to a larger scale was available. As it took in a lot of ground on one sheet, it gave a general picture of the theatre but very little detail, and was useless for artillery work. The 29th Division and others leaving the UK in March 1915 were supplied with 1:250,000 sheets of Turkey, as well as the one-inch map of Gallipoli. Copies were sent to Cairo, and in 1915 the Survey of Egypt made a poor reproduction of the *Gallipoli* sheet to provide stocks for the Anzacs. These were stamped '¼-inch' on the reverse.

Maps of the Bulair area and Lines

The 1877 map at four inches to the mile (1:15,840), which covered the whole neck of the Peninsula, was *TSGS 2052 Survey of Defensive Position near Bulair shewing the lines constructed by the Anglo-French Army in 1855. Sketched December 1876 by Lieut. Cockburn RE and Lieut. Chermside RE. Corrected June 1905. Confidential.* It was reprinted for the 1915 operation (as GSGS 2052) and overprinted with the Army's squaring system in red; each square had 500-yard sides.[41] This map, appended to the 1909 *Report on the Defences of Constantinople*, was closely form-lined, with spot-heights. Maunsell, military attaché in Constantinople, who corrected it in 1905, had drawn two panoramic sketches in March 1904 which were added to the foot of the map. Had more time been available, this map could have been redrawn at the War Office or the Survey of Egypt with contour lines (with height values) more appropriate for modern field artillery use. On the Western Front, a five-metre contour interval was considered appropriate for large-scale (1:10,000 and 1:20,000) trench and artillery maps.

Perhaps because insufficient numbers of Sheet 3 of the 1:40,000 map were printed, the Royal Naval Division, assigned to the diversionary attack at Bulair on 25 April, continued to use the one-inch map (GSGS 2285) showing the Bulair Lines, which carried the army squaring, and possibly had the four-inch map as well. In the event the Division only made a brief feint at Bulair on 25 April and, apart from Freyberg's one-man diversionary operation, did not land. Thus the shortage of 1:40,000 sheets with naval squaring was not critical.

Accuracy of British maps

Why were the one-inch and 1:40,000 maps considered 'inaccurate and of little use'? In the 1908 British redrawing and reduction from 1:50,000 to one-inch (1:63,360) scale, the contour (form-line) interval had unaccountably been reduced from ten metres (about 32.5 feet) to 100 feet (about 31 metres), and this had the visual effect of suppressing the impression of relief and eliminating many important under-features. It appears that this wide interval was the result of a policy decision for all one-inch topographical maps at this time, based on the Ordnance Survey policy for the map of the United Kingdom.

However, it was clearly stated in Close and Cox's *Textbook of Topographical Surveying* (1913)[42] that 'the weight of [international] authority is in favour of a contour interval of about 50 feet [about 15 metres] for a 1-inch scale [map]. . . These considerations have led to the decision to adopt the same rule for military sketching, both on its own merits and because sketches will necessarily be used in conjunction with government maps.' Indeed the new and widely admired 1:50,000 map of France of the period incorporated an interval of ten metres (thirty-two feet), while in the USA it was twenty feet. The 1908 one-inch map of Gallipoli did not therefore meet this 1913 specification, although it did conform to earlier Ordnance Survey practice. As a counsel of perfection, it would have been advantageous to have used hill-shading, hachures or rock-drawing to emphasise inland cliffs and gullies; this could have been done only to a limited extent without air survey or a close ground survey. All-in-all, it might have been better to reproduce directly the old 1:50,000 contours.

The 1913 *Textbook* stated that the uses of maps in war were:[43]

1. For strategical purposes;
2. For finding the way;
3. To give the Commander of a force topographical information concerning roads, villages, woods, hills, streams, bridges, ferries, railways, water supplies, &c.;
4. To enable a general outpost, offensive or defensive position to be taken up;
5. And generally to convey information which cannot be given at the moment by the eye alone.

It is clear that, as a general rule, large scales are not required.

This last statement was dramatically disproved within a year or two, when the opening operations of the First World War on the Western Front and elsewhere demonstrated that as soon as operations bogged down in trench or position warfare, an accurate, large-scale contoured and gridded map was absolutely essential for artillery and other tactical purposes in modern war. This remained the case throughout the 20th century and into the 21st. A map with five-metre or ten-metre contours was found absolutely essential for artillery work; the Second World War and subsequent operations up to the present day have confirmed this. Modern weapons imposed their own requirements; the map became part of an integrated weapons system, part of a 'revolution in military affairs'. The best example of this phenomenon in the pre-war period was the Russo-Japanese War of 1904–5, which was closely observed on the spot by Sir Ian Hamilton, who also wrote a book about it.[44] He did not, however, appear to have learned the lessons himself.

In general, though, the one-inch map of Gallipoli, and its 1:40,000 derivative, fulfilled the 1913 *Textbook* conditions. However, the problem of the wide contour interval was exacerbated by the lack of any specific interval information, although the values were printed by the contour lines. That said, careful study of the map's contours and spot-heights, particularly in conjunction with visual reconnaissance, air photos and topographical descriptions available in the handbooks, should have given sufficient information to troops landing and moving inland. The form-lines showing relief on the 1854 map were not the result of an accurate contour survey, but were nevertheless carefully sketched in. Although not technically accurate, they gave a very good idea of the steep sides and depth of features such as Gully Ravine and the broken country around Sari Bair.

It was unfortunate that the 1915 Gallipoli operations occurred at a crux in the development of artillery survey and air survey (not to mention battlefield communications), and it is worth remarking that the same problems were experienced on the Western Front. It might just be argued that an air survey should have been made in the pre-war or early-war period; this question is examined in Chapter 7. Had the Gallipoli operations taken place two years later, by which time air survey techniques had considerably developed – as evidenced by good maps being produced from air photos on the Western Front (where, however, a relatively good topographical base existed), and in Egypt, Palestine and Mesopotamia – it might have been a different story. Even on the Gallipoli Peninsula, later in 1915, maps were being produced based on an Allied triangulation with additional control points obtained from air photos. Such maps, however, take a long time to prepare. Lack of time (and surprise) was the problem with the initial landings at Gallipoli.

The topography of the Peninsula remained relatively unchanged over the period 1854-1914, though coastal erosion continually modified the coastline and other forms of erosion also occurred. The coastline shown on the 1854 map differed significantly from that on the 1908 and the 1915 maps, and the reasons for this need to be identified.

A further problem was the suppression of detail when the 1854 map was redrawn and reduced in 1908; control points such as churches, mosques and windmills shown on the 1854 map were omitted. Suppression of contours and detail is not unusual when reducing a map, but its need can certainly be questioned when the reduction is by such a small percentage (about twenty percent in linear terms). The problem was compounded by the later enlargement from 1:63,360 to 1:40,000 at the Survey of Egypt – i.e. to a scale larger than that of the original 1:50,000 map. Such an enlargement

should, if anything, be accompanied by an increase in detail and closer contours, but this did not necessarily happen in 1908 – some detail was omitted
but new detail, notably the 1906 submarine cable to Imbros and telegraph
lines, was added. Some detail on the Asian side, around Kum Kale, was
taken from the Admiralty chart. In addition, the secret edition carried a red
overprint of the Turkish fixed defences. Clearly an attempt had been made
to include detail of military significance, but the problem was that the terrain itself was of great military significance and needed to be represented
as accurately as possible. In 1915 the Survey of Egypt presumably did not
have access to the 1854 map, or its later reprints; Dowson, in Cairo, may not
have known of these maps. The 1908 map gave no clues as to its forebears in
any marginal inscription. The French force did, however, carry copies of the
1854 map, but these were not apparently studied by Hamilton or his Staff.

Given that the Peninsula had not been accessible to the overt operations of British or French surveyors in the decades since the Crimean War,
apart from a brief interlude in 1876–80 (and perhaps later in the case of
the French), the one-inch map, despite the stated deficiencies, was simply the best available, and was not a bad reconnaissance map for rapid
unopposed or lightly opposed landings and exploitation operations. Like
most maps of most theatres in those days it was not suitable for position
warfare, but it had never been intended for trench warfare or prolonged
operations.

The evaluation given by the Official History of the 'War in the Air' was
incorrect in places, and only partly justified:

> If the observer in the air were studying the peninsula from the only maps
> which the Allied forces possessed in the early days of the campaign, he
> would soon be aware that, although the main features might be cor-
> rectly shown, the multitudinous folds in the ground, and the rivers too,
> were given at best approximately, and often incorrectly. Some important
> features were omitted altogether. For example, the vast Gully Ravine,
> fifty to a hundred yards wide and extending some three miles, with
> precipitous banks a hundred feet high, was not even indicated. And this
> ravine was to prove one of the vital tactical features in the campaign. The
> complete unreliability of the maps was, for long, a serious handicap to
> the airmen who were called upon to reconnoitre and to report the effect
> of the [Naval] fire.[45]

It was untrue to state that Gully Ravine was not indicated; although the
wide contour interval understated the rugged nature of the country, the
feature was clearly shown by a watercourse and two close contour lines
on either side, indicating a very steep drop of over 100 feet. It was also
shown clearly on Chart X93 of the Helles area, which the commanders
studied. Close study of the map, combined with an awareness of the

contour interval (it was printed on the one-inch map but not the 1:40,000; on the latter, contour values in feet were printed by the contour lines, which gave the necessary information about contour interval) should have given sufficient information, particularly when supplemented by aerial reconnaissance and photographs.

Many 1:40,000 sheets were augmented, corrected and personalised by the addition of further defence details or layer-colouring to emphasise the relief before the landings – for example those used by Hamilton and his Staff. The formation and unit headquarters also modified their printed maps with manuscript additions, and there are many examples of such in The National Archives[46] in London and the Australian War Memorial collections. One of the latter, used by Monash, was layer-tinted and annotated with Turkish defences dated 18 and 20 April, and another used by Blamey was layer-tinted.[47] Yet another was used by Captain A M Ross, Staff Captain of 3rd Australian Brigade, to plan that Brigade's landing at Anzac on 25 April. In this way some of the perceived inadequacies of the printed maps were overcome.

It has been suggested by Tim Travers[48] that inaccurate maps, as well as disagreement as to the intended landing place, may have led to the Navy landing the Anzac Corps too far to the north. He based his argument on a signal from de Robeck to Churchill on 4 May: 'Admiralty map does not extend sufficiently far North to include this [Anzac] position also land features on map are inaccurate. Military squared one [1:40,000] is being used.'[49] The actual criticism is unclear. The 'Admiralty map' was Chart X95, an enlargement based on the 1871 chart, and the topography was only shown in general terms by horizontal hachures. In fact, it included the southern part of the Anzac bridgehead area. Given that the 1:40,000 map was in general use by the Navy, attention should focus on that. But why blame the map? The cliff feature on Gaba Tepe with its look-out station and poled telegraph lines, was shown very clearly on the map. Travers was taking de Robeck's statement out of context; the Admiral was merely explaining to Churchill how to follow the operations on his charts and maps in London. The Navy was very familiar with this coast, had reconnoitred it for months and produced panorama drawings, and had identified the key coastal features necessary for a correct landfall. It is more likely that the current and approach in darkness led to navigation problems which could not be rectified at the last minute. If the approach had been buoyed, an insecure thing to do, the Turks might well have moved the buoys, as they were known to do in some places.

Brig.-General C Cunliffe-Owen (the Anzac Commander Royal Artillery) noted that three days after the landing at Anzac he held a conference of ships' captains, gunnery lieutenants and land observers, in which the point was made that explaining targets by map was very difficult 'as there was an error of 400 yards in compass bearings taken' (clearly this error increased with the range). On 29 April he noted that 'it was unfortunate that our squared map was not accurate, as ships depended on compass bearings'.[50] On 4 May he 'sent Jopp, my staff officer, ashore to fix certain points, and our line by compass bearings... locating our line in such precipitous country was practically impossible from the sea'.[51] After the war, speaking of artillery work on the Peninsula, he claimed that:

> the chief difficulty was the absence of a reliable map. The map we had was one that had been done in 1840, I think [he was probably confusing the 1854 survey with the hydrographic survey executed fifteen years earlier by Captain Graves RN]. It was divided into two mile squares, with smaller squares marked by letters, and each subdivided by nine numbers. These maps did not agree with the ground, and what was most important for ships fire, the compass bearing was two degrees out.[52]

There are two issues here. One is the topographical inaccuracy, and the other is the supposed faulty alignment of the compass roses. The former was a result of the original hasty survey undertaken in 1854, and the subsequent redrawing in 1908 and enlargement in 1915; apart from the unhappy decision to space the contours at only 100-feet vertical interval, the map was compiled from the best available sources. As far as the compass roses were concerned, they were superimposed, together with the Naval grid, at the Survey of Egypt, which was faced with a difficult task as the Naval charts were plotted on the Mercator projection, while the Army's map was on the Bonne. The 1:40,000 sheets did, however, carry a statement explaining the distortion factor.

The Intelligence Department in Egypt

As early as August 1914, Ernest Dowson, Surveyor-General of Egypt, had been asked by Colonel Hedley (MO4) to undertake general map work and reproduction for the 'Near Eastern Theatre'.[53] Until reasonable maps and information about the Ottoman Empire had been obtained or made, and operations were being considered at several widely spaced locations (not necessarily the Dardanelles), Maxwell's staff officers tried to compensate for the absence of maps of Asia Minor, Syria, Palestine and Arabia by scouring the shops of Alexandria and Cairo for guide books.[54] In March 1915, and while Hamilton's Force was reloading its ships at Alexandria, the one-inch map was enlarged by the Survey of Egypt to 1:40,000 (a standard British Western Front scale), in three sheets.

These were beautifully printed sheets, on strong linen-backed paper, with topographical and tactical detail (roads, villages, the Bulair Lines, Turkish forts, barracks, trenches, batteries, cables and telegraph lines and other defence information) printed in purple, form-lines (at 100-feet verti-cal interval) in bistre, hydrographic information for the Navy, including large numbers of soundings, in black, and coastline, watercourses and marsh in blue. Tactical information such as batteries, not shown on the normal edition of the one-inch map, was taken from the secret edition. Additional 'going' information such as 'steep sandy bluffs' and 'thick scrub' was again taken directly from the one-inch map. As the map was intended for use by the French as well as the British, the 'instructions for the use of squares' were bilingual. No indication was given about sources or the degree of accuracy, other than the statement that it was a copy of a War Office map – i.e. the one-inch map.[55]

The Survey of Egypt thus had a great deal of work to do in a very short time, as these new 1:40,000 sheets were not begun until after Maxwell received the news in February that a special force under Birdwood was to be sent to the Dardanelles. This was well before the decision made after 18 March to land a large force (under Hamilton) on the Peninsula. Sheet-lines had to be recast, colour-separations made, new tactical information added, lithographic plates prepared for each colour (including another plate for the red artillery squaring system), and thousands of copies of each sheet printed, folded and packaged for distribution.

The sheetlines were recast, with considerable overlaps, so as to enable each of the main landings (29th Division at Helles and the Anzac Corps from Gaba Tepe north to Fisherman's Hut) to have its own sheet, which included their respective landing areas and the Kilid Bahr Plateau. These were Sheets 1 and 2 respectively. The larger Sheet 3 covered the Peninsula from the Narrows to east of the Bulair Lines, and hardly overlapped with the other two sheets. This arrangement shows that considerable care and thought had gone into the process.

Although not as accurate, in detail and ground forms, as later large-scale maps produced from captured Turkish material, these 1:40,000 sheets gave good indications as to the difficult terrain to be encountered by any landing troops attempting to push inland.[56] Squared and unsquared edi-tions were printed, including a first squared edition carrying an artillery squaring system in red on the Western Front model. Unfortunately the Navy objected to this army grid and, as the Navy was the principal source of fire support, the whole first edition had to be scrapped and the maps reprinted with the Naval grid and compass roses with 1915 magnetic variation superimposed.[57] As C Cunliffe-Owen noted, compass bearings taken from the map were two degrees out, but a 'distortion note' on the map clearly explained this. To enable correct bearings to be taken from the map, the note explained that the reference squares and protractors (compass roses) printed on the map had been distorted to correspond to the map distortion (Bonne projection), and gave 'combined corrections' for sectors of the compass.

Map supply from London and Cairo

All the 1:250,000, one-inch and 1:40,000 sheets supplied by the War Office, the Ordnance Survey and Survey of Egypt were printed on excellent, hard-wearing, linen-backed paper, as were the 1:20,000 sheets printed after the landings. The British could not be accused of providing maps which were poor in this respect. Questions of accuracy have already been dealt with. While initial map supplies were generally adequate, there is some evidence of insufficient quantities of 1:40,000 sheets being printed before the first landings. However, scales-of-issue at this time were relatively small in every theatre; it was only as the war went on that they became more lavish. In early 1915, whether on the Western Front or in Gallipoli, the Staff worked on the basis that each officer should carry one copy of each sheet. GSGS at least cannot be faulted on this score.

Troops of the Royal Naval and 29th Divisions leaving England for the Dardanelles were supplied before they left with copies of the one-inch map, overprinted with red 'artillery squares' on the Western Front model, and with 1:250,000 sheets. The first two battalions of the Royal Marines 'Special Force', part of the Royal Naval Division, intended to form landing parties to destroy guns, left England on 6 February; most of the rest of the Division left Avonmouth on 1 and 2 March. The Royal Naval Division was informed on 24 February by Colonel Hedley (MO4) that its maps were ready, folded and in packets, to be collected by an officer. They were:[58]

1-inch Gallipoli Peninsula Sheets 1 & 2 300 copies of each
1-inch Constantinople Sheets 1–4 1,000 copies of each*
¼inch [1:250,000] sheets Constantinople, Gallipoli & Rodosto 300 of each

*300 for the use of RN Div, remaining 700 of each of 4 sheets to Egypt in reply to a request, to be handed over on arrival.

On 21 February, on being informed of impending operations against the Dardanelles, Maxwell cabled the War Office in London: '621E. Your 3180 Cipher. We have no maps available here. Please supply.'[59] In reply, the War Office in London informed Maxwell on 9 March 1915:[60]

Following maps have been sent from here:		
Gallipoli	scale 1-inch to mile.	
Constantinople	scale 1/250,000	
Rodosto	-do-	700 copies on 'Dunluce Castle'
Gallipoli	-do-	
Gallipoli	1-inch squared with 1000 yard squares	1000 copies on 'Minnetonka'

All the troops from home will be supplied with similar maps.
Copy to GOC's file 10/3/15
Copy to Maps officer –do-
GOC A&NZ Corps

The 1:250,000 sheets, 700 copies of each of which were on the *Dunluce Castle*, were those being sent out with the Royal Naval Division and referred to in Hedley's letter of 24 February.

Twenty-two cases of maps were on board the *Minnetonka*,[61] which sailed on 8 March for Lemnos, carrying elements of the Royal Naval Division. In the case of units of the 29th Division, which left Avonmouth around 17 March, the maps of Turkey arrived just two days before departure.[62] The 29th Division was issued with the one-inch map, smaller-scale maps, and various handbooks. Brig.-General Hare of 86th Brigade noted that before leaving Coventry they were issued with 1:250,000 maps of Turkey and one-inch maps of the Gallipoli Peninsula, as well as the *Manual of Combined Naval and Military Operations, Handbook of the Turkish Army* and *Murray's Guide*.[63] Given that British practice at this time was to issue maps to all officers, but as a rule not to NCOs, the War Office (GSGS/MO4) had made good provision for mapping-up the Force which left the UK.

It is not known exactly when the reproduction work for the 1:40,000 sheets was carried out by the Survey of Egypt, but on 10 March Birdwood's Anzac Staff received a cablegram about maps from the War Office (probably a copy of the one above, passed on by Maxwell), to which they responded by deciding 'to proceed with preparation of Gallipoli squared map in spite of this – as new map squares would be smaller'.[64] Clearly by this date the production of the 1:40,000 sheets in Egypt was already in its early stages. With the naval fire-control squaring, the sub-squares on the 1:40,000 were about ⅝-inch, whereas if the army squaring of the one-inch map had been enlarged proportionately to the map, at 1:40,000 they would have been ⅞-inch. Smaller squares implied greater accuracy in fire-control. The Navy in any case wanted its own squaring to be used.

The production of 1:40,000 sheets in Egypt was delayed by the scrapping of the first edition with the Army squaring and the printing of a new edition with naval squaring. No record of printing dates has survived, but stocks of the final edition were issued to the Anzac Corps over several embarkation days starting on 4 April. On that day, the Anzac Staff sent Mr Cairns, their printer borrowed from the Survey of Egypt (with the newly formed Printing Section), to Alexandria with instructions, taking maps for the Anzac HQ and for the Australian Division transports. On the 4th and 5th, special arrangements for them having been made, the maps for the covering force, the 3rd Australian Brigade, were obtained and issued to the OC troops on board the *Osmanieh*. On 5 April maps for the Anzac HQ and New Zealand Division were received and issued. The Anzac Staff informed

Sinclair-MacLagan, the commander of 3rd Australian Infantry Brigade, that: 'A box of maps is sent herewith. The maps are made up into parcels for delivery to the ships of your force. The maps of Gallipoli (Sheet 1) handed to you at Mudros by Major Wagstaff, should be put aside and kept quite distinct from the maps sent to you now for issue.' These were probably the one-inch squared maps brought out from England. On the 8th, stocks of 1:40,000 Sheet 2, obtained from the Egyptian Survey, were packed and issued to the New Zealand Division. Maps were also ordered for troops on board *Surada*, and the Corps General Staff office finally packed up. The Australian Division's maps were distributed at sea on the 10th.[65]

Thus it appears that the production of the 1:40,000 sheets continued through the whole of March and into April. Either mapping-up requirements and scales-of-issue of the 1:40,000 sheets had not been properly thought out beforehand, or there had been insufficient time for printing, as there was a critical shortage of Sheet 3, covering the Gallipoli–Bulair area. On 10 April Hamilton's Intelligence Chief, Lt-Colonel Ward, telegraphed from Mudros to Cairo asking for more copies: 'At least 500 copies of Sheet 3 of Gallipoli urgently required by GHQ. 500 more copies of Sheet 1 [Helles–Kilid Bahr] and as many more copies as you can of Sheet 2 [Anzac–Suvla] at an early date. Advise despatch to base and GHQ.'[66] No figures survive for the total numbers of 1:40,000 sheets supplied from Egypt, but several thousand were printed. These continued in use during the early weeks of the campaign, being gradually superseded by new 1:20,000 sheets copied from captured Turkish maps.

It must be remembered that Kitchener and the War Council envisaged military operations beyond the Gallipoli Peninsula – indeed all the way to Constantinople. On 10 April Hedley (MO4) advised Clayton in Cairo that more small-scale (1:250,000) maps were on the way: '3968 Cipher. M.O.4/384. Following left on P&O Osterley April 9th. 71 cases, 1400 each, Constantinople, Rodosto, Gallipoli, Adrianople, 1000 Ismid, 500 Gumuljina.'[67] This was further evidence that MO4 was being thorough in its preparations.

Further evidence that all was not well with map supply from Egypt surfaced on the 13th, when Ward again telegraphed to Cairo about supplies of 1:40,000 sheets:

> 250 Sheet II [Anzac–Suvla], addressed GHQ received yesterday. Were any squared copies sent for use of Navy, if so, on what date and to whom addressed? Navy will be requiring 250 more squared unfolded copies of Sheet I [Helles] and a total of 500 each of Sheets II [Anzac–Suvla] and III [Bulair]. Sheet III squared urgently required. Please stamp 'squared' or 'unsquared' on future folded copies.[68]

Such stamping was duly carried out, as surviving copies attest. The Navy needed unfolded, squared copies for its fire-support operations.

The War Office was still despatching maps on 16 April. MO4 telegraphed to Clayton on the 17th:

4090 Cipher M.O.4. 393 – Following despatched by P&O Egypt April 16th

¼-inch	Constantinople, Rodosto, Gallipoli, Adrianople		2600 of each.
1-inch	Constantinople	4 sheets.	3000 of each.
General Map Balkans.			500 copies.

Your I.G./128 March 5th. Charts asked for except Persian Gulf No. 2862.[69]

I.G. (or I.g.) was the section of Clayton's Intelligence Department dealing with geographical matters, including maps.

The Royal Naval Division's Order No. 1 of 21 April referred only to 'Sheets Rodosto & Gallipoli 1/250,000'.[70] However, other RND orders referred to the one-inch map. Given that the RND was to be taken round to Helles and landed there after its demonstration at Bulair, it was probably issued with sheets of the 1:40,000 map. However, copies of both sheets of the one-inch map survive which were apparently used by the RND at Bulair and at Helles, perhaps because of shortages of the 1:40,000 sheets.

Following the landings, Turkish maps were captured which were immediately reproduced by the Printing Section at Hamilton's GHQ, using its limited hand-litho facilities, and were also sent back to Cairo for more sophisticated reproduction in large quantities on the powered presses of the Survey of Egypt. Map production during the Campaign is dealt with in Chapter 9.

Maps produced by Hamilton's GHQ Printing Section before the landings

The GHQ Printing Section is dealt with in Chapter 9; suffice it to say here that it was equipped in Egypt with hand-lithographic and duplicator printing equipment, and reproduced vitally important intelligence maps (utilising the results of aerial photography and reconnaissance) and diagrams in black for the assault force before the landings. The principal intelligence maps were:

1. 1:40,000 'Sketch map Square 177 Showing defences of Achi Baba correcting former reconnaissances on 13/4/15'; printed to update existing maps.[71]
2. Successive editions of a 1:40,000 lithographed sketch map of Turkish field defences, from 14 April in the Helles, and from 18th in Anzac,

sectors, based on RNAS air photos and visual reconnaissance; dated 14, 18 and 20 April:[72]

3. *Z2010 Gallipoli Peninsula. Sketch plan showing results of Air Reconnaissance to 14 April 1915. Issued 14-4-15. Note. Coastline taken from 1:40,000 supplied by the War Office (683).* [Unsquared. Helles sector only]

4. *Z2011 Gallipoli Peninsula. Sketch plan showing results of Air Reconnaissance to 18 April 1915. Issued 18-4-15. Note. Coastline taken from 1:40,000 supplied by the War Office (683).* [Unsquared. Helles sector only]

5. *Z2012 Gallipoli Peninsula. Sketch plan showing results of Air Reconnaissance to 18 April 1915. Issued 18-4-15. Note. Coastline taken from 1:40,000 supplied by the War Office (683).* [Squared. Includes area northwards to Anzac Cove]

6. *Z2012A Gallipoli Peninsula. Sketch plan showing Amended results of Air Reconnaissance to 20 April 1915. Issued 20-4-15. Note. Coastline taken from 1:40,000 supplied by the War Office (683).* [Squared. Includes area northwards to Anzac Cove]

7. A further edition was produced before the Second Battle of Krithia (6 May): *Z2013A Gallipoli Peninsula. Sketch plan showing Amended results of all Air Reconnaissance to 3 May 1915. Issued 3-5-15. Note. Coastline taken from 1:40,000 supplied by the War Office (683).* [Squared]

8. Copies of one or two untitled 1:40,000 squared lithographed sketch maps, carrying details of Turkish defences obtained from air reconnaissance, of the Gaba Tepe–Anzac–Suvla–Maidos area, were specially printed by the GHQ Printing Section for the Anzac Corps before the landings. One was dated 18 April.[73] These showed clearly the development of the Turkish entrenchments on the Peninsula. As they showed the area right across the Peninsula, they were clearly intended to be used for the Corps' main thrust to Mal Tepe, to cut off the Turkish forces in the Helles sector.

Conclusion

Controversially, in the face of received wisdom, it can be said that the maps produced by the Allies in advance of the landing were the best available – the only ones available – for their attempt on the Dardanelles, that the expedition had been well 'mapped-up', and that the map supply was adequate for swift operations. The intelligence maps supplied by GHQ provided crucial tactical intelligence, updated at frequent intervals from air photos. Much maligned by historians of the campaign, the maps became a convenient scapegoat, and with minute scrutiny of their shortcomings, have remained so for the past 100 years. But there was other terrain intelligence available, from the air and on the sea, and ultimately, from the capture of the newly issued Ottoman maps themselves, as we shall see in the succeeding chapters.

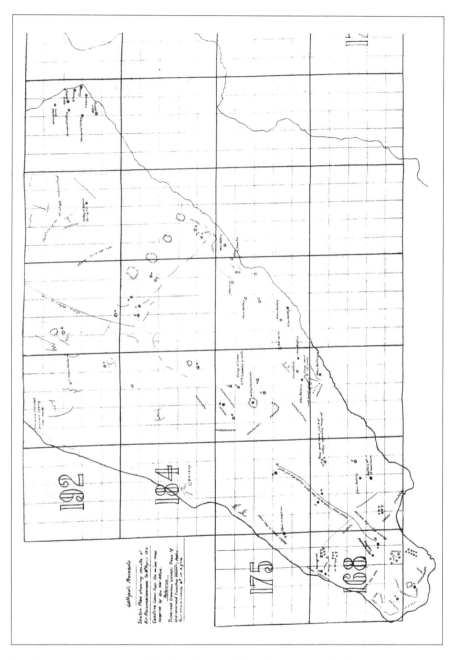

Intelligence map prepared before the April landings from air photos; revised to
18 April and reproduced by the GHQ Printing Section

Notes

1. Chasseaud, Peter, 'Mapping for D-Day: The Allied Landings in Normandy, 6 June 1944', *The Cartographic Journal*, London, 38(2), pp. 177–89.
2. Ibid.
3. Pritchard, Maj.-Gen. H L, *The History of the Corps of Royal Engineers*, Vol. VI, Chatham: Institution of Royal Engineers, 1952, p. 15.
4. Nasr, Seyyed Hossein, *Islamic Science*, London: World of Islam Festival Publishing Co., 1976, pp. 27–48.
5. War Office (1944), *Notes on Maps of the Balkans*, July 1944, Confidential, Directorate of Military Survey, London, p. 40.
6. Anon. (probably Col. Mehemmed Shevki Pasha), 'The Topographical Service in the Ottoman Empire and the Modern Turkish Cartography', *L'Universo*, No. 1, 1920, pp. 127–36.
7. Ibid.
8. Ibid.
9. *Planheft Südosteuropa, Südlicher Teil, 1 Juli 1943* (German Military Survey), Berlin, given in War Office (1944), *Notes on Maps . . .*, op. cit.
10. MI4 (1924), *Latitudes of the Turkish Mapping System*, typescript note by MI4, dated 8/8/1924, in MCE, RE.
11. *Plates to Accompany the Military report on Eastern Turkey in Europe and the Ismid Peninsula [General Staff, War Office, London] (Second Edition, 1909). (B414) 200 6/09 H & S 454-2WO*. Foolscap, maps, plans and photographs covering Constantinople, Central Plains (Adrianople, etc.), Istranja Balkan District, The Eastern Rhodope District. TNA(PRO) FO 881/9513X.
12. Col. Mike Nolan, in his unpublished notes '1907–1917 – The Golden Years in the Development of Cartography in the Ottoman Empire' (2000), states 'printed between 1910 and 1911 or 1913–1914'.
13. Dowson, E M, *Mapping from Aeroplane Photographs in Gallipoli*, Secret, duplicated typescript report with maps and photos, Survey of Egypt, c.Sep 1915, p. 3.
14. MI4, op. cit.
15. Anon, op. cit.
16. VA11 War Diary, Bayerisch Hauptstaatsarchiv, Kriegsarchiv, Munich.
17. See Chasseaud, Peter, *Artillery's Astrologers – A History of British Survey and Mapping on the Western Front 1914–1918*, Lewes: Mapbooks, 1999 for artillery survey in the period before and during the First World War.
18. Two copies are held in the Australian War Memorial collection.
19. Copy in Australian War Memorial; photograph of this in TNA(PRO) WO 153/1058.
20. Cunninghame, Minutes of Evidence to the Dardanelles Commission, p. 1155, TNA(PRO) CAB 19/33.
21. Sheets J8 (Kuchuk Keui), J10 (Hissarlar), K10 (Chamlija), L10 (Maltepe and Islands), in TNA(PRO) WO 301 pieces 171, 177, 187, 192, respectively.
22. F Cunliffe Owen to The Secretary, Army Council, 27-9-1927, in IWM Department of Documents.
23. A 1:100,000 contoured sheet in TNA(PRO) WO 153/1058 has no graticule; it carries a 1915 print date.
24. Anon., op. cit.
25. Nicholas to Hedley, TNA(PRO) WO 301/46.
26. In TNA(PRO) WO 153 and WO 301.

27. Anon., op, cit.
28. *In Report from Major R.H. Phillimore, R.E. (8th Field Survey Co., R.E.) on Turkish Staff Maps 1:25,000 and 1: 5,000 of Gallipoli and Chanak Kale, with list of Conventional Signs Employed. 20/2/1919.* MCE, RE.D 30, 3(4).
29. Nicholas to Hedley, 8 May 1915, in TNA(PRO) WO 301/46.
30. TNA(PRO) WO 153/1055.
31. War Office (July 1944), *Notes on Maps of the Balkans*, op. cit.; *Planheft Südosteuropa*, op. cit., and other sources.
32. TNA(PRO) WO 153/1058.
33. MI4 (1924), op. cit.
34. *Carte de la Presqu'Ile de Gallipoli* (in two sheets); published in 1854 by the Dépôt de la Guerre, Paris, under the direction of Colonel Blondel (engraved by Erhard, 42 rue Bonaparte), printed Chez Kaeppelin, Quai Voltaire.
35. *Reports and Memoranda relative to Defence of Constantinople and other positions in Turkey. Also on Routes in Roumelia. Strictly Confidential, Printed at the War Office by Harrison & Sons. 1877. [0631] 103 WO.* TNA(PRO) FO 358/1; FO 881/3676; WO 33/29.
36. Memorandum on the Passage of the Dardanelles by Major J C Ardagh RE, in Paper No. 797, *Seizure of the Dardanelles as a means of coercing the Porte*, War Office, 1880, in TNA(PRO) WO 33/35.
37. *Reports and Memoranda*, op. cit.
38. *The Dardanelles Commission 1914–16*, London: The Stationery Office, 2001, p. 118.
39. Callwell, Maj.-Gen. Sir C E, *The Dardanelles*, London: Constable, 1919 (2nd edn 1924), pp. 47–8.
40. *Catalogue of Maps Published by the Geographical Section of the General Staff*, War Office, London, 1923, p. 7.
41. Gallipoli Campaign 1915, Maps, TNA(PRO) WO 301/473.
42. Close, Col. C F and Cox, Capt. E W, *Text Book of Topographical Surveying*, 2nd edn, London: HMSO, 1913, p. 183.
43. Ibid, p. 180.
44. Hamilton, Sir Ian, *A Staff Officer's Scrap Book During the Russo–Japanese War*, 2 vols, London: Edward Arnold, 1905.
45. Jones, H J, *The War in the Air*, Vol. II, London: OUP, 1928, p. 2.
46. Gallipoli Campaign maps in TNA(PRO) WO 153 and WO 301.
47. Bullen, John, List of Maps of Gallipoli Campaign, n.d., in the Australian War Memorial, Gallipoli, Vol. I, p. 8.
48. Travers, Tim, *Gallipoli 1915*, Stroud: Tempus, 2002, p. 68.
49. De Robeck to Churchill, 5 May 1915, 13/65, Chartwell Papers, Churchill College, Cambridge.
50. Diary and papers of General C Cunliffe Owen, p. 18. TNA(PRO) CAB 45/246.
51. Ibid, p. 19.
52. Ibid, Extracts from a lecture on Artillery at Anzac, given at the R.A. Institution by Brig. Gen. C. Cunliffe Owen, p. 1.
53. Dowson, E M, 'Further Notes on Aeroplane Photography in the Near East' *Geographical Journal*, 58, 1921, p. 359.
54. Moorhead, Alan, *Gallipoli*, London: Hamish Hamilton, Four Square edn, 1963, p. 108.
55. Peter Chasseaud's study of Sheets 1, 2 and 3.
56. Ibid.
57. Dowson, 'Further Notes . . .', op. cit.

58. Royal Naval Division misc. correspondence & arrangements for embarkation 1915, p. 39, PRO ADM 137/3088A.
59. Anzac Corps General Staff War Diary, TNA(PRO) WO 95/4280.
60. Secretary, War Office, London to GOC-in-C, Egypt, rec'd 9/3/15, in TNA(PRO) WO 158/574.
61. Ibid.
62. Hickey, Michael, *Gallipoli*, London: John Murray, 1998, p. 58.
63. Diary of Brig.-Gen. S W Hare, GOC 86th Brigade, 29th Division.
64. Anzac Corps General Staff War Diary, op. cit., referring to 'Copy of W.O. Cablegram 4008 (recd 9th) – re maps'.
65. Anzac General Staff War Diary, op. cit.
66. Lt-Col. Ward, Mudros, Lemnos to Maps Officer, W.O. , recd 10/4/15, in TNA(PRO) WO 158/574.
67. Secretary, War Office, London to Director of Intelligence, Cairo, recd 10/4/15, in TNA(PRO) WO 158/574.
68. Col. Ward [GHQ Mudros] to Int. Dept Maps Section [Cairo], recd 13/4/15, in TNA(PRO) WO 158/574.
69. Secretary, War Office, London to Director of Intelligence [Cairo], recd 17/4/15, in TNA(PRO) WO 158/574.
70. Royal Naval Division, General Staff, War Diary, TNA(PRO) WO 95/4290.
71. Anzac Corps, Intelligence War Diary, TNA(PRO) WO 157/678, Appendix Z12.
72. TNA(PRO) WO 301/499-503, Gallipoli Campaign 1915, maps.
73. Anzac Corps, Intelligence War Diary, in TNA(PRO) WO 157/668 & 678.

1. Butler's air photo of Turkish defences at Achi Baba on 24 April, the day before the landings (IWM HU 81412).

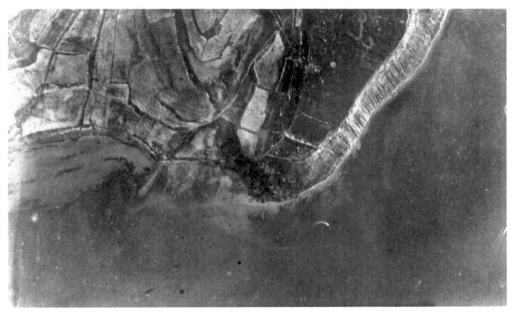

2. Butler's air photo of De Tott's battery and the landing at S Beach, 8am, 25 April (IWM HU 81414).

3. Butler's air photo of Sedd-el-Bahr and the beached River Clyde, 25 April (IWM HU 81413).

4. Butler's air photo of Turkish defences at V Beach (Helles) on 21 April, four days before the landings (IWM HU 81411).

5. River Clyde at V Beach, Sedd-el-Bahr (RE Institution).

6. Observation across the entrance to the Dardanelles and the Asiatic shore (RE Institution).

7. View of X Beach and the dominating limestone cliffs at Helles (RE Institution).

8. General view of the Helles Sector, along the Krithia Road, looking north-east (RE Institution).

9. View from A Beach (Suvla) south to Lala Baba, with the Sari Bair range in the background (Peter Doyle).

10. View from Plugge's Plateau (Anzac) towards the south-west, showing Gaba Tepe and the cliffs of the Helles sector (Peter Doyle).

11. The Maidos coastal road, heading eastwards towards Kilye Bay, with the imposing cliffs of the Kilid Bahr Plateau to the left (Peter Doyle).

12. The Sphinx dominating the view from Walker's Ridge (Anzac) towards Ari Burnu (Peter Doyle).

13. Ocean Beach, Nibrunesi Point and the Salt Lake (Suvla), from Walker's Ridge (Anzac); the Kirech Tepe Ridge dominates the skyline (Peter Doyle).

14. The scrub-filled Monash Valley from The Nek (Anzac) (Peter Doyle).

15. W Beach looking south-east, showing the Helles lighthouse and memorial situated on the Guezji Baba hill (the southern knoll of Hill 138) (Peter Doyle).

16. The entrance to Gully Ravine at Gully Beach (Peter Doyle).

CHAPTER 7

Gallipoli from the Air

It might be thought that the introduction of the air dimension and imagery intelligence would dispel the fog of war. Despite the initial air intelligence failure (the British lack of appropriate photogrammetric techniques, photographic equipment, personnel and material) the air dimension was a crucially important one at Gallipoli, with several different services and units being involved. British and French seaplane and aeroplane squadrons supplied vital photographs and intelligence, as well as spotting for naval gunfire. However, it was a matter of too little, too late, for this to make a great difference to the quality of the maps, or to the outcome of the landings.

Early operations suffered from the British services' failure to develop their air photographic, and photogrammetrical, capability before the war. They lagged significantly behind the French, and even further behind the Germans. Nevertheless, borrowed apparatus and improvised methods led to air survey for trench mapping became highly developed from late-May, even if not at this stage of the war an exact science.

Air surveys

Could it be argued that the British, or the Allies, should have made an air survey of the Peninsula in the pre-war or early war period? Unfortunately the Allies had not developed their photogrammetry to a sufficient extent by early 1915, by which time they were only just beginning to develop crude techniques for the graphic plotting of the planimetry from air photographs, and even then they needed a fairly dense net of ground points to which to fit the air photo detail. Such control points might conceivably have been obtained from the new Turkish 1:25,000 survey, but the trigonometrical data were not available to the Allies. Interpretation of relief from air photos only began to be developed from 1915 onwards through comparative shadow analysis and the study of stereo-pairs. The use of precision instruments to plot points and contours from air photographs was only slowly achieved during the war (by the Germans, but not by the Allies who were not even considering instrumental air photogrammetry) as the war drew to a close.[1]

The remarkable pioneering work of Scheimpflug, an Austrian, was completely ignored by the Allies, even though they were aware of it. Using rectified vertical and oblique air photos taken with a special seven-lens camera, he was able not only to plot planimetry but also to draw contours using a stereocomparator.[2] Even had the resulting map not been as accurate as necessary for artillery fire, it would still have given the command a compelling terrain model on which to base their plans. It was clear that the British flyers over Gallipoli were convinced, from what they could see from the air, that the terrain was particularly difficult from a tactical point of view. A close-contoured plan or photo-map might well have convinced the command of the impossibility of the endeavour. The experience of studying air photos during this and the subsequent Salonika Campaign led Alan Ogilvie and T C Nicholas to write a pamphlet on interpreting ground-forms from air photos. There is no reason why this could not have been done at an earlier stage if better air photographic resources had been made available.

Questions of international law in transgressing Turkish air space apart, an air survey in the 1913–14 period should not have been out of the question but, although considerable progress had been made in this direction, particularly in Austria and Germany, the British and French lagged behind and had few resources for such a venture. While Scheimpflug had already developed his system for stereoscopic photogrammetric mapping and contouring from air photos before the war, the RFC and RNAS were only just beginning to organise their air photography, which was still in the experimental stage, and in any case were thinking of reconnaissance rather than mapping. This is not to say that in different circumstances, with imagination, will and resources, an air survey map of great operational value could not have been produced, but rather to ignore the political, cultural and financial realities of the time. Such a map would not have been of great accuracy, particularly in terms of relief and terrain depiction, but would have given an invaluable picture of the difficult terrain, and been much more accurate than the 1908 one-inch map of the Peninsula. From this point of view, a photo-map or mosaic would have sufficed. Unfortunately, this did not become a feasible proposition until mid-1915, by which time better cameras and gathered experience had revolutionised the situation.

The air dimension and photogrammetry problem

The advantage of the bird's eye view for intelligence and mapping had been obvious to the military mind for centuries, and we have seen that in

1862 Captain Grover RE, who reconnoitred the Suvla– Gaba Tepe–Maidos route on foot in 1877 was a prime mover in starting British Army ballooning. To see the terrain spread out below, withholding few secrets, was worth much expenditure of money and effort. The enemy's defences could be identified, as could his movements and dispositions. Key features of the terrain could also be picked out, though variations of relief were subdued in the view from the air. At certain times of day, when the sun was low, the shadows thrown by terrain features gave a striking picture of relief. In theatres where the terrain was inaccessible and relatively unknown, no commander would wish to have to make do with no aerial reconnaissance – to be blind. Even where he knew the ground, air reconnaissance was still crucial, as experience on the Western Front, notably the Battle of the Marne, had already shown in August and September 1914, for identifying the enemy's positions, movements and strengths.

An Italian airman, Captain Tardivo, had taken air photos in 1911 at Tripoli for operational mapping purposes during the war with Turkey, when Italian gunboats also got inside the Dardanelles and attacked shore installations. Subsequently, aeroplanes were used for reconnaissance during the Balkan Wars of 1912–13, when pilots from Britain, France and other European powers flew with the armies of both sides. However, there was no air survey of the Gallipoli Peninsula, systematic or otherwise, though it is possible that the Bulgarians photographed the area of the Bulair Lines during their operations against them.

The British services had no permanent organisation in place before the war, as the German Army and Navy did by 1914, for the taking, analysis and evaluation of air photographs.[3] Serious British experiments in the taking of air photographs were under way in the RFC and RNAS in 1913–14 (e.g., a photographic survey of the Isle of Wight and Solent), but not in plotting from them. Knowledge of plotting from air photographs existed within the international scientific community. A 'state of the art' defence of the British would not stand up to scrutiny in this respect; if the technology existed, the question is why the British did not exploit it. The answer has to be sought in cultural attitudes and official complacency and parsimony.

There is no doubt that suitable airships, aeroplanes and cameras existed by 1914. Unfortunately in Britain neither the military nor the political imagination and will existed to put these to use, no institute or university department of photogrammetry had been set up as in Germany, and there was no trained body of air photographers and photogrammetric draughtsmen. Neither was there an air survey unit in the forces. All that existed was an experimental photographic section; in 1913 Victor Laws, an NCO, took overlapping photos of the Basingstoke Canal with the new, experimental, Watson camera. Churchill was presumably aware of this when, in March 1914, he advocated a photographic survey from an airship of trade routes in Somaliland, and proposed to order photographic gear and equipment.[4] A simple air survey of the Gallipoli Peninsula could perhaps have been made prior to the war, or in the first few months, when there was very little chance of Turkish (or German) interference from anti-aircraft fire or air interception. Such an air survey, even if insufficiently resourced, might at least have warned the command about the difficult terrain of the Peninsula and forced them to reconsider the wisdom of a landing operation.

By contrast, the Germans had early begun serious research into the military applications of photogrammetry. In 1901 the Prussian Survey had adopted terrestrial photogrammetry for fortress and siege war-fare, especially for artillery map-shooting, a stereoscopic method using Pulfrich's photo-theodolite providing the first practical results. In 1903–4 it established sections for fortress artillery surveys and to produce artillery *Planmaterial* – i.e. a dense, gridded 1:25,000 trigonometrical and topo-graphical framework including fixed points of the fortress area, battery emplacements and observation posts, for use in German fortresses and attacks on enemy fortresses.[5] After the start of army aerial photography in 1911, enemy battery positions and other targets were plotted from air photographs. The Photogrammetric Section arranged for survey practice in fortresses. Two Survey Detachments (*Vermessungs-Abteilungen*), incor-porating Photogrammetry Sections, were set up in 1912 and practised ter-restrial and aerial photogrammetric cooperation from airships, balloons and aeroplanes at Wahn (near Cologne) and Thorn in East Prussia. In December 1912 Moltke issued an instruction 'Reconnaissance and Survey in Siege Warfare', Fortress Survey Detachments (*Festungsvermessungs-Abteilungen*, or *FestVAs*) being formed in 1912–13 for frontier-fortress artil-lery photogrammetry using balloon and aeroplane photographs. In March 1914 three *FestVAs*, created from the Photogrammetry Department of the Prussian Survey, existed at Cologne, Metz and Strassburg,[6] the Survey's photogrammeters being transferred to the *FestVAs* on mobilisation.[7] Much of the German lead in photogrammetry can be traced to this development, for the *FestVAs* became the nuclei of the wartime survey units with the field armies. Unlike British and French practice, aerial photogrammetry featured in German survey units from the start of the war.

By 1914 the Germans and Austrians were significantly ahead in aerial photogrammetry, notably with two more developments full of significance for the future. The first was the Scheimpflug multiple-lens camera, made in Austria. The lack of suitable lenses for air cameras at first meant a very restricted field of view, and even the development of wider-angle lenses did not satisfy the demands of the map-makers for photographs which would cover large areas with a single exposure. This led to the invention of multi-lens air cameras; Scheimpflug's comprised seven oblique lenses surrounding a central vertical lens. This was used experimentally before and during the First World War, fitted to a Zeppelin gondola, the concept of using a 'survey airship' as a 'spy-plane' being widely discussed in Germany before the war;[8] a Zeppelin captured in France in 1914 was carrying an aerial camera.[9] However, mechanical problems and lack of suitable aircraft meant that the use of the multi-lens camera was never extensive, and it was not until 1918, when Major Bagley (USA) invented the tri-lens camera, that a practical multi-lens camera was available.[10] The second important development was the Zeiss 1909 'balloon camera', a survey camera with which gun-flashes, shell bursts, enemy positions, observation posts, etc., could be photographed from high ground, balloons or Zeppelins. Plotting was initially done by hand, and later with the stereoautograph. A 'photo-plane-table', incorporating a photogoniometer (an angle-measuring instrument), was developed to be used in conjunction with this camera, on the Porro-Koppe principle to eliminate lens distortion.[11] The photogoniometer method was to be further developed during the war by Hugershoff and Cranz, and later by Zeiss, becoming a key feature of post-war precision instruments for air survey. Soon after German military flying sections were created in 1911, the first vertical and oblique air survey photographs were taken from aeropanes.[12]

Despite F V Thompson's pioneering work on terrestrial stereophotogrammetry and automatic plotting in 1907–8, and a growing awareness of the German lead in technical education, optics and applied science, the British attitude to terrestrial and air photogrammetry was remarkably sceptical in the period before, during and even after the war. It was summed up by a British reviewer of a new German publication on this subject in 1913 who remarked in the highly regarded Royal Geographical Society's *Geographical Journal* that 'photo-surveying is more akin to an amusing game than to a useful art'.[13] By 1914 surprisingly little progress had been made in Britain in air survey, considering the developments in airships and aeroplanes in the previous decade and progress in other countries. The British were only dimly aware of progress in Germany and Austria – to them these crucial applications of technology to military cartography might have been occurring on another planet. This makes Thompson's contribution even more remarkable.

Air support for the Dardanelles

When Hamilton was summoned by Kitchener, on 12 March 1915, to be given command of the Force supporting the naval action in the Dardanelles, Braithwaite insisted on the importance of having a better air service than that of the Turks in case fighting over the Gallipoli Peninsula became necessary, and asked for modern aeroplanes crewed by experienced pilots and observers. Hamilton famously recorded that Kitchener, who was determined to reserve RFC support for the Western Front, retorted, with flashing spectacles, 'Not one!'[14] The only air support therefore came from the Admiralty, at Churchill's insistence. At first, apart from the seaplanes, Commander Samson's RNAS machines, and initially with only one camera, were all that would support the expedition.

Despite the fact that Royal Naval Air Service (RNAS) aerial photography was very much encouraged by Churchill (First Lord of the Admiralty from 1911) before and during the war, Britain still lagged behind the Germans in this respect. At an Admiralty conference on 3 April 1915, during a discussion of aircraft types, Churchill 'pointed out that an additional very desirable attribute for the reconnaissance types was a photographic apparatus to enable detailed photographs to be taken of the enemy's country. This point was strongly emphasised.' Commodore Sueter, Director of the Air Department and Inspecting Captain of Airships, stated that this had already been considered, and 'a start had been made by sending out the expert Photographer of the Air Service, with an assistant and complete photographic outfit (including a cinematograph and a telephoto camera), to the Dardanelles to enable photographs of the minefields to be taken. . . .' He was presumably referring to Flight Lieutenant Butler of Samson's No 3 Aeroplane Squadron, or Lieutenant W Park RNVR of *Ark Royal*. Churchill then 'again emphasised the great importance of developing aerial photography as quickly as possible; and said that we must not let the army get ahead of us in this'.[15]

Churchill, however, like Kitchener, had his eyes not just on Gallipoli but also on Naval operations and the Western Front, and certain of his strictures about air photography were to do with operations in the North Sea, RNAS operations from Dunkirk, his plans for building up a massive strategic bombing in the west, and the great double-pronged Allied land offensive, planned for May, in Artois and Champagne. On 3 April, after seaplanes from Dover and Dunkirk had bombed German submarine facilities at Antwerp, he minuted the War Council that he attached great importance to the development of photography, which was certain to be required for important reconnaissances (in connection with North Sea operations) from May onwards. He emphasised that the Navy should keep fully abreast of the latest army progress in air photography and artillery spotting. The Navy should take every opportunity of learning from the more experienced RFC.[16] Again, on 24 April, two days after the German gas attack at Ypres opened the desperate Second Battle there, he demanded that Sueter tell him what he had been doing about aerial photography. Churchill had heard that only one officer was actively engaged in such work, and that the RNAS had not yet taken any satisfactory photographs (on the Flanders coast). He stressed the great importance and urgency of the matter, and asked Sueter to see General Henderson (GOC RFC) immediately, and ensure that the RNAS was ready, by borrowing cameras or photographers from the RFC, to take photographs after 1 May.[17]

Here Churchill was referring to impending operations off the German coast. In Gallipoli, where the landings took place the day after he wrote the last instruction, the army had no cameras or photographers to lend, and Flight Lieutenant Butler of No. 3 Squadron had been hard at work taking photographs over the Dardanelles and the Peninsula since early April.

Ark Royal, commissioned as a seaplane carrier on 9 December 1914, had sailed from Sheerness on 1 February, arriving at Tenedos on the 17th. It is not clear whether Sueter was referring to Park and *Ark Royal* or Samson's squadron when speaking of the photographers and cameras; reports from *Ark Royal* covering this period make no mention at all of air photography. However, photos were taken of the *Ark Royal*'s seaplanes, of the seaplane carrier *Aenne Rickmers* and of the balloon ship *Manica*, in this period, by one or more of *Ark Royal*'s complement and sent back to Sueter with a report covering the period up to 22 May.

It is, however, possible that the RNAS seaplanes made use of cameras before Samson's aeroplane squadron arrived on 23 March. Park was responsible for photographic and mapping work, but it is unclear at what stage the various cameras were introduced. Park himself was an architect in civilian life, and reckoned to be 'a very skilful and accurate observer from the air'.[18] At a later stage, a hand-held Ross half-plate camera was used in the Short seaplanes. This had originally been designed for use in airships, and in the seaplanes was used for obliques or verticals, the latter through a hatch in the bottom of the fuselage. An excellent German camera captured in France was also used, but this was seriously damaged by sea-water when one of the Sopwith Schneider seaplanes crashed. Also used was the RFC A-type cameras, heavy and unwieldy, introduced in France at the end of February 1915 but not available at the Dardanelles for many months. Given that only fifty-five photos had been taken by the end of October over the Gallipoli Peninsula by the *Ark Royal*'s seaplanes, most of these of the Anzac area,[19] it is unlikely that many, if any, were taken before the initial landings. They may, however, have been taken of the forts, minefields and during naval bombardments.

A post-war Admiralty report, part of which was written by Samson, stated baldly that as far as aerial photography was concerned:

In this branch of aviation [the enemy] were in 1915 certainly ahead of the British and possibly of the French. Photographs taken during the campaign were seen at Constantinople [after the war], and they are much better than ours of this period, although taken at 8,000 feet, whilst ours were taken at 4,000 feet. They are more distinct and give clearer details.[20]

Ark Royal and RNAS seaplanes

The RNAS was active in the eastern Mediterranean theatre from the outbreak of hostilities. In late November 1914 the Navy reported that Tenedos was the only potential aeroplane (as opposed to seaplane) base near the Dardanelles.[21] The Tenedos airfield was at the west end of the island, on low, flat ground about half a mile from the landing beach. It was only 300 yards square,[22] but this was sufficient for all the aeroplanes which were to arrive in the theatre except for the *Ark Royal*'s Sopwith Tabloids. The airfield was ready for use just days before Samson's No. 3 Squadron arrived at the end of March 1915.

The *Ark Royal*, a converted merchantman, was the Navy's first seaplane carrier. A report written before she arrived at the Dardanelles indicated that she carried 'six seaplanes and four land machines'. The seaplanes had a speed of about 60 knots in still air and an endurance of three to four hours; two of the large seaplanes could be fitted to carry Lewis guns. The Sopwith single-seater aeroplanes could take off and land from a 400-yard field, reach 85–90 mph, carry four 20-pound bombs or steel *flechettes*, and had an endurance of three and a half hours. They could also take off from the ship's deck, but not land there. No information was given about cameras.[23]

Ark Royal arrived at Tenedos on 17 February 1915, with Squadron Commander R H Clarke Hall, carrying eight aircraft – three large 200 HP (one Short, two Wight) and three lighter 100 HP Sopwith two-seaters seaplanes and two Sopwith Tabloid single-seater aeroplanes. The Short was the only one up to the work, the others being 'sadly inefficient for the work they would be called upon to do'.[24] *Ark Royal*'s Sopwith Tabloids, needing a large, smooth field from which to operate, could not fly from Tenedos; the 400-yard field there was too rough for them to take off.[25]

One of her aircraft, out of four attempts, managed to take off on 17 February, the very day of *Ark Royal*'s arrival, when a seaplane reconnaissance of Forts 1 to 6 at the entrance to the Dardanelles was carried out; trenches were seen in the Cape Tekeh area, and south of Fort 4 several new batteries were spotted from 4,000 feet. The machine received several hits from rifle fire.[26] Two days later an aircraft attempted to use wireless to spot for the fleet's gunfire during the bombardment of the forts, but the set failed.[27] On this day, 19 February, a reconnaissance of the whole coast from Gaba Tepe southwards to Cape Tekeh and across the mouth of the Dardanelles to Besika Bay was carried out to locate Turkish defences, and gun emplacements were reported in naval grid squares U36 and 2C.22; one, three quarters of a mile north of Cape Tekeh, was for three guns, while the other on Gaba Tepe had no guns in position. However, the seaplanes failed in their naval fire-spotting task because of adverse weather conditions which prevented further flying until 25 and 26 February. On the latter day, *Ark Royal* noted: 'Sent seaplane to reconnoitre for trenches, troops, howitzer batteries . . . Trenches observed running inland from coast about 3 miles to S of Fort 4 (South Coast). North Coast – many trenches round Cape Tekeh.' Sketches were made of trenches seen in the Cape Tekeh area.[28] Such visual reconnaissance was better than nothing, but had no pretensions to accuracy.

Most of the initial work was visual reconnaissance and spotting for the Navy's guns. By early March the *Ark Royal*'s seaplanes, heavy, slow and underpowered, with little capacity for climbing to any great altitude (3,000 feet, gained slowly, was a great achievement), had been found practically useless for reconnaissance sorties due to their unreliability and the lack of experience of their observers.[29] They were sitting ducks, and on reconnaissance missions were always within range of rifle-fire from the ground.

The shortage of aircraft led to desperate signals to London and Egypt for more. On 26 February the War Office in London signalled to Maxwell in Cairo: ' . . . Navy have four aeroplanes besides seaplanes off Dardanelles. We have none available.'[30] *Ark Royal* located trenches and field guns south of Gaba Tepe on 5 March, and on 8 March reported: 'Objects, possibly mines, 18 in number, seen in position as previously reported by seaplanes (Narrows – Fort 13 area).'[31] On the same day, the War Office sent a further signal to Maxwell on the subject of air support: 'Admiralty are sending out 12 aeroplanes and 12 pilots, also 1 kite balloon section.'[32] This was a reference to Samson's No. 3 Squadron RNAS, and to No. 1 Kite Balloon Section in the *Manica*. On 9 March Carden signalled to the Admiralty that he could not make any further progress against the Dardanelles defences until his air service was reinforced.[33]

On 1 and 4 March seaplanes identified the moves of mobile 6-inch howitzer batteries.[34] On 4 March seaplane observers visually located old trenches at Sedd-el-Bahr, behind the Old Castle.[35] On 10–12 March, air reconnaissances of Saros Bay and the Bulair Lines were carried out; at Bulair a seaplane reported four lines of traversed trenches and an entrenched camp with two redoubts.[36] The sortie on the 12th was directed at the area from the Kavak river to the Bulair Lines and beyond, but low cloud and mist prevented any detailed reconnaissance. It was, however, determined that the Kavak Bridge, which was viewed from a low altitude, was still intact. As far as the Bulair Lines were concerned, *Ark Royal* reported that a large camp and two new earthworks were located, as well as trenches between Kavak and Bulair. Old earthworks marked N, S. and R1, on map plate 58 of NID Report 838 were reported to be in disrepair and full of water. Forts Sultan and Napoleon were little damaged, and two gun emplacements were located protecting the landing places in naval grid square 2.D.33. Further, 'A considerable amount of flying over this area will be necessary to locate and map various trenches, works, etc.'[37]

The RNAS seaplanes practised spotting mines submerged at various depths near *Ark Royal*, and made further visual minefield and other reconnaissance flights daily from 13 and 17 March. On the 13th, five lines of mines were seen running halfway across the channel between the Kephez Light and the Swandere river, but the Asiatic side of the Straits was reported clear. The experiments with locating mines by visual observation were inconclusive; it all depended on the weather conditions. Even a slight breeze would ripple the surface of the water and prevent a view below the surface to where the mines were moored a few feet down. On the other hand, in good light and still conditions, a remarkably clear view could be obtained.

Terrain information was also reported: 'a swamp with standing water of about 400 yards each way was seen in squares J and K 64 and 65. Swandere and Avulzar Rivers contain water.' A sketch map showing the lines of mines was forwarded the following day. On the 14th further details of batteries, trenches and topography were acquired.[38] Although *Ark Royal* made successful visual experiments to locate Turkish mines below the surface, the technique could not be guaranteed as the current and other surface anomalies often rendered this impossible. It was intended that photography would be used, but it is not confirmed that this actually took place; the same problems would have been encountered as with visual reconnaissance. An air camera was not available until Samson's RNAS No. 3 Aeroplane Squadron arrived at the end of March, and even then it was not until around 11 April that the first useful photos of the Peninsula were obtained. On 15 March *Ark Royal* reported to Sueter that information had been obtained and guns and mines only located by the most careful use of binoculars and squared maps by the observer, and that the pilot without an observer would have brought back no information of any value. On the same day she reported that 'experiments with mine sunk near *Ark Royal* seen at 5-feet, 10-feet and 18-feet depths at 1,500, 1,000 and 3,000 feet respectively, but conditions of light and sea were very favourable. Appearance similar to objects seen in Dardanelles.'[39]

The results of all visual reconnaissance sorties flown to 19 March were plotted on an outline map covering the Peninsula as far north as Gaba Tepe, and as far east as Nagara Point on the Asiatic Shore; this showed trenches and field guns south of Gaba Tepe, a gun emplacement at the cape between Gaba Tepe and Helles, and two emplacements at Helles, as well as trenches and two field gun positions. An emplacement was shown at De Tott's battery, and plenty more trenches, emplacements and camps along both shores of the Narrows. On 31 March *Ark Royal* reported that 'Commander Samson's aeroplane squadrons [sic] have now commenced work from Tenedos. Work in Dardanelles will now be delegated to aeroplanes. *Ark Royal*'s seaplanes will be used for more distant reconnaissance etc.' During February and March, *Ark Royal*'s eight seaplanes logged seventy-four sorties, during only twenty-nine of which was useful information obtained. Total time in the air was 60 hours and 28 minutes, and in this period there were no fewer than thirty-two engine failures.[40]

On 7 April Lieutenant Bromet took *Ark Royal*'s Wight Seaplane No. 172, with Lt-Commander Hornby as observer, in an attempt to reconnoitre the Bulair Lines and the town and port of Gallipoli, but engine trouble forced a return after a flight lasting only thirty-six minutes.[41] This type of problem plagued the seaplanes. The shortage of aircraft in the Aegean led to a demand by Birdwood, and then by Hamilton, for some of the French machines in Egypt to be sent to the Dardanelles. On 8 April Kitchener signalled to Maxwell: 'Admiralty here think you had better keep the seaplanes for service in Egypt and explain through Hamilton to de Robeck the necessity of their remaining if he wants your Brigade' (Cox's Indian Brigade).[42] Hamilton was having to do some horse-trading with Maxwell to get what he and de Robeck wanted. On the same day, de Robeck signalled to Maxwell: 'Request seaplanes, urgently required for French Army, be sent ASAP. They will be returned immediately they can be spared.'[43] On the 9th Hamilton signalled to Maxwell: 'Certainly will do my best about the seaplane.'[44] The next day some Schneider Cup Sopwith single-seater seaplanes arrived, and *Ark Royal* noted that *Minerva* and *Talbot* would also operate with seaplanes.[45] Hamilton signalled again to Maxwell: 'It is all right about your getting the seaplanes.'[46] From 17 April *Doris* also worked with seaplanes, and *Ark Royal* announced that she was now responsible for five types of seaplanes and three types of engines.[47]

In April *Ark Royal*'s seaplane operations became more efficient than in February and March; eight seaplanes flew seventy sorties in that month, obtaining useful information during forty-eight of these. Ten days were unsuitable for flying owing to bad weather, but due to being at sea or erecting new machines at Tenedos, flying only took place on sixteen days; total flying time was 72 hours and 42 minutes, and there were only twenty engine failures. During April one machine was lent at different times to *Minerva* and *Doris*.[48] On the eve of the landings, *Ark Royal*'s seaplanes kept the landing places under close observation. At 9.30pm on 24 April Anzac Corps HQ received a report from *Ark Royal* that Gaba Tepe was quiet and that no guns had been seen.[49] The Turks were lying low, but they were also watching and prepared.

Kite balloons

In April the *Manica*, a tramp steamer converted to a balloon ship, arrived with No. 1 Kite Balloon Section, equipped with a Drachen-type kite balloon for observation purposes; two or three observers were carried in the basket, in telephone communication with the ship. It was used primarily for spotting for naval gunfire, though general reconnaissance was important. As far as is known, no photography was done from the kite balloon. This was an activity much practised by the French and Germans before the war but, despite various experiments extending over decades, Britain lagged seri-ously behind by 1914.[50] *Manica* was at Lemnos on 16 April,[51] and was later joined by *Hector*, which left Liverpool on 2 June. On 25 April the landings of the Anzac Corps were supported by naval gunfire directed by kite balloon observation, no aeroplanes being able to operate this far from Tenedos.[52] A report on the work of the kite balloon ships at the Dardanelles made no mention of photography, but emphasised the importance of observers pos-sessing a geographic capability, including knowledge of:

> The appearance and characteristics of modern earthworks and emplace-ments, and of troops in the open; cavalry, infantry and artillery... Map-reading, contours and visibility of ground. Use of the Compass... Estimation of distances, and the effect of rising and falling ground on the fall of shot.[53]

Samson's No. 3 Squadron RNAS, and the first air photos

On 26 February Sir James Maxwell asked the War Office, in view of possi-ble landings at Gallipoli, if aeroplanes were to be sent for Birdwood's force in Egypt. The War Office replied the following day that no aeroplanes were available, but the Navy had four aeroplanes besides their seaplanes off the Dardanelles (but they could not take off from Tenedos). Churchill had already completed plans for sending Commander Samson's No. 3 Squadron RNAS, consisting of twelve naval aeroplanes and pilots, then operating in Flanders, to the Dardanelles. On 8 March the Admiralty sent these out, supplementing them with a kite-balloon section.[54] En route, Samson collected ten new French Farman aeroplanes at Marseilles, but finally arrived at Imbros on 23 March[55] with only five out of the twenty-two in a serviceable condition. The French were sending six aeroplanes to Mudros from Egypt, but these did not, apparently, arrive until May.[56] By 23 March, the day that Samson's Squadron arrived by sea at Imbros, an airfield had already been prepared at Tenedos, and de Robeck was plan-ning to continue the naval operations.[57]

Samson himself arrived two days after the fleet bombardment of the Dardanelles forts, but the rest of his squadron took another two weeks to arrive, and the first British aeroplane (as opposed to seaplane) flight did not take place until 27 or 28 March. Even then, apart from Butler's private camera (first used on 4 (Jones) or 14 (Aspinall-Oglander[58]) April), good photographs were not available for another fortnight. Samson allotted him a Henri Farman machine, which he regarded as 'quite suitable for this single seated work',[59] and the intelligence picture was gradually built up on the 1:40,000 base map. Butler did his own processing, assisted by an amateur photographer, the Squadron having no specialist photographic unit attached. At first the photos were regarded as tools for detecting Turkish batteries, mines and other defences rather than as a means for accurate defence and terrain mapping. This view rapidly changed, as it became clear that only air photography could create a detailed picture of the beaches and hinterland, the terrain and the growing defences.

Butler's first photographs may have been experiments made with locating underwater mines, and it was not until 11 April that No. 3 Squadron first attempted to locate trenches and batteries in the Helles and Anzac areas, and even then this was a visual rather than a photographic reconnaissance. The first definite mention of photographic reconnaissance was on 14 April, when an intelligence report stated:

> Aeroplane report 14 April; Flights [sorties] carried out:- One spotting flight. One flight taking photographs. One flight taking major Villiers Street to Gaba Tepe. Two reconnaissance flights. Flight with camera 11 a.m. Photographs developed not very good owing to age of films. Prints will be sent tomorrow showing position around Sedd-el-Bahr neighbourhood.[60]

GHQ issued an 'Aeroplane Reconnaissance' report on the same day, covering entrenchments located, and also roads:

> An excellent road has been made from Sedd-el-Bahr to Krithia, and other roads not shown on map of Gallipoli have been constructed. A map of these roads is being sent from Tenedos, and will be forwarded when received.[61]

A further eighty-minute 'camera flight' took place on the morning of the 17th, when Flight-Commander Marix took Butler up as an observer, but no information was given about the photos obtained.[62] Specific photographs of the beaches and their exits were taken at a late stage just before the landings (Table3).

Table 3: Examples of air photos taken before the landings[63]

Date	Location and notes
14 April	[see above – no details]
17 April	[see above – no details]
19 April	Trenches in square 155 a, g. [hills at In Tepe, on Asiatic side of Straits]
20 April	Morto Bay & Eski Hissarlik, square 169 v, w, x. [Morto Bay & area north of De Tott's Battery]

185

21 April	Morto Bay, square 168 t, u, y, z. [area inland of Morto Bay, including road to Krithia]
21 April	Beach, square 168 c, h. [mouth of Gully Ravine & beach to south]
21 April	Beach, square 176 b, g. [south of Sari Tepe, towards Y Beach]
21 April	Cape Helles and part of Sedd-el-Bahr, showing trenches, redoubts, etc.
21 April	Sedd-el-Bahr.
24 April	Achi Baba, showing entrenched all-round defence position, etc

Butler's German plate camera – a small, folding, hand-held Goertz-Anschutz taking small, narrow-format exposures only about 3¼ x 5¼ inches (8.3 x 13.4cm) – provided contact prints at a scale of roughly one-inch = 280 yards (1:10,080) from negatives exposed at about 4,000 feet. Anti-aircraft fire later forced the aircraft to fly at 7,000 feet and over, at which height the resultant prints would be at a much smaller scale (1:17,640) and of correspondingly less use from a tactical point of view. The focal length of his camera was 12cm (scale = f/h, where f = focal length and h = height).[64] Photos taken later with the French camera, focal length about 12 inches (30cm), were significantly larger, 120 x 170mm format.

It does not appear that Butler had enlarging equipment with him, and there was probably no local civilian professional photographer at Tenedos. Dowson, at the Survey of Egypt, could easily have supplied such equipment, but there is no evidence that it was asked for. In this respect the expedition was remarkably ill-equipped. The contact prints supplied Hamilton and de Robeck with an absolutely indispensable picture of the Turkish defences (including trenches and battery positions), the terrain of the assault beaches, their exits and hinterland, and of the interior. They also made it possible to correct the map, as it became clear, for example, that there were two redoubts, and in fact two hills (observation from the sea would already have made this clear), at the locality at Helles known as Hill 138. These twin hills had been shown correctly on the French 1854 map but, due to the wide contour interval on the British one-inch and 1:40,000 maps, only as a single spot-height on these. Given the primitive state of air photo interpretation at this time, it is probable that full value was not extracted from the images, even though some of the prints were of remarkably good quality. There was no trained or experienced air-photo-interpreter in the theatre except for the RNAS people themselves, who were learning as they went along, for the simple reason that this branch of intelligence work was only just beginning; the British armies in France were only just realising the need for air photo experts at this time, the first being appointed in July.[65]

Visual and photographic air reconnaissance was absolutely crucial before the landings. Army and Navy intelligence officers, themselves going into the air, and marking reconnaissance results on landing on a master intelligence map, supplied vital information. Much could be confirmed from a close study of the photos. From this master map, continually updated, the Intelligence Staff prepared duplicated, and later lithographed, squared sketch maps which could be issued to the troops, and to the Navy for fire support. Several problems remained. One was that, viewed from the air, the rugged nature of the ground was lost – it seemed much flatter. Others were the poor quality and non-verticality of the air photos, the lack of accurate map detail against which to plot new information, and the lack of experience in interpreting air photos. All these improved immeasurably over the next few months.

On 2 April, in Alexandria, de Robeck cabled Hamilton that the 'Navy was making reconnaissances and sketches of all possible landing places, and asking for Staff Officer to be sent to assist arrangements for cooperation'. Hamilton replied that '2 trained aeroplane observers were being sent in the *Paros* today: also that Staff officer would be sent whenever he could be sent for'.[66] The observers, destined for Samson's No. 3 Squadron, were Major R E T Hogg, Central India Horse, who arrived at Tenedos on 10 April with Captain Jenkins to join No. 3 Squadron. Both were experienced observers, attached to the Royal Flying Corps, who had worked with French seaplanes in Egypt.[67] They were joined before 11 May by 2nd-Lt the Hon. Knatchbull Hugessen RHA, of 'B' battery RHA (29th Division) who was specifically appointed to spot for British land batteries once the troops were ashore. Working with No. 3 Squadron until August, he used a 1:40,000 map sheet to mark up trenches and targets around Krithia, and later used 1:20,000 sheets over the Suvla area.[68]

Air reconnaissance

The Official Historian of the air war, drawing on Samson's reports, summarised the air intelligence and mapping role:

> Systematically the officers plotted the enemy positions; they controlled a part of the ships' fire against enemy batteries, especially those in the difficult country on the Asiatic side; they procured some crude but useful photographs of the landing beaches and the ground in their immediate neighbourhood, and they wrote descriptions of the beaches as they appeared from the air; they corrected the inaccurate maps; and they dropped bombs on batteries and camps. All the information that was brought in was passed on to head-quarters at once, but the squadron commander [Samson] kept also a map which was supplemented and

brought up to date from the air reports, from day to day, and this map was handed to Sir Ian Hamilton before the landings.

Most of the photography, which was of an experimental kind, was done by one officer, Flight Lieutenant C. H. Butler, who began on 4 April [more likely the 14th] with a small folding Goertz-Anschutz camera. A better camera was later borrowed from the French squadron, which under Captain Cesari had come out in May, and Butler fixed this alongside his seat outside the nacelle. Until the end of June, when he was badly wounded, he exposed in all some 700 plates, piecing groups together to form maps of each important area, and these maps, from time to time, were passed to army head-quarters. It was not until the end of August that a regular photographic section was organised; thereafter the progress of aerial photography was rapid.[69]

This, however, was after the Suvla landings.

It appears, therefore, that Butler may have taken scores of air photos of the minefields facing the navy, the forts, the beaches, their exits, and Turkish defences farther inland, before the landings on 25 April,[70] by which time his Squadron had flown forty-two reconnaissance and eighteen photographic sorties.[71] The Squadron appears to have flown an average of three sorties per day for all purposes before the 25th. From Tenedos it was some seventeen miles to Helles, thirty to Gaba Tepe, and more to Anzac; to Bulair it was sixty miles direct or seventy miles avoiding overflying the Peninsula.

The RNAS flying reconnaissance and photographic sorties from *Ark Royal* and Tenedos were later perturbed to find that, although they had been requested to concentrate their attentions, and write reports on, beach defences, Hamilton and his staff, in their final plan, decided to land their troops at some of the beaches which the RNAS had reported as being particularly well-defended by the Turks (at Helles). One writer on the campaign claimed that the RNAS report was not seen by Hamilton's Staff.[72] Not only is this hard to believe, but it does not agree with Samson's account and contradicts the Official Historian, who stated, as we saw above, that all information was immediately passed on to headquarters.

Hamilton was no newcomer to the possibilities of aeroplanes; before the war he had been given his first flight over the Fleet off the Medway on the same day that Samson had taken Churchill up for a spin. Hamilton had also visited the RNAS at Eastchurch in 1912 and 1913 and been taken for several flights. He made several visits to Tenedos, as did Hunter-Weston, among other things to assess the intelligence potential of Butler's air photos, and assess their use in operational planning. Samson noted that both generals carefully studied all the air photos, and thoroughly discussed the part No. 3 Squadron were to play in the landings.[73]

No. 3 Squadron overflew the Peninsula whenever weather permitted. Samson stated that he was told about the proposed landings on about 11–12 April, and his Squadron immediately made every effort to secure good photos and make sketches of all possible beaches, including any defences located. Prior to the landings they provided clear reports on all beaches, and Samson gave Hamilton his own map on which was plotted all reconnaissance results and photo intelligence.[74] The only failure was at Sedd-el-Bahr, where well-sited and concealed trenches were not located from the air. Samson noted that they could have obtained better results with the improved cameras used later in the war.[75] Butler's folding camera was still in use on 23 May; the French squadron, from which a camera was borrowed, did not arrive until May, and the first photos taken with it seem to have been taken about 28 May.[76]

Thus RNAS mapping activity in the air was at first confined to making sketches and filling in traces (the Survey of Egypt printed squared 1:40,000 skeleton traces to overlay on the maps, so that visual reconnaissance information could be added), but reconnaissance photographs were taken as soon as possible. As well as spotting for the ships' guns, Samson's machines had to perform reconnaissance work for the Fleet, attempt to locate mines, and also undertake further reconnaissance to assist the army in making plans for landings.

Major Hogg, reporting on No. 3 Squadron's work before the landings, stated that at first 80 horse-power Henri Farman machines were used, but these were so underpowered that it was often impossible to fly more than eight to ten miles up the Peninsula from Cape Helles. Later 100 horse-power Maurice Farmans arrived, and reconnaissance sorties were then flown up to the line across the Peninsula from Nibrunesi Point to Maidos, which included the Anzac sector, and also along the Asiatic Shore as far as Chanak at the Narrows. When this initial reconnaissance was completed, a complete map was sent to Hamilton's Staff at Lemnos. Hogg also made one reconnaissance as far as Bulair, about sixty miles from Tenedos, in a Maurice Farman with a 120 horse-power engine, and spotted for the Navy in a wireless-fitted machine.[77]

On 11 April, following the arrival of Hogg and Jenkins, No. 3 Squadron made the first attempt to locate the Turkish trenches and field gun positions in the Helles and Anzac areas. Samson considered the results to be fairly good, and forwarded a tracing to Hamilton's GHQ. A 'Sketch map 1/40,000 Square 177 Showing defences of Achi Baba correcting former reconnaissances on 13/4/15' was soon issued, and this was probably drawn from air photos.[78] On the same day, General Hunter-Weston (GOC 29th Division) and his GSO2 sailed in the cruiser *Dartmouth* to Tenedos where, at the aerodrome, they conferred with Samson, studied the air reconnaissance results, and arranged for a copy to be sent to 29th Divisional HQ the next day.[79] Successive editions of an outline 1:40,000 intelligence map of the Turkish field defences in the Helles and Anzac sectors, based on RNAS air photos and visual reconnaissance, were reproduced by the MEF Printing Section and distributed to the troops before the landings; these were dated 14, 18 and 20 April (see Chapter 6). Assaulting formations and units were thus provided with 'defence' supplements to their operations maps. Air photos were probably only supplied to Hamilton's HQ Staff, not to lower formations or units, before the landings though they were studied at Tenedos by formation commanders.

Thoroughly alerted by naval bombardments and minesweeping attempts, the Turks worked feverishly on their defences throughout the months before the landings. The Anzac Corps Staff reached Mudros on 12 April, and found that they were to land in the Gaba Tepe area. The next day, Hamilton signalled to de Robeck:

> Will you please have two of the available aeroplanes placed at the disposal of the GOC the ANZAC, Lt Gen. Sir W. Birdwood whose HQ are on board HMT the *Minnewaska*, and one at the disposal of the GOC 29th Div, Major General Hunter Weston HMT the *Andanian* for the forthcoming operations.[80]

An air reconnaissance from Tenedos was made on 14 April by an Anzac staff officer, Major Villiers Stuart,[81] and on the same day the first sketch map showing the results of aerial reconnaissance was lithographed and distributed, only days after air photography began. On 15 April Hamilton spent almost two hours at Tenedos with Samson and Keyes (de Robeck's Chief of Staff) 'trying to digest the honey brought back by our busy aeroplane bees from their various flights over Gallipoli.'[82]

Photography of the beaches

It was naturally suggested that air photos should be used for reconnaissance of the beaches and their exits. From the time when the first air photos were taken of the land defences, few days were left to form a good picture of the terrain and the Turkish defences before the landings. This was clearly a very difficult task with only one camera. On 16 April Hamilton asked de Robeck 'for further information as to length, breadth of Cape Helles beaches and preparations for defence from seaward of ravine in Sq. 184, S, T, X, Y. [Sari Tepe area, north of Krithia, running inland from coast]. Suggested photographs of beaches might be obtained from aeroplanes.'[83] Samson was critical of the joint naval and military policy as regards the use of his aircraft, believing that had they been permitted to concentrate solely on close reconnaissance of the landing beaches, they would have produced much more complete results.[84] In this he does not seem to have thought the lack of cameras a constraint though clearly, besides shortages of plates or film, paper and chemicals, having only one camera and one experienced photographer at this stage was a serious limitation.

The landings and after

Samson considered, in the light of his constant flights over the Peninsula, that the landings would be impossible.[85] He was mistaken. The landings, though difficult, were possible. What was impossible, given the total loss of surprise, was the break-out from the beach-heads. His pessimism was shared by Hamilton's intelligence staff, and by most of the generals, who had also seen the air photos, maps and intelligence reports. On the 25th Samson's aircraft photographed the landings in progress, and on that and the following few days, the aircraft photographed important inland positions, spotted for the Navy and reconnoitred the whole Peninsula as far as Bulair, and also the Asiatic coast,[86] watching particularly for Turkish troop movements towards the bridgeheads. On the 26th and 27th Samson noted that 'we could see the Turks digging in all across the Peninsula. Trenches used to spring up like magic.'[87]

Although the pre-landing attempt at airfield reconnaissance at Helles had failed when the landing parties encountered strong opposition, after the main landings a suitable, if rough, landing place was soon identified next to Hill 138 (Hunter-Weston Hill), about half-a-mile from W Beach (Lancashire Landing), and used daily, but was under continuous shellfire and, from 29 June, was only used for special purposes and as an emergency landing ground. Samson noted that it was always shelled when in use, and four planes were destroyed there by 2 May; another was lost there later.[88]

Following the April landings, further air photos were taken which were used by the GHQ Printing Section during the land operations for making the important 'trench diagrams', showing the Turkish trenches, battery positions, etc., which served much the same purpose as trench maps on the Western Front. Through most of 1915, however, the trench diagrams were not sufficiently accurate to be used for the direction of artillery fire, and the 1:20,000 map (taken from captured Turkish 1:25,000 maps) was used for this.

On 2 May Samson wrote that the Army had found Butler's 'wonderful photographs' of the enemy positions extremely valuable.[89] As a result, a new sketch map of Turkish defences was printed and issued the following day.[90] Air photos were at first only supplied to GHQ, but in May or June, lower formations such as the 29th Division received such photos of, for example, the Gully Ravine area. The RNAS did not, at this stage, have the capacity to make large numbers of prints from each photographic plate.

The photographic unit which arrived with the French squadrons may have helped the British with printing.

Hogg reported on 11 May that since the landings they had been flying reconnaissance sorties and spotting for ships and land batteries, under the orders of de Robeck (Navy) and Hunter-Weston (29th Division), and that Knatchbull Hugessen had been appointed to assist in spotting for the army's batteries in the Helles sector. He made it clear that No. 3 Squadron was working for 29th Division in the Helles sector, while 'the *Ark Royal* with seaplanes is working with the Australian force on the West Coast near Nibrunesi Point and is entirely distinct from No. 3'. When VIII Corps was formed (under Hunter-Weston) on 24 May, covering the Helles sector, No. 3 Squadron worked for this new formation.

Hogg also remarked on air photography and on the inadequacy of the 1:40,000 map:

> Photography. – The maps of Turkey [i.e. the Gallipoli Peninsula] are very indifferent, many natural features are not marked, and roads and paths inaccurately shown. This has been corrected to some extent by sketches from aeroplanes. The country however presents very few landmarks such as prominent farmhouses, woods etc. and it is extremely difficult from Observation Posts on the ground to spot works that have been plotted on the map by aeroplane. Observation. The observer has to plot in the position of patches of gorse, a green field or any such indication which may help the location of a trench from the ground.
>
> We have only one camera, private property, a Naval Pilot [Butler] has been taking photos with this. The first experiments were not satisfactory, but latterly excellent results have been obtained, and are of the greatest value. The photos, in addition to their value to the General Staff, correct the map and enable the observer to place the enemy's positions and trenches with greater accuracy.
>
> Developing and printing are done here by the owner of the Camera.[91]

He thus makes it clear that no other camera was yet in use by 11 May. By 28 May, however, Butler was using the French camera, fixed to his machine in a vertical position, which enabled him to obtain sharper and more vertical photos. These good-quality images were used to plot the first of the 'trench diagrams', that of the Krithia sector dated 1 June. Photographs taken over the Peninsula from May, with this camera, and later repro-duced in Dowson's 'Secret Report' (see Appendix VI), show the 'fiducial marks' at the middle of each side typical of survey cameras; these would have enabled the principal point of each photograph to be identified, and radial triangulation to be undertaken had the British understood the nature of this photogrammetric technique.

Before the attack of 4 June, No. 3 Squadron flew reconnaissance and artillery spotting sorties, and Butler took photos of the complex network of Turkish trenches south of Krithia. From these, large-format and large-scale trench diagrams (1:6,000) were lithographed by the GHQ Printing Section, the first being dated 1 June, and delivered by air to Advanced GHQ at Helles. The Squadron's pilots used these 'photographic maps' to direct artillery fire.[92]

On 10 June Hogg reported some organisational changes; formerly the Squadron had been working directly under 29th Division, but since then the new VIII Corps had been formed so they were now working under the orders of the Corps CRA (Commander, Royal Artillery) for reconnaissance and spotting purposes, a rather anomalous position for the observers as they were now 'practically absorbed into No. 3 Aeroplane Squadron, the O.C. of which [Samson], though directly under the orders of the Admiral [de Robeck], meets the requirements of the CRA as far as possible'. He emphasised that the Turkish anti-aircraft guns were getting more accurate, were scoring 'a good many hits', and that as a result sorties were having to be flown at 7,000 feet or over, rather than the earlier 4,000 feet. As the seaplanes were no longer working in this sector, they also had to fly submarine-spotting sorties. Describing one German submarine, he noted that near the surface there was 'no disturbance of the water visible, but her hull showed up greyish green, and an under-water bow wave, as she dived, showed up the direction which she was going in – Then she disappeared.'

Hogg also remarked on the utility of powerful binoculars for artillery observation work: 'The 12 Mag[nification] Binoculars . . . are excellent; the smaller field [of view] is a disadvantage for general work, but for examining gun emplacements particularly, the high power is of immense value.' As far as camouflage and concealment were concerned, he noted:

> Our gunners conceal their guns much better than the Turks. The latter in nearly every case cover their emplacements with quantities of brushwood, making hard distinct outlines which attract attention. One or two judiciously placed branches and a cover painted to harmonise with the surroundings are probably more efficacious.[93]

In his next report, on 25 June, Hogg gave details of the development of their photographic work:

> Photography. – This is all done by one pilot, Lieutenant Butler RNAS in a Henry [sic – Henri Farman]. The French have lent him a camera, which he fixes alongside his seat outside the nacelle. Plates are brought back here for development; he has the assistance of an amateur: there is no regular photographic establishment, as the French have. Results have been very satisfactory. He pieces the photos together to form a map,

which is sent to [Hunter-Weston's VIII] Army Corps HQ. Trench reconnaissance is now done in this way exclusively. Its value is so great that a
regularly equipped photographic section attached to each squadron or
other unit appears to be indicated.

This is the first reference to photo-mosaics being made; this implied that
photography was being done in a relatively systematic way, overlapping
verticals being taken from a constant altitude, which also enabled 'trench
diagrams' to be traced off. However, in the absence of control points on
the ground, these were far from accurate in a planimetric sense, and also
carried no height data. On 25 June he wrote that an Henri Farman machine
was being used exclusively for photography, but that 'they are of very
little use for our work here'. He had earlier noted that with these under-
powered 80 HP Henri Farmans it was impossible to get more than eight to
ten miles up the Peninsula to plot Turkish trenches and gun positions. On
25 June he also reported that a second French squadron had just arrived,
and he had heard of a third on the way.[94]

After Butler was wounded at the end of June, his photographic work
was taken over by Flight Lieutenant Thomson. The borrowed French camera, which produced excellent clear prints, was damaged in an aeroplane
accident before 30 July; this was most unfortunate given the impending
diversionary operations at Helles on 6 August in connection with the
Suvla landings and Anzac attacks. On 30 July Major-General Douglas,
commanding 42nd Division and now commanding VIII Corps in the
Helles Sector, since the departure of Hunter-Weston in mid-July, was
reduced to asking the French for the loan of existing photos of 'certain
areas' not covered by British photos.[95]

The French Air Service

The first French aeroplane squadron to join the RNAS at Tenedos was
Captain Cesari's squadron, l'Escadrille 98T, which arrived at the Dardanelles
early in May. The first French air photographs were taken about mid-
May, Lieutenant Saint André specialising in this work, which provided
sufficient data for the reproduction of rudimentary, but approximately
accurate trench diagrams of the French and Turkish trenches. The French
squadrons at Gallipoli, gradually building up from one to at least three,
not only took their own photos for mapping by the French Topographical
Service, but in May lent a good air camera, focal length 30cm (12 inches) to
the British. From 4 August, and probably earlier, series of air photos were
being taken specifically for mapping.[96]

Seaplane work during and after 25 April

The duties of *Ark Royal*'s seaplanes, apart from spotting for naval gunfire, included the reconnaissance of all roads leading to the Turkish front positions as far north as Taifur Keui (thirty miles from the tip of the Peninsula), and as far east as Maidos, watching for troop movements and reinforcements. They also included the location of enemy battleships in the Dardanelles, and reconnaissance of permanent fortifications and field gun positions. Little success was obtained with the latter, 'partly owing to the nature of the country which is much broken and covered with thick low scrub in which the guns are carefully concealed, and partly owing to the fact that the enemy refrained from firing their field guns to any great extent when an aeroplane was in a position to observe'.[97] After the landings, *Ark Royal*'s seaplanes concentrated on supporting the Anzac sector.

Towards the end of May, *Ark Royal*'s seaplanes continued with spotting, photography and reconnaissance. The seaplane carrier *Ben-my-Chree* joined *Ark Royal* on 12 June,[98] and was the base for the Short 184 seaplane used by Flight Commander C Edmonds to torpedo a Turkish ship on 12 August, the first occasion a ship had been torpedoed from the air. He struck again on 17 August. Such headline-making strikes were of little significance when set against the routine but crucial work of reconnaissance and photography.

Air spotting for naval bombardment was developed during the campaign using aerial photography as a base. After vertical and panoramic photos had been taken of the targets on which seaplane spotting observation was required, the observer using these photos with a transparent scale showing the actual distances on the ground could immediately locate the target. First flying over the ship to set the scale to the line of fire, he placed it over his vertical photograph in its correct orientation and could then plot the fall of each shell on the photograph and read off the range and deflection errors.[99]

Air work for the Suvla operations

Concern for secrecy restricted opportunities for air reconnaissance before the Suvla Bay landings. Good photographic coverage of the Suvla Bay area was flown from Imbros, but as the time of the landings approached, for security reasons only brief high-altitude reconnaissance flights were flown, low-level flights being forbidden.[100] Nevertheless air reconnaissance and photography accurately identified the smallness of the Turkish garrison, precisely located the weak Turkish defences and provided the most detailed and accurate information about them, and about Turkish troop movements and the concentration of enemy forces after the

195

landings.[101] They did not, however, give much detailed information about the terrain, and their results were not interpreted with this in mind. Apart from the beaches and their exits, observers and air photo interpreters were not instructed to consider the terrain.[102]

As the Suvla area was too far from Tenedos for effective cover, and the previous reliance on *Ark Royal* to cover the Anzac sector was unsatisfactory, the RNAS aeroplane unit established a new airfield on Imbros. On 4 August Capt. A A Walser noted all existing trenches and gun emplacements (most of which he identified as unoccupied), made a sketch of the position from the air, and handed this to GHQ. The next day Knatchbull Hugessen confirmed the information about the gun emplacements and reported that the trenches north of the Salt Lake were unoccupied. Detailed photos were taken of the Chocolate Hill defences, one of the landing's first objectives. On 6 August the only enemy troops seen were moving away from the area.[103]

While overflying the area was kept to a minimum so as not to arouse Turkish suspicions, several of the good air photos taken with a French camera showed little or nothing in the way of enemy trenches or other defences except at Lala Baba. Knatchbull Hugessen wrote against two of these photos taken just before the landing: 'Note complete absence of all trenches, etc.'[104] Samson flew low over the area on 23 July, seeing little activity and few trenches.[105] GHQ's *Final Instructions* of 29 July to Stopford's Corps made a specific reference to 'an aeroplane photograph [which] has also disclosed the presence of a few trenches on Lala Baba. A sketch of these trenches, which have apparently been constructed for some months is attached.'[106] The air photos confirmed the Intelligence staff in their belief that the area was only lightly held.[107] Unfortunately this did not prevent Stopford and his Chief-of-Staff from adopting a cautious rather than aggressive attitude.

Colonel F H Sykes RFC and No. 2 Wing RNAS

Col. F H Sykes RFC arrived from England on 24 June to study the air situation, and sent his report to the Admiralty on 9 July. Among other reasons, the fact that he was RFC while Samson was RNAS created much bad blood. He emphasised the need for a huge expansion of the air forces in the theatre, and recommended that six A-Type air cameras, as used in France, with personnel to form a photographic section, should be sent out.[108]

From early August, as a Wing Captain, Sykes took over command of air operations, commanding RNAS Eastern Mediterranean Station. As a direct consequence of his report, No. 2 Wing RNAS under Wing Commander E L Gerrard was, in August, sent from Dunkirk to Imbros. It operated independently of Samson's No. 3 Wing and, building on its Flanders experience, rapidly developed an expertise in photography while No. 3 Wing specialised in reconnaissance and bombing.

Its photographic officer, Flight Lieutenant C F Lan-Davies, described the sorry state of affairs when he arrived:

> There were a few stores and tools available, and only by going round personally begging from the *Ark Royal*, Egyptian Engineers, Maps Office, etc., was I able to get started. I finally succeeded in getting a darkroom built and equipping it. The best method of attachment of the camera to a machine presented difficulties, as the idea at home had been to hold the camera in the hand. This was clearly impossible on Morane Parasol machines, where the camera, in order to avoid cutting off, must be on the outside. I arranged a suitable bracket for holding the camera, and proper boxes to hold the plates, and also built onto the cameras sent out from England a direct vision viewfinder. The finders sent out were of no use, and without one the amount of country included in each photograph and the proper overlapping cannot be at all correctly estimated. I carried out a number of trials to find the correct exposure and, as results of some kind were urgently needed, started work. From plates exposed on one day, clear bright prints were supplied to the Maps Office by the next day, and in some cases enlargements were made. A number of trench and other maps have been made from them, and I may fairly claim that the work turned out is really satisfactory and of use to the General Staff. Observers from the *Ark Royal* and captains of the monitors have asked for copies of many of the photographs, which they found of considerable value. No. 3 Wing has for long been photographing, but No. 2 Wing results and volume of work turned out compare favourably.[109]

No. 2 Wing took over 1,500 photos between 26 August and 19 November; of these 160 exposures failed and a further 120 were lost because of damage incurred by aircraft. In the course of photographic sorties, two cameras were destroyed in accidents to aircraft.

By the end of August a new airfield had been constructed at Kephalo Point on Imbros. This was used by Nos 2 and 3 Wings until the evacuation. On 1 November *Ark Royal* moved to Mudros, and thence to Iero Bay, Mitylene. From here, her seaplanes flew reconnaissance and photographic missions over Smyrna, before she was ordered to Salonika on 7 November, arriving the following day.[110]

The importance of the Air Service for photo-reconnaissance and mapping cannot be overstated; in a memorandum dated 21 October 1915, Sykes noted:

> At the beginning of the campaign the Air Service was based at Tenedos. This base necessitated an oversea flight of 18 miles for work on the

Peninsula and was distant from the strategically important area north of [it?]. It had however the advantage of being near the local base of operations which was then situated on that Island. The transference of the aircraft base to Imbros proved to be a great advantage. The service flight to Helles was shortened by 8 miles and the position is far more central both as regards the new Suvla–Anzac area and the wider strategical area N. and E. of the Gallipoli Peninsula.

As the operations developed it became apparent that the centres of gravity for air work were four, viz. Helles, Anzac–Suvla, the Dardanelles and the Asiatic shore, the Gulf of Saros and the area NNE and NW of it. As far as possible separate units have been allotted to these areas. The distribution has proved very satisfactory and it is proposed to retain it unless further developments necessitate alteration. [section follows about air observation of Naval gunfire on land targets]… both the Naval and Military forces are peculiarly dependent upon [the RNAS]. Its efficiency and adequacy are matters of vital importance to the success of the operations as a whole, apart from the fact that it carries out all strategical and tactical reconnaissances, and directs the greater part of the fire both of sea and shore guns, it is the sole agent for the supply of reliable maps. This applies to ordinary maps as well as to trench maps.[111]

Samson, reporting from Imbros on 23 November 1915 on the work of No. 3 Wing RNAS during the Dardanelles operations, noted that 'photographs have been taken of the whole sphere of operations'.[112] He was critical of the maps provided for the campaign, noting that: 'The great difficulty we encountered in the Dardanelles was the bad maps available: in time we got out our own maps, and towards the end of the campaign an excellent one was produced by the Survey Department [of Egypt] from our photographs.'[113]

Conclusion

The use of air reconnaissance at Gallipoli was to add diversity to the data in the hands of Hamilton and his General Staff, further adding to, elucidating and correcting that already received from MO2 and GSGS (MO4) in London and that obtained by intelligence officers in theatre. The value of this approach cannot be overstated, especially when combined with the results of other surveys, such as those made from the sea. These form the subject of the next chapter.

Notes

1. Chasseaud, Peter, 'German Maps and Survey on the Western Front, 1914–18', *Cartographic Journal*, London, 2001, 38(2), pp. 119–34.
2. Berger, Jos. Viktor, *Luftfahrzeuge im Dienste der Geländeaufnahme*, Kriegstechnische Zeitschrift 1913, pp. 171–9, 261–72.
3. Chasseaud, op. cit.
4. Churchill, Proposed Aircraft Expedition to Somaliland, TNA(PRO) CAB 37/119/47.
5. Albrecht, Oskar, *Das Kriegsvermessungswesen während des Weltkrieges 1914–18*, Deutsche Geodätische Kommission, Munich, 1969, pp. 6–7.
6. Bundesarchiv-Militärarchiv, Freiburg-im-Breisgau, files PH9XX/47, *Übungen der Vermessungsabteilungen in Wahn und Thorn 1912, mit photograph*; PH9V/98 & 99, *Erkundungs- und Vermessungstätigkeit im Festungskrieg. – Entwurf einer Dienstvorschrift in Zusammenarbeit mit dem Kriegsministerium und dem Chef des Generalstabes der Armee*, Bd. 1, 1913–14, & Bd. 2, Jan. 1913 bis Apr. 1914.
7. Albrecht, op. cit., p. 7.
8. Eckert, M, 'Meine Erfahrungen als Geograph im Kriegsvermessungs- und Kriegskartenwesen', *Kartographische und schulgeographische Zeitschrift*, 1922, 1 & 2, 7–10.
9. Roussilhe, H, *Emploi de la Photographie Aérienne aux Levées Topographiques à Grande Echelle*, Enyclopédie Industrielle et Commerciale, Librarie de l'Enseignement Technique, Léon Eyrolles, Paris, 1930, p. 30; *Manual of Photogrammetry*, American Society of Photogrammetry, 1952, p. 8.
10. *Multiple Lens Aerial Cameras in Mapping*, by the Technical Staff of the Fairchild Aerial Camera Corporation, Fairchild Corporation, New York, 1933.
11. Schumann, R, 'Die Entwicklung der photogrammetrischen Geräte in Jena von Jahrhundertwende bis zum Jahre 1945', *Kompendium Photogrammetrie*, 18, Leipzig, 1986.
12. Albrecht, op. cit., p. 33.
13. Hills, E H, review by 'E.H.H.' of *Die Geschichtliche Entwicklung der Photogrammetrie und die Begründung ihrer Verwendbarkeit für Mess- and Konstruktionswecke* by Weiss, M; Strecker & Schröder, Stuttgart, in *Geographical Journal*, 42 (2), 1913, p. 189.
14. Hamilton, Gen. Sir Ian, *Gallipoli Diary*, Vol. I, London: Edward Arnold, 1920, pp. 7– 8, 25; Rhodes James, Robert, *Gallipoli*, London: Pimlico, 1999, pp. 52–3.
15. Extracts from Minutes of Conference Held in the Admiralty on 3 April 1915, TNA(PRO) ADM 1/8497.
16. Minute to War Council by Churchill, 3-4-15, Milner Papers, Bodleian, Box 122, Folio 129; also quoted, with slight differences, in Churchill, W S, *The World Crisis*, Vol. 2, London: Butterworth, 1923, pp. 540–1.
17. Churchill, op. cit., p. 552.
18. *Report on Naval Bombardment Procedures in the Helles Sector*, TNA(PRO) WO 95/4263.
19. Report by Lt Park RNVR on HMS *Ark Royal*'s photographic work; referred to in Nolan, Col. Mike, *The Gallipolian*, Winter 1994, p. 15.
20. 'Mitchell Report', *C.B. 1550 Report of the Committee Appointed to Investigate the Attacks delivered on and the Enemy Defences of the Dardanelles Straits*, 1919.

Admiralty, Naval Staff, Gunnery Division, April 1921, pp. 513–14. TNA(PRO) ADM 186/600.

21. Dardanelles. 1914 Sept–Dec. TNA(PRO) ADM 137/881.
22. Major Hogg's Reports, HQ, RFC, ME, Gallipoli & Asiatic Mainland 1915, TNA(PRO) AIR 1/2119/207/72/2.
23. Particulars of HMS *Ark Royal*, unsigned and undated (probably early 1915), TNA(PRO) AIR 1/361.
24. Jones, H J, *The War in the Air*, Vol. II, Oxford: OUP, 1928, pp. 10–11.
25. *Reports from HMS* Ark Royal, *Dardanelles Operations, Feb– May 1915*, Print code: 0(35) AS 140 Pk 1300 250 8/15 E&S, blue printed paper cover, in TNA(PRO) AIR 1/2099/207/20/7.
26. Hickey, Michael, *Gallipoli*, London: John Murray, 1998, pp. 51–2.
27. Corbett, Sir Julian S, *History of the Great War, Naval Operations*, Vol. II, London: Longmans, Green, 1921, p. 147.
28. Reports from HMS *Ark Royal, Dardanelles Operations*, op. cit.
29. Rhodes James, Robert, *Gallipoli*, London: Pimlico, 1999, p. 46.
30. Sec. W.O., London to GOC in C, Cairo. 3324 Cipher M.O. 179. Your 653 E. Feby. 26th, in TNA(PRO) WO 158/574.
31. *Reports from HMS Ark Royal*, op. cit.
32. Sec. W.O., London to GOC in C, Cairo. Rec'd 8.3.15. 3443 Cipher M.O. 192. March 8th. Your 683 E. March 4th, last paragraph. TNA(PRO) WO 158/574.
33. Aspinall-Oglander, Brig.-Gen. C F, *History of the Great War, Military Operations, Gallipoli*, Vol. I, London: Heinemann, 1929, p. 86.
34. Saunders, H St G, *Per Ardua. The Rise of British Air Power 1911–1939*, London: OUP, 1944, p. 62.
35. Corbett, op. cit., p. 176.
36. Ibid, p. 206.
37. *Reports from HMS Ark Royal*, op. cit.
38. Dardanelles 1915 Jan–April (H.S. 1089), items 289/25, 26 and 27, TNA(PRO) ADM 137/1089; *Reports from HMS Ark Royal*, op. cit.
39. *Reports from HMS Ark Royal*, op. cit.
40. Ibid.
41. Ibid.
42. Kitchener to Maxwell, Cairo, Rec'd 8.4.15. 3925 Cipher. Your telegram 861E. TNA(PRO) WO 158/574.
43. Vice-Admiral (via Mudros) to Maxwell, Cairo. Rc'd 8.4.15. Your 173N. TNA(PRO) WO 158/574.
44. Hamilton to Maxwell, Cairo, Rc'd 9.4.15. MF 101 8th. TNA(PRO) WO 158/574.
45. *Reports from HMS Ark Royal*, op. cit.
46. Hamilton to Maxwell, Cairo, Rc'd 10.4.15. MF 105 10th. Your Telegram 867E. TNA(PRO) WO 158/574.
47. *Reports from HMS* Ark Royal, op. cit.
48. Ibid.
49. Anzac Corps General Staff War Diary, TNA(PRO) WO 95/4280.
50. Chasseaud, Peter, unpublished PhD thesis, *British, French and German survey and mapping 1914–1918*, University of Greenwich.
51. *Report on the Working of the Kite Balloon Ships at the Dardanelles*, Paper on Kite Balloons, 19 October 1915, TNA(PRO) AIR 1/2103.
52. Aspinall-Oglander, op. cit., p. 139.

53. *Report on the Working of the Kite Balloon Ships at the Dardanelles,* Paper on Kite Balloons, op. cit.
54. MEF Dardanelles, Gen. Staff (GHQ) War Diary, 1915 Feb–1915 Apr. Appendices. O(b). TNA(PRO) WO 95/4263.
55. Samson, Charles Rumney, *Fights and Flights,* London: Ernest Benn, 1930, p. 218.
56. Corbett, op. cit., p. 208.
57. Ibid, p. 229.
58. Aspinall-Oglander, op. cit., p. 137fn.
59. Samson, op. cit., p. 227.
60. Anzac Corps Intelligence War Diary, 15–30 April 1915, TNA(PRO) WO 157/678, Appendix Z4.
61. Ibid, Appendix Z1.
62. Ibid, Appendix Z4.
63. Information on Butler's photos obtained from MS inscriptions in album of photographs in IWM Dept of Photographs (Accession No. 9008-06), and internal evidence of the photos in that album.
64. Ibid.
65. Chasseaud, Peter, *Artillery's Astrologers – A History of British Survey and Mapping on the Western Front 1914–1918,* Lewes: Mapbooks, 1999, p. 119.
66. MEF Dardanelles, op. cit.
67. Major Hogg's Reports, op. cit.
68. Chasseaud collection.
69. Jones, H J, *The War in the Air,* Vol. II, Oxford: OUP, 1928, p. 28.
70. The authors have only seen eight photos or references to specific photos taken before 25 April; photos and MS inscriptions in album of photographs in IWM Dept of Photographs (Accession No. 9008-06).
71. Samson, op. cit., pp. 232–3.
72. Rhodes-James, op. cit., pp. 80–1.
73. Samson, op. cit., pp. 230–1.
74. Notes on interview with Air Commodore C R Samson, DSO., at the Grosvenor Court Hotel, Davies Street, on 15th March 1923. Operations Section. 16th March, 1923, TNA(PRO) AIR 1/724/76/6.
75. Samson, op. cit., p. 228.
76. MS inscriptions, dated 23 & 28 May, in album of No. 3 Squadron air photos in IWM Dept of Photographs (Accession No. 9008-06). The earliest photograph seen by the authors taken with the French camera was dated 28 May.
77. Major Hogg's Reports, 11 May, op. cit.
78. Anzac Corps Intelligence War Diary, TNA(PRO) WO 157/678, Appendix Z12.
79. 29th Division General Staff War Diary, TNA(PRO) WO 95/4304.
80. MEF Dardanelles, Gen. Staff (GHQ) War Diary, op. cit., Appendix 13 April. TNA(PRO) WO 95/4263.
81. Anzac Corps General Staff War Diary, op. cit.; Aspinall-Oglander, op. cit., p. 166.
82. Hamilton, op. cit., p. 109.
83. MEF Dardanelles, Gen. Staff (GHQ) War Diary, op. cit.
84. Samson, op. cit., pp. 232–3.
85. Ibid, p. 231.

86. Jones, op. cit., p. 45.
87. Samson, op. cit., p. 237.
88. Jones, op. cit., p. 52; Samson, op. cit., pp. 238–9.
89. Roskill, Capt. S W (ed.), *Documents Relating to the Naval Air Service*, Vol. I, 1908– 1918, London: Navy Records Society, 1969, p. 205; TNA(PRO) AIR 1/361.
90. Roskill, op. cit., p. 258; TNA(PRO) AIR 1/664.
91. Major Hogg's Reports, 11 May, op. cit.
92. Jones, op. cit., p. 52.
93. Major Hogg's Reports, 10 June, op. cit.
94. Ibid, 25 June.
95. General Douglas to French CEO, 30-7-15, in TNA(PRO) WO 95/4273.
96. Dated from MS entries in album of No. 3 Squadron air photos in IWM Dept of Photographs (Accession No. 9008-06).
97. *Reports from HMS* Ark Royal, op. cit.
98. Jones, op. cit., pp. 56–7, 64–6.
99. Ibid, p. 73.
100. Rhodes-James, op. cit., p. 248.
101. *Notes for Observers*, Royal Flying Corps, 1915, p. 11. Copy in Sykes papers, Vol. I, RAF Museum, Hendon. See also Sykes, F, *From Many Angles: An Autobiography*, London: Harrap. 1942, p. 166, and Rhodes-James, op. cit., p. 255.
102. Sykes, op. cit., pp. 157–73.
103. Jones, op. cit., p. 59.
104. MS inscription against photos 456 & 457 in album (Vol. VI – Gallipoli & various) of air photos collected by Capt. Hon. M Knatchbull MC, on loan to IWM Dept of Photographs.
105. Samson, op. cit., p. 256.
106. Appendix 3 (Final Instructions from GHQ to IX Corps for the Suvla Operations, 29 July) of OH Military Operations, Gallipoli Vol. II, Maps and Appendices, London: Heinemann, 1932, p. 19.
107. Aspinall-Oglander, op. cit., pp. 29, 165.
108. Jones, op. cit., p. 57.
109. Lan-Davies to J H Dallmeyer Ltd, October 1915, in *British Journal of Photography*, 18 April 1919.
110. Jones, op. cit., p. 74.
111. Roskill, op. cit., pp. 241–6; TNA(PRO) AIR 1/654.
112. Ibid, p. 258; TNA(PRO) AIR 1/664.
113. Samson, op. cit., pp. 227 –8.

CHAPTER 8

Admiralty Hydrographic Surveys

While attempts to gather detailed hydrographic and other intelligence were made by the Naval Intelligence Department (NID) at points on the German coast, at the Dardanelles, apart from the regular charting operations begun by Spratt and continuing up to the outbreak of war, little additional inshore hydrographic intelligence was acquired, and the post-war Naval report ('Mitchell Report') on the Dardanelles operations included an appreciation of the hydrographic knowledge of the western side of the Gallipoli Peninsula, its coast, soundings, maps, etc., considered it to be 'most inadequate' in February 1915.[1] As this was 'the principal area from the point of view of naval war operations', it was a serious omission:

> The coast was incorrectly charted and the soundings were not only sparse, but did not in any way give an idea of the configuration of the sea bottom. No detailed survey of this area had ever been made, a survey by Captain Graves in 1840 having been confined to the immediate approaches of the Dardanelles and the Island of Tenedos, with the Archipelago and waters contiguous to it.[2]

However, while later hydrographic surveys by Wharton and others remedied some of these deficiencies, the Navy had to acquire such additional information as it required during the preliminary operations themselves.

Existing charts

Spratt's remarkable charting, mapping and other operations have been described in Chapter 2. A medium-scale Admiralty Chart (one-inch to the nautical mile, or 1:72,960) No. 2429, *The Dardanelles (Ancient Hellespont), From the West Entrance to Cape Nagara*, was published in 1871. This crucial chart was compiled from an 1840 survey by Commander T Graves, and a specific survey by Captain T A B Spratt, assisted by Lieutenant A L Monsell, J Stokes (Master), G R Wilkinson (Acting Master), and E W

Brooker (Second Master), in the paddle steamer HMS *Spitfire* (which Spratt had taken over from Graves in 1850) in 1855, covering *The Narrows*; the latter portion was separately incorporated as a larger-scale (1:29,136) inset.[3] The Gulf of Saros (Xeros) portion had been surveyed by Commander Copeland RN in 1833, and 'The remainder from various documents in the Hydrographic Office.' The chart carried a cautionary note: 'As there has been no complete survey of the Strait to the Eastward of Cape Nagara, the chart of that part must be used with caution.' This deficiency was soon remedied, for later editions stated that the section from Nagara to Gallipoli [port] had been surveyed in 1872 by Commander W J L Wharton RN, Navigating Lieutenants J Millward and C H C Langdon, Lieutenant C J Fellowes and Midshipman E P Chapman, of HMS *Shearwater*. In 1880 Captain Wharton observed the latitude of Cape Helles Light and found it was 7 seconds south of the chart position.[4]

The chart *The Narrows* was also produced by the Admiralty at 1:22,600 in 1856,[5] while another sheet, *Dardanelles and Tenedos Channel* was published in London by J Imray & Son in 1864 and again in 1868.[6] The land details were crude and inaccurate, and clearly did not incorporate the French 1854 survey. The Salt Lake at Suvla was not shown.

The 1871 chart gave a good, firm depiction of the relief of the Gallipoli Peninsula, using hachures for which the copper plate was a very suitable medium.[7] The source of information for the land area of the Peninsula was given as a 'French Imperial Survey of 1854–5,' clearly that by the *Dépôt de Guerre*. Although the hachures were based on the contours of the 1854 French survey, the outline, relief and the little detail shown of the Peninsula differed significantly from the 1854 map, and some may well have been retained from Stratt's surveys. Spot-heights and the aqueduct and 'fountain' in the Helles area agree with the French map. This 1871 chart was subject to later corrections, the last before the campaign being 13 November 1913. A new edition appeared in 1914.[8] It was also used by the Admiralty in February 1915 as the base for enlargements X93, 94 and 95. These are dealt with below.

No further charts of the Dardanelles had been prepared or issued before February 1915, except that an old three inches to a nautical mile (1:24,320) chart, F.019 *Isthmus of Boulaïr, with adjacent anchorages*, dated 1887, was issued in early 1915, as was a smaller-scale chart designated F.064, *The Dardanelles and western approaches* (one inch to nautical mile, or 1:72,960), which included *The Narrows* (2½ inches to nautical mile, or 1:29,184), issued on 22 February 1915 as an inset.[9]

The important report *NID 838, Turkey Coast Defences, May 1908*, Part II of which covered the 'Coast Defences and Resources of the Dardanelles', contained four charts covering the Dardanelles, one of which (Chart 3 – based on the 1871 chart) showed the fixed defences updated to December 1914, the new additions being in red.

A decision having been made in early 1915 to attack the Dardanelles, and it initially being assumed that the Navy should be able to force the Straits without help from the Army, which at this stage had no troops available, the Hydrographic Department of the Admiralty under John F Parry rapidly produced a set of three special large-scale (1:24,320) fire-control charts, based on the 1871 chart, for the bombardment of the Dardanelles forts, having worked out a system for square-referencing and reporting fall-of-shot before the war.

On 5 February 1915 Admiral Sir Henry Jackson sent a memo to DAD (Director, Admiralty War Staff), DID (Director, Intelligence Division), Signal Section, COS (Chief of Staff) and Parry the Hydrographer, stating that:

A large scale chart is being prepared on a scale of 3 inches to a nautical mile, for use in the event of a bombardment of the Dardanelles Forts by the Allied Fleets, to assist spotting from ships, air craft, or land stations. The most recent practical experience has been considered in connection with the preparation of the charts, and the draft notes or explanations and instructions to be printed in the margin are attached herein for consideration and suggestions.[10]

These charts were all named *Dardanelles from the entrance to Nagara Kalessi* (Nagara Point is east of Maidos, beyond the Narrows), and were numbered X 93 (Sheet 1), X 94 (Sheet 2) and X 95 (Sheet 3). The date of production given by the Hydrographic Department for all three sheets was 16 February 1915.[11] The 'X' designation indicated that these were 'important and sensitive' but 'non-confidential' fleet charts but, as fleet charts, they were not to be made public ('Y' Charts were confidential and 'Z' Charts were secret).

The Draft Instructions[12] described the squaring system in detail. Each large numbered square was subdivided into twenty-five lettered five-inch squares (omitting 'e'), each of which contained nine dots (in three rows of three); a typical reference to a point was 69 M 4, the last figure being the 'dot numeral' or, more accurately, 69 M 55-30, the four last figures representing coordinates in yards from the south and west sides of the squares (i.e. giving northing before easting, the reverse of the newly-evolved British Army practice). On the later 1:40,000 chart-map produced in Egypt in March from the War Office one-inch map, the equivalent large squares would have sides of about three-inches; because of projection differences, the squares on this chart-map had to be distorted in order to match on the ground the squares on the original 1:24,320 chart.

A note, dated 6 February 1915, by Murray F Sueter on this memo read: 'The proposed system of dividing the chart and the W/T signals to be used are concurred in, as they are in general accordance with those at present in use in the air service.' On 8 February Jackson suggested that 100 sets of these charts be prepared, together with sixty celluloid scales.[13] On 19 February the Hydrographer was able to report that:

> 3 charts have now been prepared . . . X 93, 94 and 95, were required to cover the whole area concerned. . . . 100 numbered sets, of 3 charts in each set, together with 60 boxes of celluloid scales, each containing 2 scales, have today been handed to Commander The Hon. L. J. D. Lambert, RN for transmission to the Mediterranean.[14]

On the same day, the Admiralty signalled to Limpus in Malta: 'An officer carrying secret charts is proceeding from Toulon for Malta either on the 22nd or 23rd by a collier or by a French destroyer. The charts should be despatched to Admiral Carden as soon as possible, and as they are urgently required a special vessel should be sent if necessary.'[15] Jackson noted: 'The promptness with which these charts have been prepared is very creditable to those concerned.'[16] These charts were used for the preliminary landings at Sedd-el-Bahr and Kum Kale and the Navy's big attempt to force the Narrows on 18 March, and continued in use after this date.

The failure of the purely naval operations in February and March led to the overprinting with naval squaring of the 1:40,000 maps of the Gallipoli Peninsula, being prepared in Egypt, to aid artillery spotting, and the addition to these maps of the most up-to-date hydrographic data, turning them into an early form of chart-maps. Ernest Dowson, Director-General of the Egyptian Survey Department, initially had the 1:40,000 maps overprinted with the Army's artillery square system for use once the force was ashore, but had to reprint them all with the Navy's different system at the latter's insistence, as the Navy was going to provide all the covering fire, at least until the force was well-established ashore. As the Mitchell report noted:

> The maps supplied by the GSGS (squared and numbered) were admittedly imperfect and operations charts prepared by the Hydrographic Department of the Admiralty from the Admiralty charts also squared and numbered with a view to Naval gunfire, were also based on imperfect work. Moreover, there was no common system of squaring or numbering of the two departments' productions.[17]

Clearly two different fire-control systems could not be used, as this would only lead to a disastrous confusion.

The Mitchell Report appears to underestimate the early hydrographic work, as the charts of the area not only included Graves's work, but also, as we have seen, surveys of the Narrows by Spratt and others in 1855, while the Gulf of Xeros had been surveyed by Copeland in 1833, and 'The remainder from various documents in the Hydrographic Office'. The section of the Straits from Nagara to Gallipoli was surveyed in 1872 by Wharton and others, and Wharton did further work in 1880. Nevertheless, Mitchell's assessment of the accuracy of the soundings must be taken seriously. The Greeks had planned to attack this very coast, but there is no record of Admiral Kerr in Athens being able to provide up-to-date hydrographic or beach intelligence. This does not mean that no information was passed. There were close relations between the Greek and Royal Navy personnel in the Dardanelles area and at Tenedos, British officers were serving on Greek naval craft, and there is no doubt that some information was acquired in this way.

The Suvla Bay area had been charted by earlier Admiralty hydrographers from the time of Spratt and Graves, but little specific hydrographic work was done in that area before the April landings or for the Suvla operation in August. It was feared that any obvious survey work would merely alert the Turks and induce them to strengthen their defences in this zone, as had happened at Helles. However, there were more general hydrographic data available for the Suvla Bay area, as Turkish maps had been captured, and since April there had been months of close observation by the Navy's fire-support ships as well as aerial reconnaissance, air photography and landing parties.

Commander Douglas and his survey work

The Hydrographic Department fully recognised the inadequacy of the existing maps and charts and, when it was learned that active operations were in prospect, Commander Henry Douglas, Superintendent of Charts at the Admiralty, was appointed Surveying Officer on the staff of the Vice-Admiral commanding the Eastern Mediterranean Squadron (at first Carden, then de Robeck) to try to 'rectify matters on the spot'. Douglas arrived at the Dardanelles on 24 February, and the only material he had to work with were proofs of the new Naval operations charts (X93–X95), the GSGS one-inch and 1:250,000 maps, and knowledge of the extent to which the surveys of Graves in 1840 could be considered accurate. In fact Graves' surveys formed a sound basis of all new work in 1915, being found to be 'most accurate as regards scale and bearing'. Douglas did a great deal of survey work before the Army's landings of 25 April and later during the subsequent operations. He carried out beach surveys prior to the landings,[18] and also some survey work in connection with fleet gunnery, notably to assist *Queen Elizabeth* to fire 'indirect' across the Peninsula.

As land reconnaissance was impossible before the April landings, the selected landing places at Helles, Anzac and Kum Kale had to be examined as closely as possible from the sea. Much data had to be acquired:

charts had to be checked, shoal water carefully sounded, and anchorages organised for the many transport ships involved. In addition, to acquire as much general intelligence as possible, the Navy and RNAS had to keep the whole Peninsula under close surveillance, and Turkish defensive work had to be disrupted by naval bombardment.[19]

Douglas's log for the period before the landings, which also recorded the weather and sea conditions, shows the variety of work done by him, including hydrographic survey:[20]

5–6 March   *Queen Elizabeth* bombarding by indirect fire
17 March   Boat work – surveying at Mudros
25 March   Laying buoys for firing
26 March   Surveying coast in *Grampus off the Gallipoli beaches*[21]
29 March   Surveying – no location given [possibly of Suvla Point to Bulair[22]]
30 March   Anchored at Imbros after surveying
31 March   Surveying and sketching; Mudros at dusk
 1 April   Surveying Gulf of Adramyti
13 April   To Tenedos in *Dartmouth* with General Hunter-Weston etc
14 April   Examining coast; then to Mudros
15 April   Admiral and General over in *Triumph* to bombard
18 April   Over in *Dublin* with General Hunter-Weston and other officers to view Peninsula, returning to Mudros

This may, however, under-record the survey work; some was certainly done before 5–6 March to enable *Queen Elizabeth* to start her indirect firing.

As we have seen, various panoramic sketches of the possible landing places were drawn from the sea. The Navy's reconnaissance sketches took the form of a set of drawn panoramas which were soon lithographed on tough linen-backed paper by the GHQ Printing Section. There were at least six of these:

- *General View of West Coast of Gallipoli Peninsula south of Gaba Tepe (S.S.E. 2 miles)*; this indicated various landmarks, 'trenches, precipitous cliffs, Blockhouse, battery behind ridge, Achi Baba', etc. On the same sheet was also an oblique, contoured sketch-map, probably the result of air reconnaissance and possibly sketched from an oblique air photo: *Rough sketch showing General Idea of the Topography from Gaba Tepe southwards to C. Helles, Gallipoli Peninsula*. This indicated 'Good sandy beach, steep cliffy coastline, Mal Tepe (conspicuous), Achi Baba', etc.
- *Sketch No.1 showing general view from proposed position of covering ship* [Gaba Tepe to entrance to valley (Chana Orasi)]. *See also Sketch No.2*.
- *Sketch No.2. View looking into valley of Chana Orasi (bearing SbE 1' from shore)*.

- *Sketch No.3. View showing position WNW of Cape Tekeh to cover Karethia Plain.*
- *Sketch No.4. View showing suggested landing places at C. Helles and position of Covering ship.*
- *Sketch No.5. View showing position for covering ship and landing places* [Helles].

These assault panoramas are evidence of the considerable thought, preparation and cooperation which were put by the Army and Navy into the brief, intense period before the landings. Butler, of the RNAS, was also taking oblique and near-vertical air photos in considerable numbers during April.

Douglas 'rendered most valuable services in connection with the reconnaissance of landing places in the Gallipoli Peninsula prior to the landing',[23] and may have been responsible for some, if not all, of the panoramic drawings listed above. On 3 March *Irresistible* put out a surveying party in boats, to examine and buoy the approaches to Camber Beach at Sedd-el-Bahr, which had previously been avoided owing to the presence of a reef. On the beach the party found a battery of destroyed field guns.[24] Landings took place the next day, but little success was achieved. Demolition, survey (including survey of potential airfield sites) and beach parties were landed from *Inflexible* and *Ocean* under Lt Commander Giffard. A Royal Marine covering force (one company) tried to move forward to a line extending for a mile and a half from Morto Bay to the 'fountain' north of Tekke Burnu (the westernmost tip of the Peninsula), which it intended to hold for three hours while the demolition and survey parties did their work, but as Turkish fire prevented the covering force from advancing, the parties pulled out.[25]

Some ten days after the 25 April landings, in conjunction with Lieutenant T C Nicholas, Hamilton's Maps Officer, Douglas produced a 'Plan of SW end of Gallipoli Peninsula' showing the Turkish defences at Helles as they existed on the morning of assault. This was printed in colour by the Survey Department, Egypt,[26] and later appeared, in slightly modified form, in the Military Operations Official History.[27] It included a panorama drawing of the Helles sector, drawn by Douglas.

Indirect fire surveys for battleships and monitors engaging land targets

Douglas also executed surveys to assist indirect fire on enemy forts and batteries, both before the landings and during the subsequent operations. This important work, which he further developed later off the Flanders coast, also included surveys for the indirect fire of monitors. On 5 March 1915 the Navy planned to use a cairn on the summit of Haji Monorlo Dagh as an aiming point for *Queen Elizabeth,* laying the fire of her 15-inch guns over the Peninsula.[28] Douglas undertook survey work for *Queen Elizabeth*'s indirect fire bombardment of the forts guarding the Narrows at Chanak and Kilid Bahr. This involved extending the triangulation across the Peninsula between 26 March and 3 April by taking sextant angles from points offshore.

Later in the campaign, Commander C V Robinson, formerly of the *Natal,* and Lieutenant Bowen, who had spent two years in the Hydrographic service, both serving in the *Edgar,* worked with Lieutenant Park of *Ark Royal* to produce some remarkably accurate naval bombardment results. Bowen obtained from the Anglo-French survey (see Chapter 9) the list of coordinates of points they had fixed on both sides of the Dardanelles, so that he could fix the *Edgar*'s position to within twenty-five yards. He plotted these points on his chart, and used them to cut in a series of sextant angles to certain terrain features, thus obtaining good aiming points.[29]

There were four distinct phases of naval gunnery surveys for indirect fire, with all of which Douglas was closely involved, and which were described by him in a report written soon after the evacuation, *Notes by Captain H. P. Douglas, R.N. on Methods Employed by H.M. Ships When Engaging Enemy Batteries:*[30]

1. *Queen Elizabeth* on Chanak and Kilid Bahr Forts, before 25 April.
2. Battleships and cruisers against Turkish field batteries on Gallipoli Peninsula, after the landings.
3. 14-inch and 9.2-inch Monitors anchored off Rabbit Islands firing at Asiatic batteries.
4. Ships under way off west coast of Gallipoli Peninsula.

In September 1915 Douglas was promoted to Acting Captain, and when the surveying ship *Endeavour* (Capt. Lieutenant-Commander Edgell) arrived in October he was put in charge of all theatre hydrographic surveys. At the end of 1915 his promotion to Captain was confirmed, and he was awarded the 'Italian Silver Medal for Military Valour' for his services in the Mediterranean.[31]

Table 4: Relevant Naval Charts

Number	Notes
No. 1608	c.1 inch to mile, showing Tenedos and part of Turkish coast to east
No. 2429	(1 inch to nautical mile, or 1:72,960) *The Dardanelles (Ancient Hellespont),* 1871, with subsequent additions. Also edition with defence overprint.

Number	Notes
F. 019	3 inches to a nautical mile (1:24,320) *Isthmus of Boulaïr, with adjacent anchorages*, 1887, reissued in early 1915.
F.064	(1 inch to nautical mile, or 1:72,960) *The Dardanelles and western approaches*, including inset *The Narrows* (2½-inches to nautical mile, or 1:29,184), issued 22 February 1915.
X.93	*Dardanelles from the entrance to Nagara Kalessi*, enlarged and
X.94	redrawn from
X.95	2429. Also edition with defence overprint.

Notes

1. Mitchell Report, *C.B. 1550 Report of the Committee Appointed to Investigate the Attacks delivered on and the Enemy Defences of the Dardanelles Straits. 1919. Admiralty, Naval Staff, Gunnery Division, April 1921*. P522. TNA(PRO) ADM 186/600.
2. Ibid.
3. British Library Map Library, Maps SEC.5. (2429).
4. 1914 edition, BL Map Library, Maps BAC6. (2429).
5. BL Map Library, Maps SEC.5. (2429).
6. BL Map Library, Maps 43980. (7) and (8).
7. Dardanelles, Charts and tracings used by the Eastern Mediterranean Squadron 1914 –1916. TNA(PRO) ADM 137/787.
8. BL Map Library, Maps BAC6. (2429).
9. *A Consecutive List of Fleet Charts and Miscellaneous Diagrams, Charts and Plans, issued for Fleet Purposes, 1915, Corrected to 1st April 1915. Hydrographic Department, Admiralty. (Compiled April 1915)*: pp. 4–5, 10–11.
10. Dardanelles 1915 Jan–April (H.S. 1089), item 100. TNA(PRO) ADM 137/1089.
11. *A Consecutive List . . .*, op. cit., pp. 24–5.
12. Dardanelles . . ., op. cit., items 101–2.
13. Ibid, item 100.
14. Ibid, item 103.
15. Dardanelles Commission, p. 351, No. 29, signal 264. TNA(PRO) CAB 17/184.
16. Dardanelles . . ., op. cit., MS note on item 103. TNA(PRO) ADM 137/1089.
17. Mitchell Report, op. cit.
18. Denham, H M, *Dardanelles. A Shipman's Log 1915–16*, London: John Murray, 1981, pp. 72–3.
19. Aspinall-Oglander, Brig.-Gen. C F, *Military Operations, Gallipoli*, London: Heinemann, 1929, p. 127.
20. *Weather Report by Captain Douglas RN*, in Additional statements and documents produced by witnesses after giving evidence to the Dardanelles Commission, TNA(PRO) CAB 19/32.
21. Denham, op. cit., p. 72.
22. Ibid, p. 73.

23. *Memoirs of Hydrography*, Part III. Typescript, Ch. VII, p. 72. Hydrographic Department, 920: 528.47 JAC.
24. Corbett, Sir Julian S, *History of the Great War, Naval Operations*, Vol. II, London: Longmans, Green, 1921, pp. 172–3.
25. Ibid, p. 176.
26. Dardanelles, Charts. TNA(PRO) ADM 137/787.
27. Aspinall-Oglander, op. cit.
28. Corbett, op. cit., p. 176.
29. *Report on Naval Bombardment Procedures in the Helles Sector*, TNA(PRO) WO 95/4263.
30. *Notes by Captain HP Douglas RN on Methods Employed by HM Ships When Engaging Enemy Batteries, C.B. 1202, Confidential, 1916, Admiralty, Gunnery Branch, G. 01701/16. May 1916.* TNA(PRO) ADM 186/26.
31. *Memoirs of Hydrography*, op. cit.

CHAPTER 9

Captured Maps and New Maps

Once the landings had taken place on 25 April and the position had been consolidated, the need was primarily for an accurate map for shore-based artillery and on which to show trenches and other targets. For accurate location of enemy batteries, artillery observation posts or flash-spotting survey posts had to be fixed accurately to a regular survey grid, to which one's own batteries, and those of the enemy, also had to be fixed. By the end of 1914 it had been recognised that artillery survey had to become a normal part of operations, and survey sections for this purpose, as well as for map-making, had to be included in war establishments. However, the first British survey section at Gallipoli, under Nugent, did not start work until June.

New 1:25,000, 1:20,000 and 1:10,000 mapping was produced with commendable speed, both at Imbros by the GHQ Intelligence Staff and Printing Section, and in Egypt. The production of even larger-scale trench diagrams, from air photos, followed in late May and June. This remarkable achievement was not initially accompanied by a realisation of the need for an overarching survey organisation and standardised geodetic and cartographic data for the theatre. Survey and mapping developed on an *ad hoc* basis, as operations developed, at Helles, Anzac, and later at Suvla, and also independently by the French and the British, as well as by the Army and the Navy. No one possessed the geodetic data on which the Turkish surveys and maps were based; no trig lists had been captured, and the captured maps contained very few fixed points.

Captured maps

The British 1:40,000 map, in three sheets, of the Gallipoli Peninsula was recognised as inadequate, being essentially nothing more than an enlargement of the 1908 one-inch map but, as no Turkish large-scale maps were captured by landing parties during the preliminary raids, nothing better was available until various maps were captured following the landings on 25 April. These Turkish maps, apart from a few at 1:20,000, followed German practice by being reproduced at 1:25,000 and 1:50,000. They had Ottoman script, and were rather torn and illegible. Nevertheless, they were re-photographed in Egypt, the script transliterated into English and, after preliminary and provisional editions, were reprinted with the naval grid as a new edition.[1]

Lt Tresilien Nicholas, Hamilton's 'Maps' Officer, had started the war as a research geologist at Trinity College, Cambridge, and went to the Geographical Section at the War Office in January 1915 as a bowler-hatted civilian. After a few weeks, he was warned that he might have to take a Printing Section, with hand-operated litho and letterpress equipment, to the Dardanelles, so was put into uniform in mid-February, collected a revolver from the Tower of London, and on 22 March 1915 embarked for Mudros in the *Arcadian* with 'A' Printing Section RE, which had been formed at the School of Military Engineering at Chatham. Although he returned with Hamilton to Imbros before the landings, his Printing Section did not arrive at GHQ MEF at Imbros until 12 May (it had been held in Egypt because of lack of base facilities at Imbros). Here it joined the 'Anzac Printing Section' which was already at work. On 8 May Nicholas explained the initial confused situation regarding captured maps:

We have captured several Turkish maps, some of which are improvements on our own. One of these includes the Gallipoli Peninsula from Cape Helles to a little South of Maidos. It is on the scale of 1 in 25,000, outline, water and contours in brown, names in black. It is contoured every 10 metres and looks a very nice map, but the contours have a slightly conventional look and it is difficult to decide how much has been done by the draughtsman. No date is given. Another map captured was a 1 in 20,000 map of the area around Maidos and Kilid Bahr, contoured every 10 metres and printed rather roughly, and evidently hastily, in black. It, too, looked very nice at first sight, but on comparing it with the other I found a difference of 30–40 metres in several of the heights; the topography differed considerably, and a test measurement of a length of about 4 km. showed a difference of 20%. One map is evidently lying, and perhaps both. The result has been to make me rather suspicious of elaborately contoured Turkish maps.

We are having the 1 in 25,000 map reproduced roughly by the Printing Section, chiefly for its roads and names of places, but the Staff are against making any general distribution of a new map now that operations have begun.

Among other captured maps are three of the Turkish 1/25,000 series of the Bosphorus; one of these is the Kuchuk Keui sheet, but the other two are Constantinople and the sheet to the North, which will go a long way to filling up the gap along the Bosphorus. I am sending them to Cairo with one of your maps as a pattern and asking for them to be reproduced in the same style. I have asked that they be sent on to M.O.4. when finished with. I would have sent them direct to you but for the distance. I believe there is a good photographic department at Cairo and plenty of draughtsmen.[2]

The sheets of Constantinople and the Bosphorus were a vital addition to the MEF's resources, given the expectation that operations would extend to that area – which was indeed the aim of the expedition.

As a first step towards producing new operations maps, the first captured maps were used for a new printing by Hamilton's GHQ Printing Section at Imbros early in May; this was a black lithographed, squared, outline 1:40,000 sketch map, entitled '*Sketch Plan of the Gallipoli Peninsula*', and was used to mark up the latest intelligence – particularly Turkish trenches, wire, batteries, etc., obtained from sea and air (visual and photographic) reconnaissance.

For the Helles sector, sheets derived from the 1:40,000 operations map were soon replaced by reproductions of captured Turkish maps. Several sheets were captured by the Australians on 19 May, including a good and crucial large-scale, contoured map of the Anzac and Suvla area found on the body of a Turkish officer,[3] and these were later incorporated into the new British *Gallipoli* 1:20,000 series (see below) printed at the Survey of Egypt.

Nicholas wrote to Hedley on 12 June, explaining these developments:

Not long after landing we began to capture maps, which proved the Turks to be far better equipped in this regard than we were. We captured a copy of a map on the scale of 1/25,000, extending from Cape Helles to the North edge of the Kilid Bahr Plateau, where it was finished off in a manner which suggested strongly that the survey had been continued further North. The map bore evidence of having been produced in a hurry, and was printed entirely in brown, except for the names, but it was contoured at 10 metre intervals, and, as far as could be judged from inspection, the contouring seemed well done and highly detailed. The Printing Section produced a number of editions of this map, and I spent many long hours making tracings of it.[4]

This map, of part of an area extending to the north edge of the Kilid Bahr Plateau, was apparently surveyed and printed before the regular Turkish 1:25,000 series. It differed in significant details from the later Turkish survey, and was on different sheetlines. It was rapidly and crudely redrawn in May by Nicholas and reproduced in three sketch-map sheets by the 'Printing Section, GHQ Med. Ex. Force' (serials 19, 20 and 21) as the black 1:25,000 *Preliminary map of Southern Gallipoli Peninsula showing names, Roads, Telegraphs and 50 metre Contours* (see below);[5] the very wide contour interval is worth noting.

The early productions by Nicholas's Section were:

← 1:25,000 (Z.2015, Printing Section GHQ MEF), *'Preliminary map of southern portion: Gallipoli peninsula showing names, Roads, Telegraphs and 50 metre Contours'.*[6] Ungridded black contoured map of Helles–Krithia area. One copy showed British and Turkish trenches in manuscript to the west of Krithia.[7]

← 1:15,840 (4 inches to the mile) (Z.2016, Printing Section GHQ MEF), *'Sketch Map compiled From Photos and Aerial Reconnaissance'*, showing Turkish trenches, covering the Krithia–Fusiliers' Bluff–Kereves Dere area. This was the prototype for a new type of map – showing detail and trenches plotted from air photos.

← 1:10,000 (Z.2018, sheets 1-4, Printing Section GHQ MEF), enlargements of Z.2015, 'Artillery Maps'.[8]

The capture of a second sheet later in May led to this being sent to Egypt, to be rapidly reproduced in twelve hours (though GHQ did not receive them for seven days) in an edition of 1,000 copies as the 1:20,000 *Southern Gallipoli, From a Turkish Map, Provisional Edition*, with heights in metres and contours at ten-metre interval. This replaced the *'Preliminary map'*. It was a large, ungridded sheet with topographical detail and contours, unusually, printed in blue, and compass roses in black. As it did not reproduce photographically, such a blue background was normally used as a base for inscribing further detail or lettering, as part of the process of creating a new printing plate. There were no names at this stage – presumably they had not yet been transliterated and transcribed onto the printing plate. One copy had Turkish positions marked in MS for 24 April – i.e. before the landings, a retrospective addition.[9] The scale of 1:20,000 seems to have been chosen, like that of 1:40,000 for the earlier sheets, because it had been adopted as a standard British operations scale on the Western Front (where these scales had been adopted from the Belgian national survey). This provisional edition was very soon followed by a definitive edition of this sheet. This was reproduced over a five-day period (Nicholas called it 'an admirable piece of production') with greater care as the 1:20,000 and (in four sheets) 1:10,000 *Map of Southern Gallipoli from a Captured Turkish Map*. Nicholas also noted that applying the British Naval squaring to the reproductions of Turkish maps proved difficult, as the latter were very different from the British 1:40,000 map.[10]

The capture of sheets of the regular Turkish 1:25,000 survey in early June led to the British adoption at the end of July of the Turkish sheetlines of this series as standard for their 1:20,000 topographical sheets. Of this episode, Nicholas noted on 12 June:

. . . during the last few days we have captured 6 sheets of yet another Turkish map on the 1/25,000 scale, differing considerably from the first, and as these extend to Ejelmer Bay and Ak Bashi Lemain, the C.G.S. [Braithwaite] decided that they should be sent off at once to Cairo for reproduction and issued as the operations map in substitution for sheets 1 and 2 of the 1/40,000 map, so we are faced with another impending change of map.[11]

GHQ issued a memorandum about mid-July, stating:

A new issue of maps will shortly be made in substitution for Sheets 1 and 2 of the 1/40,000 map of Gallipoli. The new map will be on the scale of 1/20,000 and will be issued in 7 sheets. Five of these are reproduced from captured sheets of a newly surveyed Turkish map, while the 6th and 7th sheets (*Krithia* and *Sedd-el-Bahr*) are a provisional edition taken from the present *S. Gallipoli* 1/20,000 map, and will be replaced by a more correct edition as soon as the necessary material is collected. Other sheets will be prepared if the originals can be obtained. The system of squares has also been improved and 600 yards adopted as the unit in place of 675 yards. These maps will be issued throughout the Med. Exped. Force and on a given date of which due notice will be given they will be taken into use as the Operations Map and substituted for Sheets 1 and 2 of the 1/40,000 map and for *S. Gallipoli* 1/20,000 and 1/10,000 which will then be withdrawn. 7 sheets:- *Anafarta Saghir, Kurija Dere, Boghali, Dainler* [*Damler*], *Chanak, Sedd-el-Bahr, Krithia.*[12]

These sheets carried a note explaining the new naval grid (squaring) used on the series, which differed from the grid carried on the old 1:40,000 series.

The withdrawal of Sheets 1 and 2 of the 1:40,000 map and the large 1:20,000 *Southern Gallipoli* sheet took place at the end of July, so that the new series would be issued and in place before the Suvla and Anzac operations of early August. Braithwaite issued Force Order No. 21 to all formations of the MEF on 27 July:

1. The new 1/20,000 Map of Gallipoli issued in seven sheets will be taken into use as the Official Map of the Mediterranean Expeditionary Force from midnight 31st July/1st August. After that date all references in orders, reports, or other documents will be understood to refer to this Map unless another Map is specifically mentioned.

2. All previous orders regarding the Maps to be used by the Mediterranean Expeditionary Force will be cancelled as from midnight 31st July/1st August.[13]

The new 1:20,000 contoured sheets were produced in Egypt (as series GSGS 4000), with transliterated names. These eventually covered the whole Peninsula and Asiatic Shore of the Dardanelles. The *Krithia, Provisional Edition* sheet was followed by a small *Krithia Extension (Provisional Edition)* sheet to the west, covering Cape Helles. Soon, both these sheets were recast together as one standard sheet in the series, which finally comprised eighteen sheets. A second edition, though not distinguished as such, in a new *Dardanelles* series (on the same sheetlines), was later produced of five of the sheets (with additional and revised detail, green compass roses, etc). Place names were not standardised on the maps and in orders, and several Force Orders were issued on this topic. Larger-scale trench diagrams, plotted as accurately as possible from uncontrolled air photos, were inaugurated and remained on non-standard scales and sheetlines for the time being. In addition a 1:50,000 'orographical map' (GSGS 4001) was produced in Egypt in two sheets from captured Turkish 1:25,000 sheets.[14]

Printing and Survey Sections

The *History of the Corps of Royal Engineers*, which is sometimes misleading and not totally to be relied on, stated:

> Early in 1915, a field survey section was got ready for the expedition, but was not eventually taken. As a consequence, operations and particularly artillery co-operation were hampered by the lack of any reliable survey. Fortunately, a moderately good and fairly recent map was found upon a captured Turkish officer. This was promptly reproduced by the Survey of Egypt and distributed. Arrangements were then made with this very efficient department to send Mr Meldrum, with the rank of captain, to undertake original surveys. Later a maps and printing section (corresponding to the 1915 organisation on the Western front) was sent to the Dardanelles from Egypt, under the command of Lieutenant A G Ogilvie (later Professor of Geography at Edinburgh University). This section was, however, independent of the survey section under Captain Meldrum. It is probably true to say that in no other theatre of war were overlapping and lack of touch in survey matters so marked.[15]

It will be seen that this judgement is largely supported by the contents of this chapter.

The first field survey unit to work with the Gallipoli expedition was the 'Anzac Printing Section', which had been formed from civilian personnel and equipment of the Survey of Egypt (including a printer, Mr Cairns, and a Turkish compositor). Birdwood sent a secret message to Maxwell on 6

March 1915 about 'The sequence of embarkation indicated by the possible employment of the Force leaving Egypt' which included the following terse statement: 'Army Corps HQ – including printing and litho sections'. Clearly the Section had not yet been formed, for on the 9th the Anzac Staff noted: 'Question of Printing Section taken up. AQMG Egypt sent telephone message saying that matter should be arranged by Army Corps with Egyptian Survey Dept.' Things moved rapidly, for the next day the Anzac Staff noted: 'Arrangements made with CE [Chief Engineer] and Egyptian Survey Dept for a printing and litho section', and the day after: 'Further arrangements made for raising a printing & litho section'. On 1 April the Anzac Corps Staff sent a message to GHQ about the Printing Section, and two days later a further message was sent warning them of its despatch.[16]

On 7 April the Anzac Printing Section, comprising civilians from the Survey of Egypt equipped with hand-operated letterpress and litho press, embarked on the *Arcadian* at Alexandria.[17] This Section, which was handed over to Hamilton on the latter's arrival in Egypt, would print many of the panoramas, sketch maps and trench diagrams before the assault and during the operations. The Section's equipment and personnel were supplied by the Survey of Egypt, and came under the command of Nicholas, Hamilton's Maps Officer at Imbros. It was used for the lithographic printing of diagrams and tactical intelligence maps before the landings, and topographical and trench maps afterwards. It was therefore rather a misnomer to call it the Anzac Printing Section; as Nicholas emphasised, it was completely manned by civilian litho draughtsmen and letterpress printers from the Survey of Egypt.[18] 'A' Printing Section RE, brought out from England by Nicholas, was delayed in Egypt for lack of transport, and only joined the Anzac Printing Section at Imbros on 12 May.

Apart from topographical maps printed in Cairo, all other lithographed maps (trench diagrams and intelligence maps) were printed on the hand presses at GHQ on Imbros, where conditions for map reproduction were not ideal. A manuscript note, probably by Nicholas, on a 1:6,000 scale map (dated 26 June 1915) of the Turkish trenches stated that it:

> ... includes position northwards from the Straits up Kereves Dere through the French zone towards Krithia. The [litho] draughtsman received this map at 9pm. Drawing was finished at 4am and 50 copies pulled ready for despatch by 7.30am. Light very bad for drawing and sand and dust everywhere.[19]

Nicholas supervised the joint Printing Section until 10 August 1915, when Lt Alan Ogilvie RFA (T), from 1912 to 1914 a junior demonstrator in geography at Oxford (he joined the Territorial Army as a gunner in 1911), who subsequently served in Macedonia, took over its command.[20] Nicholas was retained at Imbros as Maps Officer until the evacuation in January 1916. He worked in Egypt until mid-May mapping sand dunes in the Suez Canal area, and was then sent on leave to England, arriving at the end of May. He persuaded Hedley to let him take a Printing Section from Southampton to France for the new 5th Field Survey Company RE, attached to Reserve Army (later Fifth Army), to which he was posted as Maps Officer. Nicholas's Gallipoli experience was invaluable when it came to plotting trenches, rectifying air-photos, and deducing the relief on Reserve Army's 1:5,000 trench maps; he had done precisely this for the 1:6,000 trench diagrams of the Turkish area.[21]

Conditions were not easy back in plague-ridden Egypt. On 29 June Lawrence wrote to George Lloyd at Hamilton's HQ, noting among other things that more captured maps of the Asiatic side were required, that individual captured maps could be sent back to Egypt for reproduction rather than waiting for sets to be put together, and that the Survey of Egypt printer, Cairns, was required by Dowson to return to Egypt, owing to deaths among the printers, draughtsmen and photographers there.[22] The Printing Section remained at Imbros until after the evacuation, when it was transferred to Salonika. At some stage, probably after moving to Salonika, the GHQ Printing Section's light printing equipment (hand-presses) was entirely replaced from Egypt by letterpress platen presses and a flat-bed litho machine and heavy hand-presses, thus greatly increasing output, and much use was made of the 'vandyke' process for transferring map drawings by transmitted light to sensitised printing plates.[23]

Together with Ogilvie, Nicholas compiled a valuable set of notes on reading relief, and related points, from air photos, studying shadows on photos taken at different times of the day. This practice of deriving terrain forms from shadows appears to have begun with the French. Captain J H Cole and Lt W M Hayes from the Survey of Egypt also helped with the Gallipoli mapping at Imbros, notably with map drawing and plotting from air photos.

Map and trench diagram production in the field

With printing facilities available at Imbros in the form of the combined Anzac and British Printing Sections under Nicholas, it was possible for tactical maps to be printed with defence information. Once it was realised that a rapid breakthrough of the Turkish defences was not imminent, it was considered necessary to create large-scale trench diagrams (the planimetry could not initially be made accurate enough to dignify them with the name of maps or plans). The first step was to produce a reasonably accurate large-scale topographical map onto which trenches could be plotted from air photographs.

Trench mapping in the Gallipoli Peninsula began before any Allied triangulation or control framework had been started. It arose through the requirement for a detailed and relatively accurate artillery map, and immediately pointed up the necessity of a rigorous trigonometric control. There was a great need to improve the accuracy of artillery work on the Peninsula; thus far targets which could not be identified in the difficult terrain on the 1:40,000 sheets were being shelled ineffectually – a terrible waste of scarce ammunition. It was the 'shell shortage' in France which had led to artillery survey being introduced on the Western Front, to save wastage of ammunition in ranging – every shell had to be 'fired for effect'. However, although new British 1:25,000, 1:20,000 and 1:10,000 sheets from captured Turkish originals soon came into use, positions and aiming points could not always be identified on these with sufficient accuracy.

Captain Walter Vivian Nugent RFA, who had sailed from England on the Staff of 29th Divisional Artillery, had previously worked on boundary commissions and in MO4, and on arrival in the theatre immediately began to gather topographical intelligence. On 5 April in Alexandria, he had compiled sufficient information, some of it vitally important for the movement of artillery and other transport, to present a report on the Peninsula to 29th Division HQ. At Gallipoli, like other army and naval gunners, he found the squared 1:40,000 map useless for the direction and control of fire. This led him first, in May, to compile from some good near-vertical air photos taken by Butler, a map of the area of his own batteries. The planimetry of this experimental map was crudely drawn, without any control framework, by tracing the outline of the main features and trenches from a photo-mosaic onto drawing paper with the point of a steel aeroplane *flêchette*, or anti-personnel dart, and pencilling in the scored lines before inking them up to form the trench diagram. The scale had to be carefully calculated from the height at which the photos were taken (about 6,000 feet), obtained from aneroid readings, checked by known distances on the ground whenever possible.

When tested by the gunners in action, this diagram proved an enormous advance on existing maps; for the first time a detailed picture of the ground was available, showing the main features and the relative positions of the Turkish trenches. If the gunner observer now saw shells burst on the edge of a poppy field, he could find the position of that field on the map; it was not only thus localised, but also relatively accurately located, and its shape and distance and bearing to the target could be closely determined. This was a great boon to both ground and air observers.

From Nugent's 29th Division batteries in May, the use of the new trench diagrams spread first to VIII Corps (formed on 24 May) and then to the whole Helles front. They were first lithographed for use in offensive operations, corrected to 1 June, in the Third Battle of Krithia on 4 June. More significantly, the question of the lack of a reliable ruling triangulation had arisen, and it was recognised at the highest level that this was vital for accurate artillery work and as a control for the trench diagrams – a major step towards the construction of an accurate map. By the time (July) that Ernest Dowson, of the Survey of Egypt, visited Hamilton's GHQ to see what further help Egypt could give on survey and mapping questions (Appendix vii), Nugent had been appointed to GHQ as GSO3 in charge of an embryonic Survey and Maps Section.[24]

On 12 June Nicholas wrote to Hedley that the:

> … reproductions of the Turkish maps, though far better than the 1/40,000, had been found to be inaccurate in many respects, and the almost complete absence of fixed points upon them makes the location of trenches and taking of bearings a highly difficult task. Numerous aeroplane photographs have been taken and with their aid highly detailed trench plans constructed. The greatest difficulty is experienced in placing these in their proper position on the map, and the results have differed so considerably that suspicions are entertained as to the correct placing of even the few fixed points which the original Turkish map does show.

Nicholas went on to explain how this situation led to the creation of an artillery survey section under Nugent:

> Representations to this effect were made from those on shore, particularly from the 29th Division and Artillery, to G.H.Q., and a request made that a proper Survey Section should be obtained from home. Capt. Nugent, who was on the 29th Division Staff, was sent for by the G.O.C., as being an expert, and after a consultation, a cable was despatched to the War Office (Troopers), asking for a Survey Section to be sent out, and that Capt. Nugent should be appointed to I.C., to supervise the sub-section. He would be required more specifically to superintend and co-ordinate the numerous small pieces of survey work which were being started both by the British and French.[25]

The cable (No. M101) was sent by GHQ MEF to the War Office, London, on 31 May, and gave as a reason for needing a survey section the need 'to carry out the triangulation and correction of our present map, which is hopelessly inaccurate?'.

From the end of May, the trench diagrams were continually extended and improved, both by the development of the trigonometrical control framework, and by a sequential process of progressive approximations, by which detail was refined, augmented and placed ever more precisely relative to the fixed control points. During July Dowson, in collaboration with Nugent, whom he had known from the pre-war Sinai survey, developed encouragingly successful methods of utilising air photos. These, however, were not taken to any survey specification, and did not meet the rigorous requirements for making accurate maps.

They also inaugurated a trigonometrical framework, extending into enemy territory, as a control for the air photographs, and Dowson sent to the Survey of Egypt for a 'Bahel'-pattern reducing and correcting apparatus which had been used for reconciling old maps of government land with contemporary topography. This was found invaluable for correcting air photos for scale variations and tilt distortion; the photographs were projected by lantern onto a ground-glass sheet in their correct map position, traced onto tracing cloth and reproduced using the vandyke process. Using this method, 1:6,000 scale trench diagrams could be supplied to the troops the day after the photos had been taken.[26]

The further stages that remained to be carried out were the addition of accurate heights and contours, integration with the Anglo-French Survey and the 1:20,000 map derived from captured Turkish sheets, and the extension over the whole Peninsula in a regular series of sheets. The evacuation occurred before all this was achieved.

From trench diagram to Anglo-French survey

The MEF was fortunate in having two expert regular army surveyors to put artillery survey on a proper footing – the gunner, Captain (later Major) Nugent, and the sapper, Major Stewart Francis ('Skinface') Newcombe RE, an experienced survey officer who had also worked on the Sinai survey, and on the southern Palestine survey with Lawrence and Woolley just before the war, who was with an Anzac Corps Field Company. Neither was at first used on the Peninsula in his expert survey role, but the need for accurate ranging and control of artillery fire and the insufficiency of the existing maps for trench warfare soon changed their tasks. Nugent, as related above, was the first to revert to survey work.

It seems probable that part of the impetus behind GHQ's request for a survey section was the imminent despatch by Churchill of a 15-inch howitzer, which it was hoped would be able to deliver carefully surveyed plunging fire onto the Kilid Bahr forts. Hitherto the heaviest British guns on the Peninsula were 60-pounders and old 6-inch howitzers, whereas the Navy provided every calibre up to the 15-inch guns of *Queen Elizabeth*.

It was very significant that, according to Hedley of MO4, the initial request for a Survey Section for the Gallipoli expedition was refused when the MEF was first mooted (as we have seen from the aeroplane episode, Kitchener was extremely reluctant to allocate resources for Gallipoli), but was later sent when wired for.[27] The response in England to the MEF's request was extremely rapid, the No. 2 Ranging & Survey Section RE (the 1st Ranging Section RE had been formed in England in late October

1914) being formed early in June at the Ordnance Survey from regular RE personnel, and embarked on 8 June for the Dardanelles, just over a week after receiving the request.

No. 1 Section in France had originally been tasked with locating enemy batteries by cross-observation onto signals dropped by aircraft, but as wireless signalling replaced the former role, the artillery survey and mapping role took over. As soon as it arrived later in June, No. 2 Section set to work on topographical surveys under Nugent, who in June was appointed General Staff Officer (GSO3) at GHQ, MEF (Maps and Survey Officer). He conducted trig survey work at Cape Helles (and later at Suvla), and trench surveys at Anzac, and in November was promoted GSO2.[28] He was therefore the key British survey figure in the theatre, and the point of liaison with the French for their joint survey. Newcombe, as we shall see, became involved in mapping at Anzac, but his prime responsibility remained the command of a field company. Later in the war he worked closely with Lawrence, whom he already knew from their southern Palestine survey days, in Arabia, and he was captured by the Turks in Palestine in 1917 while serving with Allenby.

At Imbros, Nugent worked with Nicholas to develop further ways of accurately mapping the topography and Turkish trenches using air photos taken by Butler's successor, Flight Lieutenant Thomson RNAS. As no trig data were yet available, there was no control (apart from the Turkish 1:25,000 map which showed very few identifiable points, whose precise values were not known) on which the air photos could be hung. Dowson visited them from Egypt in July and spent a month trying to get the Gallipoli survey and mapping onto a sound footing (Appendix VII), later sending Captains Cole and Meldrum and Lt Hayes from the Survey of Egypt to assist. Dowson, later in 1915, wrote a 'Secret' paper, 'Notes on mapping from aeroplane photographs in the Gallipoli Peninsula', which he issued at the end of September 1915 (see Appendix VI).[29]

The new trigonometrical surveys were made in conjunction with de Larminat's surveys of the French sector of Helles and the Asiatic Shore (see below) which resulted in an Anglo-French 1:20,000 map. They included the islands off the Peninsula and southwards to Tenedos, and were also of great value to the Navy, which supplied the bulk of heavy artillery support. The triangulation was later linked via Imbros to the Anzac and Suvla sector. The progress of this Anglo-French survey, and its related mapping, was slow, despite the fact that survey photographs were being taken from the air in early August. On 5 November VIII Corps (Helles) issued the following information: 'An accurate survey, showing both our own and the Turkish trenches, on a scale of 1/10,000, is in course of preparation by GHQ and, when ready, will supersede the present 1/20,000 map and the 1/6,000 trench diagram.'[30]

The Survey Section from Gallipoli was, following the evacuation, shipped to Salonika and ultimately developed into the Field Survey Company, British Salonika Force (later 8th Field Survey Company) under Lt-Col. Henry Wood RE who had previously commanded 1st Field Survey Company in France. It was Wood who would return to Gallipoli after the Armistice to check the accuracy of the Turkish maps. Nugent was awarded the DSO for his survey work on the Peninsula; Newcombe was also decorated, not for survey work but for rescuing Anzac tunnellers from a gas-filled mine.

VIII Corps mapping in the Helles sector

Weeks before Nugent set to work, in fact only ten days after the landings of 25 April, Commander Henry Douglas RN and Lieutenant Nicholas (Maps Officer, GHQ) went ashore to survey the topography of Helles and the Turkish defences, partly as a matter of historical record. The result was a 1:9,000 (4 inches to 1,000 yards) scale 'Plan of S.W. end of Gallipoli Peninsula Showing Turkish Defences as existing 25 Apr. 1915', dated 5 May 1915, augmented by a panoramic drawing entitled 'General View of S.W. end of the Gallipoli peninsula before the landings.' These were beautifully lithographed on one sheet in several colours by the Survey Department, Egypt.[31]

We see in Gallipoli in late May and early June the creation of an entirely new type of very large-scale (1:600) trench map, or 'trench diagram', necessitated by the fact that operations had, because of the firepower of modern weapons (mostly rifles and machine guns), immediately degenerated into trench warfare, as on the Western Front. They had to show as much topographical detail as possible in order to locate Turkish defences from air photos. A precisely similar procedure was begun at about this time in France.

For the Third Battle of Krithia early in June, the first such trench diagram was prepared by Captain Nugent, covering the area in front of Krithia, with the sea on the left, printed by the GHQ Printing Section at Imbros, and issued with VIII Corps Orders on 3 June. This was the first of a long series of such diagrams progressively improved and completely plotted from air photos, which were the equivalent of the 'trench diagrams' and later 'trench maps' in use on the Western Front. It was entitled 'Diagram Showing Advanced Turkish Trenches & Communications', and carried a note explaining that 'The diagram is based on information available up to the afternoon of June 1st. Reliance however, must not be placed on the diagram showing every Turkish trench.' The 'Reference' key showed British Trenches, Turkish Trenches, Communication Trenches, probable Turkish machine guns, Roads, Tracks, Watercourses and Wire entanglements. A further note stated that: 'The relative positions of the trenches are correct within small areas, but the diagram should not be used to measure long distances or bearings.'[32]

Similar trench diagrams were issued dated 17 June, 22 June, 26 June, and at frequent intervals thereafter. While the first one (1 June) was lacking in detail, it did indicate roads, sunken roads, tracks, nullahs (watercourses), Gully Ravine, vineyards, orchards, olive groves, the village of Krithia, ruined houses, woods, hedges, areas of scrub, as well as the trenches and other tactical detail indicated in the Reference. As the series developed, successive editions showed ever more and more accurate planimetric detail, such as field boundaries, and also gave a better portrayal of the relief aspects of the terrain through more accurate depiction of nullahs, cliffs and so forth. They were not, however, contoured.

We saw above that in July, in conjunction with the French, Dowson and Nugent started a trigonometrical framework, extending into enemy territory, for artillery work and as a control for air photos, and Dowson obtained a 'Bahel' restitution apparatus from Egypt.[33] Most of this work was in connection with the Helles sector.

One map – 'Map Showing British & French Trenches, Gallipoli Peninsula, Southern Zone 7th July 1915, Secret, 8th Army Corps' – according to the Western Front surveyor F J Salmon, 'was produced by the Engineer Unit of the Royal Naval Division and is merely a diagram, having been compiled from sketches, sextant and prismatic compass work'.[34]

The VIII Corps 'Maps' Officer on 25 August was Captain H M Chrystall.[35] This may have been a local rank only, for a Lieutenant H M Chrystall RE served with 3rd and 5th Field Survey Companies RE in France as a Trig Officer in 1918.[36] A secret lithographed foolscap VIII Corps 'Trench Diagram of Left and Centre Sectors' (6th Series, 5 November, scale 6 inches = 1 mile), showing detail in black and British trenches in red, was drafted at Royal Naval Division HQ by 'J.H.L.'.[37]

The Anglo-French survey only slowly resulted in new mapping of the Helles sector. On 5 November Brig.-General Street of VIII Corps General Staff issued an 'Instruction on maps and survey' asking lower formations to produce 1:2,500 sketch maps which would be used to produce 1:5,000 Corps diagrams showing trenches and communications, and noting that an accurate 1:10,000 survey showing Allied and Turkish trenches was being prepared by GHQ. This would replace existing 1:20,000 maps and 1:6,000 trench diagrams, and in future all sketch plans should be at some denominator or multiple of this 1:10,000 scale.[38]

French maps and the Anglo-French survey

Despite the close pre-war relationship between the French *Service Géographique de l'Armée* and the Turkish survey department in

Constantinople, the French were as cartographically ill-prepared as the British. The original map served out for the landings was, as we have seen, the British 1:40,000 based on an earlier one-inch map which was, in turn, based on the French Crimean War 1:50,000 survey.

The French Government agreed that their Army and Navy detachments serving at the Dardanelles should come under British command; the French military force was designated the *Corps d'Expéditionnaire d'Orient* (CEO), and when this departed from France on 2 March 1915, its *Service topographique* comprised only a *Section de Topographie* consisting of Captain de Larminat (Infantry) and his clerk, Corporal de Jerphanion. From this date up to the end of April, i.e. during the crossings and the landings (at Bizerta 6–10 March; Mudros 15–26 March; Alexandria 28 March–16 April), it was concerned with coordinating the information already received about the location of Turkish divisions, and showing these graphically on enemy-order-of-battle maps.

The French landed at Kum Kale on 25 April as a diversion, but immediately pulled out and took over the British right flank at Helles. On 2 May de Larminat installed himself with d'Amade's French Force HQ in the ditch of the ruins of the 'Old Castle' at Sedd-el-Bahr. He used the Crimean War 1:50,000 map reproduced by the *Service Géographique de l'Armée* in Paris, and also the British 1:40,000 map derived from it, 'both of which needed serious alterations to meet the requirements of trench warfare'. As soon as British 1:20,000 and 1:10,000 sheets, based on captured Turkish maps, became available, they were supplied to the French Section.

The first French operations maps were crudely reproduced on a composition duplicator, protected only by a tarpaulin stretched against the wind and the dust, or in a tent. These were merely 1:5,000 and 1:10,000 sketch maps, enlarged from the 1:40,000 and 1:50,000 maps, showing the situation and new tactical information – including French positions, trenches, and enemy batteries. Copies of these were sent to Hamilton's GHQ at Mudros.[39]

Captain Cesari's squadron, *l'Escadrille 98T*, arrived at the Dardanelles early in May, joining the RNAS at Tenedos. The first French air photos, taken about mid-May by Lieutenant Saint André, provided sufficient data for the reproduction of rough diagrams of the French and Turkish trenches. These were accurate enough in their detail, but like those of the British were not based on any triangulation network; this did not yet exist, as the Allies had not captured any Turkish trigonometrical data.

The inadequacy of the existing maps led to an expansion of the Section, and a shift of location into the *Deuxième* (Intelligence) *Bureau*'s HQ tents until better accommodation was found in June. The strength of the Section at the end of May was eight. Only de Larminat and de Jerphanion, his deputy, were trained topographers; three of the others were draughtsmen. On 1 July Captain Thomas (trig officer and topographer), Boudineau (topographical draughtsman) and Desoye (litho draughtsman) arrived from Paris. Thomas, a colonial artillery officer, was a geodetic survey expert and was responsible for most of the artillery survey and the creation of the new *plan directeur*, or artillery map. These three were followed by Sgt-Major (*adjutant topographe du cadre du Service Géographique*) Léopold Martin on 9 July; he was later promoted to *sous-lieutenant*. By 11 July some thirty unsquared 'situation' trench diagrams had been plotted and reproduced at scales varying from 1:2,500 to 1:20,000. The normal scale of issue totalled seventy-four copies, but this was sometimes exceeded.[40]

Towards the end of June, General Gouraud, who had taken over command from d'Amade and was concerned about Turkish artillery fire from the Asiatic Shore, ordered an artillery survey to be made so that these guns could be accurately located and dealt with. This solution was the same as that which had to be applied on the Western and other fronts in 1914–15. Work therefore began on the trig survey which was to form the foundation of the Anglo-French 1:20,000 artillery map (and an excellent gridded *plan directeur*). De Larminat, who was promoted *chef de bataillon* (major) on 15 July, measured a base starting from the western end of Cape Tekke plateau, and built onto this, using a small theodolite and a steel surveyor's tape, a triangulation of the French area, extending this to the limits of visibility. Conspicuous points were fixed by theodolite observations, and calculated in rectangular coordinates. He executed a network of nine trig stations covering the Allied tip of the Peninsula, and by 11 July had added seven more stations.

He later extended this network to include Rabbit Islands (a group of small islands between Tenedos and Cape Helles) and Tenedos, and from these southern stations intersected points on the Asiatic side of the Dardanelles. Meanwhile Thomas completed the network within the Peninsula, where some sixty trig stations were eventually established. The work was obstructed by the almost instantaneous disappearance of every trig signal they erected, as this small area – the French sector at Helles extended on a 1-km front to a depth of 3.5 km – was overcrowded with troops. Martin carried traverses from these stations to the French heavy batteries, the same technique used by the French on the Western Front.[41]

Integration with naval surveys

The triangulation proved extremely useful to the Army and Navy. By 11 July twenty-four points on the Asiatic Shore had been fixed, and by October, seventy-five. On Tenedos itself, seven points were fixed, and three on Rabbit Islands; these ten points were initially not as reliable as the others, being observed in bad weather conditions. Their purpose was to help French naval gunnery, and the gunnery officer of the *Saint Louis* expressed his appreciation. In October the triangulation was recomputed, the new values being based on later, more carefully observed rays.[42]

The British Fleet also used the French triangulation for its shooting, and Ramsey, de Robeck's Flag Commander, informed de Larminat on 30 July that:

> ... we have been served by your triangulation for all our shooting from Rabbit Island, and I found it not only useful but much more accurate than our own. The French naval liaison officer has passed it to me, and I have since heard that the 14-inch guns of *Roberts* have been ranged onto a target with a sight elevation which, following your triangulation, had to be 14,025 metres and which the aeroplanes had ranged to 14,050 metres, a difference probably due to the wind. Our topographer on board *Roberts* has fixed himself according to your calculations, and he has already triangulated a portion of the coast around the Island of Mavro. We now have another 24cm [9.2-inch] monitor. Benefiting from your valuable work, they are also able to fire accurately by night as well as by day and I am confident that the result will contribute to making life very pleasant in the French camps as on the beaches.[43]

A British report on the spotting work of British seaplanes observing the fire of the monitor *Roberts* from 22 July stated that:

> The range was first measured off geographically by a very careful triangulation and survey ranges reached 19,500 yards (10 nautical miles), probably the longest at which guns have been fired in naval warfare.[44]

The Turkish batteries on the Asiatic Shore opposite Helles were located with the help of a map based on an air-photo mosaic, made by Lt Saint André, fitted onto the observed points. This comprised some thirty same-scale, near-vertical photos. Batteries near fixed points were relatively easy to plot, ten such being fixed by 11 July. Around In Tepe, near Toptash Burnu on the Asiatic Shore, the density of fixed points and the large number of air photos on which these could be identified enabled a mean photo-scale to be established and new detail points on the photos to be plotted. Thus the original 'high-order' triangulation was progressively amplified, admittedly with 'lower-order' points, from the photo-restitution, and a dense 'canevas de restitution' was developed, again in a similar way to the Western Front.[45] Farther to the west and south, where there were fewer fixed points, overlapping strips of photos between points were taken at the fixed scale of 1:6,000 (implying a constant altitude during the sortie). On these adjusted strips, grid cuts were plotted between the fixed points, and detail traced from the photos as described below.[46]

The lack of accurate maps of the Gallipoli Peninsula made the restitution of air photos very difficult, as the British also found. Various methods of graphic restitution, such as *craticulage* or *faiscaux anharmoniques* used on the Western Front, were unsatisfactory in Gallipoli because they depended on an existing reliable planimetric framework. Thomas developed a technique based on the points of the new triangulation. Starting with pairs of trig points on the 1:20,000 map which could also be identified on an air photo, he measured the distances along a line joining the two points to a grid line, and transferred these proportionately to a line joining the same points on the photo, thus plotting grid cuts and enabling the reconstruction of the map grid on the air photo. The photographic detail was next drawn onto the map relative to the grid. Not only topographical detail, but trenches and enemy batteries could be plotted in this way. Despite its approximate nature, the method was justified by its speed, by the fact that many near-vertical photos were available, by the relatively level ground, and by the lack of alternative methods.[47]

Vertical relief (ground-forms) was more difficult to depict accurately than planimetry because stereoscopic air-photogrammetric methods had not yet been developed, but the contours of captured Turkish maps were extremely useful. Otherwise, the usual practice was to interpolate form-lines using the network of points for which planimetric and height values had been obtained. Air photos were also studied to assist the contouring of dead ground. In the In Tepe area, air photos taken when the sun was low enabled shadows to be utilised to identify features of the terrain, identified by visual reconnaissance from the air, and their approximate three-dimensional forms to be reconstructed. This method was extended along the west coast past Besika Bay, amplified by data from drawn panoramas made from the islands.[48]

This triangulation enabled a new 1:20,000 map to be created, based on ground surveys at Helles, combined with the 1854 survey and air photos. This new map of the Allied zone extended a long way into enemy territory, and was lithographed in colour by the Survey of Egypt. A further 1:20,000 map of the Asiatic coast, covering about 150 square km from Erenkeui on the Asiatic Shore opposite Helles, past Kum Kale and Besika Bay to the coast abreast of Tenedos, was simpler than the one of the Peninsula and was entirely based on French air photos. It was fixed onto a triangulation and was printed on a small hand-press of the *Deuxième Bureau* (Intelligence). Detail was in black, and for this area hachuring was used rather than contouring, for which there was insufficient data, apart from captured Turkish maps, owing to a faulty theodolite incapable of taking vertical angles.

In October Thomas produced a provisional 1:10,000 gridded and 5-metre contoured *plan directeur* for the Helles sector showing Allied and Turkish trenches and Turkish batteries, almost indistinguishable from those in use on the Western Front. This was reproduced by the British GHQ Printing Section, and was also used by British units.[49] Thomas interpolated contours as described above, also using the drainage pattern and other data derived from Turkish maps.

Following the formation of the French Salonika Army, Commandant de Larminat and Captain Thomas were both attached to the *Armée d'Orient* and left Sedd-el-Bahr for Salonika on 4 October. The *Service (or Bureau) Topographique des Dardanelles* was then directed up to the evacuation in December 1915 by de Jerphanion.[50]

The Anzac sector

Mapping the Anzac sector was extremely difficult because of the rugged, tangled terrain and limited perimeter; any attempt at forward mapping using normal ground survey techniques would be greeted with ferocious sniper and shrapnel fire. Even more than at Helles, therefore, captured Turkish maps were vitally important, and were first utilised by straight copying or enlarging, with transliterated place names. An unsquared black 1:10,000 contoured sheet was soon produced, entitled *Map of Area occupied by Australian & N.Z. Army Corps, Enlarged from a Turkish map* (Z.2021, one copy with MS trenches dated 15 June: British in red and Turkish in green[51]), followed by another (Z.2024A), still unsquared, with the same title and scale with brown contours at 40-foot (heavy at 200-foot) intervals, at least one copy of which had trenches in MS: British (i.e. Anzac) in red, and Turkish in green. The brown contour plate was registered with needles, as was standard army practice using hand-press stone-litho processes.[52] A further black 1:10,000 map, *Koja Chemen Tepe*, covering the Chunuk Bair and Biyuk Anafarta area north-east of Anzac Cove, was clearly from a captured Turkish map, and was both contoured and squared (Squares 92, 93, 80, 81). Some zones on this map were hatched to show wooded areas.

Major Newcombe, formerly a survey and intelligence officer, was, as commander of 4th Field Company RE (2nd Australian Division), heavily involved with mining operations at Anzac. He was awarded the DSO for an act at the end of October:

> For conspicuous gallantry and devotion to duty near Anzac, Gallipoli Peninsula, on 29th October 1915. During rescue operations he entered a mine tunnel soon after the first casualties were reported, and, although suffering from the effects of fumes, he continued to lead rescue parties till he was completely disabled by the gas. One officer lost his life on this occasion in the attempt at rescue.[53]

Newcombe, as the officer at Anzac most experienced in survey, was made responsible for the mapping of the sector in addition to his Field Company duties. Many of the printed sketch maps and trench diagrams at Anzac carried the inscription: *Any additions or corrections to be sent to Major*

Newcombe, 4th Field Coy, 2nd Aust. Div. For example, *Trench Map 1/1800 from Chatham's Post to Lone Pine (Provn.), Compiled from Photos and Traverses. Contours compared with enlargement of 1/20,000 Turkish Plan.*[54]

As the Anzac sector included the most difficult terrain encountered in the Peninsula, the fact that a report on its large-scale mapping survives is of particular significance. After the evacuation, Newcombe wrote a report on Anzac Trench Mapping and 'the system of squaring' for trench maps,[55] which was sent back to Hedley in London. This described the techniques and equipment used to produce three categories of plans:

The following maps or plans were made by the 2nd Australian Division at Anzac.

1. Trench plans 30-feet to 1-inch (1/360) to show tunnels and mines, for engineer use only.
2. Trench plans 60-feet to 1-inch (1/720), reduction of above showing communication trenches in addition, and more comprehensive, for Divisional staff, Brigadiers and for planning accommodation tunnels, etc.
3. A general map 150-feet to 1-inch (1/1800) to show our firing line with known places marked for reference, and the enemy trenches with the ground to our front contoured with 10-foot intervals.

No.1 was made by tape measuring and compass, and 2 was a reduction of 1. No. 3 required a small triangulation survey, but owing to the difficulty of observing from conspicuous points, a tacheometer traverse was carried right through the firing line. This traverse was tied on to the triangulation and the reduction of 1 was then tied on to the fixed tacheometer points. Thus a fairly accurate map of the firing line was obtained.

From this base and using the points fixed by tacheometer, conspicuous points in the enemy trenches or enemy country were fixed by plane-table using a periscope. Aeroplane photographs of enemy trenches were enlarged using our firing line as a base, and the points fixed by plane-table for tying in. Thus an accurate plan was obtained.

For contouring, the Turkish 1/25,000 map was enlarged. And where necessary the 10-metre contours slightly shifted to fit the ground as observed from the plane-table or photos. The 10-foot contours were drawn in by plane-tabling, usually by using Abney's level without a periscope, as the latter was found to be too inaccurate. The 10-foot contours were only for the ground near our trenches, more distant ground being shown by the 10-metre or 30-foot contours of the enlarged Turkish map. Valleys and other features were put in either by plane-table or from the photographs.

. . . Of these 1/800 maps, two issues were made, one showing all our communication trenches as well as the enemy's and issued only to Staff and Engineers, the other omitting all behind our firing line, issued to every infantry officer. This was to prevent plans of our trenches being captured.

The copy attached [not present; possibly 'Trench Map 1/1800 from Chatham's Post to Lone Pine (see above)] was a provisional issue only, a second and improved edition was being prepared when the evacuation took place. The scale of the map was large because enemy trenches were so close that a smaller scale would not have shown the detail so conveniently; it was possible to use it for giving direction for tunnels intended to undermine desirable points beyond enemy trenches.

1/1800 or 50 yards to 1-inch was used because every officer has an inch scale in his note-book, and other maps had already been used on that scale.

It was intended to show:

All conspicuous points in enemy country, such as prominent trees, peculiar piles of sandbags, noticeable overhead cover etc. to enable officers to read the map easily.

Known points in our own trenches require marking to enable the map to be sited.

All names used for our own or enemy trenches are put in.

For artillery a map on 1/3600 was being produced, reducing the 1/1800 and extending its area by fixing points by plane-table and enlarging the photographs. This map was not quite ready but would have included all the area over which our artillery fired.

A special officer was detailed to go round artillery observation posts or batteries to mark their positions on the map given them, to see that every one entitled to a map had one, to assist certain officers to read them and to collect and put on the map any fresh names or conspicuous points or pet places which artillerymen made use of, to enable them to pick up objects more rapidly. Battalion Intelligence officers also were asked for names or special objects to be shown in a second edition.

The map was especially useful to new units coming to the trenches, to Intelligence officers and others who were able to describe enemy trenches to within 12 yards and to telephone immediately positions of enemy mortars or guns accurately. They were useful also for mining operations and in one case of a captured Turkish tunnel, the officer in charge was enabled to know what direction to take when he got into an enemy trench.

In case of a planned attack, the value for staff operations is obvious.

It was found possible to enlarge the photographs to 60-feet to 1-inch [1:8640] by fixing accurately from a base in our trenches 2 or more points in enemy trench and enlarging the line between those points. Hence position of our tunnels with reference to enemy line was correct to about 5 or 10 feet.

In addition to this map, it was intended to issue a photograph of the area by adjusting together several aeroplane photographs and making one large photograph [mosaic]. Copies were to be issued to Staff and all battery commanders.

Experience showed, especially in the peculiarly indented country, that the study of the photograph assisted materially the understanding of the country while the map gave distance and direction.

Though the photograph of the enemy's country may be considered particularly secret, there could be no more objection to issuing them than the maps, since the latter gave equal detail of enemy's trenches and probably the enemy have photographs themselves.

The following instruments were used:

3-inch theodolite, 300-foot steel tape. Periscope with glasses absolutely parallel: wooden from painted black inside. Tacheometer and staff. Small plane-table with telescopic legs, Abney's level. The compass was used for traversing, but owing to [the proximity of] steel [snipers'] plates and rifles, was often found inaccurate.

Conclusion

In the use of intelligence sketch maps and trench diagrams of an entirely different series from the standard contoured topographical sheets, the maps used during most of the Gallipoli Campaign repeated the early mistake made in France. The initial lack of a dedicated survey unit, and prolonged absence of an integrated and coordinated Allied survey organisation, prevented the early creation of an artillery triangulation, thus denying effective artillery support and retarding the production of good maps. The lack of early provision for air survey also impeded progress.

The 1:20,000 topographical maps were incompatible with the larger-scale trench diagrams, and this was a major cartographic error that had serious implications for operations. The obvious solution, to combine all the information onto one, reliable, gridded base map, was arrived at in mid-1915 on the Western Front with the creation of the British 'regular series' 1:10,000 trench maps. However, trenches were not overprinted on to the 1:20,000 maps until the end of 1915. It was not until 1916 that there was identical topographical and tactical detail on both 1:10,000 and 1:20,000 maps of the Western Front. Towards the end of the Gallipoli Campaign, we see the beginnings of a similar trend, with the creation of a 1:10,000 regular series.

Notes

1. Dowson, E M, 'Further Notes on Aeroplane Photography in the Near East', *Geographical Journal*, 58, 359.
2. Nicholas to Hedley, 8 May 1915, in TNA(PRO) WO 301/46.
3. Aspinall-Oglander, Brig.-Gen. C F, *History of the Great War, Military Operations, Gallipoli*, Vol. II, London: Heinemann, 1932, p. 20; Rhodes James, Robert, *Gallipoli*, London: Pimlico, 1999, p. 220.
4. Nicholas to Hedley, 12 June 1915, in TNA(PRO) WO 301/46.
5. TNA(PRO) WO 301/508, 505, 507 respectively.
6. TNA(PRO) WO 301/505–508.
7. In TNA(PRO) WO 153/1199.
8. TNA(PRO) WO 301/ 509–513.
9. TNA(PRO) WO 153/1199.
10. Nicholas to Hedley, 12 June 1915, op. cit.
11. Ibid.
12. Anzac Intelligence War Diary, Appendix No. JY 21, TNA(PRO) WO 157/681.
13. Ibid, Appendix No. JY 37.
14. Later special editions of this sheet, overprinted with Turkish fortifications and other defences and the positions of Allied ships on 25 April, were published in London; those carry the designation: 'NS (GTD) C.B. 1550', etc. (Naval Staff (Gunnery Training Division) Confidential Book) were from the post-war Mitchell report.
15. Pritchard, Maj.-Gen. H L, *The History of the Corps of Royal Engineers*, Vol. VI, Chatham, Institution of Royal Engineers, 1952, p. 15.
16. Anzac Corps General Staff War Diary, TNA(PRO) WO 95/4280.
17. Orlo Williams Diary, 7 April 1915, IWM.
18. T C Nicholas tapes, IWM, Dept of Sound Records.
19. In TNA(PRO) WO 301.
20. 'A' Printing Section Outline War Diary, RE Institution Library, Chatham.
21. Nicholas tapes, op. cit.; 10475/3/1-3.
22. T E Lawrence to Capt. G Lloyd, 29 June 1915, Churchill College, Cambridge; noted by Mike Nolan in *The Gallipolian*, Spring 1994, p. 15.
23. 'A' Printing Section . . . Diary, op. cit.
24. Dowson, E M, Director-General, Survey of Egypt, *Notes on Mapping from Aeroplane photographs in the Gallipoli Peninsula, Secret*. [c.September 1915], initially issued not earlier than 22 September 1915. Over 40 foolscap pages, illustrated with maps, diagrams and four air photographs, 'taken by the RNAS in Gallipoli for mapping purposes', reproduced typescript, in MCE, MRLG. Also in TNA(PRO) WO 317/13 and AIR 1/2284/209/75/10.
25. Nicholas to Hedley, 12 June 1915, op. cit.
26. Dowson, E M, *Notes on Mapping . . .*, op. cit.
27. Hedley typescript, para 11, sub-section (a).
28. No. 2 Ranging and Survey Section Outline War Diary, RE Institution Library, Chatham.
29. Dowson, E M, *Notes on Mapping . . .*, op. cit.
30. Royal Naval Division General Staff, Correspondence, Reports & Operations Orders, Dardanelles 4/15 to 1/16, p. 33, TNA(PRO) ADM 137/3087.
31. TNA(PRO) WO 301/527.

32. TNA(PRO) WO 301/578. See also Dowson, *Notes on Mapping* . . ., op. cit.
33. Dowson, *Notes on Mapping* . . ., op. cit.
34. Salmon Collection, Royal Geographical Society. Belgian, French and German Maps – Miscellaneous Maps No. 143A.
35. Note on MS map in TNA(PRO) WO 153 1199.
36. 5th Field Survey Company RE War Diary, TNA(PRO) WO 95 492.
37. Royal Naval Division General Staff, Correspondence . . ., op. cit., p. 67.
38. Ibid, p. 33.
39. Service Géographique de l'Armée, *Rapport sur les Travaux exécutés du 1er août 1914 au 31 décembre 1919. Historique du Service Géographique de l'Armée pendant la Guerre*, Paris: Imprimerie du Service Géographique de l'Armée, 1924, pp. 245–7.
40. Reports on Section de Topographie in 3M 569 – *Service Géographique; Armée d'Orient, mission du Service Géographique dans les Balkans*, Service Historique de l'Armée de Terre, Château de Vincesses, Paris.
41. Service Géographique de l'Armée, op. cit., pp. 245–7.
42. Reports on Section de Topographie, op. cit.
43. Service Géographique de l'Armée, op. cit., pp. 245–7.
44. Report of work by Short seaplanes in support of firing by HMS *Roberts*, TNA(PRO) AIR 1/665/17/122/714.
45. Service Géographique de l'Armée, op. cit., pp. 146–61.
46. Reports on Section de Topographie, op. cit.
47. Ibid.
48. Ibid.
49. *Presqu'Ile de Gallipoli – Plan Directeur du Secteur Français, 1:10,000, Edition Provisoire, octobre 1915*, TNA(PRO) WO 301/612.
50. Service Géographique de l'Armée, op. cit., pp. 245–7. See also Reports on the work of the Section de Topographie in 3M 569 – Service Géographique: *Armée d'Orient, mission du Service*, op. cit.; and also de Larminat, E, *La topographie chez l'ennemie. Comment nous dressions la carte du terrain occupé par l'adversaire*, Paris: Lavauzelle, 1920. BL Ref: X.619/10050.
51. TNA(PRO) WO 301/551.
52. In Collection of Gallipoli Maps, GHQ-MEF, BL Map Library, Maps 43336. (21).
53. *London Gazette*, 22 January 1916.
54. TNA(PRO) WO 153/1055.
55. Report by Major S F Newcombe RE, with GSGS Map Room stamp dated 17 March 1916; TNA(PRO) WO 301/45.

CHAPTER 10

Repeating the Mistakes: the Suvla Landings

The preparations for the Suvla Bay landings in August had several advantages over those for the April assault, including possession of captured large-scale Turkish maps, months of additional reconnaissance opportunities, excellent air photographic coverage and accurate intelligence about Turkish defences and dispositions. The failure to break out of the Suvla beach-head cannot in general be laid at the door of intelligence failure, though intelligence and maps were not always distributed effectively. The failure, rather, is clearly ascribable to the inexperience of the troops, particularly in night operations, and lack of positive leadership, above all on the part of General Stopford, commanding IX Corps, the force designated for the landings. That said, it is important to identify the sources of intelligence, and the ways in which it was used. This is an area which has received little dedicated study.[1]

Suvla Bay as a landing place

We saw in Chapter 3 that Grover in 1877, and Ardagh in 1880, had both identified the Suvla Bay area and the beach south of Nibrunesi Point as good potential landing zones, and that this was confirmed by several subsequent reports. Grover had stated that his large-scale map (four inches to the mile) showed:

> ... the coast between Kaba Tépé and Suwla Bay, on the west side of the Gallipoli Peninsula, opposite Maïdos, which seems suitable for the landing of a force to attack, in rear, the batteries of Kilid Bahr and Boukali, as a means of land – co-operation with a naval effort to force the passage of the Dardanelles. The selected coast is low, and affords easy access to the interior, for an extent of nearly two miles, on the west of the villages of Böjök Anafarta. It is here protected from the prevalent north-east winds, and the Admiralty Chart appears to show sufficient depth of water, and good anchorage, for the proposed operation.[2]

Suvla Bay was again specified as a landing place in the 1909 War Office *Report on the Defences of Constantinople,*[3] and this report actually included a panoramic drawing from the sea, indicating the landing place. The Greeks also envisaged a landing here. It was not included in the April 1915 landings because at that season the Salt Lake was impassable, being full of water, and because the route inland east of Sari Bair was believed to be strongly held and would therefore require a large force to force through, and could not be supported by the Fleet's guns.[4] In addition, the Navy was concerned about lack of accurate hydrographic data, and feared shoals, rocks and reefs.

Sight is often lost of the fact that, following the Helles and Anzac landings in April, it was still hoped to push the Fleet through to Constantinople, that the Russians might yet land a corps at the Bosphorus, and that the Greeks or Bulgarians might declare war against Turkey.[5] There were still, therefore, distinct strategic possibilities despite the lack of progress in fighting up the Peninsula.

However, even more so than for the April landings, the lack of a clear strategic aim and purpose for the Suvla and Anzac attacks on 6 August and subsequent days led to confused objective-setting and muddled operational planning. Were the operations intended to lead to a break-out and a dash across the Peninsula to the Narrows, combined with a further attempt by the Fleet to force its way through to the Marmara and Constantinople? On 29 June Hamilton was telling Kitchener that he envisaged using additional divisions to turn the Turkish right flank at Anzac (i.e. break out around the north side of the existing Anzac position) and to push forward east and south-east to occupy a position right across the Peninsula from Gaba Tepe (south of Anzac) to Maidos (on the Narrows), capturing the Kilid Bahr Plateau in order 'to clear the Asiatic shore subsequently of big guns' (something he should have done in April). He also wanted to make a landing on the Asiatic Shore.[6] Or were they intended merely to improve the existing position and to secure a base-area and harbour at Suvla?

A lack of strategic clarity had obvious implications for the survey organisation responsible for making or ordering the required maps, and for the distribution of such maps. There was also a disastrous imbalance between the secrecy requirement and operational efficiency. Both of these factors – strategic muddle and obsessive secrecy – restricted or curtailed opportunities for gathering geographical information and for studying the terrain. As usual, the consequence of all this was failure, with heavy casualties among the attacking infantry.

In his Despatch of 11 December, Hamilton retrospectively defined his aims and objectives as:

1. To break out with a rush from Anzac and cut off the bulk of the Turkish Army from land communication with Constantinople [i.e. the primary attack, to capture the key height of Koja Chemen Tepe (the highest point of the Sari Bair ridge) as the key to the capture of the line across the Peninsula from Maidos to Gaba Tepe].
2. To gain such a command for my artillery as to cut off the bulk of the Turkish Army from sea traffic whether with Constantinople or with Asia [i.e. capture the Kilid Bahr Plateau].
3. Incidentally, to secure Suvla Bay as a winter base for Anzac and all the troops operating in the northern theatre [i.e. a secondary attack; diversionary operations were also carried out at Helles].

Point No. 2 was connected with the desire, expressed by Churchill, to emplace heavy and super-heavy artillery (9.2-inch guns and 15-inch howitzer) in positions where it could destroy the Turkish defences and forts in the area of the Kilid Bahr Plateau. Churchill had minuted as early as 14 May that:

> The operations have now reached a point where they may easily develop into a great siege similar to that of Port Arthur, though not so formidable. Our preparations should therefore consider and cover the following points: . . The provision of heavy artillery, which could be used against the semi-permanent works, and the mounting on shore of heavy long-range naval guns which can, from the existing positions held by our troops, bring accurate fire to bear on the permanent defences.

On the same day he minuted to Fisher and his Chief of Staff: 'The fifth 15-inch howitzer with fifty rounds of ammunition, should go to the Dardanelles with the least possible delay. . . The two 9.2-inch guns will go to the Dardanelles, either in the two monitors prepared for them or separately, for mounting on shore. . .'[7]

In the event, the 15-inch howitzer was sent to Mudros but, even if landed, did not reach the Peninsula and never fired a shot. The naval guns were never mounted on land but, together with a 14-inch gun, mounted in monitors performed very useful service against Turkish batteries on the Asiatic side. Unfortunately the enthusiasm of Churchill and Keyes (de Robeck's Chief of Staff) was not matched by that of others in key positions, notably Stopford and Reed (Stopford's senior staff officer). And by the time of the Suvla operations, Churchill was no longer at the Admiralty. These memos to Fisher, allocating more naval resources to the Dardanelles, had finally triggered the resignation of the First Sea Lord, bringing about Churchill's downfall a few days later, when he was replaced at the Admiralty by Balfour. As Chancellor of the Duchy of Lancaster, however, he remained influential, retaining a seat on the War Council (now renamed the Dardanelles Committee).[8]

Various questions arise from Hamilton's statement. The strategic aim was much the same as it was in April. But was the Navy to cooperate, and what was the role of the other Allies? And what of terrain difficulties? The capture of the Sari Bair range committed Hamilton's force to operations in almost impossible country, as he well knew from the Anzac experience in the Sari Bair foothills. Did the corps commander understand his instructions? General Stopford was persuaded by his orders, and by conversations with Hamilton and Braithwaite, that his main task was to secure a harbour and base area, so his operations did nothing to support the attack from Anzac and did not form part of a synergetic whole. As a result he failed to drive forward from Suvla to crown the surrounding heights (how he thought he could secure the area without doing this remains obscure – he had made it clear to Hamilton that he fully recognised the need to capture the hills) and push southwards past Anzac to the Narrows before Turkish reinforcements could arrive. Stopford's over-cautious approach was also coloured by his view – flying in the face of all intelligence reports – that a heavily entrenched Turkish position, supported by heavy artillery, had to be tackled in a Western Front manner.[9]

A major contributor to early failure was the excessive secrecy, in defiance of field service regulations which stressed that the need for secrecy had to be balanced against possible loss of operational efficiency. The Suvla operation, at first a mere afterthought to a big attack from Anzac and mostly planned, like the April landings, by Aspinall, Dawnay and Deedes, was cloaked in such secrecy that the formation commanders themselves were kept in the dark for far too long. Several senior officers remained unbriefed until 30 July, and many didn't see a map before the landing. The same concern for secrecy had restricted opportunities for land, sea and air reconnaissance (low-level reconnaissance flights were forbidden[10]) to a minimum far below the absolute minimum required for conduct of operations. Thus most commanders, officers and men were totally lacking in an understanding of the ground over which they had to operate.

Knowledge of the Suvla terrain and Turkish defences

The terrain of the Suvla Bay area was fairly well known and appreciated before the landings, but it could be argued that, as at Anzac, no amount of terrain intelligence would compensate for lack of experience in fighting in these conditions. This is particularly true of the ground encountered once troops had left the flat Suvla Plain.

In his letters to Kitchener, his Despatch, and subsequently, Hamilton makes much of the difficult terrain, particularly the dense scrub, with the implication that he had not been fully aware of this before the operation.

In fact he was in possession of a great deal of terrain intelligence from various sources. The 1909 War Office Report[11] stated (emphasis added):

> South of Cape Suvla is the wide bay of the same name, well sheltered from the northern winds which frequently prevail, and having a sandy beach suitable for landing. A good beach runs south of Nibrunesi Point also, and from both these places access is fairly easy to the villages of Biyuk and Kuchuk Anafarta, and thence into the plain about Turshtenkeni and Selvili. A rough coast track leads south also.
>
> *Suvla Bay.* The northern shore of the bay is lined by low, rocky cliffs, some 30 feet high, and rocky hills covered with low scrub extend along the coast to the east. Between the cliffs and the mouth of the Salt Lake is a stretch of firm, sandy beach, 900 yards in length, on which a landing could easily be effected in calm weather or when the wind is north. In a southerly wind landing would not be practicable, but northerly winds are prevalent, especially in winter, and from these the bay is quite sheltered. Deep water extends close up to the beach, but there are occasional shoals. A landing on the north side of the bay gives access to a stretch of sandy hillocks, covered with tufts of grass, which offer no obstacle to the passage of guns or wheeled vehicles; 800 yards inland cultivation (principally maize) is reached, with firm ground passable for all arms. The hill [Lala Baba] between Salt Lake and Nibrunesi Point is of sand and stones, *covered with low scrub*, and has an old tomb on the summit. The plain between the Topalin Mezar Dere and the Kizlar Dere is covered with cultivation and dotted with large trees, oak and walnut. Low *scrub-covered* hills of sandy soil descend to the plain from the south and east. The Salt Lake or Lagoon is ordinarily dry in summer, but with a south wind it may fill up again. From November to April it always contains water. When dry its bed is easily passable for infantry. The opening to the sea is 80 yards wide, and also becomes dry in summer.

Further extracts from the 1909 report are given in Appendix III, including information about the Sari Bair range immediately to the south, where the Anzacs had encountered impossible terrain and a tough Turkish defence.

Of the area north of Suvla Bay, the British 1:50,000 map (GSGS 4001) produced in the late-summer (possibly August) of 1915 by the Survey of Egypt and based on captured Turkish 1:25,000 originals, carried this description (possibly written by Nicholas or Ogilvy, clearly with a geologist's eye):

> The sharp ridge running from the neighbourhood of Ejelmer Bay to Suvla Point is formed of beds of hard sandstone alternating with less

resistant rocks and dipping to the S.E. The seaward slopes are steep, rocky and in many places precipitous, while the S.E. slopes are more gradual but corrugated by numerous minor parallel ridges, where the harder beds crop out. *The whole ridge is covered with low scrub. . . . Hills around Anafarta Sagir are covered with thick scrub* and traversed by ridges of hard rock with a general E–W trend.

Although the map was printed after the Suvla landings, the information was available before August; it was also printed on the British 1:20,000 sheets of the GSGS 4000 *Dardanelles* series, some of which appeared in August.

Reconnaissance by landing parties and patrols from Anzac

As early as 30 April, the Navy landed a fighting patrol from a destroyer on Suvla Bay's southern beach to deal with Turkish artillery observers directing fire onto the Anzac beach, and this patrol attacked a Turkish piquet entrenched on the summit of Lala Baba and cut a telephone wire. This feat was repeated inside the bay two days later by Captain C Cribb and fifty men of the Canterbury (New Zealand) Battalion, landed by the destroyer *Colne*, who surprised sleeping Turks in the Lala Baba trench. The New Zealanders searched the area, discovering two trenches covering the beach to the south of Nibrunesi Point, and also a spring on the western side of the hill, before successfully re-embarking.[12]

Two brave and adventurous ground reconnaissances made from the northern flank of the Anzac beachhead during May – the first by Major Overton and Corporal Denton on 15–16 May, and the second by Major Overton and Captain Hastings on 27 May – proved that the terrain was practicable for a left-flanking movement towards Chunuk Bair, and that the Turks considered the terrain to be so difficult that the area was undefended. Only old and unoccupied stretches of trench were seen on Chunuk Bair.[13] More incredibly, a New Zealand reconnaissance patrol under Lieutenant G R Blackett was landed from a trawler on the night of 20 June at Nibrunesi Point, the tip of the southern arm of Suvla Bay under the northern slopes of Kiretch Tepe, to locate Turkish artillery positions on the western hills. After successfully crossing the Suvla Plain, they returned to their trawler, after locating an abundant water supply on Kiretch Tepe, without encountering any Turkish soldiers or defences. Turkish patrol activity was reported, but there were few enemy forces north of the Anafarta Spur.[14]

Invaluable terrain intelligence, which was to form the foundation of the Anzac and Suvla operations in August, was gathered through these reconnaissances. More information could have been gathered in this way, but as it was feared that frequent patrolling might alarm the Turks, reconnaissance patrols were discouraged in the weeks before the landings. Thus new confirmation regarding the paucity of the Turkish defences, which might have encouraged Stopford and Reed to adopt a more forward operational approach, was not acquired. It has also been argued that the many wells and other water supplies should have been located and verified by patrols before the landings,[15] but not only is it unlikely that the Turks would have countenanced this degree of activity, but it is also probable that they would have taken more effective steps to render these supplies unusable.

Hydrographic intelligence and landing places

While there is disagreement regarding the accuracy of existing Admiralty charts and other hydrographic information for the Suvla area, there is no doubt that the Navy could have collected more data before the landings had it been warned to do so.[16] Again, excessive concerns about secrecy may have played a part in this, but given that a force was landed at Anzac, just to the south of Suvla Bay, in April, and maintained in that position thereafter, there were ample opportunities for further hydrographic reconnaissances off a land area where Turkish forces were extremely thin on the ground.

According to Aspinall, the hydrography of Suvla Bay itself was largely unknown, and the old Admiralty chart was unreliable. We have seen that although the Suvla Bay area had been charted in the 19th century, little specific hydrographic work in that area was done before or in April 1915, or for the Suvla operation in August, as it was feared that any obvious survey work would alert the Turks and lead to stronger opposition. Hamilton was extremely angry when a destroyer fired a shell into the Salt Lake to test the hardness of its surface before the August landings, believing that this would give the game away to the Turks.

The Navy originally rejected the idea of landings at Suvla Bay because it believed that shoal waters and reefs made landings too hazardous, and that the charts were poor and insufficient accurate hydrographic data were held. On the other hand there were now more general hydrographic data compared with April, as Turkish maps had been captured, and there had been months of close observation by the Navy's fire-support ships as well as aerial reconnaissance (seaplanes and aeroplanes), air photography and landing parties, which all contributed their bit to the overall picture.

Naval reconnaissance suggested that the northern shore was rocky and not suitable as a landing place, while in the southern area around Lala Baba it was decided that the low cliffs bordering the sandy beach ruled it out also as a landing place. A further adverse factor was that the sea near the shore at Lala Baba was very shallow. A suitable landing place was located just north of 'The Cut' (the apparently dry watercourse connecting Suvla Bay with the Salt Lake) on the eastern side of the Bay. Here a long, wide beach looked very promising, while there was an apparently easy exit from the beach to the Suvla Plain across low sand-dunes.[17] The Salt Lake itself was known to be dry in summer, and between The Cut and Lala Baba was separated from Suvla Bay by a low and narrow ridge of sand-dunes.

However, the Navy's considered view was that, owing to shallow water and the possibility of rocks, no landings should be attempted within Suvla Bay. Instead, they advocated landings on the excellent beach, over a mile long with easy exits to the Suvla Plain, south of Nibrunesi Point, the southern arm of the bay. This firm sandy beach, with its deep-water approaches very close to the shore, was well-known to the Navy, through close observation by the destroyers guarding the Anzac northern flank.[18] Visual reconnaissance and sketches made from the sea gave a useful general impression of the terrain, but 'the distance prevented any useful information being gained'.[18] While the beach seemed to have an easy, almost flat gradient, it was difficult to estimate distances and heights, and the sketches did not disclose any Turkish defences.

In the event, despite its misgivings and although certain beaches were shelving or difficult in other ways and some of the approaches were bad, the Navy found that it was able to land Stopford's Corps in the face of weak opposition. New purpose-built, shallow-draught landing craft, originally designed for Fisher's pet Baltic operation, were used. Because of their pairs of narrow, extending ramps, giving the appearance of antennae, they were known as 'Beetles'. Most of Stopford's force was landed south of Nibrunesi Point, the Navy's preferred beach, but Hamilton's plan was changed at Stopford's insistence to land Sitwell's 34th Brigade inside the bay north of The Cut, at the beach earlier identified. This Brigade, however, ran into trouble. The covering force destroyers anchored in the wrong positions, and as the Navy had feared, an uncharted reef was encountered, two of the special landing craft 'Beetles' struck the reef, and their troops had to wade shore in neck-deep water. The net result of all this was that the landing was made south of The Cut. Despite the usual chaos associated with troops (and these were relatively untrained and inexperienced) landing in the dark, good footings ashore were made against light opposition, but bad leadership and a failure to push on meant that the initial successful landing was not exploited. The 'Beetles', as well as tank landing craft (the tanks specially modified to climb the sea wall), were later prepared to make coastal landings in Belgium in mid-1917, but as Haig's Flanders offensive failed to make sufficient progress this operation was cancelled.[20]

Air photography and reconnaissance, and the Turkish defences

Aerial reconnaissance and photography provided the most detailed and accurate information about the Turkish defences and troop movements, and revealed the small size of the garrison defending the Suvla area.[21] They did not, however, give much detailed information about the terrain, and their results were not interpreted with this in mind. Apart from the beaches and their exits, observers and air photo interpreters were simply not told to consider the terrain.[22]

Details of air reconnaissance and photography at Suvla were given in Chapter 7, but it is useful to summarise them here. On 23 July Samson flew low over the area and saw little activity and few trenches.[23] On 4 August all existing trenches and gun emplacements were identified (most were unoccupied), and the position sketched from the air. The next day the information about the gun emplacements was confirmed and it was reported that the trenches north of the Salt Lake were unoccupied. Photos were taken of the Chocolate Hill defences, one of the first objectives. The air photos generally showed little or nothing in the way of enemy defences except at Lala Baba, and Knatchbull Hugessen recorded: 'Note complete absence of all trenches, etc.'[24] On 6 August the only enemy troops seen were moving away from the area.[25]

The results of earlier reconnaissance by landing parties had not necessarily been well-collated or appreciated; the *Final Instructions* issued on 29 July from GHQ to Stopford's IX Corps made a specific reference to 'an aeroplane photograph [which] has also disclosed the presence of a few trenches on Lala Baba. A sketch of these trenches [not reproduced in the Official History], which have apparently been constructed for some months is attached.'[26] The air photos confirmed the Intelligence staff in their belief that there were only some 4,000 men and a few guns to oppose a landing by a whole British corps of over 20,000 men, and also revealed which localities and hills were undefended, and the relative strength and dispositions of those which were defended.[27]

To summarise, the Suvla Bay area was weakly fortified by the Turks and there were no continuous lines of trenches. We have seen that various isolated stretches of trenches existed, that these had already been identified by reconnaissance, and that it was appreciated that there were only weak Turkish forces in the area. Nevertheless the British prepared 'dispositions' maps or traces showing what Turkish defences had been located by air photography and other reconnaissance. The Turkish force (the Anafarta Detachment) defending the Suvla area, commanded by the Bavarian Major Willmer, comprised four battalions, no machine guns, little barbed wire and a few pieces of artillery whose effect he maximised by changing positions frequently and also using dummy guns. He had established strongpoints on the Kiretch Tepe ridge north of Suvla Bay, Hill 10 north of the Salt Lake and Chocolate Hill east of the Salt Lake, while Lala Baba was entrenched and piqueted by a look-out party. His main force was in a line about a mile north of the western hills, parallel with the sea, barring the way to the Tekke Tepe heights, north of Anafarta Sagir.[28] Thus in the immediate landing zone, one Turkish brigade was to be assaulted by a British corps which might have been considered an overwhelming force.

In the area of the British and New Zealanders' attack from the Anzac beachhead, the old shallow Turkish trench on the summit of Chunuk Bair, had been severely damaged by British naval bombardment.[29] The *First Instructions* from GHQ to IX Corps, dated 22 July, noted that 'Latest photographs show that the Turkish trenches on this [the Chunuk Bair] ridge, do not extend further north than Chunuk Bair, and it is unlikely that the higher portions of the ridge are held in great strength'.[30]

For their associated Lone Pine attack at Anzac, the Australians had prepared an accurate, detailed map of the position from the excellent air photos now available, and indeed such trench maps had been prepared and improved ever since the first landings in April, although at first the lack of air photos delayed progress. Unfortunately in this case the photos were poorly interpreted, the timber cover, showing clearly on the photos, of the Turkish front trenches remaining 'unidentified,' and the significance of a steep ravine (later called The Cup, in which the Turkish headquarters and reserves were situated, forming the main communication with the front on the left of the Lone Pine position) branching from Owen's Gully, was not appreciated by the Intelligence staff evaluating the photos; the reverse slopes of this ravine were untrenched, and a breakthrough here would have led directly into open country.[31]

Maps for the Suvla operation

By the end of July, excellent 1:20,000 topographical maps, copied by the Survey of Egypt from captured sheets of the recent Turkish 1:25,000 survey (see Chapter 9), were available for the Suvla landings as well as for the Anzac and Helles sectors. These British topographical maps did not, however, show the Turkish defences. While trench diagrams had been plotted for the Helles and Anzac sectors, as the result of close study of, and plotting from, aerial photos over a period of three months, simple lithographed intelligence sketch maps were prepared for the Suvla landings by MEF GHQ showing Turkish defences, reflecting the lack of plottable defences on the ground, as identified by land, sea and air reconnaissance. This information turned out to be accurate.

An overdone obsession with secrecy (lack of surprise was a major element in the failure of the April landings) meant that, for the Suvla landings, maps were either only issued to assaulting troops on the afternoon prior to the landings (British company commanders were only issued with maps at Mudros at 2.30pm on the eve of the assault[32]) or, even worse, in some extreme cases, on the day itself after they had disembarked on a hostile beach.

A deception plan, involving the issue of reports and maps of the Asiatic coastline, was put into operation, 11th Division being concentrated at Mitylene, to threaten the Smyrna district. These maps had to be ordered from, and printed in, Egypt, and their production priority led to a disturbing delay in the arrival of the maps actually required for the real operations.[33] Nevertheless, the Suvla maps were available a full week before the landing, allowing plenty of time for study had they been distributed with this in mind.

Following the consolidation of the beachhead and linking up with Anzac, trench diagrams were created for the new operations area on the pattern of those already established at Helles and Anzac.

Water supply

Water supply was perhaps the most problematic aspect of the terrain, and considerable forethought went into planning for the eventuality that there would be severe shortages in the initial phase of the Suvla landings. However, divided responsibilities and failure to inform troops of the probable location of wells and sub-surface water supplies led to a crisis which severely affected operations. The Dardanelles Commission was extremely critical of the arrangements made.

The Suvla Plain north of the Salt Lake appeared flat and arid, while in the Azmak Dere valley the terrain was greener and supported several tree-ringed farmsteads. Water supply, particularly in the trying heat of August, was from the start a serious point for consideration.[34] Greek peasants employed as guides by the Anzac Corps, described as 'uneducated and cannot read a map but are intelligent', gave information on water supply in the area between Suvla Bay and the Anafartas, stating that it was abundant between Biyuk and Kutchuk Anafarta, the main supply coming from wells exploiting water in the alluvial sediments of the Suvla Plain. Some of these wells were to be 'poisoned' by proximity to dead Turkish soldiers.[35] Water supply was also stated to be good, even in July, in the area of any break-out from the Anzac perimeter.[36]

Captured Turkish maps indicated many wells in the Azmak Dere valley, but there were few in the plain and on the northern and southern arms of the bay. Intelligence reports provided the welcome information that there were good springs on Kiretch Tepe, and it was also believed that there was a good sub-surface water supply which could be reached by shallow excavation. On balance, short-term supply remained a cause for much concern, given the large number of troops that would be landed, and it was appreciated that they would have to be supplied from the sea during the early phase of operations.[37]

On 14 July Hamilton asked the War Office for an expert 'water-diviner' to be sent out to assist in finding water after the landings. Lieutenant-Colonel Brady RE, the officer at the War Office responsible for Works and Services for the BEF in France, considered that a more scientific approach was required and, after consulting Sir Aubrey Strahan, Director of the Geological Survey of Great Britain, arranged to send out three Survey geologists (Cunningham, Pocock and Whitehead) together with water-boring equipment (drive tube wells) from the specialist firm of Thompson and Hunter.[38] Two of these geologists had joined the army, and were extracted from their units to send to the Dardanelles, while the third was from the Geological Survey. Strahan also, at Brady's request, collected geological data on the Gallipoli Peninsula and nearby islands. Mr A Beeby Thompson, head of the firm, placed orders for the appropriate equipment on 23–24 July and left England with an assistant on 26 July. Brady kept Hamilton informed of all this, but on 22 July was told that a 'diviner' was wanted, not geologists. Brady replied that 'I did not trust such important work to diviners,' and went ahead with his arrangements. He later reported of the geologists that 'I believe they all did very useful work.'[39] This was apparently the first occasion on which geological assistance and information was solicited for the Gallipoli operations.

Conclusion

After the experiences of the April landings, and the operations and reconnaissances of the subsequent months, there should have been little doubt about the difficult nature of the terrain. Many contemporary sources cite difficult terrain as impeding the operations following the landings at Suvla Bay, and the fact that troops lacking experience of fighting in this theatre were landed in this area undoubtedly hindered operations. The War Diary of 11th Division noted 'rough stony ground, cut up into a tangled succession of steep ravines', and 'dwarf ilex . . . with limbs frequently as thick as a man's arm, and with foliage through which it was impossible to force one's way'.[40] This terrain description would have been familiar to anyone who had fought at Anzac, and indeed was prefigured in the various pre-war reports. Yet Suvla looked enticing. Apparently open ground where cultivated, it soon descends into scrub-covered wilderness, with small hills of harder rock providing vantage points for the defender. Even if such terrain information had been distributed, the inexperienced troops would have found the ground heavy going; they had had no training in fighting in similar terrain configuration.

Despite all the anxious pre-landing staff work regarding water supply, the troops seem to have been poorly informed about the existence of sub-surface water, and how to reach it. There is no doubt that conditions were fearful in the heat of August, but sufficient warning had been given for these to have been overcome; in the words of a critical participant, John Hargrave, 'the landing should not have relied, fatally, on seaborne replenishment'.[41]

Notes

1. An unpublished paper by Sarah Nicholas, providing a useful tour d'horizon, may be the first serious study of this; Nicholas, S, *British Military Intelligence at Suvla Bay, August 1915*, 2000 (unpublished dissertation).
2. *Reports and Memoranda relative to Defence of Constantinople and other positions in Turkey . . .*, 1877, pp. 147–8, in TNA(PRO) WO 33/29.
3. *Report on the Defences of Constantinople*, Secret, London, General Staff, War Office, 1909.
4. Aspinall-Oglander, Brig.-Gen. C F, *Military Operations, Gallipoli*, Vol. I, London: Heinemann, 1929, p. 313.
5. Aspinall-Oglander, op. cit., Vol. II, London: Heinemann, 1932, p. 6.
6. The Dardanelles Commission, 2001, p. 150.
7. Churchill to 1 S.L., C.O.S., in Evidence to the Dardanelles Commission, TNA(PRO) CAB 19/28, Appendix B1, p. 210.
8. Rhodes James, Robert, *Gallipoli*, London: Pimlico, 1999, p. 187.
9. Travers, Tim, *Gallipoli 1915*, Stroud: Tempus, 2001, p. 142.
10. Rhodes James, op. cit., p. 248.
11. *Report on the Defences of Constantinople*, 1909, op. cit.
12. Aspinall-Oglander, Vol. I, op. cit., p. 313.
13. Rhodes James, op. cit., p. 219.
14. Aspinall-Oglander, op. cit., Vol. II, p.130.
15. Nicholas, op. cit.
16. It is possible that Commander Douglas carried out at least a reconnaissance of the area on 29 March, while on board the destroyer *Mosquito*; see, Denham, H M, *Dardanelles. A Midshipman's Diary*, London: John Murray, 1981, p. 73.
17. Aspinall-Oglander, op. cit., Vol. II, pp. 129–30.
18. Ibid, p. 132 & fn.
19. Hammersley, report on 11th Division's operations, TNA(PRO) WO 32/5123.
20. Wolf, L, *In Flanders Fields. The 1917 Campaign*, London: Longmans, Green, 1958; Edmonds, J, *Military Operations, France and Belgium, 1917*, Vol. II, London: HMSO, p. 117.
21. *Notes for Observers*, Royal Flying Corps, 1915, p. 11; copy in Sykes papers, Vol. I, RAF Museum, Hendon. See also Sykes, F, *From Many Angles. An Autobiography*, London: Harrap, 1942, p. 166, and Rhodes James, op. cit., p. 255.
22. Sykes, op. cit., pp. 157–73.
23. Samson, Charles Rumney, *Fights and Flights*, London: Ernest Benn, 1930, p. 256.
24. MS inscription against photos 456 & 457 in album (Vol. VI – Gallipoli & various) of air photos collected by Capt. Hon. M Knatchbull MC, on loan to IWM Dept of Photographs.

25. Jones, H J, *The War in the Air*, Vol. II, London: OUP, 1928, p. 59.
26. Appendix 3 (Final Instructions from GHQ to IX Corps for the Suvla Operations, 29 July) of *OH Military Operations*, Gallipoli Vol. II, Maps & Appendices, London: Heinemann, 1932, p. 19.
27. Aspinall-Oglander, op. cit., Vol. II, pp. 29, 165.
28. Rhodes James, op. cit., p. 255.
29. Ibid, pp. 284–5.
30. *OH Military Operations, Gallipoli*, Vol. II, op. cit., Appendix 2, p. 17.
31. Rhodes James, op. cit., p. 264.
32. Ibid, p. 257.
33. Nolan, M A, *The Gallipolian*, Spring 1994, p.16.
34. Aspinall-Oglander, op. cit., Vol. II, pp. 129–30.
35. Hargrave, John, *The Suvla Bay Landing*, London: John Murray, 1964, p. 115.
36. Anzac Intelligence War Diary, Bulletin, JY 15, dated 7 July, Intelligence Note on Roads, water Supply, etc. TNA(PRO) WO 157/681.
37. Aspinall-Oglander, op. cit., Vol. II, pp. 129–30.
38. Strahan, A, 'Introduction. Work in Connection with the war', *Memoirs of the Geological Survey*, London: HMSO, 1919; Beeby-Thompson, A, *Exploring for Water*, London: Villiers Publications, 1969, p. 253.
39. Lt-Col. Brady's evidence to Dardanelles Commission, TNA(PRO) CAB 19/28, p. 100.
40. 11th Division War Diary, TNA(PRO) CAB 45/258.
41. Hargrave, op. cit.

CHAPTER 11

Retrospect

As we have seen, there is much evidence to suggest that intelligence material (maps, reports, plans and reconnaissance) were all available to Hamilton and his General Staff, both before and after the landings. In retrospect, the terrain described in Chapter 1, in terms that would not be alien to any commander, can be seen to have exercised a significant factor in the outcome of battle; in the words of Australian historian Ashley Ekins: 'At virtually every stage of the campaign the advantages and limitations imposed by terrain dominated the battlefield and largely determined the outcome.'[1]

Terrain and the Gallipoli Campaign

As was discussed in Chapter 1, the role of terrain is an important factor in the following considerations: (1) tactical position; (2) mobility; (3) ground conditions; (4) resource provision and hazard mitigation. These are discussed below in relation to what actually happened during the Gallipoli Campaign, assessing the role of terrain overall in its outcome.

Tactical position

The three main zones of conflict, Cape Helles, Anzac Cove and Suvla Bay, each had its own problems associated with tactical position. All three were within range of enemy shelling, and unlike the Turks, who had unlimited space for resting troops in the well-watered valleys behind the lines, there were no adequate rest camps.[2]

Cape Helles and Achi Baba. The landings at Cape Helles were to be made at narrow beaches leading into narrow, constrained valleys which rise up the slopes of the Kilid Bahr Plateau with the intention of capturing the plateau top, threatening Kilid Bahr below. The limestone cliffs are steep to near

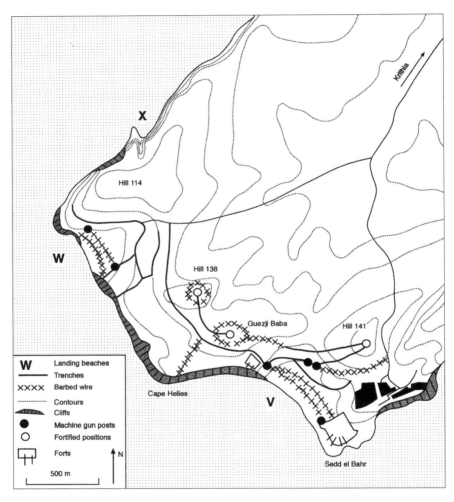

Helles Sector, showing Turkish defences and the funnelling effect of V and W beaches and the excellent use of Terrain by the Turks; based on survey made by Nicholas and Douglas just after the landings in April

vertical and unscalable coastal cliffs, and therefore the only access to the slopes of the Kilid Bahr Plateau was through the incised valleys, particularly as there is only one low-lying area at Morto Bay. The two main landing beaches selected, V and W, have only relatively narrow stretches of open beach (200–300 metres) which funnel directly into narrow gorges surrounded on both sides by the limestone slopes characteristic of this land system.

Defence of the valleys by the Turks was relatively straightforward, given the ability for enfilading fire from both sides of the valley, and the narrowness of the beaches. Turkish preparations in the month after the cessation of the naval bombardment exploited small hills (Hill 114, Hill 138 and Guezji Baba) as strongpoints, surrounded by trenches and extensive barbed wire entanglements mounted on angle-iron stakes. Trenches contoured the valley sides so as to provide the mutual enfilade fire promoted by the practitioners of the day.[3] Machine-gun emplacements were installed on the cliff tops at the mouth of both valleys, providing crossfire.[4] To the attackers, the enfilade fire produced by both the infantry in the trenches and the machine-gun posts was decimating. Vegetation on the beaches was insufficient to provide much cover, and the only natural breaks in slope were some raised beach material on V Beach, which enabled the attackers to shelter. The commanding hills and Turkish positions were only captured three days after the initial landing when the steep cliffs and slopes characteristic of the Helles sector were turned to the attackers' advantage in providing cover, although the nature of the crossfire was such that such cover could never be a hundred percent efficient.

The beach designated 'X' by the Allies was largely undefended by the Turkish forces simply because it was extremely narrow, and the slopes were precipitous and densely vegetated. This meant that the attacking forces were able to come ashore largely unopposed and, if it had not been for poor leadership and inadequate communications, might have assisted in the capture of Hill 114, thereby compromising the Turkish defences. This was not to be. A similar situation was encountered on the other side of the Peninsula at Morto Bay (S Beach), which was also lightly defended. The landings at X and S beaches were not considered by the British to be as important as those at V and W beaches, presumably because here at least the beaches were slightly wider, and access to the dip slope of Achi Baba easier.

Once ashore, the troops had to fight up the dip slope of Achi Baba, part of the Kilid Bahr Plateau. Failure to exploit this more open terrain reflects resourcing difficulties and the tactical advantage for the Turks of the possession of the higher ground. The Allied troops were advancing up what was a relatively gentle slope, but were hampered by inadequate land-based artillery and ammunition, and decreased efficiency of naval artillery due to the flat trajectory used. Limited successful advances on the flanks of the plateau, in the spurs and gullies of the undulating topography typical of plateaux, also meant that often the flanks of the Allied advances were left 'in the air' and in danger of being outflanked. The Turks for their part were opposing the Allies on a forward slope, and were able to direct their artillery and machine-gun fire with greater accuracy. After a series of attritional battles which mimicked the Western Front, trench systems became more or less static, and Achi Baba was never captured.

Gaba Tepe and Anzac Cove. The intended landing site of the Anzac troops was to be north of Gaba Tepe on the open beach initially designated Z beach, later to be called Brighton Beach by the troops. The plan was to exploit the lower slopes of the Sari Bair Plateau, rising up the less steep, but still deeply incised valley systems of the southern margin of the plateau in order to reach the summit and overlook Kilid Bahr and the Dardanelles beyond. In fact, as is well known, the landing actually took place much farther to the north in Anzac Cove. This was unfortunate, as it is the only stretch of coast where the soft sediment cliffs of the Peninsula plateaux meet the sea, and although the Turkish defenders had not strongly defended this stretch of coastline, it was topographically challenging.

The tactical implications of the mistaken landing are serious. After initial successes on the day of landing, the Anzac troops did not ever manage to control the heights of the plateau, and as at Cape Helles, a parallel line of trenches was dug along the coastal slopes, the Turks always having the observational advantage of high ground. The final Anzac line actually ran north-eastwards paralleling the fault scarp which was the north-eastern expression of the plateau. The effectiveness of the Anzac position was therefore severely constrained by the nature of the slopes, particularly with regard to the steepness and level of dissection of the plateau, extremely difficult for the attacking troops to ascend. Turkish forward trenches, positioned as they were at the crest of this slope, provided a clear view of the low ground beneath them. The dissected dip slope leading up to the plateau also presented problems, the dissection producing north-west–south-east trending narrow ridges separated by steep-sided gullies. The broken ground provided by this topography made communications difficult, and the further construction of Turkish defensive positions on the higher slopes, surrounding the peaks of Chunuk Bair and Koja Chemen Tepe, meant that advances by the Anzac troops were difficult and costly; typical examples being the battle for the Lone Pine and the charge of the Australian Light Horse at a narrow subsidiary ridge known as the Nek. The constant observation of all the Anzac lines by the Turks meant that there were no safe rest camps close to the line, and even swimming parties were under constant threat from Turkish artillery. Finally, the narrowness of the beach at Anzac Cove produced its own problems with respect to resourcing and storage of men, material and pack animals from the sea.

Suvla Bay. The landing at Suvla Bay, made in August 1915, was meant to exploit the previously untried landing beaches of the bay, and to allow troops to deploy rapidly across the flat Suvla Plain before taking the high ground which surrounded the plain in the form of the Anafarta and Karakol ridges. The landing was, unfortunately, bodged such that troops from different commands became hopelessly mixed, and no decisive military decisions were taken that day, and as we have seen, even the hard lessons of the landings in April were not learned.

In fact the Turkish defenders were small in number, and were deployed in small outposts to the north and south of the Suvla Plain, exploiting small knolls and hillocks of harder rock sticking above the plain. The British troops did eventually traverse the open and flat Suvla Plain, and not even the Salt Lake was an obstacle to progress, by foot at least, as it was seasonally dry. However, although they were to take up their positions at the foothills, they were never to take the commanding peaks which overlooked the Suvla Plain, and consequently they wasted a valuable opportunity to break out of the constrained area. A later offensive in August tried to break out of the Suvla Plain by attacking the so-called Chocolate, Green and Scimitar hills, and the north-western facing scarp of the Sari Bair Plateau. However, these attacks failed at least in part because of the observational advantage possessed by the Turks who were now deployed in force, and ultimately this led to the decision to withdraw from the Peninsula completely.

Mobility

Unlike the situation on the Western Front, trafficability was never a major issue in the Gallipoli Campaign, due to a variety of factors. Importantly, the level of troop movements was limited inland, as the majority of supplies were derived from shipborne sources, including water supplies, as is well known. Movement of supplies inland was in the main by mule transport, although some wheeled traffic was used more extensively at Cape Helles, where there was the maximum Allied penetration. Therefore, it was important to construct piers for the landing of stores, and for the construction of roads capable of taking wheeled artillery pieces, as there were no real roads on the Peninsula at that time. These roads and paths were mostly constructed by slope excavation, and there is no record of elaborate construction methods being used. However, road construction using crushed stone aggregates was carried out by the Royal Engineers on Lemnos, and may also have been used on the Peninsula.[5]

Ground conditions

Ground conditions are most important in the development of permanent or semi-permanent entrenchments and other defensive positions. Three basic sets of ground conditions existed, primarily associated with the plateaux, limestone cliffs, and hard ridges of the Peninsula. These affected the construction of temporary, shallow-scrape 'foxholes', and more permanent defensive trench positions. Importantly, the nature of the ground conditions allowed for the development of tunnelling and offensive mining.

Trench and dugout construction. The necessity to establish secure beachheads after the first landings at Gallipoli ensured that trench warfare would become an important aspect of life for both sides during the Gallipoli Campaign. Initially, trenches were dug to provide protection for the newly landed and battle-weary troops, but by the end of the campaign, trench systems took on a complexity which in many ways mimicked that of the Western Front and was intimately associated with the intricacies of the local terrain.

On the Anzac front, the relatively soft sediments of the Sari Bair Plateau enabled the fairly rapid development of rudimentary trench systems, although this was hampered in the opening hours of the campaign by an absence of adequate construction tools, and by the degree of root penetration. By the end of the campaign, the trench systems were complex with a parallel underground system of tunnels and saps. In addition, many terraces were cut in the reverse slope to provide rudimentary dwelling areas. In general, few drainage problems were encountered, due to the paucity of rainfall, in the summer months at least, the relative permeability of the trenches, and the absence of ground water close to the surface – itself a major issue. Revetment was usually achieved using locally derived or shipped-in timber, and both sides used covered trench systems, roofed by timber baulks and earthworks, in order to mitigate the effects of shrapnel and small arms fire, although largely useless against direct hits from high explosive shells. Covered trench systems made extensive use of loopholes for snipers. New trenches were often dug by the use of shallow tunnels which were then roofed with timber before the cutting of loopholes. As with the Western Front, dugouts varied from the deep, shell-proof dugout to the shallow recess or 'funk-hole' intended only as a limited shelter. Extensive dugout systems were cut into the seawards slopes of the Sari Bair Plateau providing shelter for a variety of administrative and service personnel.

At Helles, the initial landings encountered the relatively hard limestones of land system II and this meant that in many cases there was insufficient depth for protection without the use of heavy tools not immediately available. Blasting was used later in the campaign.[6] However, the subsequent advances from the Helles beachhead enabled the construction of trenches in both soft sediments and harder limestone rocks. Extensive dugout systems were also constructed, and much use was made of the incised 'gullies' on the dip slope of the Kilid Bahr Plateau, particularly at Gully Ravine. At Suvla, trench construction was commenced tactically earlier than it should have, before the high ground was captured and exploited. Support lines protecting the landing beaches were also dug adjacent to the Salt Lake, and these were undoubtedly more difficult to maintain, given the proximity of standing water, marshes and sand-dunes. Lala Baba, composed of the same hard rocks that making up Kirech Tepe Ridge was also heavily defended.

Offensive mining. Offensive mining is characteristic of protracted trench warfare, and was extensively used on the Western Front.[7] Mining was also employed, intensively but on a smaller scale, at Gallipoli, on both the Helles and Anzac fronts.[8] There were few geological problems with these tunnelling activities, as they were exclusively cut through the relatively workable sediments of sands and clays, with harder bands serving to roof the tunnels.[9] On both fronts, and by both sides, mining activities were developed after the failure of the summer offensives. On the Anzac front, mining and tunnelling activities led to the development of an extensive underground tunnel system which sent forward a series of saps under the enemy lines which were to be packed with explosives and blown at appropriate moments. In addition, and in an attempt to solve the overcrowding of the Anzac Cove area, an extensive tunnel system was constructed under the Anzac trench lines to provide quarters for the men, storage facilities, and the ability to move about without being observed. These tunnels were constructed by tunnelling companies of the Royal Engineers attached to the Anzac Corps. A special corps of Australian tunnellers was also raised, but were formed too late to take an active part in the Gallipoli Campaign. Similar tunnels and offensive mining techniques were employed at Cape Helles, although there was less need for an extensive system for storage and habitation. As on the Western Front, the opposing troops carried out a series of countermining techniques in order to both detect and deal with the mining activity, using shallow 'camouflet' mines designed to destroy the tunnels without producing a surface crater.

Resources

The provision of resources to the invading armies was a particular problem for the Allied forces. In most cases, elaborate supply lines were constructed which brought food, water and ammunition from Imbros. A system of semi-permanent piers and jetties was constructed, mostly from anchored inshore craft, but also from pile-driven steel girders driven deep into the beach sediments, the remains of which can still be observed today.

Potable water. Water supply was a major consideration for the Gallipoli Campaign. The Allies were forced from the beginning to plan for the provision of an adequate supply of potable water to serve both its men and animals. Water was derived from three sources: (1) surface water; (2) ground water, and (3) imported supplies. As we have seen, the search for potable water supplies initiated some of the earliest reports on the geology of the Gallipoli Peninsula, commissioned directly from the Geological Survey of Great Britain.

Surface water supplies were extremely variable and for the most part, insufficient. There are few flowing rivers on the Peninsula, the majority of them being seasonal. Ground water supplies were more promising. The majority of ground waters were derived from: (1) limestone/sandstone strata at depth; (2) beach and riverbed sediments, and (3) from clay layers capturing water in the otherwise dry deposits at Anzac.[10] The water-bearing limestone strata of the coastal area provided the resources for much of the Cape Helles operation. However, as the British advanced up the slopes of Achi Baba, groundwater became more difficult to obtain. Wells tapping this aquifer also existed around the south-eastern margins. Beach and river sediments were found to be a good source of water on the Suvla Plain by Beeby-Thompson,[11] and these provided some limited resources at Anzac Cove, and more abundant supplies at the eastern margin of the Suvla Plain. Salt water spoiling water resources was a problem within the central part of the plain itself occurring seasonally, and due to excessive water abstraction. Much of the Suvla Plain and Karakol water supplies were derived from the hard sandstones that formed the ridge.

One of the biggest problems was a lack of reliable groundwater supplies at Anzac Cove. Here, the valuable water-bearing limestones are at depth, and seasonally supplies perched on impermeable strata, difficult to accurately locate, were the norm, together with some exploitation of seasonally dry rivers. These were ephemeral, however, and many of the wells dug in the surrounding gullies began to dry up with the approach of summer, though others were found at depth. This meant that the daily ration from local sources in the 1st Australian Division was rarely more than one third of a gallon per man. Except on the extreme northern flank, wells were even scarcer in the area occupied by the New Zealanders, on the northern slope of the Sari Bair Plateau. Most water supplies for these areas were from imported water and large water-lighters used to be towed from Alexandria and Malta and moored alongside the piers at Anzac Cove. The water could then be pumped by hand into iron tanks on the beach, whence it was taken by mules to other tanks in the hills, and thence by hand to

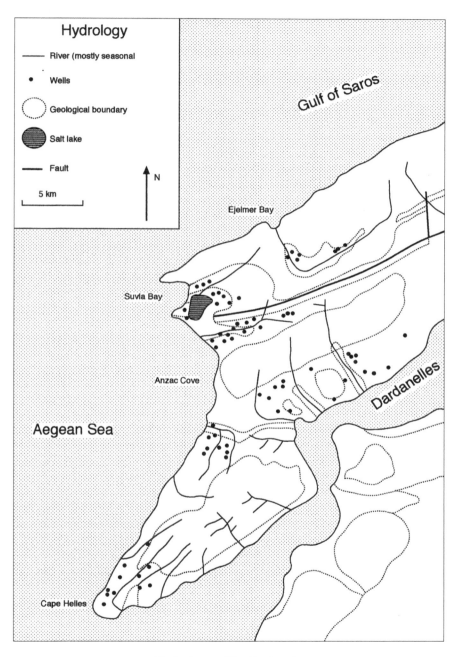

Hydrology

— River (mostly seasonal
• Wells
⋯ Geological boundary
⬤ Salt lake
— Fault

↑ N

5 km

Gulf of Saros

Ejelmer Bay

Suvla Bay

Anzac Cove

Dardanelles

Aegean Sea

Cape Helles

Hydrology of the Peninsula

the troops holding the line. Later, a pumping plant and a number of larger storage tanks were obtained from Egypt.[12] These were hauled to specially constructed platforms on the slopes of Plugge's Plateau, Walker's Ridge and other points near the front line. They were connected to the beach, and thereafter water could be pumped straight into them from the lighters, and then distributed to smaller tanks by gravitation.

The lessons learned at Anzac Cove led to the development of elaborate plans for water supply at Suvla Plain, despite the existence of more abundant groundwater supplies. Four fifty-ton water lighters specially fitted out in Egypt were towed across from Imbros by a water tank steamer, itself capable of carrying 200 tons of water, and which would fill the lighters when empty. Each lighter had been fitted with troughs, pumps and 120 feet of hose, and was manned by a crew of Royal Engineers. To enable the water to be carried forward to the troops, the bazaars in Egypt had been ransacked for every imaginable kind of water-carrying receptacle, and large quantities of milk cans, petrol tins, camel tanks and water bags had been shipped over. Unfortunately, these plans did not assist the landing in August, as the lighters grounded a long way out, and it was late in the day before water could be landed, causing much suffering amongst the troops.

Mineral/aggregate resourcing. The Gallipoli Campaign was fought over a relatively limited timescale, and there was little development of the kind of static positions developed on the Western Front which required concrete and other construction materials. In fact, the majority of permanent defensive works were built using timber and earthworks, although breastworks and sangars were created where the rock strata, limestones and sandstones could be broken into slabs. Road and jetty construction mostly utilised locally derived materials won when the initial cuttings were created, or when paths were widened, and in other cases broken and crushed stone may have been used.[13]

Hazard mitigation. The most important natural hazard which affected the troops was the flash flooding of the parallel aligned dry valley systems of the plateaux that dominate the centre of the Peninsula. This was particularly prevalent in the winter months, with increased rainfall, and unexpected floods led to the deaths of many men in the incised Gully Ravine later in the year. Little was done to mitigate such hazards, which occurred in the winter months following the break in the summer drought, and it is unlikely that they were expected.

Beaches and terrain

As has been argued by most historians, if the Peninsula was to be captured then Hamilton had no real choice but to land where he did. The capture of the high ground was of clear importance, and Hamilton's plan, to capture the Kilid Bahr Plateau using a pincer movement from Gaba Tepe and Helles and exploiting the low slopes of the coastal areas, appears sound. However, the beaches at Helles, developed at the mouth of the narrow, ravine-like valleys are clearly more suited to the defender, and the terrain multiplication effect magnified the excellent fire discipline of the Turkish troops to create a maelstrom into which the 29th Division landed during the 'Battle of the Beaches' on 25 April 1915.

The choice of Gaba Tepe makes sense from the perspective of terrain, using as it does the low slopes that would ultimately lead to that strategic prize, Maidos and the Narrows, but the use of the Anzac beaches does not. It must therefore be recognised of course that this was beyond the control of the commander once the landing was in place. Here, at the only place where the soft cliffs of Sari Bair reach the sea, the landing was made. As it happens, the landing here was a surprise, but as with Cape Helles in the south, the advantage was not pressed home, and after the initial surprise the tactical advantage soon passed to the defenders, controlling as they did the high ground.

The real mystery is why neither commander fully appreciated the value of Suvla Bay as a landing site earlier in the campaign. This has the benefit of both relatively wide beaches for the landing of men and material, and the Suvla Plain – flat but with sufficient cover for rapid deployment, and with a ground surface sufficiently dry for movement on foot or with animal transport, although damp and muddy in places. This mystery is partly answered by the fact that Suvla was some distance from the main objectives – the Turkish guns on the Dardanelles shore – and that the Allies appeared to have had little knowledge of either the terrain or the landing beaches themselves. For example, the Admiralty had little information upon the nature of shoaling of the coastal area, and the military commanders had minimal understanding of the nature of important water resources. In fact the opposition to landing at Suvla appears to have mainly come from the Navy. When the British finally landed in August 1915, the control of the high ground to the east, which ultimately could be used to outflank the Turkish positions on the Sari Bair Plateau overlooking Maidos and the Dardanelles, was in their grasp. Poor generalship led to the loss of this advantage, to the subsequent costly and unsuccessful battles for the heights of the Anafarta Ridge and the Sari Bair Plateau, and ultimately to the admission of defeat by the Allies.

Once ashore, and having become resigned to a stalemate at Anzac and Helles at least, the local use of terrain for resource provision and defensive works was reasonably handled. The most important problem lay in the provision of water supplies from groundwaters. This was only really a major problem at the Anzac front, where groundwater supply was limited and ephemeral. All previously known or newly dug wells exploited either the water-bearing limestones of the coastal areas or the alluvial/lacustrine sediments of the river valleys, beaches and coastal plains. The geologists attached to or advising the Allied forces were conversant with the problem, and the only effective solution was the use of imported supplies, clearly a costly and hazardous exercise.

The use of terrain for defensive purposes was efficiently handled on the Anzac and Helles fronts, particularly in the construction of adequate trench systems and in the use of tunnelling and dugout construction in slopes out of sight of the opposing Turkish forces. However, the inability to provide suitable rest camps close to the front line led to a severe diminution in the health and well-being of the troops. A clearly inadequate understanding led to the use of the dry seasonal ravines on the dip slope leading from the summit of Achi Baba. Many men were killed and much material lost in the flooding of the wet, winter season, adding to the discomfort of the troops.

Terrain intelligence

We can conclude from the evidence of Francis Maunsell, Frederick Cunliffe Owen, Charles Woods, Major L L R Samson, the War Office, the Naval Intelligence Division and many other sources that a British intelligence attack on the target of the Dardanelles defences and Gallipoli Peninsula was in operation in the early 20th century. However, it is also apparent that this intelligence effort did not have a high priority, was not properly resourced, directed or coordinated, and although it achieved a great deal, particularly in terms of technical information on the coastal defences and topographical information on landing places and the terrain of the Peninsula itself, it did not succeed in obtaining a copy of the recent Turkish large-scale survey of the Peninsula, or a fully detailed copy of the Greek plan for capturing the Peninsula. Further, the intelligence was not processed in such a way as to inform operational planning. Indeed, apart from the various Greek and Anglo-Greek plans there was no effective combined operational plan until one had been formulated in-theatre by Hamilton, after conferring with de Robeck following the failure of the naval attack on 18 March.

There were also at least two disastrous diplomatic failures. The first was the failure properly to appreciate and respond to the significance of the Young Turk revolution and the associated Turkish inclination towards Germany, which a more aware British policy might have prevented, and in so doing have secured Turkish neutrality. This in turn could have maintained Balkan neutrality. The second was the failure to install a military attaché at Athens from the beginning of the war, a failure which Cunninghame considered fatal from the point of view of securing Greek support; an early surprise attack on the Gallipoli Peninsula and the Dardanelles, using Greek troops and British ships, had a good chance of success. While the Germans had successfully appreciated the great strategic benefits of a proactive foreign policy to assist their *Drang nach Osten*, the British were sadly lethargic. As so often in Anglo-Islamic relations in the 20th and 21st centuries it was a case, as J K Galbraith might have put it, of private affluence and public squalor. Many influential private individuals were strongly pro-Turkish, and in a different context pro-Arab, but at diplomatic level, despite many warnings, relations were allowed to moulder.

Although a great deal of information was collected at the War Office before the war, and during the early months of the war, it was not properly collated, analysed, evaluated and distributed. The strange, catatonic, almost comatose condition of the War Office under Kitchener in 1914–15 has yet to be completely understood, but it is clear that the General Staff system had broken down, that most senior officers were in dread of that charismatic commander and statesman, and that initiative and forethought were non-existent. In Callwell's Directorate of Military Operations (MO2), frequent changes of key personnel had destroyed much of the corporate memory and, except for the brief flurry of activity at the beginning of September, the many relevant individual documents and reports lay secure and undisturbed in their safes and pigeonholes until mid-March 1915, when Hamilton and Braithwaite were suddenly summoned, briefed and despatched. Even after this date, there is evidence that the MO2 staff officers were not at all clear what information they already had – on water supply, firewood, roads, etc. – at their fingertips. That these officers were mostly staff-trained before the war, and were designated as 'passed staff college' (psc) in the War Office List, seemed to be of little significance when it came to handling intelligence material. The American Thomas G Fergusson, whose excellent book on British Military Intelligence[14] gave fulsome praise to this aspect of pre-war work, recognised this deficiency: none had received much specific training in intelligence work, and there had been no Intelligence Corps in peacetime. They had however, at the Staff College, been instructed in combined operations.

Besides the material in MO2, crucial intelligence, books, documents, photographs, maps and charts also lay in Huddleston's MO5 Library, in Hedley's Geographical Section, and also at the Admiralty and the Foreign Office. More open source material was readily available at the Royal Geographical Society, the Geological Society and Geological Survey, the British Museum Library and elsewhere, had any 'theatre intelligence section' existed to gather and collate it. An impressive dossier could easily have been compiled at this stage. As it was, the material supplied by Callwell was very impressive, as we know from the dramatic moment when, having asked to be recalled before the Dardanelles Commission to put the record straight, he produced a bag full of the relevant documents and poured out the contents in front of the commissioners. This material included the 1905 *Report on Eastern Turkey in Europe*, the Naval Intelligence Division Report (*NID 838*) of 1908, the secret War Office *Report on the Defences of Constantinople* of 1909, with its voluminous appendices of photographs, maps, plans and charts of the Peninsula, and much more. We do not have a definitive list of the documents which Callwell and MO2 provided, but all the evidence suggests that it was an impressive collection. More information and documentation was sent after Hamilton and Braithwaite had left London, and still more was being gathered by Maxwell's Intelligence under Clayton in Egypt.

A good medium-scale (one-inch) initial operations map, compiled in 1908, was provided by MO4 (Geographical Section), and this was enlarged to 1:40,000 by the Survey of Egypt. While Hedley at MO4 had properly arranged for a survey section to go out with the expedition, it was decided at a higher level that this should not proceed, and it only followed much later when it was apparent that survey was vital for artillery work. Following the landings, much better and larger-scale maps were prepared in Egypt from captured material, and even larger-scale trench diagrams were compiled from air photos and lithographically printed at GHQ MEF. An Allied trigonometrical survey was also initiated which, before the evacuation, covered the whole Allied zone, the Asiatic Shore and the Peninsula up to the Achi Baba line. Systematic air photographic coverage was flown to provide the detail to hang onto this trig framework. The survey and mapping service performed extremely well in the face of serious shortages of men and *matériel*, but there is no doubt that it would have done even better if there had been proper forethought at the highest levels at the War Office. Hedley knew what was needed, but Kitchener (himself a surveyor who should have known better) was not anxious to send scarce resources to the Dardanelles. The evidence of every previous war had indicated that survey support should be provided right from the beginning, and that it was a false economy to hope that operations could proceed without it, or with one starved of resources. As *The Times History of the Anglo-Boer War* pointed out, the British Army suffered at the outset of that war from lack of cartographic preparation; it also noted: 'accurate mapping is not a very expensive operation: at any rate its cost bears a very small proportion to the total cost of preparing for or conducting a campaign.'

In the period lasting many months when the General Staff and Admiralty should have been formulating a coordinated plan for combined operations and making vital preparations, nothing was done. The expedition's ships were not loaded for an assault landing. The attempt by the Navy to go it alone in March resulted in the loss of what surprise remained, and triggered frantic efforts by the Turks to fortify the Peninsula. Henceforth it would be a much tougher nut to crack.

Comparisons with D-Day, 1944

Having documented in this book the lamentable preparations for the tragic Dardanelles operations, it is instructive to compare and contrast the intelligence, mapping and planning aspects of the Gallipoli and D-Day operations. Operation OVERLORD, with NEPTUNE, its naval counterpart, was the largest amphibious assault in history, and could not have been more different from the Gallipoli landings of 1915. On 6 June 1944, after years of joint planning and benefiting from the topographical preparations for, and experience of, the earlier landings in North Africa, Sicily and Italy, over 150,000 men landed from more than 4,000 ships along eighty kilometres of Normandy coastline. Careful examination of existing maps revealed that because of its relatively flat terrain and lack of obvious physical obstacles, the area was the most suitable for an Allied invasion.[15]

While the Gallipoli operations plans were hastily cobbled together in a few weeks following the failed naval attack in March 1915, the preparations for D-Day took place over a period of two or three years, which began once the invasion threat to Britain had faded following the German invasion of Russia in June 1941. In this period vast quantities of new maps – many drawn up from existing maps, postcards and photographs, and updated using aerial photos and intelligence from various sources – were prepared. The defences were carefully studied in a special Theatre Intelligence Section which prepared the defence overprints for the assault maps. The Allies revised and extended existing map series, and also augmented these with new series, new types of maps and other forms of geographic support, benefiting from the topographical preparations for, and experience of, the Dieppe raid (RUTTER and JUBILEE) of August 1942[16] (for which 1:12,500 and 1:25,000 sheets with defence overprints were prepared from air photographs) and the landings in North Africa (TORCH) in November 1942, and Sicily (HUSKY)[17] and Italy in 1943. General Montgomery, commanding the ground forces in Normandy, commended the D-Day survey effort, stating that 'at no time did map supply fail or prejudice the conduct of operations'.[18] In turn, the planning and experience of the Normandy landings informed the preparations for Operation ANVIL, the landings in the South of France on 15 August 1944.[19]

Apart from the special requirements for the amphibious operation of the landing itself, the essence of the problem was the same as that which had faced the British Army in the First World War – the need to create an accurate topographical base map, at a large scale suitable for artillery work and target location, on which could be pinpointed and overprinted the intricate enemy defences. Smaller-scale maps would be required for movement and for air operations. The most up-to-date editions of available pre-war French, and pre-war and wartime British, map series provided the cartographic base for the Normandy operations,[20] and continual and increasing air photograph coverage and provision of photogrammetric resources underpinned the mapping and geographical support programme – particularly the wide variety of oblique and vertical sketches and plans of the beaches, sheets of the 1:25,000 artillery map and 1:12,500 sheets of the immediate invasion area. British, Canadian and American army mapping and admiralty charting agencies, air forces and field survey units were all involved in the preparations of the previous two years.[21]

The range of map types required was enormous, as was the air support for intelligence gathering and mapping. Again, the comparison with the Dardanelles could not be more striking. For D-Day, aircraft generally required 1:1,000,000 and 1:2,000,000 plotting maps for navigation, and 1:500,000 and 1:250,000 topographical air maps. Army/Air editions, layered in purple with emphasised spot-height boxes, were produced of all these scales, and also at 1:100,000. Fighters of the Allied air force needed 1:1,000,000 scale high-altitude topographical maps. Bombers, troop carriers, transport aircraft, night fighters and reconnaissance aircraft had to be provided with 'lattice' charts for radar navigation and maps for 'gee' navigation (position fixing by radio signals from ground stations).[22] All aircrew were supplied with fabric 'escape maps' in case they were shot down. Airborne (glider and parachute) forces were issued with 1:25,000 colour-layered maps, 1:12,500 and 1:25,000 defence overprints, and night landing and dropping-zone maps, similar to bomber night target maps, which were designed and coloured to show the ground features as they would appear from the air in the dark. They were also supplied with landing and dropping zone traces to be used with enlarged photo-mosaics, photo-maps called 'fly-in maps' which included photographs of the key ground features, half-tone mosaics, 'flak' overlays showing the location of enemy anti-aircraft guns, and 1:5,000 village photo-plans.[23] Maps showing special information were used by the operational and briefing staff on the ground in charge of controlling air forces in the battle zone during the invasion. US Bomber Command demanded oblique perspective target maps.

For D-Day, hydrographic and beach-survey preparations were meticulous. Special beach gradient and obstacle maps derived from air-reconnaissance and information provided by Special Boat Service frogmen and other sources, and 'going' maps showing the terrain to assist progress once ashore, were prepared for the landing craft and assault troops. For training purposes, deception maps were printed with false place-names. Tactical overprints on the large-scale sheets showed all features of the German 'West Wall' defences, including coastal batteries, pill boxes, minefields, trenches, etc. Special charts were prepared by the Admiralty for the approaches to the beaches, and for fire-control for the naval bombardment. Some 170 million naval charts and chart-maps were produced, incorporating the results of aerial reconnaissance.[24] Further geographical support for the operations included town plans, through-way plans, Communications of Europe (1:800,000), road maps, gazetteers, guide books and relief models.[25]

As with the Gallipoli operations, it was difficult to supply the assaulting troops with the highest-quality maps, as these did not exist. Ground troops were hampered by the legacy of inadequate pre-war French maps, with many areas only covered by enlargements of the old hachured 1:80,000 sheets to 1:50,000. Prior to 1939, 're-armament' series of 1:25,000 artillery sheets had been prepared by the Geographical Section of the General Staff (GSGS), War Office, for parts of Belgium and France, and these were now revised from air photos. As ground and close-support air forces required gridded large-scale maps for attack, and medium and small-scale maps for movement, completely new series of maps had to be prepared. New 1:25,000 (codename *Benson*) and 1:50,000 series were created covering the envisaged area of operations, and also 1:12,500 sheets for likely coastal areas. The standard artillery map showed roads, tracks and footpaths, hedges, walls and other field divisions. The infantry and their supporting tanks also found these new *Benson* 1:25,000 sheets invaluable in Normandy's *bocage* countryside with its small, irregular-shaped fields and its hedges and copses, all potential defence positions for the enemy. But the lack of reliable height control and often poor relief-depiction (hachures based on 1:40,000 scale form lines) on the old French maps used as base material meant that the artillery work suffered from inadequate angle-of-sight data. Clearly maps and terrain intelligence were vital to the success of the Allied invasion of Europe.[26]

Conclusion

The Gallipoli Campaign was doomed to failure primarily because of a lack of commitment to it from the Allied high commands in London and Paris. Too few men, too little planning, inadequate munitions, and indecisiveness together with woefully inadequate communications ultimately led to the stagnation and defeat of the Allied troops. At the heart of the failure lies an inadequate understanding of the nature of the terrain. Yet this need not have been so. In the decades before the landings, reports had been compiled by men who knew their business, soldiers and sailors who had cause to consider the possibility of an attacker coming to the hostile shores of the Dardanelles.

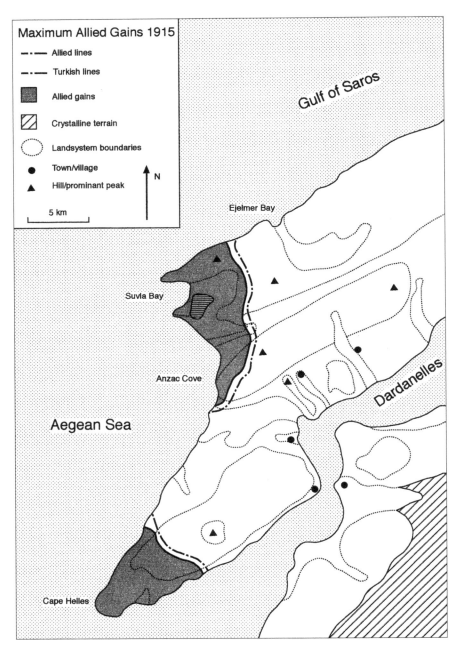

Maximum Allied Gains 1915

—··— Allied lines

—·— Turkish lines

▨ Allied gains

▨ Crystalline terrain

⬭ Landsystem boundaries

● Town/village

▲ Hill/prominant peak

↑ N

5 km

Gulf of Saros

Ejelmer Bay

Suvla Bay

Anzac Cove

Aegean Sea

Dardanelles

Cape Helles

Maximum Allied gains, 1915

As is demonstrated by the comparison with D-Day in 1944, planning was everything, and the documents and records we have examined reveal that Hamilton and his Staff had more materials to hand than have been admitted to. Within the Geographical Section of the General Staff (GSGS, MO4) there were experienced men who knew what material existed, and would surely have made it available, and the defence of Callwell and others indicates that this was achieved. The subsequent scapegoating of a map – magnified in some historians' eyes to all the maps used in the Campaign – is quite simply a method of diverting attention away from the failure of a difficult task – the landing of men on a hostile shore with the intent of attacking and gaining a Peninsula blessed with a terrain that advantages the defender. And what defenders they were – well disciplined, well-armed, well-motivated and well-led; the Turks used all the natural advantages of the Gallipoli Peninsula and sent the Allies back whence they came.

Although the strategic aims were well served by the initial plans, the terrible loss of life at Cape Helles was due to a commitment to landing on beaches which were clearly too narrow and commanded on both sides by easily fortified positions. The mistake of landing at Anzac Cove was costly, as after the initial failure to exploit early gains the positions became untenable. The vexed question of water supply was not clearly addressed and became a major issue, as was the provision of rest camps which were not overlooked by the Turkish artillery. Both of these the Turkish forces had in abundance.

The most important conclusion is a question as to why a landing at Suvla Bay had not been adequately explored, given the suitability of its landing beaches, the trafficability of the wide Suvla Plain, and the suitability of the plain in the provision of groundwater supplies. Naval opposition seems the most likely explanation. If the belated and ill-starred landing of August 1915 had been subject to better leadership, this could have changed the face of the war altogether; commanding the Dardanelles, supporting the Navy and knocking Turkey out of the war much sooner than 1918. Clearly no military campaign can hope to succeed with an inadequate understanding of the terrain to be fought over.

Notes

1. Ekins, Ashley, in Celik, Kenan and Cok, Ceyhan (eds), *The Gallipoli Campaign, International Perspectives 85 Years on*, Canakkale Onsekiz Mart University, p. 7.
2. Aspinall-Oglander, Brig.-Gen. C F, *History of the Great War, Military Operations, Gallipoli*, Vol. I, London: Heinemann, 1929.
3. Pressey, H A S, 'Notes on Trench War', *Royal Engineers Journal*, 29, pp. 297–315.
4. Kenan Celik, noted Turkish historian of the campaign, disputes that machine guns were used by the Turks, but contemporary British accounts are firm on this, noting the presence of machine-gun belts.

5. Anon [GLC], 'Engineers at Gallipoli, 1915', *Royal Engineers Journal*, 111, pp. 31–9.
6. Ibid.
7. Barton, Peter; Doyle, Peter and Vandewalle, Johan, *Beneath Flanders Fields. The Tunnellers' War 1914–1918*, Staplehurst: Spellmount, 2004.
8. Grant Grieve, W and Newman, B, *Tunnellers*, London: Herbert Jenkins, 1936; Murray, Joseph, *Gallipoli As I Saw It*, London: William Kimber, 1965; Anon [GLC], op. cit.
9. Observations underground by Peter Doyle in the Anzac sector, 2002.
10. Beeby-Thompson, A, *Emergency water supplies for military, agricultural and colonial purposes*, London: Crosby Lockwood & Son, 1924.
11. Ibid.
12. Pritchard, Maj.-Gen. H L, *History of the Corps of Royal Engineers*, Vol. VI, Chatham, Institution of Royal Engineers, 1952.
13. Ibid; Anon [GLC], op. cit.
14. Fergusson, Thomas G, *British Military Intelligence 1870–1914. The Development of a Modern Intelligence Organization*, London: Arms & Armour Press, 1984.
15. Chasseaud, Peter, 'Mapping for D-Day: The Allied Landings in Normandy, 6 June 1944', *The Cartographic Journal*, London, 38(2), 2001, pp. 177–89.
16. Clough, Brig. A B (comp), *The Second World War 1939–1945, Army Maps and Survey*, London: War Office, 1952, p. 376. Copy in BL Map Library.
17. Fryer, Brig. R E, *Survey Notes on Operation 'Husky', 22 Feb to 10 Jul 1943*, 1 August 1943, Survey Directorate GHQ Middle East Force, M.D.R. Misc. 6520, Reproduced by 512 Fd Survey Coy, R.E., August 1943. Copy in DGIA, Defence Geographic Centre Library.
18. Clough, op. cit., p. 462. Maps provided for the Dieppe raid are also covered in *The Dieppe Raid Combined Report* (the basis for 'Battle Report 1886', sometimes referred to as CB 04244), p. 9, Combined Operations Headquarters, Directorate papers, TNA(PRO) DEFE 2/551. See also 'Confidential Book 04157F' with which was issued a series of standard and overprinted maps, town plans, defence traces, photographs and mosaics of the operational area.
19. *Report of Beach Intelligence Work for Operation Anvil* (1945). Mapping Section, Intelligence Division, by the Beach Intelligence Sub-Section, Mapping Section, Office of the Chief Engineer, ETOUSA, printed by US 656 Engr Topo Bn (Army) 5675 ETO, 8/4/45.
20. *Notes on GSGS Maps of France, Belgium & Holland*, Directorate of Military Survey, War Office, London, December 1943. Copy in BL Map Library.
21. Chasseaud, op. cit.
22. Clough, op. cit., pp. 562–4.
23. Ibid, pp. 603–4.
24. Collier, Richard, *D-Day, June 6, 1944. The Normandy Landings*, London: Cassell, 1999, p. 92.
25. Clough, op. cit., pp. 388–90, 398.
26. Chasseaud, op. cit.

Appendix I

Extracts from: *Military Report on Eastern Turkey in Europe. 1905. Confidential.* Prepared by the General Staff, War Office. A 1027. I 38535. 150.-11/05. Fk. 728. E.& S. A2. Small 8vo. Hard buff covers. [Chapter VI (pp.53–72) is on The Gallipoli Peninsula.] Copy at TNA(PRO) FO 881/8589.

[The Preface, written by Colonel 'Wully' R Robertson for the Director of Military Operations, to the 1905 Report on Eastern Turkey in Europe stated that: 'This Report has been prepared by Lieut.-Colonel G F Milne, DSO, General Staff. With the exception of Chapters I and VI, the information given has been entirely taken from valuable reports furnished by Lieut.-Colonel F. R. Maunsell, C M G, R A, Military Attaché at Constantinople. In the preparation of Chapter VI [Gallipoli Peninsula and Dardanelles Defences] use has been made of Admiralty Publications. . . .' This was a reference to successive NID Reports, of which an updated version (NID 838) would appear in 1908.]

Chapter VI [dealing with the Gallipoli Peninsula and the Dardanelles Defences, included several pages (53–57) by Maunsell on the topography and on possible landing places. Significantly, he did not consider Cape Helles as a possible landing place. He distinguished between principal and minor landing places]:

General Description

The Gallipoli Peninsula, from Bulair to Cape Helles, has a length of 47 miles and a breadth varying from 14 miles at the widest part to 6,000 yards at a point 1½ miles south-west of the village of Bulair. From here it gradually spreads out, and at the northern extremity, where it joins the continent, attains a breadth of 10 miles.

Owing to its geographical position along one side of the Straits of the Dardanelles this Peninsula has great strategical importance, as its occupation would command the entrance to the Sea of Marmara.

Across the narrow neck of land which connects it with the mainland lies the defensive position of the Bulair lines. The earthworks, thrown up by the French and English troops in 1855, are still traceable, and have been strengthened by some modern works.

A spur of the Tekfur Dagh, 900 feet high, crosses this neck, and falls rapidly towards the Bulair position, in front of which is a small valley scarcely above the level of the sea. Near the village of Bulair commence the rounded slopes of the position, on a prominent crest of which are the old lines stretching from shore to shore.

West of the lines, the hills rise steeply; the principal range (1,400 feet) follows the northern shore, falling almost perpendicularly into the sea.

Rough spurs are thrown out towards the southern shore, the steep slopes of which, covered with brushwood, overlook the straits, from the western extremity of the Narrows at Chanak.

The high ground continues to Cape Helles. The ridges are difficult to traverse, and the only roads are rough cart-tracks. One valley, the Kurtumus Dere, breaks through the northern line of hills, and enters the sea at the little bay of Ejelmar, or Arapos Mermedia.

A succession of small valleys, draining into the straits, cuts across the Peninsula at right angles.

Near Gallipoli are the valleys of the Aiwali Su and other small streams, which drain the rounded cultivated spurs behind the town and in rear of the Bulair lines. The Kaya Su crosses the Peninsula from the rough country round Shaitankeui. Its valley is narrow, with steep sides at its lower end, and the stream enters the sea by a flat marshy delta near Galata Burnu.

Between it and the Karakova Dere, a valley commencing about Taifur and Bergas, are some rough hills forming the Karaman Dagh and rising to 1,050 feet.

The Ilgar and the Ak Bashi, valleys separated by spurs, also traverse the Peninsula above the Narrows.

From the Kilid Bahr promontory, overlooking the Narrows of Chanak, on which most of the European batteries of the Dardanelles defences are situated, the ground rises very steeply, and a high ridge with a scarped summit, rising above Maidos Valley, crosses to the Aegean coast.

The population of the Peninsula consists of Turks and Greeks, the latter predominating.

Towns and Villages

Gallipoli

Gallipoli, a place of 15,000 inhabitants, Turks, Greeks, and Jews, is the capital of a sanjak under Adrianople, and the seat of the mutesarrif. It is without defences, but contains an old citadel used as government offices. The town is built on a flat-topped promontory, rocky to seaward, with an open cultivated plateau to the north.

A bay, with a sandy beach, lies to the north-east of the town, along which runs the Bulair road.

The barracks, which can contain one battalion, are on the south-west side of the bay, adjoining the Bulair road. In the town are other small barracks.

The port is on the south side, and is of ancient construction, once defended by walls, with a narrow entrance into an outer basin, 60 yards by 100 yards; under an arch is an inner basin 80 yards square. The approaches to the quay are fairly easy, but very crowded. The port is 6 foot to 8 foot deep, and is used by small sailing craft and lighters. A Turkish torpedo-boat is usually stationed here.

One good street, passing through the commercial part of the town near the port, circles round the promontory about 100 yards from the shore, and then joins the Bulair road.

West of the town are some small valleys from the north, with fruit orchards, vineyards, and cultivation.

There is usually a small private stock of coal for the use of steamers, also about 11 lighters and 90 small sailing craft in the port.

Several steamship lines touch here.

Maidos

Maidos (Aji Abad in Turkish) is a small town of 900 houses, or about 5,000 inhabitants, all Greeks, in a bay behind the Kilid Bahr promontory. It is the seat of the kaimakam of the small kaza comprising the lower half of the Peninsula.

Small villages

Around Maidos the villages are mostly Turkish.

Kilid Bahr, consisting of 230 houses, and Sedd-ul-Bahr, of 90 houses, are both situated on the straits; Boyuk and Kuchuk Anafarta, overlooking the bay of that name, contain 100 houses each, Ilgar Keui and Turshen Keui have 50, Sivli about 35.

In the northern portion of the Peninsula the villages contain more Greek inhabitants; Bergas has 80 houses and Galata 100, while Bulair and Ekshemil are large villages of about 300 houses each. A cart track over bare cultivated country runs from Maidos to Sedd-ul-Bahr.

Resources

Most of the cultivated portion of the peninsula produces corn but cotton is also grown. Timber is scarce but about 12 miles below Gallipoli, at Ungardere and Yalova, are small fir woods. Water is generally plentiful in the valleys.

Communications

The roads are nothing but cart-tracks which, in the northern part of the peninsula and in the low ground, become in winter almost impassable owing to the mud. A telegraph line runs the whole length of the Peninsula, there being four wires between Bulair and Gallipoli and two between Gallipoli and Kilid Bahr.

In addition to the track from Maidos to Sedd-ul-Bahr via Krithia, there is also a track passable for wheels from Kilid Bahr, in rear of Yildiz Tabia and along the west heights to Sedd-ul-Bahr. From Gallipoli to Maidos Bairkeui is a fairly good road passable by native carts.

There is also a route from Gallipoli via Bergas, Taifur, Karnabi, and Uzun Dere to Maidos, which forms the shortest route, and is in good order during dry weather.

From Karnabi down to Ejelmar Bay the road is passable for wheels over flat country. From Gallipoli cart tracks run to Sheitan Keui and Yenikeui.

Landing-places

Owing to the steep nature of the country on the northern shore of the Peninsula, there are only a few small bays where a landing could be attempted.

The principal landing-places are –

(a)   Baklar Bay, at the neck of the Peninsula and outside the Bulair Lines;
(b)   South of Anafarta or Suvla Bay, and immediately north-west of Kilid Bahr near Gaba Tepe [Brighton Beach – Anzac].
(c)   Port Baklar is said to afford a good landing-place, which, however, would be under fire from the main position and heights near Bulair village. The port itself is full of extensive shoals, the whole shore being skirted here and there by rocks. The actual landing-places are somewhat limited, and consist of about 2,000 yards of coast available near the tile factory and another strip of 500 yards about 1½ miles further east. Easy cart tracks lead up to Bulair village, where they join the chaussée.
(d)   This landing-place lies between Gaba Tepe and Suvla Bay on the west of the Peninsula opposite Maidos. The coast is low and affords easy access to the interior for an extent of nearly 2 miles. It is protected from the north-easterly winds but exposed to the westerly. From a landing on the open beach south of Gaba Tepe, an advance could be made directly on the ridge above Kilid Bahr, whence the principal defences would be commanded from the rear. At about 1 mile inland a tolerably good road leads to Kuchuk Anafarta and Maidos, whence a good road leads to Gallipoli. In winter all these tracks become very difficult on account of mud.
　　　The country inland is open with very few trees, gently undulating and mostly under cultivation of cereals; it is unenclosed, and the only obstacles to a march are the channels cut in the sandy soil by mountain streams. The chief of these, the Asmak Dere, has a channel 8 to 10 feet in depth and from 20 to 30 feet wide, but the very soft nature of the sandy soil renders the cutting of ramps easy and the streams themselves unimportant as obstacles. The roads are merely cart tracks. The Gaba Tepe–Eski Keui road, after crossing the Kalkmes Dagh, advances through a fertile, fruit-producing valley direct on Maidos, but this road is impracticable for artillery on the south side of the Kalkmes ridge, owing to the steepness of the gradients, the shortness of the zigzags and the bad condition of the road, which is paved in parts with ill-laid boulders.

In addition to the above main landing-places there are three minor ones, viz:-
(1)   Suvla Bay, which offers fair landing, but the Lagoon renders access inland difficult and limited.
(2)   Mermedia or Ejelmer Bay, about 6 miles north of Cape Suvla, which has about 1,200 yards of beach available for landing, is small but well sheltered, and leads into easy country in the Kurtumus Dere from which good tracks lead to Maidos.
(3)   On the coast south of Baklar Burnu, or Cape Xeros, where there is a cove admirably suited for landing troops. A strip of only 500 to 600 yards of beach is available, and it is 800 to 1,000 yards from the end of the Bulair Lines to the north.

At the time of the Greek War some small earthworks were thrown up overlooking Anafarta and Ejelmar Bays, but the guns have been withdrawn and the works no longer maintained.

In the strait itself the ground rises very steeply along the shore from near Sedd-ul-Bahr to Kilid Bahr, and no landing could be effected, except for small boats just inside Sedd-ul-Bahr itself.

From Kilid Bahr to Maidos, inside the Narrows, the shore is mostly low-lying, backed by steep hills, and landings could be made at several points, also in the head of Kilia Bay and in front of Boghali Kale.

Thence to Gallipoli small landing places could be found on shingly beach at the mouths of the small valleys, but otherwise the coast is very steep.

[The rest of the chapter is on the Dardanelles coast defences, and is similar to material in NID publications. Three maps were included with the Report, in a pocket at the back:]

Sketch Map of Eastern Turkey in Europe [TSGS 2007, 1:800,000, Confidential;
    Defences (including those of Dardanelles) in red]
Survey of Defensive Positions near Bulair [TSGS 2052, 1:15,840, Corrected June
    1905]
Sketch Map of Fortress of Adrianople [TSGS 2079, 1:40,000, by Capt. Townshend,
    British Consul, Adrianople]

Appendix II

Summary of relevant contents of: *Naval Intelligence Department: N.I.D. 838, Turkey. Coast Defences and Resources; Coast Defence Ordnance and Arsenals, May 1908.*

[A copy of the text of NID 838, Turkey. Coast Defences, &c., Parts I, II and III, is in The National Archives at TNA(PRO) ADM 231/49, but the maps, charts, plates etc., although listed in the contents, are lacking. NID 838 superseded NID 458, December 1896 and NID 458a, June 1901, an indication of the length of time the Naval Intelligence Department had been gathering detailed intelligence on the Dardanelles, and other Turkish defences.]

Outline of Contents, & Maps, Plans and Charts:

1. Turkey in Europe, Asia and Africa, including Red Sea, showing Defended Areas, Submarine Cables, Railways, etc.
2. Defences of Prevesa, Saloniki, Smyrna, Tripoli, and Ras Sheikh Syed.
3. Dardanelles [Sea] Defences [1907], including Besika Bay and Tenedos. [Later corrected in red to 1914].
3A. Gallipoli Peninsula, showing defences of Dardanelles [Military Map – GSGS 2285 1-inch in 2 sheets, secret edition].
4. Outline Map of Dardanelles, Defences (area of fire, etc.).
5. Bosphorus Defences.
6. Black Sea Defences.

Part I, covering the Coast Defences and Resources of Turkey in Europe, Asia and Africa, took up 90 pages. Part II, covering the Coast Defences and Resources of the Dardanelles, Sea of Marmara, Constantinople, The Bosphorus, the Land Defences of Constantinople, and the Black Sea, was 169 pages, and included a description of the Gallipoli Peninsula, its land defences, and the Bulair Lines. It was supported by 7 maps, plans and charts, of which 4 covered the Dardanelles, and 82 plates (maps, plans and photographs), of which 46 were of the Dardanelles. Appendix I to Part II covered the History of Submarine Defences in the Dardanelles and Bosphorus up to 1896. Part III covering Coast Defence Ordnance and Arsenals, was shorter than the first two Parts.

Part II (169 pages) of the report dealt specifically with the Dardanelles. As this was a naval report it naturally concentrated on the coast defences and the various threats to a fleet, but it did contain a section on the 'Land Defences of Gallipoli Peninsula', which made specific reference to Map 3A, the secret edition of the 1-inch map showing the Turkish coastal defences, and Plates 57 and 58 covering the Bulair Lines and area. Pages 50–52 contained a 'Short Description of Peninsula', including sections on 'topography, nature of country, streams, roads, telegraphs'. It also noted that 'In this description the spelling of the names of places in the Gallipoli Peninsula has been made to conform with the spelling on the M.O.D. [Military Operations Directorate] Map (Map 3A) accompanying this report'. This was clearly done with combined operations in mind.

A long section (pages 52–63) covered the Bulair Lines and their garrison, and pages 63–69 dealt with 'Submarine Defences in the Dardanelles', including mines. The rest of the section included:

Other defences

69	Torpedo battery
69–70	Lights
71–2	Garrison of Dardanelles
73–5	Communications
76–85	Sea of Marmara
	Bulair Lines
76–7	Rodosto
	Other towns.
86–94	Constantinople
95–125	Bosphorus
126–30	Land Defences of Constantinople [including Chataldja Line]
131–54	Black Sea
155–8	Appendix I was a 'History of Submarine Defences in the Dardanelles and Bosphorus' (up to 1896).

[The plates relating to the Dardanelles Defences were]:
11.   Besika Bay.
12.   Port Tenedos, Fort and Battery.

Dardanelles

13.   Map showing position of 'Fort Seddul Bahr' in its relation to 'Cape Helles' and 'Field Gun' Batteries.
14.   Cape Helles Battery and Field Gun Battery.
15.   Fort Seddul Bahr, New Field Gun Battery.
16.   – do –
17.   – do –
18.   Mining Station at Eski Hissarlik. Orkhanieh Tabia and Field Gun Battery.
19.   – do –
20.   Map showing position of 'Kum Kalessi' in its relation to 'Orkhanieh' and 'Yeni Shehr'.

21. Kum Kalessi Tabia.
22. Fort Kum Kalessi (approaching from the west).
23. – do – (– do – from the north-west).
24. Mount Dardanus Q.F. Battery.
25. Yildiz or Tekeh Tabia.
26. Relative positions of 'Yildiz Tabia', 'Rumili Medjidieh', 'Hamidieh II', 'Namazieh', 'Derma Burnu', and adjacent batteries, &c.
27. Rumili Medjidieh Tabia.
28. – do – (approaching from the south-west).
29. Hamidieh II. (Toprak Tabia).
30. Fort Namazieh.
31. – do – (left of south front).
32. – do – (south front).
33. – do – (east front).
34. – do – (approaching from the north-east).
35. – do – (interior, south front).
36. – do – (interior, east front).
37. Bilas Baba Tabia (Kusghum Baba Tabia).
38. Relative positions of 'Hamidieh I', 'Hamidieh III', 'Medjidieh Avan Tabia', Anadolu Medjidieh, &c.
39. Hamidieh I. Tabia.
40. – do – (west by south view).
41. – do – (north-west view).
42. Hamidieh III. Tabia (Fort Sultanieh).
43. – do – (south front view).
44. – do – (west front view).
45. Derma Burnu Tabia.
46. Medjidieh Avan.
47. Anadolu Medjidieh.
48. – do – (view of interior).
49. Defences. Panoramic view of European shore.
50. Cham Burnu Tabia. Maitos Tabia. Sari Tabia.
51. Map showing positions of 'Mal-Tepeh' and 'Nagara Baba' Batteries in their relation to 'Nagara Kalessi'.
52. Mal-Tepeh Tabia. Nagara Baba Tabia.
53. Nagara Kalessi.
54. – do – (view from south-west).
55. – do – (view from north-east).
56. Ak Tabia. Agh Bashi Tabia.
57. The Lines of Bulair from the north by west.

[The maps, plans and photo-plates were printed at the Ordnance Survey.]

Appendix III

Extracts from:

Report on The Defences of Constantinople. General Staff. Secret. 1909. War Office.
[A 1311. (B 369) 100 2/09 H & S 400WO].
[xii + 151 pp. 'Copy No. 3 D.M.O.' is in The National Archives at TNA(PRO) WO 33/2333.]

[The introduction to this 1909 Report noted: 'The European side of the Dardanelles is formed by the remarkable Peninsula of Gallipoli, which is connected with the mainland by a very narrow neck of land. In order to protect the Dardanelles forts from an attack from the rear, a line of works, known as the Bulair Lines, has been constructed across this neck. In following report each of the above systems of defence [of Constantinople] will be dealt with in a separate chapter, and in addition the Gallipoli Peninsula will be specially considered from the point of view of a possible attack upon the Dardanelles defences from the rear.'[xi–xii]. One third of this Report was concerned exclusively with the Gallipoli Peninsula and the Dardanelles, as were 4 out of the 8 maps and 33 out of the 72 Plates.

The Contents of the Gallipoli Peninsula part of the Report were vital information for the 1915 landings:]

[Chapters V–VIII dealt with the Chatalja Lines, Positions to North and West of Constantinople, the Bosphorus Defences, and Landing Places on the Black Sea Coast, and Defensive Positions which might be taken up to oppose landings.

The Report contained a good deal of topographical information. Under 'Physical features' it provided the following description, which was studied by Hamilton and his staff, of the Peninsula: 4–7.]

South-west of the Bulair Lines begins a chain of hills which extends along the north-western shore of the Peninsula, as far as Cape Suvla. These hills, which attain at some points a height of 1,300 feet, fall almost perpendicularly towards the sea in the Gulf of Xeros.

Rough spurs are thrown out towards the south, the steep slopes of which, covered with a little oak and pine forest and much brushwood, overlook the Straits, until Maidos Bay (Kilia Liman) is reached, just north of the Narrows.

Between the spurs a succession of small valleys, draining into the Straits, traverse the Peninsula at right angles. Near Gallipoli are the valleys of the Aivali Dere and other small streams, which drain the rounded, cultivated spurs behind the town, and those in rear of the Bulair Lines. . .

The southern part of the Peninsula, from Cape Suvla and Maidos to Cape Helles, has rather different characteristics. In this part the highest ground is along the south-eastern coast, overlooking the Straits, while the Aegean coast is bordered throughout the greater part of its length by a shelving beach.

The Kilid Bahr plateau . . . is situated in this part of the Peninsula. Its western edge overlooks the Peren Ovasi and the Chana Ovasi, the flat cultivated valley round Ibrahim Agha's farm. The plateau lies at a height of from 600 to 700 feet above the sea. The Kalkmaz Dagh is a prominent isolated feature just north of Maidos, and forms a spur of the plateau, but at a lower level.

From the head of Maidos Bay (Kilia Liman) to Kaba Tepe on the Aegean a well-marked depression, slightly above sea level, runs across the Peninsula, dividing the Kilid Bahr plateau from the hills farther north.

North of this depression is the Saribair Hill, a steep, rugged ridge, which rises to 970 feet, and dominates very steeply the village of Biyuk Anafarta. It is seamed with many ravines, covered with brushwood, and generally difficult of access, except on the southern spurs about Kojadere and Boghali, which are somewhat easier.

South of Cape Suvla is the wide bay of the same name, well sheltered from the northern winds which frequently prevail, and having a sandy beach suitable for landing. A good beach runs south of Nibrunesi Point also, and from both these places access is fairly easy to the villages of Biyuk and Kuchuk Anafarta, and thence into the plain about Turshtenkeni and Selvili. A rough coast track leads south also.

The Kaba Tepe is a prominent headland on this coast, rising to a height of 110 feet above the sea. There is a look-out station on it which has a garrison of one lieutenant and 33 men, and it is connected by telegraph with Kilid Bahr.

The ground at the end of the Peninsula about Cape Helles is generally open and undulating, with much cultivation around Krithia. Achi Baba is a prominent hill, rising to over 600 feet, just east of this village. Near Sedd-el-Bahr, at the entrance of the Straits, is the small sandy bay of Morto; but from Eski Hissarlik Point to the Narrows the shore rises very steeply to a height of 600 feet from a narrow strip of beach. The slopes are covered with brushwood, and only steep paths up the small ravines lead to the summit. Two larger ravines, known as the Jambaz (Avuzlar) Dere and the Soghan Dere, having steep sides covered with brushwood, and both rather difficult of access, lead down to the coast, and render approach from the south to the Kilid Bahr plateau difficult.

. . . In the centre of the Peninsula there were formerly some extensive forests, but very little of them now remains. The several spurs from the northern hills are covered with patches of forest, principally oak and pine, and with much dense brushwood. The country is extremely rough and difficult for the movement of troops.

[This is only a fraction of the Report, but enough has been given to emphasise that it gives an uncompromising picture of the terrain. Even if troops could be successfully landed, and bridgeheads established, the message comes across that the country was very rugged and suited to defence, and would create severe difficulties for troops attempting to break out from beachheads and fight along the Peninsula towards the Narrows and Bulair. No doubt this is why Hamilton's staff, and most of his commanders, became increasingly pessimistic as they studied the problem. Under 'Communications' the Report was equally uncompromising:]

Rough cart tracks form the only communications throughout the entire Peninsula. In the northern part, about Gallipoli, where the soil is stiff clay, the tracks become almost impassable in winter owing to the mud. At the southern end the soil is rather more sandy, but nevertheless the tracks are difficult in wet weather.

The only metalled road in the Peninsula runs north-east from Gallipoli through Keshan to Adrianople, and forms an important military communication. . . Over the rough country in the centre of the Peninsula between Gallipoli and Maidos only one track is to be found which is passable for wheels. This track leads from Gallipoli through Bairkeui, the Karakova Dere, Taifurkeui, Karnabili, Kumkeui, and Boghali to Maidos. Leaving Gallipoli it skirts the low stony cliffs of the coast and descents occur at small streams, seven of these being crossed before Bairkeui is reached. They are all dry in summer except the Bituk Dere, but have steep banks and are difficult for wheels. . . . Easy communications lead towards Kumkeui and Boghali from landing places on the coast near Suvla and Ejelmer Bays. . . .

From Maidos to Kaba Tepe across the peninsula is a rough track recently improved by military labour.

From Maidos to Sedh-el-Bahr is a good track through Krithia, over cultivated country for the most part.

Cart tracks lead to the summit of the Kilid Bahr plateau from the beach near Kaba Tepe.

[The clear imputation of this is that, in the initial stages at least, a landing force attempting to move up the Peninsula and across country would have to be supported by mountain batteries and rely on pack transport. In this, operations would resemble those on the North-West Frontier of India; but this was hardly a 'small-war' against a few hundred ill-armed tribesmen, but a large-scale operation against troops armed with modern weapons, including machine guns and artillery – rather more like the Boer War, which, extending over two years, during which all the military resources of the Empire were concentrated, involved severe defeats for British troops and much hard fighting.

Perhaps the most important section of the 1909 Report was that dealing with 'The Military Importance Of The Kilid Bahr Plateau And Landing Places Adjacent To It'. After dealing with the plateau itself, it went on to deal with the core of the whole operational concept:]

It is obvious, therefore, that if this plateau could be occupied by a hostile force landed on the Aegean coast, some 6 miles to the west, the principal defences could be rendered untenable, and the Straits opened to a fleet which has got through the outer line of works. [37]

[The landing places were clearly the subject of close reconnaissance, and were dealt with under the heading]: Landing Places on the West Coast of the Peninsula. The landing places on the Aegean from which to gain access inland to the Kilid Bahr plateau are as follows: [39–42]

1. **South of Kaba Tepe Promontory, the most direct route.** [Y Beach, west of Krithia, was at the southern end of this stretch; the landing here in April 1915 was successful but unexploited, and the force was disembarked; X Beach, used in April 1915, was almost a mile north of Tekke Burnu (Cape Tekke), but was not considered practicable in the 1909 Report.]

   For 2 miles south of Kaba Tepe the beach is shelving and sufficiently wide for landing troops. The mouth of the Asmak Dere, close under Kaba Tepe, is most favourable for landing field or heavy guns, as the approaches inland are easy up the valley of the stream. Farther south, a steep slope of friable soil ascends from the strip of beach, and is quite practicable for infantry to ascend. The lower part of the Asmak Dere and adjoining country is intersected by several deep, steep-sided watercourses, over which field guns could perhaps be hauled by hand; short ramps, however, could be dug without much difficulty in the sandy soil. For 2 miles south of Kaba Tepe the ground is undulating and cultivated. A ridge, about 100 feet in height and covered with olive groves, skirts the shore between the upper part of the Asmak Dere and the sea. Landing parties would have to ascend this on first leaving the beach; it would form the first covering position. The ground in the Asmak Dere becomes very heavy in wet weather. According to the chart, there is sufficiently deep water near the shore, 5½ fathoms being marked ½ a mile off, and there are no rocky obstructions. The narrow fringe of beach continues to the south until within 2 miles of Tekke Burnu, where the cliffs run sheer into the water. An infantry landing could take place at the wide mouth of the valley which runs down from Ibrahim Agha's Farm and the Chana Ovasi. Shallow water is marked on the chart at the mouth of this valley. The ascent from the beach is rough and steep at some points, but it is quite practicable for infantry. Krithia can be reached by the various small ravines which run down to the beach opposite that village, but the ascent is steep in each case.

2. **North of Kaba Tepe Promontory.** [Brighton Beach, the intended Anzac landing place, April 1915; the actual Anzac landing place, a mile farther north, was not considered as a practicable landing place in the 1909 Report.] For 2 miles north of Kaba Tepe is a shelving beach, some 60 yards wide, backed by steep, friable sandy cliffs from the Saibair, a very rough and difficult ridge which extends inland towards Biyuk Anafarta. Landing for troops is easy, but they would have to march south on leaving the shore and join the other troops in the Asmak Sere. A deep, sandy ravine occurs just north of Kaba Tepe, where ramps would probably have to be made to pass field guns.

3. **South of Nibrunesi Point.** [used during Suvla landings in August 1915] The beach south of Nibrunesi Point, for a distance of 2 miles, as far as Fisherman's Hut, is wide and easy for landing, but a belt of thick, low scrub, rather difficult to traverse, fringes the shore. The 5-fathom line is from 500 to 1,000 yards from the shore, and the anchorage is protected from the prevalent northerly winds. A track runs along the beach to the landing place north of Kaba Tepe, but the cliffs have fallen and blocked it at some points, although it might be made passable with difficulty. Between Fisherman's Hut and Kaba Tepe, where the hills approach the shore, the beach is generally narrow and lined with precipitous sandy cliffs [actual Anzac landing place].

4. **Suvla Bay.** [used in August 1915] The northern shore of the bay is lined by low, rocky cliffs, some 30 feet high, and rocky hills covered with low scrub extend along the coast to the east. Between the cliffs and the mouth of the Salt Lake is a stretch of firm, sandy beach, 900 yards in length, on which a landing could easily be effected in calm weather or when the wind is north. In a southerly wind landing would not be practicable, but northerly winds are prevalent, especially in winter, and from these the bay is quite sheltered. Deep water extends close up to the beach, but there are occasional shoals. A landing on the north side of the bay gives access to a stretch of sandy hillocks, covered with tufts of grass, which offer no obstacle to the passage of guns or wheeled vehicles; 800 yards inland cultivation (principally maize) is reached, with firm ground passable for all arms. The hill between Salt Lake and Nibrunesi Point is of sand and stones, covered with low scrub, and has an old tomb on the summit. The plain between the Topalin Mezar Dere and the Kizlar Dere is covered with cultivation and dotted with large trees, oak and walnut. Low scrub-covered hills of sandy soil descend to the plain from the south and east. The Salt Lake or Lagoon is ordinarily dry in summer, but with a south wind it may fill up again. From November to April it always contains water. When dry its bed is easily passable for infantry. The opening to the sea is 80 yards wide, and also becomes dry in summer.

5. **Ejelmer (Mermedia) Bay.** [Not used in 1915] About 6 miles north of Cape Suvla, has about 1,200 yards of beach available for landing, but is small and rather open to the violent north winds which are prevalent on this coast. For this reason it is not so suitable as an anchorage as Suvla Bay. Access is easy by the Kurtumuz valley to Turshtenkeui, whence good tracks lead to Boghali and Maidos. On either side of the bay rise steep hills, which form part of those on the northern side of the Peninsula. In the Dardanelles, north and north-east winds called by the Turks 'meltem', prevail, on an average, for nine months in the year. In winter, north-east winds often blow hard for several days; there are also frequent south-west winds of some violence.

[Descriptions of the 'Routes Inland From The West Coast' were then given, with going information, (42–3) and the Report then went on to consider the Cape Helles area under the following heading: (45)]

Landing Places Along The Straits. [Only those used in April 1915 are given here: S, V and W Beaches] On the Cape Helles promontory is a sandy bay [W Beach], just south of Tekke Burnu, which offers a favourable landing place from which to attack Ertroghrul Battery. North-west of the lighthouse there is an excellent landing place on a stretch of beach 150 yards long. The north-west extremity is marked by the small watercourse shown on the Admiralty chart. There is only one house shown, and this stands on the north side of the stream. The distance from this landing place to Ertroghrul Fort is rather over 1,000 yards, the intervening country being a general rise, with no trees or obstructions, so that field or machine guns could be drawn across it without difficulty. The lighthouse is the only building between the landing place and the fort. At Sedd-el-Bahr village there is a small landing jetty [V Beach; Lancashire Landing & River Clyde; not considered as a suitable landing place in the 1909 Report, presumably because it was commanded by the guns of Sedh-el-Bahr Fort]. At Morto Bay, inside Sedd-el-Bahr Fort, is a good sandy beach with easy approaches, where a landing could be made if necessary. Although the hills descend very steeply to the shore between Eski Hissarlik [S Beach, used in April 1915, was immediately under the west side of Eski Hissarlik Point, where stood De Totts Battery] and Kilid Bahr, yet they do not form a line of cliffs, and landing from boats might be effected on the narrow strip of beach at most places . . . [not attempted in 1915].

[It also noted:] From the head of Maidos Bay (Kilia Liman) to Kaba Tepe on the Aegean a well-marked depression, slightly above sea level, runs across the Peninsula, dividing the Kilid Bahr plateau from the hills farther north. North of this depression is the Saribair Hill, a steep, rugged ridge, which rises to 970 feet, and dominates very steeply the village of Biyuk Anafarta. *It is seamed with many ravines, covered with brushwood, and generally difficult of access* [authors' emphasis], except on the southern spurs about Kojadere and Boghali, which are somewhat easier.

Maps and Plates with the Secret 1909 War Office *Report on The Defences of Constantinople*

[The maps included with the Report, and listed in the Contents, were:]
  1. *Map of the Peninsula of Gallipoli and Asiatic Shore of the Dardanelles* 1/63,360 GSGS 2285 (Secret). Sh. 1. [with defence overprint]

2. *Map of the Peninsula of Gallipoli and Asiatic Shore of the Dardanelles* 1/63,360 GSGS 2285 (Secret). Sh. 2. [with defence overprint]
3. *Sketch map showing the position of the Forts at the Narrows of the Dardanelles (European shore) in relation to the Kilid Bahr Plateau.* 1/5,280. [Ordnance Survey, Southampton; form-lines given, but no vertical-interval; shows Kilid Bahr, its Old Castle, Namazie Fort, Rumeli Mejidie, Hamidie II, Khota Suyu Tabia, Yildiz or Tekke Tabia, etc., with number and calibre of guns, and MG or field gun batteries. No defences looking landward]
4. *Survey of Defensive Position near Bulair.* 1/15,840. TSGS 2052. Confidential. [Showing the lines constructed by the Anglo-French Army in 1855. Sketched December 1876 by Lieut Cockburn RE and Lieut Chermside RE. Corrected June 1905. Close-contoured (form-lined), but no vertical-interval given, with spot-heights. It is to be presumed that Maunsell himself undertook the correction in 1905]
5. *Turkey 1/250,000. Constantinople* Sheet. GSGS 2097 (Secret). [War Office January 1909, coloured, with red defence overprint: Forts and Batteries, Chatalja Lines, and Black Sea & Bosphorus Defences]
6. *Reconnaissance of the Chatalja Lines.* 1/63,360. GSGS 1736 (Secret). [1876 – corrected by Lieut-Col. F R Maunsell, Military Attaché, up to 15th March 1903]
7. *Constantinople and the surrounding Country.* 1/63,360. GSGS 2390 (Secret). Sh. 1. [with defence overprint]
8. *Constantinople and the surrounding Country.* 1/63,360. GSGS 2390 (Secret). Sh. 2. [with defence overprint]

[The Plates were:]

Gallipoli Peninsula

1. *Sketch of Suvla Bay, from the north-west.* [west on the plate; shows 'Beach for Landing'. (Print code 110. 11/08. 1381) 400 W.O.]
2. *View of Taifurkeui road, from Rematara.* [photo]

Besika Bay

3. *Sketch of Besika Bay earthworks* [drawn by FRM; shows 'sandy beach, easy for landing.' Print code as no.1]

Dardanelles

4. *Plan of Fort Sedd-el-Bahr.* 1/1500. [Ordnance Survey, Southampton]
5. *View of Fort Sedd-el-Bahr, from seaward.* [photo, Ordnance Survey, Southampton]
6. *Plan of Orkhanie Fort.* 1/1500. [Ordnance Survey, Southampton]
7. *Plan of Kum Kalesi Fort.* 1/1500. [Ordnance Survey, Southampton]
8. *View of Kum Kalesi Fort, from seaward.* [photo, Ordnance Survey, Southampton]
9. *View of Orkhanie Fort, from seaward.* [photo]
10. *View of Kum Kalesi Fort, from the south-west.* [photo]
11. *Sketch of Dardanus Q.F. Battery, from the Straits.* [drawn by FRM; same print code as no.1]
12. *Plan of Rumeli Mejidie Fort.* 1/1500. [Ordnance Survey, Southampton]

13. *View of Rumeli Mejidie Fort, from seaward* [photo]
14. *View of the batteries on Kilid Bahr Promontory, from seaward.* [photo]
15. *Plan of Hamidie II Fort.* 1/1500. [Ordnance Survey, Southampton]
16. *Plan of Namazie Fort.* 1/1500. [Ordnance Survey, Southampton]
17. *View of interior of Namazie Fort, from the rear.* [photo; Ordnance Survey, Southampton]
18. *Plan of Hamidie I Fort.* 1/1500. [Ordnance Survey, Southampton]
19. *Plan of Chanak Kalesi Fort.* 1/1500. [Ordnance Survey, Southampton]
20. *View of Hamidie I Fort, from seaward.* [photo]
21. *View of Chanak Kalesi Fort, entering the Narrows.* [photo]
22. *View of Chanak Kalesi Fort (west front), from the Narrows.* [photo; Ordnance Survey, Southampton]
23. *Plan of Derma Burnu Fort.* 1/1500. [Ordnance Survey, Southampton]
24. *Plan of Anadoli Mejidie Fort.* 1/1500. [Ordnance Survey, Southampton]
25. *Plan of Nagara Kalesi Fort.* 1/1500. [Ordnance Survey, Southampton]
26. *View of Anadoli Mejidie Fort, from the Straits.* [photo]
27. *View of Mal Tepe and Nagara Baba Forts, from Nagara Liman.* [photo]
28. *Sketch of Kilid Bahr Plateau, from the NE.* [long panorama, drawn by F R Maunsell; same print code as no.1]

Bulair Lines

29. *View of Fort Sultan, from the north.* [photo]
30. *View of Ground north-west of Bulair Lines, from head of Domuz Dere.* [photo]
31. *View of Fort Sultan and Redoubt 'E', from near Bulair Village.* [photo]
32. *View of Uzun Tepe and Port Bakla, from Bulair.* [photo]
33. *View of Port Bakla, from Bulair Village.* [photo]

Chatalja Lines

[Plates 34–46. (Plates 41 and 43 drawn by F R Maunsell Lieut. col. Nov. 1902; 39, 44 and 46 drawn by FRM)]

Positions N-W of Constantinople

[Plates 47–8]

Bosphorus

[Plates 49–62]

Black Sea Coast (European Shore)

[Plates 63–9]

Black Sea Coast (Asiatic Shore)

[Plates 70–2]

Appendix IV

Extract from: *Report on Landing Places at KABA TEPE (Gallipoli Peninsula) with two roads leading therefrom to MAIDOS and the KILID BAHR Plateau. Road traversed 8th to 10th Sep. 1910. By Major L. L. R. Samson. Adrianople. 28.9.1910. B.16/I.547.*

[A copy is in The National Archives at TNA(PRO) WO 106/1534. NB:
1. Samson uses the word 'track' to mean beach, as well as the more usual usage of unmade road or path. To avoid confusion, where he means beach, this word has been added in square brackets.
2. Part of this report was incorporated into a Report on Gallipoli Peninsula issued on 12 April 1915 to the Anzac Corps (and presumably the other attacking formations) by Medforce GHQ before the landings.]

Details of Landing Places at KABA TEPE (Gallipoli Peninsula) and of two roads leading therefrom.

Introductory

There exist two landing places at KABA TEPE from one at least of which it should be possible to get guns inland to the plateau overlooking the KILID BAHR defences.

1st Landing Place

To the north of KABA TEPE is a good firm track [beach] for a distance of about 1,000 yards, but there are indications of the presence of shoals close inland which render it inadvisable to attempt a landing except by daylight. The track [beach] is about 30 yards in depth.

Country Inland

The mainland where it joins the track [beach] consists of sandy hillocks covered with tufts of coarse grass which at the point of junction rise perpendicularly from the track [beach] to a height of 6 feet, rendering movement difficult for anything but infantry. The hillocks are 50 yards across and are succeeded by cotton fields which meet low scrub-covered hills some 300 yards from the track [beach]. The stream running into the sea here is dry in summer, its banks are vertical, some 15 feet in height.

Except on the track [beach] this stream cannot be crossed without artificial aid until the hills are reached, at which point the track to BUYUK ANAFARTA crosses it. This track connects with a road inland to MAIDOS through ESKI KEUI, particulars of which are given later in this report. This landing place might, with advantage, be used to land covering troops to move on ESKI KEUI.

2nd or Main Landing Place

The main landing place is to be found South of KABA TEPE where is a track [beach] stretching southwards for upwards of a mile. In consequence of shoals which appear to exist here, it may be considered that only 600 yards due South of KABA TEPE affords a safe landing place, being that portion of the shore between that promontory and the mouth of the ASMAKDERE. The track [beach] here is shelving, of firm sand, and about 30 yards in depth, there being deep water close inshore. It is said that there is comparatively little difference in the depth of the track at high and low tide. It is sheltered from the North wind by KABA TEPE, and to a certain extent by the promontory to the South of it, where are low sandy cliffs. The prevailing winds here are either Northerly or Southerly.

Country inland of landing place

A thin fringe of sandy hillocks covered with tufts of grass forms the boundary between the mainland and the track [beach]. These are much lower than those at the landing place previously described, and offer but little obstacle to the passage of guns on wheeled vehicles. Inland from these is cultivation, chiefly cotton fields and sesame. The soil is sandy and is somewhat heavy where the mainland joins the track [beach].

The ASMAKDERE at the point where it flows into the sea is 10 yards wide and 2 feet deep. (See Watering places).

Position to cover landing

The left bank of the ASMAKDERE, which runs North and South about one mile from its mouth, affords a position to cover the landing of a force at this point. The soil here is sandy, covered with coarse grass and occasional patches of cultivation, it is easy for entrenchments. The valley Eastwards, i.e. towards MAIDOS is dotted with large oak trees.

Roads inland. Footpath

A narrow footpath follows the left bank of the ASMAKDERE, the banks of which are low and passable anywhere for infantry, as is the stream. This path is said to lead inland to the MAIDOS–KRITHIA road, but it is passable only for infantry in file and pack animals.

Road for wheeled traffic

In order to move guns inland it would be necessary to follow a track which leaves the track [beach] 150 yards north of the mouth of the ASMAKDERE. This is an ill-defined track passing for 180 yards through rather heavy sand. Following the course of a small tributary brook of the ASMAKDERE for a short distance, it passes through patches of cultivation and joins the ESKI KEUI – BUYUK ANAFARTA road at a point a little over a mile from the landing place. The cultivation is interspersed with stretches of short coarse grass, the soil throughout being firm and sandy. The track is 4 yards wide, and there is no obstacle to moving off it in any direction, save by the banks of the brook mentioned above.

Road to KILID BAHR Plateau

The ESKI KEUI road is now followed. [Report continues]

Appendix V

Extracts from: *Manual of Combined Naval and Military Operations*, 1913.
Confidential. 40/GEN. NO./269 [A 1674] London: Printed for HMSO by
Harrison & Sons, St. Martin's Lane, Printers in Ordinary to His Majesty. (B
156) 4000 9/13 H&S 194 WO. [72pp. The second edition, dated 2 September
1913, is at TNA(PRO) WO 33/644; an earlier edition was dated 1911. Page
numbers of the extracts below are given in square brackets.]

This Manual is issued by command of the Army Council, and with the concurrence
of the Lords Commissioners of the Admiralty. It is for the use of officers only . . .
War Office 2nd September, 1913.

This Manual deals only with oversea operations which involve a landing on an
open beach and in circumstances where sea communications and disembarkation
are liable to interference by the enemy's naval or military forces. [6]

Chapter III. Plans. General Principles [emphasis added]

12. When operations oversea are contemplated by the Government, it will be
    necessary for the naval and military authorities to advise as to the forces to be
    employed for the attainment of the object, having regard to the information
    available concerning the enemy, the topography and resources of the proposed
    theatre of operations, the anchorages, landing places and harbours, and the
    districts inland. A detailed scheme will also be required for the organization and
    mobilization of the expedition; and plans must be prepared for its embarkation
    and disembarkation and, as far as possible, subsequent operations.
       Such plans should be framed with due regard to the fact that circumstances,
    such as change of weather, or concentration of the enemy in unexpected
    localities, may demand variations of procedure, and these possibilities should
    be carefully considered.
13. *In certain circumstances it may be necessary, owing to the naval risks involved
    in their execution, to change or modify the plans originally drawn up for the
    disembarkation and subsequent operations. Such alterations will, however, usually
    involve delays, and will thus reduce the possibility of inflicting a surprise, which is
    all important. It will, therefore, as a rule, be best to carry out the original plans in
    spite of the risks which must be incurred.* [10]
. . . the complicated duties of embarking and landing troops and stores can only
    be carried out successfully so long as perfect harmony and co-operation exist
    between the naval and military authorities and commanders, and when the staff
    duties devolving on both services have been carefully organised and adjusted.

Chapter IV. Reconnaissance

Preliminary Measures

20. A thorough reconnaissance of the coast line, beaches and covering positions both by day and night, and at different seasons of the year and states of the tide, should be made before the despatch of an expedition is undertaken.
21. Preliminary reconnaissances should be carried out by naval and military officers. It will rarely be possible for the whole of the necessary information to be gained at one time, or by officers of the two services working in conjunction; its collection must therefore systematically be pursued as opportunities offer.

Nature of Information Required

22. The information required falls under three headings, namely:-
  i. Anchorages and harbours for transports and warships.
 ii. Topographical conditions for landing the troops and for forming them up.
iii. Topographical conditions inland.

If a joint reconnaissance were possible, the first would be purely naval, the second joint naval and military, and the third purely military. As, however, the conditions for landing may govern the whole scheme of operations, and as the officers of either service may have opportunities for gathering intelligence of value from the point of view of the other, it is necessary that both should understand the nature of the information required under all the headings. [16]

Coast Line and Landing Places

26. Beaches and landing places should be examined with reference to:-
Exposure to hostile fire. Height and nature of cliffs. Suitability in various conditions of tide and weather. Liability of surf to rise rapidly.
The beach-slope, shelving or steep-to. Obstructions such as groynes.
Nature of the beach; sand, or mud, &c., hard or soft. Dimensions of the beach, low-water mark to high-water mark, and above high-water mark.
Length available for landing. Estimate of the number of troops that can be landed simultaneously by day or by night.
The suitability of the beach for movement, especially at night. Exits and proposals for improvement. Forming-up places. Rendezvous. Routes to forming-up places and rendezvous. Water. Positions for covering re-embarkation.
Facilities for landing at or in the neighbourhood of the landing place.
Possibility of constructing further facilities for landing or of the extension of those existing. Materials obtainable.
Tugs and boats obtainable locally.
Intercommunication. It is of especial importance to bring to notice the facilities or otherwise which the country offers for the maintenance of communication. Points likely to be of use for visual signalling, existing wireless stations, telegraph or telephone lines which may be utilized, should be noted.

27. Reports on covering positions should give information regarding:-
Distance from the beach. Routes to the covering position, and their recognition by night. Positions where opposition may be offered by the enemy.
General description of the position recommended for occupation by day and night. Estimate of the force required to hold it by day and night. Signalling stations. Probable action of the enemy. Suggestions as to support by ships' guns. Positions for covering final stages of re-embarkation. Facilities for communication both along the position and with the beach. Water.

Military reconnaissance of the country inland

28. Information regarding the country inland of the point of landing is required under the following headings:-
Topography, with special reference to the object of the expedition and to the influence likely to be exercised by natural features on its attainment, e.g.:-
General nature of country; enclosed or open; cultivated, pasture, or wooded; level, undulating, or mountainous; passable or impassable by all arms. Roads and railways, especially those by which enemy's forces would approach the point of landing. Rivers. Canals. Towns. Villages.
Supplies.- Food, forage, fuel, &c.
Transport.
Water.
Accommodation in billets in towns and villages. [16–19]

The covering force

50. The successful landing of a covering force to seize and occupy such positions as will enable the landing of the main force to proceed with security will always be a necessary preliminary to the disembarkation of an army on the enemy's coast-line. By a secret landing at night, if the nature of the coast and of the proposed anchorage are such as to render this practicable, and possibly by drawing the defenders elsewhere by means of feints, it may be comparatively easy to gain time for a covering force to effect a lodgement, and to make such dispositions for the protection of the beach and anchorage as will enable the disembarkation of the main body to be undertaken.

51. The strength and composition of the covering force will vary according to the information available as to the strength and armament of any troops likely to oppose the landing. The nature of the country, the extent and distance from the shore of the positions necessary to cover the disembarkation must also be taken into account. If the enemy has mobile artillery it will be advisable during the hours of darkness to occupy, and so deny to him, all points from which effective gun fire can be directed on the beach and transports. These may be 4 or 5 miles inland, and may also be widely separated from one another.
Rapidity in landing is of great importance. This will usually make it advisable to distribute the covering force over as many transports – the maximum number may be taken to be five or six – as can be brought in and anchored at one time in the dark, in order that the largest possible number of boats may be employed. [29–30]
Indirect fire from ships is rarely practicable. For convenience in indicating

targets, which would be visible from the ships, naval and military officers should be provided with similar maps marked in squares. [44]

Appendix I. Definitions. [48]

Beach.- The stretch of shore allotted for the disembarkation of troops and material from one or more transports. A beach may be subdivided into two or more sections and these into two or more landing places, according to their respective extent.

Forming-up place.- A place of assembly for the smaller units, clear of but close to the landing place, to which troops proceed directly they land.

Rendezvous.- A place of assembly for the larger units to which the smaller units proceed from the 'Forming-up place'.

Covering Position.- A position to be occupied by an advanced detachment of troops (covering force) at such distance from the selected landing that neither anchorage, beach, nor forming-up place are exposed to shell fire from the enemy's land forces.

Appendix VI

Extract from: *Secret. Notes on Mapping from Aeroplane photographs in the Gallipoli Peninsula. E. M. Dowson, Director-General, Survey of Egypt*

[NB: An extract from the text of this document (written after 22 September 1915; comprising over 40 foolscap pages, with maps, diagrams, and four air photographs 'taken by the R.N.A.S. in Gallipoli for mapping purposes') is given here, but not the mathematical sections, nor the accompanying photographs, diagrams and maps. Originals of this document are to be found in The National Archives: TNA(PRO) WO 317/13 and AIR 1/2284/209/75/10.]

Mapping From Aeroplane Photographs in Gallipoli

The evolution of the above is interesting and may be of value in that it arose to satisfy a local need and was quite independent of any work that had been done elsewhere.

Aerial photographs at various altitudes and inclinations had, of course, been taken by many observers all over the Near Eastern Theatre since the commencement of War, and it was a good series of these taken in a horizontal plane over the South-Western end of the Gallipoli Peninsula that first suggested to Major W V Nugent, R F A, the possibility of constructing from such photos the map which was so badly needed.

It should be explained here that the 1:40,000 map of the Gallipoli Peninsula originally supplied proved, under the test of experience, to be inaccurate and unreliable and a need, more insistent and imperative than can even have been the case in France and Belgium, arose, not only for the location of enemy positions, but for the actual mapping of areas held by them. Ships and land batteries alike found the squared 1:40,000 useless for the direction and control of fire, and hence the impulse which first incited Major Nugent to compose a map of the area in which his own battery was operating, from aerial photographs.

The first experimental map was quite crudely constructed merely by taking one series of photographs covering the area it was required to depict and tracing the salient features through on to a piece of plain drawing paper with the point of an aeroplane 'flèche'. The recessed lines were then pencilled and the rough and uncontrolled map inked in. The scale was primarily gauged from the height at which the plane was flown when photographing (about 6,000 feet) obtained from aneroid readings checked by known distances whenever possible.

On trial, this diagram – for it was not, and could not, be dignified by the name of a map, rough and uncontrolled as it was, proved an enormous advance on anything that previously existed since, for the first time, there was available some sort of a detailed picture of the ground shewing the principal recognizable features and the relative positions of the enemy trenches. If shells now burst on the edge of a poppy-field, the position of that poppy-field was, not only for the first time localized, but was actually located with a very fair approximation to accuracy, and its shape and relation in distance and bearing to the objective, closely determined.

From the battery the use of the Trench Diagram, as it has come to be called, spread first to the Corps and then to the whole South-Western front, and at the time [July 1915] I visited G H Q Med. Force to see what further help Egypt could give on questions of survey and mapping, Major Nugent had just been appointed to G H Q as G.S.O.3 in charge of an embryo Survey and Map Section. Major Nugent had worked with me previously in the survey of the northern portion of the Peninsula of Sinai which had been executed by the G.S.G.S. in conjunction with the Survey of Egypt, and we were therefore able to co-operate effectively from the start.

Incidentally it should be remarked that the position from the point of view of the provision of a reasonably accurate general operations map had been greatly improved by the capture, on prisoners, of a series of recent Turkish maps, on a scale of 1:25,000, of nearly the whole of the Gallipoli Peninsula and portions of the Asiatic Shore. These maps were sent to Egypt as captured and were reproduced here in quantity in English for supply to units. This map is being tested by the Survey and Map Section M E F in the areas occupied and the verdict seems to be that:

(a) The controlling frame-work is good.

(b) The detail comprehensive but variable in accuracy. ([footnote:] The last report received on this point, dated 22nd Sept, reads 'The main outline of the 1:20,000 has proved to be very good. The contours are not up to much and the coastline is badly out in places.' The test, of course, has only been applied to a very small area)

The map is, however, it is universally agreed, a very great improvement on the original 1:40,000 as, indeed, being based on a properly controlled, if hastily executed, survey, it was bound to be.

This unlooked for assistance at the hands of the enemy did not materially affect the problem under discussion for, while the 1:20,000 forms an exceedingly useful general map, it is far too lacking in the representation of the varied detail with which the Gallipoli Peninsula abounds, to take the place of the diagrams constructed from photoplane work.

The construction of the TRENCH PLANS gradually improved as the collection of photographs of the area multiplied, and as increased time and increased skill in reading and taking the photographs enabled better use to be made of them. In principle, however, the plans still suffered from the essential defects of being compiled from a medley of pictures of the ground, held together by no framework, taken at varying heights and at unknown departures from the vertical.

The great utility of the results, even in this crude and uncertain form, can be readily appreciated. The next steps were clearly:

(1) To provide some controlling frame-work.

(2) To devise some systematic means of:

(a) Adjusting the photographs approximately to one common scale.

(b) Correcting their more serious errors, and

(c) Extracting from them the information required and translating it as rapidly as possible to its place in the plans.

Provision of a control

The provision of the controlling frame-work was the first problem. Since it was impossible to occupy points in the territory held by the enemy the only alternative appeared to be to build up a network in areas held by us and, with this as a basis, to intersect a number of recognizable points in enemy territory, and thus obtain a number of control points. Fortunately the nature of the country at the south-western end of the Gallipoli Peninsula lends itself to this, as the points capable of such intersections are very numerous. This appears also to be the case at present at Suvla. If the enemy territory becomes the reverse slope in either case more difficulty may be experienced, but features are so plentiful that no serious lack of suitable points need, I think, be anticipated. Instrumental observing, of course, may be, and often is, difficult and dangerous, but, like other things, it is carried out.

One difficulty experienced hitherto is that the points necessarily selected for visibility and recognizability, when seen in profile are often not so easily recognizable on the view plan photographed from above. The area to be covered being, unfortunately, still small, this has not proved the difficulty it might otherwise do, as fliers and surveyors alike get intimately acquainted with the ground. In certain cases help has been obtained in spotting control points by taking photographs of the area in which they lie at an inclination from the vertical so that the points in question are partially projected in a vertical lane.

Triangulation on the above system has now been carried up to the line of the crest of Achi Baba and is being connected through Imbros to Anzac and Suvla, at which latter place it is also being pushed ahead as far as circumstances permit. A reproduction of a profile sketch made from three triangulation points on the Krithia front made with a view to assisting selection and recognition of forward intersected points is attached.

Incidentally it may be mentioned that the portion of the S.W. end of the Peninsula held by us has been re-surveyed by ordinary methods on the basis of the triangulation executed there, and the general verdict on the accuracy of the (second) captured Turkish series, referred to above, is based on this and similar tests elsewhere. This work is incorporated in the new-issues of the 1:20,000 general operations map (Krithia Sheet) as all reliable new work will be.

Adjustment and correction of photos

In the early stages of the work the map was pieced together by individual comparison of and selection from all available photographs of a given area. This was, naturally, not only very tedious but very slow and uneven.

As a first experiment an apparatus, which is essentially an adjusting camera was devised, which aimed at enabling the images, of any selected photographs to be thrown on a piece of tracing cloth on a glass slab and traced straightaway. By suitable adjustments the image can be enlarged and reduced and can also be tilted in either plane, so that any given portion of a photograph (within practical limits of variation in scale and error in inclination of exposure from the vertical) can be adjusted to fit the control points which are previously plotted on the tracing cloth to the desired scale of working.

When the image is adjusted to fall as required on the tracing cloth, such detail as it is desired to extract from it is traced and in this way a mapped area is composed and a plan vandyked therefrom, printed and issued.

In practice insufficient allowance was made in the trial apparatus for the variation in scale due to variation in altitudes of the ground; nor were the lighting arrangements for throwing up the image on to the tracing paper under conditions of tent working sufficiently considered. These and other imperfections will gradually be conquered and it is hoped a strong, portable and effective reducing apparatus designed, which will obviate, or at least considerably minimize (what it is hoped will prove for this purpose to be) the unnecessary stages of printing the photograph and making a patch-tracing therefrom, and will, in any case, accelerate and facilitate the utilization of the aeroplane photographs for mapping purposes.

Faith in the general correctness of a plan obtained by the procedure outlined involves at least three important assumptions, viz:

(1) That the relative positions of plate, lens and area photographed are (within small limits of error) unchanged during exposure.

(2) That the spread of view of the lens photographing vertically an approximately horizontal surface introduces no impermissible variation in scale within the portion of the photograph utilized.

(3) That the variation in distance of objects on the ground from the lens due to relief of the ground introduces no appreciable changes in scale or errors in vertical projection.

It is recognised that these assumptions are by no means always justifiable, even within the limits of error permissible to small scale and rough class of plan, but some such assumptions were necessary as a starting point to enable the cruder errors of:

(a) Variation in photographing height, and

(b) Bad vertical pointing,
    To be minimised in a sufficiently simple and rapid manner to facilitate – and therefore accelerate – the composition of these trench plans, while at the same time improving their homogeneity and accuracy. The utility of the plans, even in their crudest form, can with difficulty be exaggerated: the most pressing needs were:

(c) Some measure of control so that the grosser errors were at least localized, and

(d) A systematization and facilitation of the production of the plans from the photographs.

This, the procedure provisionally adopted appreciably assists in securing.

The end kept in view by the Survey & Map Section G.H.Q. in Gallipoli is the production of a reliable 1:10,000 map of the area of operations showing all recognizable detail. On this map enemy positions and trenches, as periodically corrected, are to be shown in a coloured overprint, since the basis of the map will not appreciably change while change in enemy positions is ceaseless. Proofs of such a map of a portion of the SUVLA area were produced and circulated for criticism some little time since and final copies will probably be to hand shortly.

Appended are copies of four photographs [not reproduced here] taken by the R N A S in Gallipoli for mapping purposes, the positions of these four photos in relation to the detail on (e), four successively dated trench diagrams, on (f) the reproduction (1:20,000) of the captured Turkish map, and on (g) the 1:40,000 originally supplied, are indicated on the accompanying plans. From these it will be realized far better than from any amount of explanation the radical improvement effected by the introduction of photographic mapping.

The positions of the photographs relative to the detail on the maps can only be roughly indicated chiefly on account of inaccuracies in both maps; the photographs are poor copies as the negatives were not available and indifferent prints had to be re-photographed to obtain more copies. Photos and plans alike are only intended to be illustrative of methods and not as samples of work.

On my return from visiting G H Q Med. Force the G O C in Chief in Egypt [Maxwell] approved of the continuation of experimental work in photographic mapping in Egypt, and Major Massy, R.F.C., has since co-operated most keenly in this work. This Survey provided two of the most suitable cameras that were obtainable locally [[footnote]: Description of Camera [not present]] and a number of series of aircraft photographs were taken by Lieut C A G Mackintosh over an area on the Ismailia Canal specially selected on account of its being (1) handy (2) rich in detail (3) level, and (4) surveyed recently, accurately and on a large scale (1:2,500).

Level country was deliberately chosen for the initiation of the work but it was, at the same time, arranged that subsequent series of photographs should be taken over a well featured portion of northern Sinai of which, of course, there is an excellent map based on recent work [1:125,000, surveyed 1908–13]. I understand this has since been done, but copies of the photographs are not yet to hand, and there accordingly has been no opportunity of testing their value from a map-making point of view.

Exposure was made throughout with the camera hand-held, a bubble being attached to assist in securing verticality. At first exposure was made over the side of the plane but this was very unsatisfactory since a clear view was not attainable and the conditions were too awkward to allow the operator to watch the level bubble and make his periodic exposures properly.

It was then arranged that a trap door should be provided in an available plane, and subsequent exposures were made through this with satisfactory results. The net result of the Ismailia Canal experiments was to obtain easily and regularly sets of photographs of stretches of the country which were legible and full of detail, and which compared with the map shewed remarkable accuracy, uncorrected as they were.

From a photographic point of view the photographs were poor and each had to be "nursed" individually, but this was merely lack of experience and proper apparatus and only pointed to the need of improved manipulation and machinery.

The great difficulty of varying relief of the ground was, of course, not present, but it was desirable to free the first trials from any difficulty that could be eliminated. The study, in due course, of photographs of the well-mapped boldly-reliefed country of Northern Sinai should be most instructive.

Attached are two appendices: [Not reproduced here]
I: Notes on some individual points of immediate importance still debatable, or at least worthy of further consideration.
II: An attempt to analyse the various sources of error with a view to seeing more clearly the importance and nature of each of which, accordingly, require immediate attention and which can, for the time being, be treated as negligible.

I am very strongly persuaded of the importance of the future of mapping by means of aeroplane photography, and for normal requirements as well as those of war. The opinions and views put forward are, of course, very tentative and are hurriedly put together from a limited experience, but the whole subject is still naturally in the crudest initial stages of a new form of surveying, and we must therefore obviously be careful to keep in mind alternative methods, even if for the present they appear clearly ruled out, since an advance elsewhere may at any time call for the revival of a previously discredited instrument or method.

I would, accordingly, be grateful for any criticisms or suggestions – even the sharpest and crudest – from anyone who has had experience either in:
(1) The taking of aeroplane photographs.
(2) The construction of plans or diagrams therefrom.
(3) The use of such plans in the field.

This Survey [i.e. Survey of Egypt] being in close touch with the forces in the Near Eastern Theatres of war and, naturally, being trained in, and having the machinery – human and otherwise – for, map-making, is in a position to digest and collate such criticism and experience for the benefit of those members of the Near Eastern Forces who are concerned and interested, but who have no leisure or opportunity to collect or collate such information for themselves.

[Signed] E. M. Dowson
DIRECTOR-GENERAL
SURVEY OF EGYPT

Later Addenda
Provision of Control

The chief difficulty in choosing points to intersect in the enemy's country has proved to be the difficulty of recognising the object selected from two points separated sufficiently far apart to give an accurate determination of its position, rather than the lack of prominent objects.

For instance from one point a tree may show up standing apart from a group of trees but on proceeding to the next point it may fall in line with the group and it will be impossible to distinguish which of the trees it is.

The difficulty of recognizing the intersected objects on the photographs has almost disappeared as constant practice of picking out features of importance has led to great proficiency. When any difficulty has been experienced it has always been possible to find the object by the following method:-

The map constructed from photographs is drawn up to the nearest recognisable intersected point, and the drawing is carried on approximately in pencil by reducing each photo to fit the overlapping detail already drawn on the map. This process is continued until the point is drawn on the tracing. The relative position of the plotted intersected point is then seen with regard to the neighbouring detail and this part of the photo is searched for the object. In every case in which this method has been resorted to the point has been found within 2 millimetres of the point indicated. The point having been found on the map is re-adjusted to fit it.

An example of this method is illustrated in the specimen photograph C (not reproduced here), which was known to include the prominent blasted tree (3) shown on the profile sketch. This tree could not be found until the above method was resorted to. The neighbouring photograph to the East contained both the intersected windmills at Krithia so that it was reduced to fit the tracing 1:10,000 containing the intersected points plotted to that scale. The photograph C was then reduced until the overlapping detail agreed and the plotted intersected point was found to fall in the position shown on the back by a red circle. The tree was then picked out as the black object surrounded by a white circle. This white circle has been observed round other trees which can be easily recognised and is probably due to animals walking round it whilst rubbing themselves.

With regard to the density of fixed points these should be as thick as possible and in any case should not be separated by more than one to two kilometres in order to give a rigid check to prevent the inclusion of a distorted photograph.

Instruments for reduction of photographic detail to the intersected points plotted on the tracing. Initially great difficulty was experienced in picking out detail on the image thrown on the tracing cloth.

This was due to two causes:-

1) The lack of contrast of the majority of photographs especially the earlier ones.
2) Insufficient lighting of the photos.

These difficulties have now been overcome in the following way:-

The photos are now placed under a thin glass plate having its surface covered with a transparent varnish which will hold ink. All important detail of the photograph is then traced directly on to the glass. The travelling base board of the camera has had a hole cut through it and a dispersive reflector placed behind it throwing the light directly through the hole into the lens of the camera. The glass plate carrying the tracing is then placed over the hole and focused on the tracing cloth above. This method yields a brilliant image on the tracing cloth which more than compensates for the slight additional source of error introduced by tracing the photograph twice.

Appendix VII

Rough Running Account of Visit to M E F July 7th–24th, 1915. [dates of departure from, and arrival at, Survey of Egypt]

[**Relevant extracts from** Ernest Dowson's hitherto unpublished report on Gallipoli mapping and his visit to Gallipoli, including the start of the new trig survey, July 1915. Reproduced by kind permission of Gill Dowson]

[10 July, Mudros] The handling of maps in detail from MUDROS as a centre is fairly hopeless as long as this lack of water transport prevails, and there is not the slightest apparent hope that it will be remedied as it prevails everywhere.

[11 July, Imbros] Landing from motor boat was met on pier by Cairns [printer from Survey of Egypt] who took my kit up to my tent, while Captain _____ took me up to the I. and O. (Intelligence & Operations) Mess Tent and introduced me to General Braithwaite (C G S). [Philip] Graves, recently in Cairo, came up and sat down by me and stayed while I had dinner, as also Nugent and Nicholas who came up as soon as they heard I had arrived. Among other Cairo friends and acquaintances in the Mess were [George] Lloyd, late of Egyptian Intelligence, and [Cecil] Keeling, late of Residency, now doing ciphering for I.

The Intelligence Marquee is as follows:- [sketch-plan shows tables for Col. Ward, Capt. Deed[e]s, Lloyd & Graves, Capt. Smith, Cipherers, Clerks, etc.].

Had a long walk with Nugent and Nicholas that evening and saw Nugent's trench diagrams for the first time. Their value was obvious as (was) the danger of their uncontrolled compilation [i.e. lack of trigonometric control framework].

The next morning visited C G S [Braithwaite], Colonel Ward [Intelligence], and saw over Cairns' work [Printing Section]. The lack of appreciation of the vital value of maps and accurate maps and of a large enough scale for the intricate detached operations to be followed was amazing. Both Nicholas and Nugent severally said that annoyance had been experienced [by the GS] when the first Turkish map was captured, and it needed much persuasion and long delay before it was allowed to be forwarded to Cairo for reproduction.

Nugent, who was then on the Staff of the VIII Corps (General Hunter Weston), came over on latter's orders to urge the reproduction, and walked the deck of the "Arcadia" for an hour with Colonel Ward urging it. Col. Ward wishing at least to postpone decision for a week and objecting to the substitution of any other map for 1:40,000 although latter was known to be unreliable and misleading.

The C G S [Braithwaite] was equally indifferent, and that the map was not merely suppressed was apparently entirely due to the VIII Corps and to Nicholas' continued representation.

The second Turkish map (which fortunately promises very well) was apparently subsequently chosen as a substitute on no valid ground but merely because it extended further Northward and covered probable future ground of operations. Its accuracy and reliability seem never to have been considered by the General Staff, still less was an application of any test ever imagined.

The bitter need for maps led Nugent on behalf of the Artillery of the VIII Corps to seize on a few aircraft photos that had come in and see what he could do in the way of compilation. Later General Street, Comm[anding]. Staff VIII Corps, saw the diagrams he had produced and, after trying them, the VIII Corps have been satisfied with nothing else.

The formation of a new Survey Section under Nugent, and his attachment to the G.H.Q. for Survey work, was – as far as I can see – entirely due to the urging of VIII Corps, and from no appreciation of the crying need for maps by the G.H.Q. . . .

Tuesday, 13th. Nugent and I took the morning trawler to 'W' Beach . . . After inspecting quarters and installing ourselves [in dugout on cliff above pier], we walked out to reconnoitre, and fixed main outlines of base and first series of triangulation points. In the afternoon walked out along NW coast towards rising ground on which it was hoped to get good views back to first points and good intersections on to house or trees on Atchi Baba. Were hampered in our progress by a brisk battle in progress and eventually had to give up actually reaching the site, but were satisfied it would do. Stayed on then in the main observation post for Artillery on our left flank who were shelling guns over KRITHIA, and finished up by dining with Heavy Howitzer Battery and making our way back with some difficulty in the darkness to the dug-out. . . .

Wednesday, 14th. Next morning in dug-out, drafting report for G.H.Q . . . In afternoon made our way through French rear lines to de Totts Battery and MORTO Bay. Climbed de Tott and bathed in Morto Bay. Then made our own way via SEDD EL BAHR to VIII Corps Artillery Mess, where we dined.

Thursday, 15th. Next morning more arrangement [of triangulation] in field and squaring up reports and back to G H Q . . .

Friday, 16th. Spent at G.H.Q trying to get Survey question settled. Looked through the stores which the Survey Section had bought [sic; brought from England]. . .

Saturday, 17th. Got the Survey and Printing proposals accepted without much difficulty, but with interminable delay and difficulty in arriving at a decision. . . .

Sunday, 18th. Set forth with Lloyd and Nugent on T[orpedo].B[oat]. for ANZAC. . . . Lloyd took us all [a]long right centre and to left centre (Courtneys and Quinns Posts) but there was not time to visit the left also. We lunched with S. Butler in his dug-out . . .

Having previously arranged that we would, upon arrival, go off and see Commander Douglas (Hydrographer), we signalled the "Exmouth" and went off there to dinner. Douglas' few notes appear elsewhere [location unknown]. There met dining with him Fleetwood (Navigating Lieutenant of the "Humber") and arranged to go off to his ship the next day.

Monday, 19th. At G.H.Q. in morning writing up notes for Nugent. Nugent went over to Cape Helles to get field work properly started. In evening went off to "Humber" and had a very interesting talk on range-finding and naval gunnery, and the necessity of better methods for naval fire directed against the shore. Arranged to come off next day and go out with the 'Humber' bombarding. She was detailed to cover one of the new Monitors (the 'Roberts'). Would test new map from sea and see what improvements might be made from naval point of view.

Tuesday, 20th. Seven new T2 [sheets of second Turkish map] to hand in morning captured. Discussion as to what should be done with them as there was a disposition to try and deal with them [i.e. reproduce them] at G.H.Q. This was dropped. O. (Operations Branch) complained that the new map [Survey of Egypt 1:20,000 reproduction and transliteration of captured Turkish sheets] ignored or altered names on old (1:40,000 map) to which they had got accustomed, and made a point of the names on old map being retained, however wrong. At length it was agreed that only such old names as have got into common use (e.g. ATCHI BABA) should be retained, and correct names should be added in brackets . . .

Bibliography

1. Published books, journals, etc.

Admiralty, The, *A Consecutive List of Fleet Charts and Miscellaneous Diagrams, Charts and Plans, issued for Fleet Purposes, 1915, corrected to 1st April 1915*. Hydrographic Department, Admiralty (compiled 1915).

Albrecht, Oskar, *Das Kriegsvermessungswesen während des Weltkieges 1914– 18*, Munich: Geodätische Kommission, 1969.

Allen, Capt. G R G, 'A Ghost from Gallipoli', *RUSI Journal*, May 1963, 108(630).

American Society of Photogrammetry, *Manual of Photogrammetry*, Falls Church VA, 1952.

Andrew, Christopher, *Secret Service. The Making of the British Intelligence Community*, London: Heinemann, 1985.

Anon., *The Dardanelles for England: the true solution of the Eastern Question*, in War Office Library Catalogue, 1912, Part III (copy in British Library).

Anon. [probably Colonel Mehemmed Shevki Pasha], 'The Topographical Service in the Ottoman Empire and the Modern Turkish Cartography', *L'Universo*, No. 1, 1920; typescript translation in MCE, RE (now DGIA), Ref. D30/H1/A5.

Anon. [GLC], 'Engineers at Gallipoli, 1915', *Royal Engineers Journal*, 111, 1997.

Aspinall-Oglander, Brig.-Gen. C F, *History of the Great War, Military Operations, Gallipoli*, Vol. I, & separate Maps and Appendices volume, London: Heinemann, 1929.

_____, *History of the Great War, Military Operations, Gallipoli*, Vol. II, & separate Maps and Appendices volume, London: Heinemann, 1932.

Baedecker, Karl, *Guide to 'Konstantinopel . . . Kleinasien' etc.*, a 2te Auflage. Maps and plans. Leipzig, Karl Baedecker, 1914.

Barton, Peter, Doyle, Peter and Vandewalle, Johan, *Beneath Flanders Fields. The Tunnellers' War 1914–1918*, Staplehurst: Spellmount, 2004.

Beeby-Thompson, A, *Emergency water supplies for military, agricultural and colonial purposes*, London: Crosby Lockwood & Son, 1924.

_____, *Exploring for water*, London: Villiers Publications, 1969.

Berger, Jos. Viktor, 'Luftfahrzeuge im Dienste der Geländeaufnahme', Kriegstechnische Zeitschrift, 1913.

Bidwell, Brig. Shelford, *Gunners at War*, London: Arrow, 1972.

Branagan, D, 'The Australian Mining Corps in World War I', *Bulletin of the Proceedings of the Australian Institute for Mining and Metallurgy*, 292, 1987.

Brandenburg, Erich, *From Bismarck to the World War. A History of German Foreign Policy 1870–1914*, London: OUP, 1933.

Callwell, Maj.-Gen. Sir E, *The Dardanelles*, London: Constable, 1919 (2nd edn 1924).

_____, *Experiences of a Dug-Out*, London: Constable, 1920.

_____, *Stray Recollections*, Vol. I, London: Edward Arnold, 1923.

Carlyon, L A, *Gallipoli*, London: Doubleday, 2002.

Celik, Kenan and Koc, Ceyhan (eds), *The Gallipoli Campaign. International Perspectives 85 years on*, Turkey: Cannakale Onsekiz Mart University, 2001.

Chasseaud, Peter, *Artillery's Astrologers – A History of British Survey and Mapping on the Western Front 1914–1918*, Lewes: Mapbooks, 1999.

_____, 'German Maps and Survey on the Western Front 1914–18,' *The Cartographic Journal*, London, 38(2), 2001.

_____, 'Mapping for D-Day: The Allied Landings in Normandy, 6 June 1944', *The Cartographic Journal*, London, 38(2), 2001.

_____, *An analysis and evaluation of British, French and German military field survey and mapping in the First World War*, PhD thesis for the University of Greenwich (copy in University of Greenwich Library), 2004.

Churchill, W S, *The World Crisis*, Vol. 2 (1915), London: Butterworth, 1923.

Close, Col. C F and Cox, Capt. E W, *Text Book of Topographical Surveying* (2nd edn), London: HMSO, 1913.

Clough, Brig. A B (comp.), *The Second World War 1939–1945, Army, Maps and Survey*, London: War Office, 1952 (copy in BL Map Library).

Collier, Richard, *D-Day, June 6, 1944. The Normandy Landings*, London: Cassell, 1999.

Corbett, Sir Julian S, *History of the Great War, Naval Operations*, Vol. II, London: Longmans, Green, 1921.

Crampin, S and Evans, R, 'Neotectonics of the Marmara Sea region of Turkey', *Journal of the Geological Society*, London, 143, 1986.

Dardanelles Commission, *The Dardanelles Commission*, in The World War I Collection, Uncovered Editions, London: The Stationery Office, 2001.

De Larminat, E, *La Topographie chez l'ennemie. Comment nous dressions la carte du terrain occupé par l'adversaire*, Paris: Lavauzelle, 1920 (BL Ref. X.619/10050).

Denham, H M, *Dardanelles, A Midshipman's Diary 1915–16*, London: John Murray, 1981.

Dowson, E M, *Mapping from Aeroplane Photographs in Gallipoli*, Secret, duplicated typescript report with maps and photos, Survey of Egypt, c late Sep. 1915. Copies in The National Archives: TNA(PRO) WO 317/13 and AIR 1/2284/209/75/10.

_____, 'Further Notes on Aeroplane Photography in the Near East', *Geographical Journal*, 58, 1921.

Doyle, P and Bennett, M, 'Military Geography: The Influence of Terrain in the Outcome of the Gallipoli Campaign, 1915', *Geographical Journal*, March 1999, 165.

Eckert, M, 'Meine Erfahrungen als Geograph im Kriegsvermessungs – und Kriegskartenwesen', *Kartographische und schulgeographische Zeitschrift*, 1 & 2, 1922.

Edmonds, Brig.-Gen. Sir James, *History of the Great War, Military Operations, France and Flanders, 1915*, Vol. I, London: Macmillan, 1927.

_____, *History of the Great War, 1914*, Vol. I (3rd edn), London: Macmillan, 1933.

_____, *History of the Great War, Military Operations, France and Belgium, 1917*, Vol. II, London: HMSO, 1948.

Ekins, Ashley, 'A ridge too far: military objectives and the dominance of terrain in the Gallipoli Campaign', in Celik and Koc (eds), op. cit., 2001.

English, Lt-Col. T, late RE, 'Eocene and Later Formations Surrounding the Dardanelles', *Quarterly Journal of the Geological Society of London*, 60, 1905.

ETOUSA, *Report on Beach Intelligence Work for Operation Anvil*, Mapping Section, Intelligence Division, by the Beach Intelligence Sub-Section, mapping Section, Office of the Chief Engineer, ETOUSA, printed by US 656 Engr Topo Bn (Army) 5675 ETO, 8/4/45.

Fairchild Corporation, *Multiple Lens Aerial Cameras in Mapping*, by the Technical Staff of the Fairchild Aerial Camera Corporation, New York, 1933.

Fergusson, Thomas G, *British Military Intelligence, 1870–1914. The Development of a Modern Intelligence Organization*, London: Arms & Armour Press, 1984.

Fitzherbert, M, *The Man Who Was Greenmantle – A Biography of Aubrey Herbert*, London: OUP, 1985.

Flett, J S, *The First Hundred Years of the Geological Survey of Great Britain*, London: HMSO, 1937.

Fryer, Brig. R E, *Survey Notes on Operation 'Husky', 22 Feb to 10 Jul 1943*, 1st August 1943, Survey Directorate G.H.Q. Middle East Force, M.D.R. Misc. 6520. Reproduced by 212 Fd. Survey Coy., R.E., August 1943. Copy in DGIA, Defence Geographic Centre library.

Garnett, David (ed.), *The Letters of T E Lawrence*, London: Spring Books, 1964.

German Military Survey, *Planheft Südosteuropa*, Südlicher Teil, 1 Juli 1943, Berlin, 1944.

Gibson, Stevyn, 'Open Source Intelligence: An Intelligence Lifeline', *RUSI Journal*, 149(1), February 2004.

Gleichen, Maj.-Gen. Lord E, *A Guardsman's Memories*, London: Blackwood, 1932.

Gooch, J, *The Plans of War; The General Staff and British Military Strategy c1900–1916*, London: Routledge, 1974.

Grant Grieve, W and Newman, B, *Tunnellers. The Story of the Tunnelling Companies, Royal Engineers During the World War*, London: Herbert Jenkins, 1936.

Graves, Philip, *Briton and Turk*, London: Hutchinson, 1941.

Graves, Robert, *Lawrence and the Arabs*, London: Jonathan Cape, 1927.

Guide to Greece, The Archipelago, Constantinople, The Coast of Asia Minor, Crete and Cyprus (3rd edn), London: Macmillan, 1910

Hamilton, Sir Ian, *A Staff Officer's Scrap Book During the Russo–Japanese War*, 2 vols, London: Edward Arnold, 1905.

_____, *Gallipoli Diary*, 2 vols, London: Edward Arnold, 1920.

Hargrave, John, *The Suvla Bay Landing*, London: Macdonald, 1964.

Heller, Joseph, *British Policy Towards the Ottoman Empire, 1908–1914*, London: Cass, 1938.

Hickey, Michael, *Gallipoli*, London: John Murray, 1998.

Hills, Maj. E H RE, review by 'E.H.H.' of Die Geschichtliche Entwicklung der Photogrammetrie und die Begründung ihrer Verwendbarkeit für Mess- und Konstruktionswecke (1913) by Weiss, M; Strecker and Schröder, Stuttgart: 1913, in *Geographical Journal*, 42(2).

Hinsley, F H et al, *British Intelligence in the Second World War*, Vol. I, London: HMSO, 1979.

Hogarth, D G, 'Geography of the War Theatre in the Near East', *Geographical Journal*, 45(6), June 1915.

Hope, Maj. M, 'The Defences of Dardanelles. A Report written in 1799,' *Royal Engineers Journal*, September 1918.

Hopkirk, Peter, *On Secret Service East of Constantinople*, London: John Murray, 1994.

James, Adm. W M, letter in *RUSI Journal*, November 1963, 108(632).

Jeans, Surgeon Rear-Admiral T T, *Reminiscences of a Naval Surgeon*, London: Sampson, Low & Marston, 1927.

Jones, H J, *The War in the Air*, Vol. II, London: OUP, 1928.

Kahn, David, *Seizing the Enigma. The Race to Break the German U-Boat Code, 1939–43*, Boston MA: Houghton Mifflin, 1991.

Karatekin, N, 'Hydrological Research in the Middle East', *Reviews of Research on Arid Zone Hydrology*, UNESCO, 1953.

Keegan, John, *Intelligence in War. Knowledge of the Enemy from Napoleon to Al-Qaeda*, London: Pimlico, 2004.

Keyes, Admiral Roger, *The Naval Memoirs of Admiral of the Fleet Sir Roger Keyes*, Vol. I, London: Butterworth, 1934.

Lan-Davies, letter to J H Dallmeyer Ltd, October 1915, in *British Journal of Photography*, 18 April 1919.

Leaf, Walter, 'Notes on the Troad', *Geographical Journal*, 40(1), July 1912.

＿＿＿＿＿＿＿＿＿＿, *Troy. A Study in Homeric Geography*, London: Macmillan, 1912.

＿＿＿＿＿＿＿＿＿＿, 'The Military Geography of the Troad', *Geographical Journal* 67, 1916.

Lee, John, *A Soldier's Life. General Sir Ian Hamilton 1853–1947*, London: Pan 2001.

London Gazette, 22 January 1916. DSO citation for Maj. S F Newcombe RE.

Mackenzie, Compton, *Gallipoli Memories*, London: Cassell, 1929.

＿＿＿＿＿＿＿＿＿＿＿＿＿＿, *Greek Memories*, London: Chatto & Windus, 1939.

Macleod, Jenny, *Reconsidering Gallipoli*, Manchester: MUP, 2004.

Magnus, Philip, *Kitchener*, London: John Murray, 1958.

Masefield, John, *Gallipoli*, New York: Macmillan, 1916.

Masters, John, *The Road Past Mandalay*, London: Michael Joseph, 1961.

Mead, Peter, *The Eye in the Air. History of Air Observation and Reconnaissance for the Army 1785–1945*, London: HMSO, 1983.

Miller, Geoffrey, *The Millstone: British Naval Policy in the Mediterranean 1900 – 1914; the Commitment to France and British Intervention in the War* (Vol. 3 of 'The Straits' trilogy), University of Hull Press, 1999.

Mitchell, C W, *Terrain evaluation* (2nd edn) Harlow: Longman, 1991.

Mitchell, C W and Gavish, D, 'Land on which Battles are Lost or Won', *Geographical Magazine* 52, 1980.

Moorhead, Alan, *Gallipoli*, London: Hamish Hamilton p/b edn 1963.

Morgenthau, Henry, *Secrets of the Bosphorus*, London: Hutchinson, 1918.

Murray, Joseph, *Gallipoli As I Saw It*, London: William Kimber, 1965.

Nasr, Seyyed Hossein, *Islamic Science*, London: World of Islam Festival Publishing Co., 1976.

Nevinson, H W, *The Dardanelles Campaign*, London: Nisbet, 1918.

Newcombe, Capt. S F RE and Greig, Lt J P S RE, 'The Baghdad Railway', *Geographical Journal*, 44(6), Dec. 1914.

Newcombe, Col. S F, 'T.E. Lawrence, Personal Reminiscences', *PEF Quarterly*, July 1935.

Nolan, Col. (retd) M A, series of articles on Gallipoli mapping in *The Gallipolian*: Part 1, Spring 1993 (71); Part 2, Autumn 1993 (72); Part 3, Winter 1993 (73); Part 4, Spring 1994 (74); Part 5, Winter 1994 (76); Part 6, Spring 1995 (77).

Occleshaw, M, *Armour Against Fate. British Military Intelligence in the First World War*, London: Columbus Books, 1989.

Pamir, H M, 'Hydrogeological research in the basin of the Ergene', *Proceedings of the Ankara Symposium on Arid Zone Hydrology*, UNESCO, 1953.

Parry, J T, 'Terrain evaluation, military purposes', in Finkl, C W (ed.), *The Encyclopedia of Applied Geology. Encyclopedia of Earth Sciences*, Vol. 13, New York: Van Nostrand Reinhold, 1984.

Patrick, D M and Hatheway, A W, 'Engineering geology and military operations: an overview with examples of current missions', *Association of Petroleum Geologists Bulletin*, 26, 1989.

Pears, Sir Edwin, *Forty Years in Constantinople*, London: Herbert Jenkins, 1916.

Pentreath, Guy, *Hellenic Traveller*, London: Faber, 1971.

Perincek, D, 'Possible Strand of the North Anatolian Fault in the Thrace Basin, Turkey – an interpretation', *American Association of Petroleum Geologists Bulletin*, 75, 1991.

Porter, Maj.-Gen. W, *History of the Corps of Royal Engineers*, Vol. I, Chatham: Institution of Royal Engineers, 1889.

Pressey, H A S, 'Notes on Trench Warfare', *Royal Engineers Journal*, 29, 1919.

Pritchard, Maj.-Gen. H L, *The History of the Corps of Royal Engineers*, Vols V & VI, Chatham, Institution of Royal Engineers, 1952.

Rhodes James, Robert, *Gallipoli*, London: Pimlico, 1999.

Ritchie, Rear Admiral G S, *The Admiralty Chart*, London: Hollis & Carter, 1967.

Robertson, Gen Sir W, *Soldiers and Statesmen*, Vol. I, London: Cassell, 1926.

Rohde, Lt G H, *Die Operationen an den Dardanellen im Balkankriege, 1912/13*, Berlin: Eisenschmidt, 1914 (BL Shelfmark: 9136.dd.21).

Ropp, Theodore, *War in the Modern World*, New York: Collier Books, 1962.

Roskill, Capt. S W (ed.), *Documents Relating to the Naval Air Service*, Vol. I, 1908 –1918, London: Navy Records Society, 1969.

Roussilhe, H, *Emploi de la Photographie Aérienne aux Levées Topographiques à Grande Echelle, Encyclopédie Industrielle et Commerciale, Librairie de l'Enseignement Technique*, Paris: Léon Eyrolles, 1930.

Samson, Charles Rumney, *Fights and Flights*, London: Ernest Benn, 1930.

Saunders, H St G, *Per Ardua. The Rise of British Air Power 1911–1939*, London: OUP, 1944.

Schumann, R, 'Die Entwicklung der photogrammetrischen Geräte in Jena von Jahrhundertwende bis zum Jahre 1945', *Kompendium Photogrammetrie*, 18, Leipzig, 1986.

Sengor, A M C, and Yilmaz, Y, 'Tethyan evolution of Turkey: a plate tectonic approach', *Tectonophysics*, 75, 1981.

Service Géographique de l'Armée, *Rapport sur les Travaux éxecutés du 1er août 1914 au 31 décembre 1919. Historique du Service Géographique de l'Armée Pendant la Guerre*, Paris: Imprimerie du Service Géographique de l'Armée, 1924. Also revised edn. 1936.

Stenzel, Kapt. A, *Der kürzeste Weg nach Konstantinopel. Ein Beispiel für das Zusammenwirken von Flotte und Heer*, 1894.

Storrs, R, *Orientations, 'Definitive Edition'*, London: Nicholson & Watson, 1945.

Strahan, A, 'Introduction. Work in connection with the war', *Memoirs of the Geological Survey. Summary of Progress of the Geological Survey of Great Britain and the Museum of Practical Geology for 1918*, London: HMSO, 1919.

Survey of Egypt, *Catalogue of Military Maps and Publications Stored at Map Rooms, Survey of Egypt, Giza (Mudiriya), up to March 31, 1920*, Cairo: Government Press, 1920.

Sykes, F, *From Many Angles. An Autobiography*, London: Harrap, 1942.

Ternek, Z; Erentöz, C; Pamir, H N and Akyürek, B, 1:500 000 Ölçekli Türkiye Jeoloji Haritasi. Explanatory Text of the Geological Map of Turkey. Istanbul, Ankara: Maden Tetkik ve Arama Genel Müdürlügü Vayinlarindan, 1987.

Thomson, Sir Basil, *The Allied Secret Service in Greece*, London: Hutchinson, 1931.

Travers, Tim, *Gallipoli 1915*, Stroud: Tempus, 2001.

United Nations, *Ground water in the Eastern Mediterranean and western Asia*, Natural Resources/Water Series No. 9, New York, United Nations, 1982.

von Sanders, Gen. Liman, *The Dardanelles Campaign* (trans. & comments by Col. E H Schulz, US Army Corps of Engineers), The Engineer School, Fort Humphreys, VA. 1931.

War Office, *Report on the Defences of Constantinople, Secret, General Staff*, London, 1909. Also 'Plates' volume, 1908.

_____, *Catalogue of Maps Published by the Geographical Section of the General Staff*, WO, London, 1923.

_____, *Notes on GSGS Maps of France, Belgium and Holland, Dec. 1943, Secret*, Directorate of Military Survey, WO, London, 1943.

_____, *Notes on Maps of the Balkans, June 1944, Confidential*, Directorate of Military Survey, WO, London.

Weldon, L B, *'Hard Lying'. Eastern Mediterranean 1914–1919*, London: Herbert Jenkins, 1925.

Wemyss, Admiral, *The Navy in the Dardanelles Campaign*, London: Hodder & Stoughton, 1924.

Wood, M, *In Search of the Trojan War*, London: BBC Books, 1985.

Woods, H Charles, *Washed by Four Seas – An English Officer's Travels in the Near East*, London: T Fisher Unwin, 1908.

_____, *The Danger Zone of Europe – Changes and Problems in the Near East*, London: T Fisher Unwin, 1911.

_____, *La Turquie et ses Voisins*, Paris: E Guilmoto (éditeur), Librairie orientale et Americaine, 1911.

Woolley, C L, *As I Seem to Remember*, London: Allen & Unwin, 1962.

II. Archival & Other References

Admiralty (Hydrographic Department, Taunton)
Memoirs of Hydrography, Part III. Typescript (n.d.), Hydrographic Department, 920: 528.47 JAC.

Australian War Memorial
Maps, War Diaries, etc.

Bayerisch Hauptstaatsarchiv, Kriegsarchiv, Munich
Vermessungs-Abteilung Nr.11, War Diary.

Bodleian Library, Oxford
Milner Papers, Box 122, Folio 129, incl. Minute to War Council by Churchill, 3-4-15.

British Geological Survey, Wallingford;
logs taken on the Peninsula during the period of post war British occupation. These provide information not readily available, to the Allies at least, during the war.

British Library
Keyes Papers, 5/11.

British Library Map Library
Collection of Gallipoli Maps, GHQ-MEF, Maps 43336.(21.).
The shelf marks of other maps are given in chapter endnotes.
[Maps SEC.5. (2429), Maps B.A.C.6. (2429), Maps 43980.(7) and (8)]

Carte de la Presqu'lle de Gallipoli (in two sheets); published in 1854 by the Depot
de la Guerre, Paris, under the direction of Colonel Blondel (engraved by
Erhard, 42 rue Bonaparte, printed Chez Kaeppelin, Quai Voltaire.
Maps 43335.(94.). *Sketch of Portion of West Coast of the Gallipoli Peninsula N.W. of
Maidos*. G. E. Grover. Capt. R.E. 8th February 1876. Lithd. At the Intelligence
Branch, Qr. Mr. Genl's Department under the direction of Lt. Col. R. Home.
C.B. R.E. April 1877. [1:15,840]. Stamp: Rec'd TSGS Map Room 7 Jan 1888.

Bundesarchiv-Militärarchiv, Freiburg-im-Breisgau, Germany
Files PH9XX/47, *Übungen der Vermessungsabteilungen in Wahn und Thorn 1912,
mit photograph*, PH9V/98 & 99, *Erkundungs- und Vermessungstätigkeit im
Festungskrieg. – Entwurf einer Dienstvorschrift in Zusammenarbeit mit dem
Kriegsministerium und dem Chef des Generalstabes der Armee*, Bd.1, 1913-14, &
Bd.2, Jan. 1913 bis Apr. 1914.

Churchill College, Cambridge
Chartwell Papers.

Defence Geographic Centre
Hedley typescript (1919) on *The Geographical Section of the General Staff during the
War 1914-18*, para 2.
MI4 (1924), *Latitudes of the Turkish Mapping System*, Typescript note by MI4,
dated 8/8/1924, in MCE, RE (now DGIA).
MCE, RE.D 30: 3(4). *Report from Major R. H. Phillimore, R.E.* (8th Field Survey
Co., R.E.) *on Turkish Staff Maps 1:25,000 and 1:5,000 of Gallipoli and Chanak
Kale, with list of Conventional Signs Employed*. 20/2/1919.

The National Archives (formerly Public Record Office, hence references in notes
and below given as TNA(PRO))

(a) Open Shelves
Foreign Office Lists, 1902-1913.

(b) Special Collections
TNA(PRO) 30/57/61. Kitchener papers.
TNA(PRO) 30/40/14/1. Ardagh Papers, incl. Ardagh (1896), The Eastern
Question in 1896, October 1896. pp32-4.

(c) Admiralty
ADM 1. Secret Branch: 1796 – 1826.
ADM 1/8418/90. Admiralty files on Loss of Submarine E15 on 18-4-15.
ADM 1/8497. Extracts from Minutes of Conference Held in the Admiralty on 3
April 1915.

ADM 1/8884. War with Turkey. The Forcing of the Dardanelles. 10 August 1906. Very Secret. The Forcing of the Dardanelles (The Naval Aspects of the Question). Capt. C. L. Ottley, Director of Naval Intelligence. E44924. 12.-8/06. Pk. E.& S. A. 12pp., final (third) and earlier drafts.

ADM 137/787. Dardanelles, Charts and tracings used by the Eastern Mediterranean Squadron 1914-1916, incl. Tracing Admiralty Chart No. 2429, Defences since 4th August 1914, Enclosure No. 11 in Med. Letter No./34 dated 24-12-14.

ADM 137/881. Dardanelles, 1914 Sept – Dec.

ADM 137/1089. Dardanelles 1915 Jan – April (H.S. 1089).

ADM 137/2165, 1914, Mediterranean War Records, Dardanelles.

ADM 137/4178. 1915-22, Greece, papers relating to economic and strategical position in Balkans and Dardanelles campaign – letters from Admiral Mark Kerr, etc.

ADM 137/787. (HS Vol. 901) Dardanelles, Charts relating to Eastern Mediterranean Squadron, 1914-1916

ADM 137/881 Dardanelles. 1914 Sept – Dec.

ADM 137/1089, Dardanelles 1915 Jan – April (H.S. 1089).

ADM 137/3087. Royal Naval Division General Staff, Correspondence, Reports & Operation Orders, Dardanelles 4/15 to 1/16.

ADM 137/3088A. Royal Naval Division, misc. correspondence & arrangements for embarkation 1915.

ADM 186/26. Notes by Captain H. P. Douglas, R.N. on Methods Employed by H.M. Ships When Engaging Enemy Batteries, C.B. 1202, Confidential, 1916, Admiralty, Gunnery Branch, G. 01701/16. May 1916.

ADM 186/600, C.B. 1550 Report of the Committee Appointed to Investigate the Attacks delivered on and the Enemy Defences of The Dardanelles Straits, 1919 [Mitchell Report]. Admiralty, Naval Staff, Gunnery Division, April 1921.

ADM 231/49. Text of NID 838, Turkey. Coast Defences, &c., May 1908, Parts I, II and III, but maps, charts, plates etc., are lacking. Several of these may be found in WO 301 Gallipoli Campaign Maps, and in CAB 19, Minutes of Evidence to the Dardanelles Commission. Earlier reports on Turkey Coast Defences are elsewhere in ADM 231.

Air

AIR 1/361. Particulars of HMS Ark Royal, unsigned and undated (probably early 1915).

AIR 1/479/15/312/239. HMS Ark Royal. Monthly return of Flights, April 1915, etc.

AIR 1/654 [see Roskill: 241-6]

AIR 1/664 [see Roskill 258]

AIR 1/665/17/122/714. Report of work by Short seaplanes in support of firing by HMS Roberts.

AIR 1/724/76/6. Notes on interview with Air Commodore C. R. Samson, D.S.O., at the Grosvenor Court Hotel, Davies Street, on 15th March 1923. Operations Section. 16th March, 1923.

AIR 1/2099/207/20/7. Reports from HMS Ark Royal, Dardanelles Operations, Feb – May 1915, Print code: 0(35) AS 140 Pk 1300 250 8/15 E&S, blue printed paper cover.

AIR 1/2103. Report on the Working of the Kite Balloon Ships at the Dardanelles,

Paper on Kite Balloons, 19 October 1915.

AIR 1/2119/207/72/2. Major Hogg's Reports, HQ, RFC, ME, Gallipoli & Asiatic Mainland 1915.

AIR 1/2284/209/75/10, & WO 317/13. Dowson, E. M. (1915), Director-General, Survey of Egypt, Notes on Mapping from Aeroplane photographs in the Gallipoli Peninsula, Secret. [cSeptember 1915], initially issued not earlier than 22 September 1915. Over 40 foolscap pages, illustrated with maps, diagrams, and four air photographs 'taken by the RNAS in Gallipoli for mapping purposes,' reproduced typescript, originally in MCE, MRLG (now DGIA).

(d) Cabinet Office

CAB 2/2/1. 96th meeting of the Committee of Imperial Defence, 28 February 1907.

CAB 17/184. Dardanelles Commission, Secret – The Dardanelles Inquiry. Proof. Notes for Evidence. . . The Origin and Initiation of the Joint Naval and Military Attack on the Dardanelles, April 25. The Possibility of a Joint Naval and Military Attack upon the Dardanelles. Secret. 92B. Printed for the Committee of Imperial Defence. 2 Whitehall Gardens, December 20, 1906. Part I. Memorandum by the General Staff. N.G.L. December 19, 1906. [4pp]. Part II. Note by the Director of Naval Intelligence. [1p]. February 1907. Printed at the Foreign Office by J. W. Harrison, 14/2/1907. Foolscap. Cover + 5pp.

CAB 19/28. Written submissions to Dardanelles Commission, incl. Aspinall's written statement to the Dardanelles Commission; Lieut.-Col. Brady's evidence; Minute by Churchill, 14 May 1915, to Secretary, 1st Sea Lord & Chief of Staff; Callwell's Summary of Proposed Evidence; Cunninghame to Mears, 3-3-16; etc.

CAB 19/31. Dardanelles Commission, incl. Maxwell to Kitchener, etc.

CAB 19/32. Dardanelles Commission, incl. Hamilton's evidence, & Weather Report by Captain Douglas RN, in Additional statements and documents produced by witnesses after giving evidence to the Dardanelles Commission.

CAB 19/33. Minutes of Evidence to the Dardanelles Commission, A – C, incl. Summary of Proposed Evidence of Major-General Charles Callwell, evidence of H. Charles Woods, Cunninghame, etc.

CAB 37/119/47. Churchill, Proposed Aircraft Expedition to Somaliland.

CAB 38/12/46. Minutes of 92nd meeting of Committee of Imperial Defence, 26 July 1906.

CAB 38/12/55. Minutes of 93rd meeting of Committee of Imperial Defence, 13 November 1906.

CAB 45/246. Diary and papers of General C. Cunliffe Owen.

CAB 45/258. 11th Division War Diary.

CAB 63/17 (microfilm), sheet 137. Dardanelles, including After the Dardanelles. The Next Steps. Secret. Notes by the Secretary to the Committee for Imperial Defence [Hankey], dated March 1st 1915.

CAB 63/18 (microfilm), sheet.146. Hankey's evidence to Dardanelles Commission.

(e) DEFE Files

DEFE 2/551. The Dieppe Raid Combined Report (the basis for 'Battle Report 1886', sometimes referred to as CB 04244), Combined Operations Headquarters, Directorate papers. See also 'Confidential Book 04157F', with which was issued a series of standard and overprinted maps, town plans, defence traces, photographs and mosaics of the operational area.

(f) Foreign Office

FO 358/1; FO 881/3676; WO 33/29. Reports and Memoranda relative to Defence of Constantinople and other positions in Turkey. Also on Routes in Roumelia, Strictly Confidential, Printed at the War Office by Harrison & Sons. 1877. [0631] 103 WO.

FO 371/1847. Cunliffe Owen to Mallet 24-3-14, in Mallet to Grey 24-3-14, No.201; Minute by Russell 30-3-14.

FO 881/3288, Turkey: Despatches. Defences of Gallipoli (Vice-Consul Odoni).

FO 881/8589X. Military Report on Eastern Turkey in Europe, 1905, Prepared by the General Staff, War Office. Confidential. A 1027. I 38535. 150.-11/05. Fk. 728. E.& S. A2. Small 8vo. Hard buff covers. [Chapter VI (pp53-72) is on The Gallipoli Peninsula].

FO 881/9513X. Plates to Accompany the Military Report on Eastern Turkey in Europe and the Ismid Peninsula [General Staff, War Office, London] (Second Edition, 1909). (B414) 200 6/09 H & S 454-2WO. F'cap, buff thin card folder; maps, plans and photographs covering Constantinople, Central Plains (Adrianople, etc), Istranja Balkan District, The Eastern Rhodope District.

FO 881/9666X, & WO 33/284. Reports on the Defences of Constantinople by Lieut.-Colonel F. R. Maunsell R.A. (Military Attaché, Constantinople). 1903. Secret. [A 826] 9/1903 – (B 157) – 209 WO. Intelligence Department, War Office. 12th September 1903. Hard buff covers, foolscap. 50 pp.

(g) Secret Services

HD 3/135. Foreign Office correspondence relating to Secret Service.

(h) Various Maps

MPH 1/803/2-3 from WO 33/35. Carte de la Presqu'Ile de Gallipoli – 2 sheets, 1876-80.

MPH 1/871/2. Survey of Defensive Position near Bulair shewing the Lines constructed by the Anglo-French Army in 1855. . . 1877.

MPH 1/871/5-7, 3 Maps of Gallipoli Peninsula from report of 31-1-1877 by G. E. Grover Capt RE about proposed landing place for troops south of Hanafart (Anafarta Lim).

(i) War Office

WO 32/5123. Hammersley, report on 11th Division's operations.

WO 33/29. Reports and Memoranda relative to Defence of Constantinople and other positions in Turkey. . . (1877).

WO 33/35. Paper No.797, Seizure of the Dardanelles as a means of coercing the Porte, including Memorandum on the Passage of the Dardanelles by Major J. C. Ardagh RE, War Office, 1880.

WO 33/478. Report on Certain Landing Places in Turkey in Europe. 1909. Prepared for the General Staff. War Office. (Secret). (B133) 50 6/09 H&S 158 WO. Vi + 56pp, stiff buff card covers, portrait format c4.5x6.5 inches.

WO 33/644. Manual of Combined Naval and Military Operations, 1913. Confidential. 40/GEN. NO./269 [A 1674] London: Printed for HMSO by Harrison & Sons, St. Martin's Lane, Printers in Ordinary to His Majesty. (B 156) 4000 9/13 H&S 194 WO. 72pp. Portrait format, c3.5x4 inches. Hard buff covers.

WO 33/2333. Report on the Defences of Constantinople. General Staff. Secret. 1909. War Office. [A 1311]. [(B 369) 100 2/09 H & S 400WO]. Copy No. 3 D.M.O. Hard buff covers, portrait format, c4.5 x 6.5 inches. xii + 151 pp.

WO 33/2334.Plates to accompany the Report on the Defences of Constantinople. General Staff, War Office, 1908. (B 369) 100 2/09 H & S 400-2 WO. Buff foolscap thin printed folder, containing 72 plates, including many folding plans, panorama sketches, photographs, etc.

WO 95/4309 & 4319. 2nd Lowland Field Company RE, War Diary.

WO 95/492. 5th Field Survey Company RE, War Diary [Western Front].

WO 95/4263. M.E.F. Dardanelles, Gen. Staff (GHQ) War Diary, 1915 Feb – 1915 Apr., incl. Report on Naval Bombardment Procedures in the Helles Sector, & Appendices.

WO 95/4273. Incl. General Douglas to French CEO, 30-7-15.

WO 95/4280. Anzac Corps General Staff, Special Mission War Diary, & War Diary of Major N. P. Hancock DAA & QMG ANZAC.

WO 95/4290. Royal Naval Division, General Staff, War Diary.

WO 95/4304. 29th Division General Staff War Diary, Intelligence Summaries.

WO 106/42, Military Policy in a War with Turkey, memo by Captain Grant Duff, 11 July 1906. Envelope C3, 21a.

WO 106/1462. Cunliffe Owen, Lt-Col F., file Forcing of Dardanelles, Feasibility Report on Operations in the Dardanelles, 1914.

WO 106/1463. Talbot for Callwell, memorandum The Gallipoli Peninsula, signed 'Cal DMO 1/9/14,' 'A, 'in Dallas, memorandum The Dardanelles and Gallipoli Peninsula, dated 1.9.14, 'B'. Untitled typescript memorandum signed 'Charles Callwell DMO 3/9/14,' at 'D,' Both at 'C.'

WO 106/1534. Samson, Major L.L.R. (1910), Report on Landing Places at Kaba Tepe (Gallipoli Peninsula) with two roads leading therefrom to Maidos and the Kilid Bahr Plateau, Adrianople 28.9.1910. 10pp duplicated typescript.

WO 153/1058. Maps 1914-1918. Various theatres of war, including Gallipoli Campaign. The references of individual maps are given in chapter endnotes.

WO 157/647. GHQ MEF Intelligence Summary, Dardanelles.

WO 157/667. Anzac Corps HQ Intelligence Summaries.

WO 157/668. Anzac Corps Intelligence War Diary.

WO 157/678. Anzac Corps Intelligence War Diary, 15-30 April 1915, & Appendices.

WO 157/681. Anzac Intelligence War Diary, & Appendices, incl. Bulletin, JY 15, dated 7 July, Intelligence Note on Roads, Water Supply, etc.

WO 158/574. Dardanelles Operations – Copies of Telegrams 1915 (GOC-in-C, Egypt).

WO 161/84. Birdwood to Ellison, 13 April 1924.

WO 301. Gallipoli Campaign 1915, Maps. The reference numbers of individual maps are given in chapter endnotes.

WO 301/45. Gallipoli Campaign 1915, Report by Major S. F. Newcombe RE, with GSGS Map Room stamp dated 17 March 1916.

WO 301/46. Gallipoli Campaign 1915, Reports and correspondence. Nicholas to Hedley.

House of Lords Record Office
Lloyd George MSS F/9/2/16. Reduction of Estimates for Secret Services,
Cabinet Memorandum 19-3-1920.

Imperial War Museum
a) Department of Documents
Lt.-Col. F. Cunliffe Owen to The Secretary, Army Council, 27–9-1927.
Papers of Dr. O. C. Williams (Private Diary, Started March 13 1913, of O. C.
Williams, Capt., G.H.Q., British Med. E. F.), Department of Documents
69/78/1.
b) Department of Photographs
Lieut Butler's air photos (No.3 Squadron) in album (Accession No. 9008-06).
Capt Hon. M. Knatchbull MC, album (Vol. VI – Gallipoli & various) containing
air photos of Gallipoli etc. collected by Knatchbull Hugessen, on loan to
IWM Dept of Photographs.
c) Department of Sound Records
T C Nicholas sound recording tapes. 10475/3/1-3.

Liddell Hart Archive, King's College, London
Hamilton Papers; Lady Hamilton's Diary.

RAF Museum, Hendon
Sykes Papers, Vol. I, includes copy of Notes for Observers, Royal Flying Corps
1915.

Royal Archives
RA W27/51. Haldane to Knollys, 10 December 1906.

Royal Engineers Institution Library, Chatham
'A' Printing Section RE, Outline War Diary.
No.2 Ranging & Survey Section RE, Outline War Diary.

Royal Geographical Society
Salmon Collection, Royal Geographic Society, Belgian, French and German Maps
– Miscellaneous Maps No.143A.
There are various other Gallipoli maps in the RGS archives.

Service Historique de l'Armée de Terre, Château de Vincennes, Paris
Reports on Section de Topographie in 3M 569 – Service Géographique: Armée
d'Orient, mission du Service Géographique dans les Balkans.

Unpublished Papers etc.
Bullen, John (n.d.), *List of Maps of Gallipoli Campaign in the Australian War
Memorial, Gallipoli* Vol. 1, Australian War Memorial.
Diary of Brigadier-General S. W. Hare, GOC 86th Brigade, 29th Division.
Col. Mike Nolan (2000), notes: '1907-1917 – The Golden Years in the
Development of Cartography in the Ottoman Empire.'
Diary of Carrol Romer, Romer Family; present whereabouts unknown.
Nicholas, Sarah (2000), British Military Intelligence at Suvla Bay, August 1915;
unpublished dissertation.

Index

The proper nouns Gallipoli, Gallipoli Peninsula and the Dardanelles appear on almost every page; as such, they are not listed in this index. Other common geographical terms (e.g. Aegean, France), nations' capitals, and well-used generic names (e.g. War Office, Admiralty) are also similarly not listed.